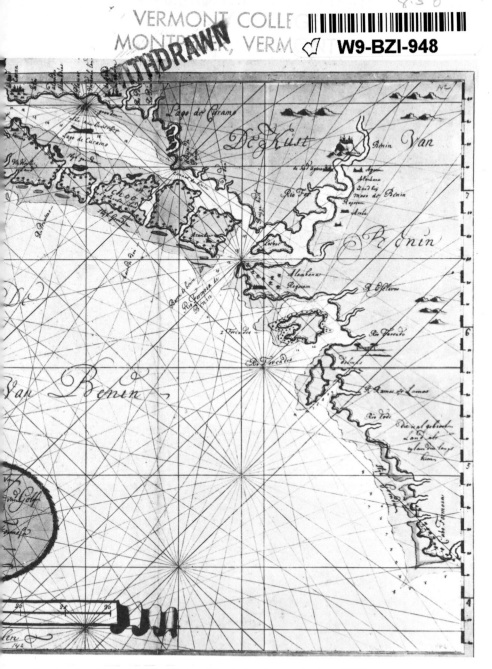

Navigational Chart of the Bight of Benin by G. van Keulen, 1716.

Benin and the Europeans 1485-1897

Benin and the Europeans 1485–1897

The present Oba of Benin, Oba Akenzua II.

IBADAN HISTORY SERIES

General Editor K. O. Dike Ph.D.

Benin and the Europeans
1485-1897

A. F. C. Ryder D.Phil.
Professor of History, University of Ibadan

Humanities Press

First published
in the United States of America 1969
by HUMANITIES PRESS INC.
303 Park Avenue South
New York, N.Y. 10010

Library of Congress Catalog Card No. 68-54523

Printed in Great Britain

Contents

Abbreviations   viii
Acknowledgements   viii
Introduction   ix

Chapter 1
The Benin Kingdom—an historical perspective   1

Chapter 2
The era of Portuguese monopoly
1. First contacts   24
2. The beginning of trade   32
3. The island trade and the first mission   42
4. The resumption of royal trade   53
5. The end of Portuguese monopoly: the second mission   65

Chapter 3
English and Dutch beginnings
1. The English   76
2. The Dutch   84

Chapter 4
The Capuchin missions
1. Spanish missionaries   99
2. Italian missionaries   109

Chapter 5
The Dutch at Ughoton
1. Trade in the main river (1650–1700)   124
2. Establishment at Ughoton   138
3. Trade and conflict   145
4. Efforts to diversify trade   156
5. European rivals and Dutch decline   164
6. We're here because we're here   179

Chapter 6
The slave-trade era
1. English and French in the mid-eighteenth century   196
2. Landolphe's enterprise in the main river   212
3. The last years of the slave trade   227

v

Chapter 7

British encroachment

1. Trade and the flag in the Benin River   239
2. The first consular visit to Benin   245
3. Retreat into the heartlands   257
4. The growth of commercial and consular pressures   260
5. The Protection Treaty of 1892   265
6. The dispute over trade   272
7. Consul-General Moor's campaign against Benin   277
8. The massacre and punitive expedition   283

Appendices
I   Fragment of the ship's book of the *São Miguel* trading
     to Benin in the year 1522   295
II   A short account of the things that happened during the
     mission to Benin 1651–2   307
III Articles of the agreement between . . . the Dutch West
     India Company . . . and the King of Great Benin 1715   316
IV   Invoice and price-list of the merchandise loaded in the
     ship *Commany* . . . 1715   320
V   Journal kept by me Fredrik Legrand at Benin in the Rio
     Formosa 1717   322
VI   Letter from the Dutch factor at Ughoton 1724   331
VII Summary for a trading venture set forth from Lisbon
     for Benin . . .   335
VIII Instructions for a voyage to the Benin River and trade
     there written by Randall Shawe 1582   339
IX   Report on a visit to Ubini (Benin City) the capital of the
     Benin country by H. M. Gallwey 1892   344

Bibliography   349

Index   359

Maps
1. The Benin Kingdom in the nineteenth century   xii
2. Lower Guinea in the seventeenth and eighteenth
   centuries   25
3. The Benin Trading Rivers in the nineteenth century   125

Plates

frontispiece
The present Oba of Benin, Oba Akenzua II

between pages 244 and 245

1. A Benin warrior chief with attendants

2. (a) A brass box representing part of the Oba's palace
   (b) Excavation showing remains of the mud walls of the
       nineteenth century palace of the Obas

3. Shrines in the main compound of the present palace

4. Sixteenth century plaques showing European traders

5. (a) A messenger of the Ogane, wearing a cross
   (b) A Benin trader

6. A war captive

7. (a) An early seventeenth century representation of a Dutch
       attack on Portuguese settlements in the bay of the island
       of Principe, December 1698
   (b) A human sacrifice to make the rain cease

8. Oba Ovonramwen, on board the Protectorate yacht *Ivy* on
   his way to exile in Calabar, 1897

Abbreviations

A.H.U.   Archivo Histórico Ultramarino, Lisbon.
A.R.   Algemeen Rijksarchief, The Hague.
A.S.C.   Archivio della Sacra Congregazione di Propaganda
             Fide, Rome.
A.T.T.   Archivo Nacional da Torre do Tombo, Lisbon.
N.W.I.C.   Archief van de tweede West Indische Compagnie.
Oude W.I.C. Archief van de eerste West Indische Compagnie.
P.R.O.   Public Record Office, London.

Acknowledgements

The publishers are grateful to the following for permission to reproduce photographs:

Dr. R. E. Bradbury, University of Birmingham, for the frontispiece; The British Museum for plate 5b; Graham Connah and the Federal Department of Antiquities, Lagos, for plates 2b, 3; The Librarian, University of Ibadan, for plate 8; Martinus Nijhow and Linschaten Vereeniging for plate 7a, from *Reis om de Wereld 1598–1601* by Olivier van Noort; Museum für Völkerkunde, Berlin, for plates 1, 2a, 4, 5a, 6.

The endpapers show a 1716 map of the Bight of Benin, by permission of Algemeene Rijksarchief, Netherlands.

Introduction

This book is the outcome of research undertaken while I was associated with the Scheme for the Study of Benin History and Culture. Begun in 1956 under the directorship of Dr. K. O. Dike, the Benin Scheme was one of the earliest interdisciplinary projects devoted to the study of the history of Africa south of the Sahara. By bringing together anthropologists, historians, ethnographers, archaeologists, and concentrating their attention upon an African state renowned for the depth of its historical tradition and the richness of its cultural heritage, the scheme purposed to demonstrate that the past of an African people may be reconstructed in exactly the same manner as that of any other people for which similar evidence is available, and that the lack of certain conventional materials of historical research did not preclude research that measured up to the standards of modern historiography. The scheme has, I believe, shown the value of the interdisciplinary—perhaps the multidisciplinary—approach in African historical studies; it has also highlighted the difficulties encountered when we try to marry the material obtained through research in one discipline with that obtained through another. With Benin, for example, we have four main bodies of evidence at our disposal: documentary material, which is entirely European in origin; oral tradition, or the accounts of the past handed down to the present by word of mouth through successive generations; the society as it is; the material remains of the past, including the thousands of brass and ivory works for which Benin is famous. Each of these categories has been studied in great detail, and our understanding of each has been much extended and deepened. Where difficulty has arisen has been in the task of relating one to the other, of fitting together these disparate elements into a coherent whole, into an integrated picture of the past. Our information about the Benin past cannot, in fact, be likened to the pieces of a jigsaw puzzle, predestined to fall neatly together once we have gathered sufficient of them; rather it must be seen as the stray components of a multi-dimensional structure seemingly held together by a few threads, although instinct tells us that it has a unity.

As knowledge in each of these spheres grows, both for Benin and for the neighbouring peoples, so will more and more links become apparent and our historical reconstruction more firmly articulated. At present I do not feel that the evidence available and our understanding of it would support a full-scale reconstruction of Benin history. Even the outline interpretation offered in the first chapter as a necessary background to the main study has had to be hedged with far more qualifications than are consonant with historical conscience or stylistic ease. Rather than inflate such a construction to unwarranted proportions, I have thought it prudent to concentrate attention upon that theme of Benin history which is at present most susceptible of investigation over a long and reasonably continuous space of time. In so doing it happens that I have fastened upon what must be accounted a minor theme in any overall view, for until the last few months of the kingdom's existence, European influences and activities were of relatively small account in all spheres of life. Nonetheless it is a theme which offers some insight into larger matters, and which may provide a starting-point for excursions into the major themes of Benin history.

My other purpose has been to attempt a study in depth of European relationships with a single West African state. From this point of view Benin offers perhaps unique advantages. In the course of four hundred years most of the colonial and commercial powers of Europe have turned their attention to this kingdom; their interests have ranged widely through commerce, missionary endeavour, and, finally, imperial ambition; and of these successive phases of enterprise there survive respectable, if sadly depleted, records. Scarcely any of this material has been published, so I have ventured to give a representative selection from it in the form of appendices.

I wish to acknowledge my great debt to Dr. K. O. Dike who first turned my attention to this field of history, and who, as Director of the Benin Scheme, made possible my research in Portuguese, Italian, Dutch and British archives. Among the many persons who gave me invaluable guidance and help in the collection of material,

I owe particular thanks to Mme Meilink Roeloffs of the Algemeen Rijksarchief, Mrs. van Caenegem, Dr. Heinrich Lutz, Father Harrington of the Società delle Missioni Africane, Cdr. A. Teixeira da Mota, and Dr. B. Siertsema. Above all, I must express my gratitude to Dr. R. E. Bradbury whose profound and unrivalled knowledge of Benin has for many years acted both as stimulant and corrective to my own essays into a field where he is undoubted master.

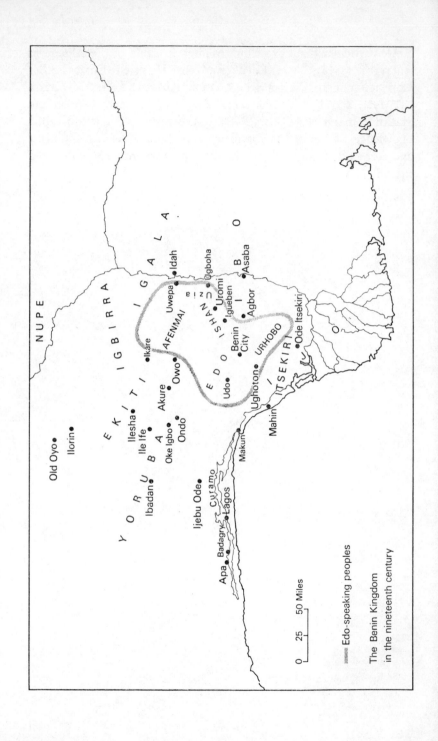

NUPE

N

IGBIRRA

IGALA

EKITI

Old Oyo ●

Ilorin ●

Idah ●

Uwepa

Ugboha

B

Asaba

Ikare ●

AFENMAI

Uromi

Igueben

Agbor

I

Uzia

ISHAN

O

Ilesha ●

Ile Ife ●

Akure ●

Owo ●

EDO

Benin

City

URHOBO

Ode Itsekiri ●

O

YORUBA

Oke Igbo

Ondo ●

Udo ●

Ughoton ●

ITSEKIRI

Ibadan ●

Mahin ●

Ijebu Ode ●

Makun ●

Curamo

Apa

Badagry

Lagos

──── Edo-speaking peoples

▓▓▓▓ The Benin Kingdom
in the nineteenth century

0   25   50 Miles

Chapter 1
The Benin Kingdom—an historical perspective

The heartlands of the old Benin kingdom are inhabited by a people who call themselves, their capital city and their language Edo. They form part and lie roughly in the centre of a larger language group to which ethnographers and linguisticians have applied the same name. This Edo-speaking group of peoples covers an area extending from the broken, hilly country that borders the Igbirra and Igala in the north, to the edge of the costal swamp forest in the south, where their neighbours are the Ijo and Itsekiri. Their other boundaries are with the Yoruba to the west, and the Ibo to the east. Linguistic evidence suggests that they have occupied this region for some thousands of years[1] in relative isolation, with the result that their language and neighbouring ones of the West Atlantic family, and even some of the dialects within the Edo group, have become mutually unintelligible. Language is not, however, the only cultural feature which the Edo-speaking peoples have in common. Dr. R. E. Bradbury has indicated three important characteristics of social organisation that distinguish all their communities, whether large or small.[2] The village settlement is everywhere the basic political unit; within the village the male population is organised into age-grades—usually three in number—which represent the fundamental pattern of authority; and in their kinship and lineage organisation there is a marked patrilineal bias and an emphasis upon primogeniture.[3] In all likelihood agricultural village

1 R. G. Armstrong, *The Study of West African Languages*. Ibadan, 1964, pp. 12–13. Calculations based on glottochronology put the period of separation between Edo, Yoruba and Igbo at between 3,000 and 6,000 years.
2 R. E. Bradbury, *The Benin Kingdom and the Edo-speaking Peoples of South-western Nigeria*. London, 1957, pp. 14–15.
3 The development of radically new political and administrative institutions since 1897 has wrought drastic changes in Edo society. Nevertheless the older institutions are still sufficiently alive to justify the use of the present tense when describing them.

communities with these features of social and political organisation characterised early Edo settlement; and such compact communities, largely autonomous in their political and economic life, still exist among them, especially in the north-western area.

In most places, however, this relatively simple pattern of organisation has been overlaid by the development of kingship, title systems and more complex political units; and it is the greatest of these more advanced polities, the kingdom of Benin, which has won renown for the Edo people. At the same time it must be emphasised that the sway of Benin seldom, if ever, extended over all the Edo peoples; less than half of them were brought into the kingdom with any degree of permanency, and some areas in the north were probably never dependent upon Benin. And if Benin was not a state embracing all the Edo, neither was it composed exclusively of Edo subjects, for to the west it encroached upon Yoruba areas, and in the east it embraced many of the Ibo living to the west of the River Niger.

The origins of the kingdom are lost in myth and antiquity, from which survives only a tradition of migration from the east that is common to many West African peoples. To reconstruct its growth it is therefore necessary to work backwards from nearer and better-known events which suggest that the process was not one of a number of groups coalescing, but the expansion of a city-state nucleus—something more akin to the emergence of states in classical Greece than in northern Europe. We have seen, however, that the city or town was an uncommon form of settlement among the Edo—in this as in many other cultural traits they resemble the Ibo more than the Yoruba—so it becomes necessary to account for the emergence of a city-state sufficiently powerful to subjugate the village-based societies around it. Benin historical tradition has tended to explain the phenomenon by assuming the existence of a city *ab initio*, and having the remainder of the Edo peoples migrate from it through the centuries. This interpretation could be supported by a detailed chronology of such settlements based upon the traditions of origin current in scores of towns and villages throughout the Edo-speaking region, for most communities now trace their origin to Benin City, often through some eponymous ancestor.[1]

---

1 The village of Idogbo, for example, derives its name from Ogidogbo, reputed to have been a son of the Oba Ozolua who was appointed ruler of the village

2

Even many non-Edo peoples on the periphery of the old kingdom take pride in circumstantial accounts of their descent from a Benin ancestor. Many of the traditions doubtless have a basis in fact, because the establishment of settlements appears to have been one of the means adopted by Benin for consolidating its hold upon a large territory. But many are equally certainly the product of a hankering after prestige, or simply the adoption of the most likely story, given the canons of traditional historiography. Outsiders have sometimes found the explanation for the rise of Benin City in an external stimulus—alien influence or conquest—establishing forms of political and social organisation untypical of the Edo. This argument is an attractive one; Benin may be the most easterly of a chain of rather similar cities running south from the Niger through Yorubaland. On the other hand, the possibility of a relatively independent growth cannot be disregarded. The village nuclei might, and have, under certain circumstances come together in groups, tribes and chiefdoms; and the single village could multiply its wards by attracting settlers as well as by the natural growth of its own population. There are indeed some indications that Benin City was not the only Edo settlement to advance towards urban development at a relatively early date; Udo, now only a large village, is said to have rivalled the capital during the first reigns of the present dynasty, and to have fallen into decay only after a long struggle.

Whatever may have been the initial impulse towards a new form of organisation, it seems clear that Benin City grew from a cluster of settlements on the site of the present town. A recent survey of the city 'walls' by Graham Connah has revealed that most of them are in fact 'linear earthworks surrounding areas of bush'—'an earthen record of a long process of fusion of semi-dispersed communities'.[1] Either from necessity, or following some foreign example, these communities evolved institutions which at once coped with the problems raised by a larger association and made possible a further expansion. A chieftaincy system appeared early in the development of the city; five of the present-day *Uzama*, the senior order of chiefs

---

after its conquest by his father. In this instance the tradition credits only the ruling lineage with a Benin origin.

1 G. Connah, 'New light on the Benin City walls'. *Journal of the Historical Society of Nigeria*, vol. III, no. 4, June 1967.

in Benin, claim to trace their titles to a period earlier than the establishment of the reigning dynasty.[1] The organisation of the city into wards based upon crafts seems to have begun with skills such as wood and ivory carving. Tradition also insists that paramount chiefs or kings, known as the *Ogiso*, emerged at a fairly early stage, though it is not clear whether they were elected or followed the same rule of primogeniture as the chiefs. The fact that thirty-one *Ogisos* are believed to have reigned, and that some of them were women, suggests that seniority, perhaps within a family, played some part in determining the choice. During this *Ogiso* phase, which may have lasted several centuries, Benin seems to have secured control of the surrounding, heavily forested country within a radius of ten or fifteen miles by establishing small, dependent farming settlements. But it was still a petty state—probably no larger or more advanced than several others among the Edo.

The *Ogiso* period is said to have ended with the banishment of the ruler. There followed a brief phase described by the traditional historian Chief J. U. Egharevba as an experiment in 'republican government',[2] by which seems to be meant a change in the method of appointing the paramount chief, so that in place of hereditary succession within a family, a choice was made by the whole body of chiefs from among their own number. This experiment proved a complete failure, for the first ruler appointed under it tried to have his son elected to succeed him, and the chiefs, having foiled that intrigue, were unable to agree on an alternative candidate from among themselves. The deadlock was finally resolved by the introduction of an alien dynasty related to that which about the same time was establishing its rule over certain Yoruba groups. Both Benin and Yoruba traditions, it is interesting to note, tell substantially the same story about Oranmiyan, the first of the new line of Benin rulers, and the circumstances in which he and his followers went to Benin at the invitation of a party among the chiefs. If such a story appears at first sight incredible, and perhaps a means of concealing a conquest, it must be remembered that instances are not

---

1 These five titles are *Oliha*, *Edohen*, *Ezomo*, *Ero*, and *Eholo n'Ire*. All the titles are hereditary, and each chief has his own compound in the city. The present dynasty has added two titles to the *Uzama* order.

2 J. U. Egharevba, *A Short History of Benin*, 3rd ed. Ibadan, 1960, p. 6.

unknown in African history when a people, perplexed as those of
Benin were, have turned to a foreign lineage credited with supernatural powers in the arts of government.[1]

There is much substance in the traditional view of Benin history
which sees the arrival of the new dynasty as the watershed between
the early petty state and the great kingdom. The aliens brought
with them new concepts, new modes of government, and probably
new weapons and methods of warfare which were to launch Benin
upon a course of expansion and conquest. Nevertheless it must be
emphasised that there was no sudden transformation. The first
Obas, as the new rulers were called, lived under the shadow of the
older regime, very much controlled by the principal Edo chiefs, the
Uzama Nihinron, who had become hereditary kingmakers. It needed
a *coup d'état* organised by the fourth *Oba*, Ewedo, to free the ruler
from his position of *primus inter pares* in relation to the *Uzama*.
Ewedo symbolised his assumption of supreme authority by several
changes in ceremonial, such as compelling all chiefs to stand in his
presence—formerly the *Uzama* had remained seated—and forbidding them to make use of swords of state (*ada*), or confer titles.
Even with their status thus reduced, the *Uzama* remained a great
power in Benin and tradition asserts that in a later reign they led a
rebellion against the ruler. Other important innovations attributed
to Ewedo are the building of a new palace apart from the chiefs'
compounds, and the organisation of a hierarchy of chiefs to serve
the palace. From these beginnings was to evolve an elaborate
structure of palace officials comprising many hundreds of men and
women devoted to the service of the Oba, and striving to ascend a
carefully graded ladder of ranks at the top of which stood a number
of individual titles which were in the gift of the Oba, and to which
he could add at his pleasure.

Although many titles and refinements were introduced into the
palace organisation over the centuries, the form it had assumed by
the nineteenth century seems still to have corresponded with the
pattern established by Ewedo. Servants of the Oba belonged to one
of three palace associations, among which were distributed the
duties of his household. The senior association, *Iwebo*, originally

---

1 The Mossi dynasty appears to have extended its power thanks to such a
reputation. cf. E. P. Skinner, *The Mossi of the Upper Volta*. Stanford, 1964.

took charge of the Oba's wardrobe, including his regalia; and in course of time, like many a similar department in the royal households of medieval Europe, it also acquired a general oversight in matters of finance and trade. Its leader was—and still is—the *Uwangue*, a title said to have been created by Ewedo. *Iweguae*, the second association, comprised the ruler's personal attendants and domestic servants under the leadership of the *Esere*. As the latter title is of more recent origin than that of *Uwangue*—almost two hundred years later according to Egharevba's chronology—it may well be that the functions of *Iweguae* were originally shared between *Iwebo* and the third association, *Ibiwe*. This latter group of retainers was in recent centuries responsible only for the service of the Oba's wives and children; the title of its senior chief, *Osodin*, is traced to Ewedo. A strict division of function and the restriction of each association to its own quarters within the palace helped to engender among them that spirit of rivalry and emulation which was an important element in the political structure of the Benin state, enabling an astute Oba to neutralise factions and preserve his independence as final arbiter among his more powerful subjects. A weak monarch, on the other hand, could become the prisoner of his own hierarchic, ambitious household.

One other feature of Ewedo's revolution in government is worthy of mention: this was his decision to rename his state *Ubini*.[1] The significance of this name is not satisfactorily explained by tradition, and it is especially interesting that it appears to be of non-Edo origin. Possibly it indicates that Ewedo and his supporters in the struggle with the Benin chiefs still represented the alien element introduced by the new dynasty, and that his victory marked the triumph of that element over the Edo after an uneasy period of cohabitation and compromise. Thereafter, at least, the two components of the state began to merge into a strong, coherent unity, even though the rulers maintained the link with their ancestral home through rituals enacted at the accession and death of every

---

1 According to tradition, the immediate area of Benin City was known as *Ogodomigodo* during the *Ogiso* period. The first ruler of the new dynasty is said to have renamed it *Ile-Ibinu* (land of vexation) because of the opposition he encountered there, and it is this name that Ewedo is supposed to have modified to *Ubini*.

Oba.[1] On the former occasions, Obas received symbols of authority cast in brass from the spiritual head of their dynasty—a potentate known in Benin as the *Oghene* or Great Lord. From this same source Oba Oguola, the successor of Ewedo, is reputed to have obtained the services of a brass-worker who established in Benin the art of *cire perdue* casting in brass, thus founding a craft which was always associated with the temporal and spiritual powers of the dynasty.[2] When an Oba died, his body, or some parts of it, were carried to the *Oghene* for ritual burial. Thus the dynasty preserved its relationship with the source of its mystical authority which had perhaps facilitated its first acceptance by the Edo.

Besides opening a new era in the political development of Benin, Ewedo also laid the foundation for its expansion by conquest, instead of by the slow process of colonisation through which it had so far attained only very modest limits. This new military power and ethos in Benin may have arisen partly from the introduction of new weapons and methods of warfare; horses are said to have come to Benin with the dynasty, and certain types of bows and swords are associated with it. New methods of organisation almost certainly played a part, with greater specialisation of function within the state and more autocratic control enabling Benin to muster its resources for war more effectively than ever before.

The century and a half which, by Egharevba's computation, came between the death of Oguola and the accession of Ewuare are among the most obscure periods in Benin history.[3] The rulers are

---

1 cf. A. F. C. Ryder, 'A reconsideration of the Ife-Benin relationship'. *Journal of African History*, vol. VI, i (1965). This article examines the evidence for and against the tradition which identifies the *Oghene* with the Yoruba Oni of Ife, and suggests that many conflicts could be resolved by ascribing a more northerly origin to the dynasty. It is further argued that the origin of the name Benin might be sought in this direction.

2 A large body of literature has gathered around Benin art; the most recent work devoted exclusively to the subject is P. C. Dark and W. and B. Forman, *Benin Art*. London, 1960. The most substantial study is F. von Luschan, *Altertümer von Benin*, 3 vols. Berlin and Leipzig, 1919. cf. also the useful discussion in W. Fagg, *Nigerian Images*. London, 1963.

3 Attempts to assign dates to events in Benin history earlier than the sixteenth century are fraught with difficulty. Egharevba places the arrival of Oranmiyan in the late twelfth century; R. E. Bradbury ('Chronological problems in the study of Benin history'. *Journal of the Historical Society of Nigeria*, vol. I, no. 4, 1959) would put it a century later.

shadowy figures to whom tradition attributes no notable achievements. Some stories told about them give the impression that their authority was still contested by the *Uzama* and town chiefs of Benin. One of them, Ohen, is said to have been stoned to death after it was discovered that he had murdered the *Iyase*, the senior town chief; his son is reputed to have fought several times with the *Uzama*. If such accounts are reliable, it might be concluded that although Ewedo and Oguola had successfully established a nucleus of royal power in the palace organisation, the more purely indigenous elements led by the *Uzama* and town chiefs remained hostile to the conception of government embodied in the new monarchy.

Such an interpretation has the merit of making more intelligible the next major event in Benin history—the seizure of the throne by Ewuare—which is surrounded by many mysteries. If tradition runs aright, this was the first of the disputed successions which later became so common a feature of Benin politics. As in all such contests, Ewuare, the challenger, based his claim against the occupant of the throne on the sound Edo principle of primogeniture, though his exact relationship to the previous Oba is obscure.[1] After a fierce struggle, which culminated in the storming and burning of Benin City, Ewuare killed his rival. Possibly this was a purely domestic upheaval in both its course and causes, yet it may be significant that it must have occurred around the middle of the fifteenth century when important dynastic changes were taking place in several states to the north of Benin. In particular, new and inter-related dynasties appear to have established themselves at that time among the Oyo, Nupe and Igala, and there is evidence of some relationship between them and the rulers of Benin who followed Ewuare.[2] It may be, therefore, that the struggle for the throne in Benin was part of a wider disturbance. The magnitude of the changes in the form of government subsequently carried through by Ewuare might also be interpreted as evidence of a new wave of foreign influence fully comparable to that associated with Oranmiyan.

Perhaps the most important of Ewuare's political reforms was the institution of an association of town chiefs similar in structure

---

1 cf. Bradbury, 'Chronological problems', p. 284.
2 cf. Ryder, 'The Ife-Benin relationship', p. 36.

to that which already existed in the palace. By this means that influential part of Benin society which had in the past often organised resistance and rebellion against the ruler was given a permanent role in government, for the town chiefs (*Eghaevbo n'Ore*) henceforth participated with those of the palace (*Eghaevbo n'Ogbe*) in the ruler's council that debated and decided matters of high policy. As individuals they also shared in the government of towns and villages,[1] and some performed important functions of state. Their leader, the *Iyase*, had by the seventeenth century become the principal commander of the Benin armies. It may seem odd that Ewuare should in this manner enhance the importance of a group noted for its opposition to the palace—a feature of its behaviour which persisted, for the town chiefs have until recently been regarded in Benin as something akin to a permanent and official 'opposition'.[2] One explanation might be that the action was designed to placate the 'town' elements and win their backing against a hostile 'palace' establishment in the aftermath of his forcible possession of the throne. But whatever his motives might have been, the new association came to play an important part in Benin political life primarily as a counterweight to the palace. Its titles, like those of the palace, were non-hereditary and in the gift of the ruler, who could also add to their number and regulate their order of precedence at will. An able ruler thus enjoyed control of a delicate mechanism through which he could reward services, satisfy ambition, stimulate loyalty, neutralise conflict and counter hostility. Indeed, much of the political history of Benin turns upon the strivings of important men and families to win place or advancement in the hierarchies of town and palace, and upon the efforts of rulers and pretenders to the throne to consolidate a following in those associations.

---

1 For administrative purposes the Benin kingdom was divided into tribute units, each controlled by a person resident in Benin City. This person, who was usually a title-holder, also acted as an intermediary between the Oba and those living in the areas for which he was responsible. In order to prevent such men becoming over-powerful, rulers took care that no one should secure control of several contiguous units. The prestige and perquisites attached to these offices made them the object of keen competition among influential citizens of Benin. cf. Bradbury, *The Benin Kingdom*, pp. 42–3.

2 cf. Bradbury, *The Benin Kingdom*, p. 43.

Ewuare is also reputed to have changed the name of his kingdom and capital from *Ubini*, the name associated with Oranmiyan and his successors, to *Edo*. That so fundamental a measure should be attributed to this ruler is indicative of his key position in traditional historiography, but it is a tradition that raises a number of problems. The story that he chose the name to commemorate a slave who had befriended him before he won the throne is not very convincing, nor does it seem likely that a name chosen in such a manner could win acceptance as the name of a people and language with a long tradition already behind them. The earliest documentary records from European sources also do not lend support to the story, for they all refer to the kingdom and city as Benin, and this some decades after the supposed change. It is possible that the story grew up in order to account for the existence of the native name *Edo* and the alien *Benin*; such problems are commonly resolved in graphic anecdotes involving well-known historical figures. It is certainly reasonable to suppose that *Edo* is the older, indigenous word for the people of Benin and their language. Its adoption by Ewuare may have been part of the same policy which led him to give a larger part in state affairs to the town chiefs; namely the policy of identifying himself with the Edo, rather than with the alien tradition of earlier rulers. If this interpretation is correct, it follows that Ewuare's measure had only partial or temporary success, for later rulers continued to use the name *Benin*, and it was not until the seventeenth century that *Edo* acquired sufficiently general currency to be recorded by a European as the name of the country.[1]

A similar fate overtook Ewuare's attempt, likewise conceived in terms of Edo custom, to solve the crucial problem of regulating succession to the throne. He tried, so tradition tells us, to apply the principle of primogeniture and buttressed it by giving formal recognition to the heir-apparent in his own lifetime. Moreover, this prince, on whom he bestowed the title of *Edaiken*, was given a place among the most ancient order of Edo chiefs, the *Uzama*, and like them had his own village on the periphery of Benin City. Here too it could be argued that Ewuare was seeking to identify his dynasty more completely with its Edo subjects. Unfortunately no

---

1 The earliest-known reference to the name *Edo* occurs in O. Dapper, *Naukeurige Beschrijvinge der Afrikaensche Gewesten*. Amsterdam, 1676, p. 122.

such device could eliminate the tensions and rivalries that inevitably surrounded the succession, and the system broke down immediately it was put to the test.[1] Nevertheless it remained an ideal which later rulers often strove to make a reality.

Egharevba describes Ewuare as 'powerful, courageous and sagacious',[2] and the Edo still tell many stories which bear witness to his prowess as a warrior and military commander. He can indeed be regarded as the founder of Benin's reputation as a formidable military power, and of its empire. Under his command the Benin armies extended their conquests beyond the Edo regions, subjugating many towns and villages of Ekiti, Ikare, Efenmai and the western Ibo, among them the important towns of Owo and Akure. In Benin City itself his power was manifested in the building of the great inner wall and ditch—perhaps the most remarkable work of fortification in southern Nigeria.[3] Tradition offers no explanation for Ewuare's military successes, except to stress the efficacy of the magical powers with which he protected his subjects and destroyed his enemies. A similar reputation attaches to the founder figures of the Nupe and Oyo dynasties with whom, as has been suggested, Ewuare may have had some connection. If a more mundane explanation is required, it might be found in his skill in organising his subjects and harnessing their energies to a war machine which became an integral and permanent part of the state. While little information is available about the military organisation of Benin at this time, the details of Ewuare's campaigns and conquests create a strong impression that there was emerging a type of militia force which engaged in regular annual expeditions, either to enforce the submission of recalcitrant subjects, or to extend the bounds of the empire still further. On this greatly extended territorial foundation Benin City grew in size and splendour—in Ewuare's reign it is said to have acquired the name of 'City'—the number of chiefs increased, and the magnificence surrounding the Oba himself was enhanced

---

1 The complicated story of the struggle for the throne among Ewuare's heirs is told by Egharevba, *A Short History*, pp. 22–3.
2 ibid. p. 14.
3 Graham Connah, 'New light on the Benin City walls', op. cit., has demonstrated that the rampart and ditch attributed to Ewuare is the only one of the 'walls' which can be regarded as a defensive fortification.

with the introduction of coral beads, scarlet cloth and carved ivory.

Despite periods of confusion following the death of most rulers, the empire of Benin continued to expand for more than a century after Ewuare. His youngest son, Ozolua—remembered as Ozolua the Conqueror—especially fostered the military character of the state. Under his leadership the armies of Benin were kept in constant activity, sometimes fighting two campaigns in the course of a year. He suffered at least one major defeat, but on most occasions divisions among his opponents, the superiority of his own forces, and his reputation as an invincible warrior gave him the victory. This sustained military pressure from Benin upon the surrounding peoples brought many areas under the permanent rule of the Oba. His most extensive conquests were made in Ishan, and he is also credited with a victory over Ijebu-Ode. Considering the distances involved and the known strength of Ijebu-Ode, it is unlikely that this success amounted to a conquest of that Yoruba city. More probably the tradition refers to a Benin victory in a border clash between two powers whose spheres of influence were now beginning to expand and overlap to a point where forcible demarcation became essential. In all his wars Ozolua was the active leader of the Benin armies, a devotee of battle; so much so that his own troops eventually wearied of his lust for war and killed him in order to end a particularly stubborn contest with Uromi in Ishan.

The royal house of Benin did not rely solely upon armed force to extend its influence. It also turned to advantage its prestige in the mysteries of government and the associated magic arts of kingship. Ewuare, it may be noted, was renowned as a magician as well as a warrior; indeed the two qualities went together. A belief that the dynasty possessed supernatural powers—a belief enhanced by military achievement—therefore enabled it to establish its offshoots in a dependent relationship farther afield.[1] Sometimes members of the royal lineage were installed as chiefs over conquered peoples, and surrounded by a court and ceremonial that borrowed many features of the parent court at Benin City. Ozolua in particular

---

[1] In this manner of expansion one may see a repetition of the process by which the Benin dynasty itself was first established. And while sending out its own branches it continued to hold fast to its parent root.

is remembered as having settled many of his sons in this manner. Thus was created a complex network of dynastic and ritual ties which bound to Benin many chiefdoms that were otherwise virtually autonomous.

One of the most important dynastic transplantations took place under another of Ewuare's sons, Olua, who preceded Ozolua on the throne. Tradition relates that Olua's eldest son, Iginua, became extremely unpopular in Benin where it was made clear that he would not be accepted as Oba. His father, therefore, determined to establish him in his own chiefdom at a safe distance from Benin, and sent him off, equipped with all the necessary royal regalia and attended by a retinue of chiefs' sons, into the swamp forest around the Benin River. Around this wandering band formed the embryonic Itsekiri kingdom, probably at first no more than a few settlements on the river.[1] In fact, Iginua's settlement among the Itsekiri may have followed the pattern of another made earlier by Ewuare when he sent an illegitimate son to Ughoton to be the first chief (*Olughoton*) of that riverside town. Besides establishing offshoots of the Benin dynasty in new regions, the Itsekiri and Ughoton enterprises were important in that they marked the awakening of Benin interest in the coastlands. The Edo had been, and indeed remained, a landfaring people with a positive distaste for activities which involved travelling by water. They relied, therefore, very much upon Ijo allies or auxiliaries who were thoroughly at home in the rivers, and who could supply the canoes which Benin lacked. What enticed them into this unfamiliar and inhospitable terrain we can only conjecture. Possibly the dynasty was pursuing a policy of proliferation on every side regardless of physical obstacles. Possibly it was influenced by the early appearances of Europeans in the Benin River.

Throughout most of the sixteenth century, the successors of Ewuare and Ozolua maintained the tradition of military kingship, and either led, or at least accompanied, their armies on the campaigns which carried the influence of Benin still farther afield. Ozolua's son Esigie is remembered for his defeat of the invading forces of Idah—a victory of great significance, for Idah was a powerful state with a system of kingship which in many ways resembled

---

1 cf. infra p. 28 and W. A. Moore, *History of the Itsekiri*. London, n.d.

that of Benin. Further more, since both Benin and Idah acknowledge a relationship between their ruling dynasties, it is possible that the war had a deeper significance than is suggested by the misogynist explanation common in Benin tradition.[1] It may, for example, have arisen from the general disturbance of the pattern of power along the middle Niger in the second quarter of the sixteenth century—upheavals which established a great Nupe state, and broke the power of Oyo for almost a century.[2] Benin weathered the storm, but not apparently without changing its relationship to the *Oghene*, and laying greater stress on the ritual powers of the Oba.[3]

In the later years of his reign, Esigie turned his attention towards the coast, securing submission or tribute from a number of petty states to the west of the Benin River.[4] Orhogbua, his son and successor, consolidated this new sphere of influence by conquering Mahin and penetrating westwards as far as the island on which Lagos now stands. In some ways expansion in this direction was a natural sequel to the earlier coastward settlements associated with Ewuare and Ozolua. Orhogbua may even have intended to found a new coastal state with himself as its ruler, for it is said that the expedition kept him absent from Benin for many years, and that he only returned to his capital at the insistence of the chiefs. Eventually the camp at Eko developed into the state of Lagos, ruled by a king who traced his descent from the royal line of Benin, though his subjects were of Yoruba origin. For almost three centuries the royal house and chiefs of Lagos maintained their association with Benin by seeking confirmation of their titles from the Oba and paying a customary tribute.

The end of the sixteenth and beginning of the seventeenth centuries saw widespread unrest in the regions to the north-west of Benin, and the reign of Ehengbuda, last of the warrior Obas. Disturbances within a number of Yoruba states—particularly Akure,

---

1 Tradition blames the outbreak of the war on the unfaithfulness of Imaguero, wife of the *Uzama* chief Oliha (cf. Egharevba, *A Short History*, pp. 28–9). The Igala version of relations between Idah and Benin is examined by J. Boston, 'Notes on the origin of the Igala'. *J.H.S.N.*, vol. II, no. 3, 1962.
2 cf. R. Smith, 'The Alafin in exile: a study of the Igboho period in Oyo history'. *Journal of African History*, vol. VI, no. 1, 1965.
3 cf. Ryder, 'The Ife-Benin relationship,' pp. 35–6, et infra pp. 70–1, 72.
4 cf. infra p. 73 n. 2.

Ilesha and Owo—and the perennial conflict between Oyo and the Nupe appear to have been the source of trouble. Benin was drawn in, and again, as in the time of Esigie, emerged victorious and enlarged. Dutch visitors in the earlier part of the seventeenth century heard of a major victory won a generation earlier over a large army of horsemen sent to invade Benin from the direction of Oyo.[1] Perhaps they were being told of an early appearance and defeat of the famous Oyo cavalry; but since the Nupe were at that time dominant in the Oyo region, it is equally possible that the reverse was inflicted on their armies. From this victory Ehengbuda won recognition of Benin suzerainty over large areas of Ekiti, and tribute from several Yoruba rulers, among them those of Akure and Owo. Another series of campaigns expanded Benin hegemony towards the Niger, as many more Ibo towns and villages to the west of the river submitted to the Oba.

The Benin empire was to grow no more. In some directions it had reached natural boundaries: the River Niger to the east, and the sea to the south. Elsewhere it now marched with other powerful kingdoms whose military and religious systems were able to resist further encroachment. The Benin monarchy itself was beginning to change, as the Oba increasingly delegated command of his armies to senior chiefs. Most of the successes achieved in the time of Ehengbuda were won under the leadership of the senior town chief, the *Iyase*, and the dangers of that development became clear when he quarrelled with the Oba. Fighting broke out in Benin City, ending with the defeat and suicide of the *Iyase*. A law forbidding any future *Iyase* to return to Benin City after making an important conquest was then passed in an effort to avoid future confrontations; and it may have been this crisis which determined Ehengbuda to take personal command of an expedition that ended in disaster when he was drowned in the creeks between Lagos and Benin. Probably as a result of that mishap, 'it was arranged that the Benin war-chiefs or warriors be commanding the Benin troops henceforth and not the Obas of Benin any more'.[2] Thus the common practice of Ehengbuda's reign hardened into custom, and the relatively secluded life to which the rulers of Benin had been

---

1 Dapper, *Naukeurige Beschrijvinge*, p. 131.
2 Egharevba, *A Short History*, p. 34.

adapting themselves now became more rigorously restricted and organised within the ample bounds of the palace. The Oba, as the pivot upon which the life of the state turned, was transformed from a figure of military might to one of supernatural powers; the two elements had, it is true, always co-existed in the Benin concept of kingship, which saw the Oba as the temporal and spiritual guardian of his people, but the emphasis now shifted decisively to the ritual functions of kingship.

In theory, the nature of the supernatural powers attributed to the Oba, and the complicated structure of palace and town associations, afforded even a secluded ruler ample means of controlling his kingdom. In practice, however, the withdrawal of the Oba into his palace—from which he emerged briefly only once or twice a year—raised great difficulties and dangers for the monarchy. Benin did not easily adjust itself to the new circumstances. For more than a century the Obas in their new role suffered a loss of power and prestige, while that of the important chiefs, especially the leading members of the palace associations and the military commanders, rose correspondingly. Benin tradition reflects these changed fortunes of the kingship, for, in striking contrast to the famous Obas of the sixteenth century, the seven rulers of the seventeenth are all obscure men, almost indistinguishable from one another. The alteration in the balance of political power within the state also seems to be reflected in a new mode of succession to the throne. Instead of following the practice of the previous century, when succession had been determined by a rule of primogeniture, the kingship was opened to several branches of the royal family. Contemporary Dutch accounts give the impression that this procedure put the final choice of ruler into the hands of the most powerful chiefs:

> When the king lieth upon his death-bed, he sends for one of his nobility, whom they call Onegwa[1] to whom he declares the right of succession, and who shall be his heir; which this nobleman does reveal to none, till a competent time after the king's death; but then takes upon him the oversight of the deceased king's goods and children, who come with great humility and salute him, not as yet knowing who shall

---

1 i.e. *Uwangue*, since the early sixteenth century, at least, one of the most influential of the palace chiefs.

inherit the crown. Every one makes address to this Onegwa with great respect, in hopes of future advantage, but he continues silent till the appointed time; when sending for the Owe-asserry,[1] that is, the General, tells him which son the deceased king appointed to inherit the crown: whereupon the General, without speaking a word, withdraws to his house; and the Onegwa sets up that son to be king; whereof the retired General receiving notice, after five or six days, he comes again to the court, and calling for the Onegwa, demands if that were the old king's will; wherein receiving an affirmative satisfaction, immediately they present the deposited inheritance of the crown, and he receives the dominion.[2]

Dapper based this account on information gathered in the early decades of the seventeenth century when the choice of heir was still restricted to an Oba's sons; later it extended to his brothers. It is hardly necessary to point out the opportunities which such a procedure offered for collusion between the leaders of the palace and town chiefs (the *Uwangue* and *Iyase*), and they appear to have taken full advantage of them. Even once installed on the throne, an Oba was not entirely secure. At least one was deposed by his chiefs for depriving them of their customary share in the state revenues and numerous perquisites. His successor, Egharevba remarks, was an Oba 'of unrestricted liberality';[3] so the lesson had obviously been taken to heart by both sides.

In these circumstances, it is not surprising that descriptions of the Benin system of government written in the seventeenth century by Dutch, Spanish and Italian observers all show the supposedly all-powerful Oba virtually confined to his palace, and hedged around by his chiefs. One of the Spanish Capuchins who went to Benin in 1651 drew this picture of the Oba's plight:

One of these officials was an old man, and a great magician, who consulted the devil on all matters, and enjoyed so much favour with the king that the latter was entirely under his influence, and nothing whatsoever was decided in the kingdom without his advice. In order that the king might not know what was happening among his subjects, he

---

1 i.e. the *Iyase*.
2 Dapper, *Naukeurige Beschrijvinge*, p. 130. I have taken the translation from John Ogilby's *Africa*, London, 1670, which is wholly, but often inaccurately, lifted from Dapper.
3 Egharevba, *A Short History*, p. 38.

had been persuaded, on the pretext of enhancing his greatness, to leave his palace only once a year, and allow no-one to see him. But so that the king might be satisfied with this form of seclusion, and neither seek nor desire outside diversions, these had been provided within the palace itself—which was very large—by a variety of musicians, and by furnishing for his carnal pleasures and debaucheries five hundred concubines; some even affirm that their number exceeds three thousand. So great was the cunning and wickedness of the official, that he might not lose his favour with the king.[1]

Allowing for a measure of exaggeration and simplification, this account agrees fairly well with that given in other sources. Oral tradition too preserves much the same memory of the Oba ruling when the Capuchins were in Benin:

> Many took advantage of his youthfulness so that the long-stored treasures of the former kings were wasted. The royal coral beads were gambled away in games of dice with Osuan.[2]

This state of affairs might have produced a monarchy on the pattern of Oyo,[3] had the chiefs been able to give their position some permanent basis independent of the throne. But they either did not try, or else they failed, to change the non-hereditary and appointive character of their titles and offices; so that, however weak an Oba might be, he, or at least his office, remained the ultimate source of all power and promotion in the kingdom. Thus he was the potential beneficiary of feuds and rivalries among the great men who surrounded him.

At length, in the last decade of the seventeenth century, there appeared an Oba determined to reassert the independence of the throne by taking advantage of bitter rivalry that had developed between the town and palace chiefs. The outcome was a civil war that raged with some intermissions for over twenty years, devastating many parts of the kingdom, including the capital. Putting together

---

1 José de Alicante, *apud* M. de Anguiano, *Misiones Capuchinos en Africa: II. Misiones al reino de la Zinga, Benin, Arda, Guinea y Sierra Leone*. Madrid, 1957, pp. 225–6. Taking this passage with information recorded by other members of the mission, it appears that the official in question was the *Uwangue*.

2 Egharevba, *A Short History*, p. 35.

3 cf. P. Morton-Williams, 'The Yoruba kingdom of Oyo', in *West African Kingdoms in the Nineteenth Century*, ed. D. Forde and P. Kaberry, Oxford, 1967.

the reports of European visitors and oral tradition—although these are not easily reconciled—it would seem that about 1690 the Oba began to take drastic action against powerful chiefs both within Benin City and in the provinces.[1] He struck particularly at the wealth of the town chiefs. Led by the *Iyase*, these chiefs with their followers and dependants rose in rebellion, and from an encampment some miles distant from the capital they harassed the Oba for several years, inflicting defeats on his armies, and on one occasion sacking the city and palace. Where the Oba found his support is not clear; probably the palace chiefs rallied to him, for oral tradition certainly exaggerates when it asserts that he was abandoned by the whole people. He also took pains to gain the favour of Europeans by encouraging the Dutch West India Company to trade in the Benin River, and by showing a willingness to receive missionaries from São Tomé.[2] It was a Portuguese who, in the last years of the century, patched up a truce between ruler and rebels, though the *Iyase* still refused to return to Benin City.

The Oba attempted to improve his incomplete victory by establishing a firm rule of primogeniture to govern succession to the throne, and thus eliminate an important means of influence which the chiefs had so successfully exploited in the past. In theory at least this rule has ever since prevailed in Benin, and has prevented a repetition of the seventeenth-century experience when the frequent choice of old men for the throne led to short reigns and fostered feeble government. A system of primogeniture could not, however, fend off struggles between princes disputing their claims to seniority. In a society where the ruler had many wives, where these were sent to villages outside the capital to give birth to the royal children, and where there was no system for recording the exact date of a child's birth, much genuine doubt and confusion might arise in the twenty years or more which could intervene between the birth of the son and the death of the father. On the other hand, there is no doubt that many disputes arose less from uncertainty as to the rightful heir than from the nature of political organisation in Benin. It can be taken as axiomatic that there were many more claims for office and favours than could be met from existing resources, especially at times when the prosperity of the

---

1 cf. infra p. 127.   2 cf. infra p. 113-4.

state and the extent of its power were diminished. Those not presently satisfied with their rank and fortune had therefore to pin their hopes on a prospective heir to the throne, and pay their court to him. Because an acknowledged heir thus tended to become a focus of opposition, many Obas were reluctant to name a successor during their lifetime, even though by neglecting to do so they greatly lessened the chances of a peaceful transfer of power. Conversely, those presently enjoying favour had either to outbid the aspirants in the favour of the heir-apparent, or else raise up at the opportune moment a candidate of their own. Conflicts within Benin society were therefore likely to break into the open on the death of a ruler, and to polarise around rival candidates for the throne. So deep-rooted was this tendency that, despite the primogeniture convention, during the eighteenth and nineteenth centuries only one Oba ascended the throne undisputed, and most had to overcome their rivals by force.

Nevertheless, the Benin monarchy did emerge stronger from the long civil war that spanned the end of the seventeenth and opening of the eighteenth centuries. General war-weariness, the humbling of the *Iyase*, who lost his function as military commander to the *Ezomo*, and the concentration of the opposition upon their efforts to put their own candidate on the throne, rather than upon modifying the political system, all combined to sap the strength of the forces opposed to the monarchy. Akenzua I, the Oba who emerged triumphant from the civil wars, was thus able, thanks to a shrewd political sense, to restore much of the former authority of the crown. Many sources of revenue which had fallen into abeyance, or into the hands of chiefs, were recovered for the ruler, with the result that, in contrast to his poverty-stricken predecessors, Akenzua is remembered as one of the richest kings ever to sit on the Benin throne.[1] Even so, the revival could not carry the monarchy and government back to the forms of the sixteenth century. Akenzua and his successors confined themselves within the palace. They maintained their authority largely by manipulating the title system, and by an increasing emphasis upon their ritual function as guardians of the nation's prosperity and security. Which is not to argue that these

---

1 A considerable growth of European trade contributed to his wealth. cf. infra p. 145.

rulers enjoyed less real power than their warrior ancestors, but that the character of the kingship had undergone a fundamental change with this growing insistence upon its majesty and mystery.[1]

Weakness in its rulers throughout most of the seventeenth century and a long civil war at its close had inevitably loosened Benin's hold upon its subject territories. Dutch records show that control over the lower Benin River—important as a centre for trade with Europeans—was lost to the Itsekiris and Ijos.[2] Information about the interior is less precise, but it seems that Ishan remained in a state of rebellion during much of Akenzua's reign; Agbor rose against his son, Eresoyen; and a major campaign had to be waged against Ugo in the reign of Akengbuda. With a state of unrest affecting territories relatively close to the heart of the kingdom, it is improbable that Benin was able to bring much effective control or influence to bear upon the peripheral regions. It must be borne in mind, however, that the Benin 'empire'[3] had a somewhat informal character. Only the central area within easy reach of the capital ever came under the permanent supervision of the Oba; farther afield his authority was exercised through military settlements, resident representatives (as in Akure), or through junior brothers who were made hereditary chiefs (*enigie*) of towns and villages. Some of these bonds between Benin and its vassals were in truth as light as air, demanding little more than a formal acknowledgement of the Oba at the beginning of his reign, and a friendly attitude thereafter. Within such a system disruption at the centre led to a loosening of ties, a lapse in the performance of customary obligations, rather than to sudden rebellion, or to wholesale repudiation of links with Benin. The loose-knit, heterogeneous character of the 'empire' helped also to ensure that revolt in one part did not flare into a general conflagration.

The greatest threat to the integrity of the Benin 'empire' came

---

1 The changed character of the kingship is reflected in a new style of brasswork produced for the palace in the eighteenth century; lightness and a certain naturalism gave way to a ponderous, rigidly stylised art.
2 cf. infra p. 135.
3 The term 'empire' is frequently used to describe the territorial and political complex of which the Oba and Benin City were the centre. There is a danger that this and other concepts drawn largely from non-African models may mislead us if they are not carefully qualified.

from neighbouring states powerful enough to attract or compel parts of it to enter their own orbit. In the sixteenth century Benin had overcome this danger by defeating or warding off her most menacing neighbours—Idah, Oyo and the Nupe. But in the eighteenth and nineteenth centuries new pressures began to develop. In the wake of the Fulani *jihad* came a fresh wave of Nupe attacks on the northern Edo areas; to the west, the break-up of the Oyo kingdom led to fighting in Ekiti; on the coast a British presence gradually established the bases which demanded and made possible an advance to the interior. Not even at the height of its fortunes could Benin have resisted the forces that were now closing upon it, so the oft-aired subject of its decline in the nineteenth century is irrelevant to the outcome. As the British grip tightened upon the coast and Yorubaland, and especially after the downfall of Jaja and Nana, an awareness of a new and overwhelming challenge developed in Benin. In response the kingdom which for centuries had cultivated and welcomed contact with Europeans sought safety in isolation. Withdrawal to the heartlands was hastened and made more complete by the breakdown of trade with Europeans and neighbouring states. Wars in the Nupe country had destroyed trading links to the north; the growth of the Royal Niger Company severed the routes to the east; in the west, the considerable arms traffic which flourished during the early period of the Yoruba wars was shut off in the eighteen-seventies by the closing of the Oke Igbo route.

From one point of view, the last century of Benin's existence as an independent state can be regarded as a period of steady and inevitable decline wherein rulers sought to maintain a grip on a shrinking state by ever more feverish manipulation of the political system[1] and a greater emphasis on human sacrifice. The hapless Oba Ovonramwen lost control altogether in 1896.[2] On the other

---

1 One measure of the overwork to which the system was subjected can be drawn from the creation of titles. Of those in existence at the end of the nineteenth century, twenty-six were in use in the reign of Ewuare, another twenty-six were added up to the time of Akenzua, nineteen more were created in the eighteenth century, and no fewer than twenty-seven by the last three Obas of the nineteenth century.

2 At his trial in 1897, witnesses agreed that Ovonramwen had tried unsuccessfully to prevent certain chiefs attacking and killing Phillips and his party. Egharevba, *A Short History*, chap. xxv.

hand, the basic, well-tried political structure had been preserved and continued to function.[1] Benin could still defend its interests effectively against reasonable odds; at the beginning of the century a major military effort had led to the reconquest of Akure, and the imposition of Benin control over much of Ekiti country; on the eve of the British conquest, preparations were in hand for an expedition to subdue a rebellion at Agbor. And at the end, resistance to the punitive expedition of 1897 confounded all the British 'Benin experts' who had confidently predicted an ignominious surrender.

1 For a detailed examination of the state in the nineteenth century see R. E. Bradbury, 'The kingdom of Benin', in *West African Kingdoms in the Nineteenth Century*, ed. D. Forde and P. M. Kaberry. Oxford, 1967.

Chapter 2
The era of Portuguese monopoly

1. First contacts

Portuguese ships first reconnoitred that part of the West African coast which now lies within the boundaries of Nigeria some time between 1469 and 1475. During those years, a Lisbon merchant, Fernão Gomes, held the lease of the Guinea trade from King Afonso V of Portugal by a contract which required *inter alia* that each year his captains should explore one hundred leagues of coastline beyond Sierra Leone, where exploration directed by the Portuguese crown had temporarily halted.[1] By 1471 the seamen in Gomes' employ had reached that part of Guinea to which they gave the name of Costa da Mina, and it was probably in the two succeeding years that they penetrated into the Bight of Benin, gained some knowledge of its principal rivers, and discovered that slaves could be bought there. The sixteenth-century historian Antonio Galvão attributed the first Portuguese voyage through the Bight of Benin to one Ruy de Sequeira in 1472,[2] the same year in which he, or another of Gomes' captains, first sighted the islands of Fernando Po, Príncipe and São Tomé.

No immediate attempt appears to have been made to exploit these discoveries. Gomes' contract finally expired in 1475, the year in which war broke out between Portugal and Castile, distracting the former from African affairs until peace was made in 1479. Then the Portuguese crown eagerly turned its attention to developing trade with the gold-producing regions of the Costa da Mina, and it was in pursuit of this lucrative traffic that its agents extended their activities eastwards into the Bight of Benin. Fleets of small vessels, mostly of the caravel type, laden with European merchandise, would work their way along the Guinea shore and anchor off one of the Fante coastal villages, where their goods could be bartered for gold.

---

1 cf. E. Prestage, *The Portuguese Pioneers*. London, 1933, reprinted 1966, pp. 184–5. J. Parry, *The Age of Reconnaissance*. London, 1963, pp. 133–4.
2 A. Galvão, *Tratado dos descobrimentos*. Porto, 1944, p. 129.

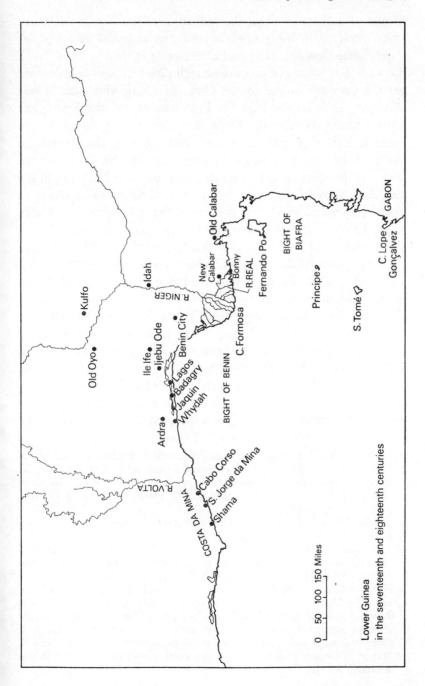

Lower Guinea
in the seventeenth and eighteenth centuries

0 50 100 150 Miles

It was soon discovered that the African merchants—many of whom were attracted to these markets from the interior—preferred, or even insisted, on receiving part of the price of their gold in slaves. Because they could not procure enough slaves to meet this demand on the outward voyage to the Costa da Mina, and since it was obviously impolitic to seize the local inhabitants, the Portuguese turned to the rivers in the Bight of Benin as being the nearest to hand, and, thanks to prevailing winds and currents, relatively easy of access. It became the practice for a few caravels, detached from the main trading fleet on the Costa da Mina, to make their way to the so-called 'slave rivers', and return with their cargo of slaves in time to complete the barter deals with the gold merchants before the entire fleet sailed for Portugal.[1] In January 1480 two caravels made such a voyage to the 'Rio dos Escravos' and obtained more than four hundred slaves, most of whom were subsequently bartered for gold. Fernão do Po commanded one of these vessels,[2] and returned in subsequent years to undertake similar voyages, including one in 1485 which is mentioned by de Barros.[3] The 'Rio dos Escravos' visited by the Portuguese in 1480 could have been any one of the 'five slave rivers' known to Portuguese pilots,[4] but is unlikely to have been the river, noted for its extremely dangerous bar and lack of trade, which bore that name some twenty years later.[5] These five rivers began with the one the Portuguese named the Rio Primeiro (First River), and included the Rio Fermoso (the

---

1 A Flemish merchant, Eustache de la Fosse, who was taken prisoner by the Portuguese when sailing to Guinea aboard a Castilian ship in 1479, has left an account of one of these voyages. 'Voyage à la côte occidentale d'Afrique en Portugal et en Espagne (1479–1480)', ed. R. Foulché-Delbosc. *Revue Hispanique.* 1897, pp. 174–201.
2 ibid. p. 186. De la Fosse calls him 'Sr. Fernand de les Vaux'.
3 J. de Barros, *Da Asia*, Dec. 1, liv.iii, cap. 3.
4 A privilege granted to the settlers of São Tomé (16 Dec. 1485) permitted them to trade 'in the five slave rivers which are beyond our fortress of São Jorge da Mina'. A.T.T. *Livro das Ilhas*, f. 109v.
5 cf. Duarte Pacheco Pereira, *Esmeraldo de situ orbis*, ed. R. Mauny. Bissau, 1956, pp. 136–8. Writing c. 1506, Pacheco Pereira described the Rio dos Escravos thus: 'This river has shallows or a shelf of hard sand which extends almost a league out to sea; on it there are two and a half, and at the most three fathoms of water. This is a very dangerous place, and a wise man will keep away from it. There is no trade, nor anything else worthy of note in this Rio dos Escravos.'

Beautiful River, now the Benin River), the Rio dos Escravos (the Slave River), the Rio dos Forcados (the Swallowtail River) and the Rio dos Ramos (Creek River), in that order from west to east. That all these rivers were named by the Portuguese does not mean that they frequented them, but that their identification was essential to accurate navigation. Miscalculation could prove dangerous, as was demonstrated in later years when a number of ships, mistaking the Ramos for the Forcados River, were wrecked on the extremely shallow bar of the former.[1] If this important factor of navigability is taken into account, together with the location of trade in later times, it would seem likely that on these early voyages the Portuguese acquired their slaves in either the Benin or Forcados Rivers.

Whichever of the 'slave rivers' the Portuguese frequented, the people they first met and traded with would have belonged to the Ijo tribe, which at that time dominated the coastal belt of swamp forest. Extending inland to a depth of thirty or forty miles in this region, and described by a later traveller as 'a morass covered with an impenetrable forest',[2] the swamp belt forced its few inhabitants to live in small groups at a bare subsistence level. Movement depended entirely upon the maze of creeks and rivers, and on canoes in which to navigate them; life depended upon what could be obtained from the waters, and from raids upon neighbouring communities. Hence the Ijo gained their reputation for ferocity and piracy, including the assertion that they practised cannibalism, which was made in the earliest Portuguese description of them, and repeated on many occasions. This first mention of the Ijo occurs in the *Esmeraldo de Situ Orbis*, a work written at the beginning of the sixteenth century by Duarte Pacheco Pereira who had acquired some first-hand knowledge of the area in the course of his service on the Costa da Mina.[3]

---

1 Pacheco Pereira, *Esmeraldo*, p. 140. The bar of the Ramos River had less than two fathoms of water.

2 J. Adams, *Sketches taken during ten voyages to Africa between the years 1786 and 1800*. London, n.d., p. 28.

3 Pacheco Pereira was governor of S. Jorge da Mina from 1520 to 1522, but it is generally believed that he wrote the *Esmeraldo* about 1506, and based it upon experience gained from an earlier spell of duty in Guinea. He was probably the *cavalleiro da casa del Rey* named Duarte Pacheco whom Bartolomeu Dias met in Príncipe on his return from the voyage to the Cape of Good Hope. He had been sent to explore the rivers of the coast, but falling ill returned with Dias. Ref. de Barros, *Asia*, Dec. I, liv. iii, cap. 4.

His account of the coast proximate to Benin reveals a distribution of peoples that has not changed radically over the centuries. To the west of the Forcados River, and some distance inland, he places the *Huela*—a word which may be related to *Iwere*, the name by which the Itsekiri know themselves; the area indicated corresponds to what is believed to be the early centre of Itsekiri settlement.[1] Farther inland, beyond the Ijo and *Huela*, lay the *Subou*, the present-day Urhobo or Sobo people, whose settlements appear to have expanded towards the sea since the end of the fifteenth century. Today much of the swamp forest still shelters only a scanty population of Ijos.

Of the peoples mentioned as dwelling around the Benin River by Pacheco Pereira, only the Urhobo belonged to the Edo-speaking group. The Benin Edo live now, as they seem to have done then, outside the swamp forest area; the southern limit of their settlement corresponds closely to the division between swamp and rain forest, and there are no grounds for believing that it ever extended nearer to the coast. Nor have the Edo of Benin ever been great river-farers or canoemen. If they depended at all upon the coastal region for supplies of such commodities as salt and fish—and it is not certain that they did—they obtained them through the Ijo and Itsekiri. In fact, at the time the Portuguese first touched the coast, Benin paid little or no attention to the sea; it was not a coastal state, and its trade and political interests drew it firmly towards the interior. Thus it was possible for the Portuguese to trade in the rivers without knowing of the existence of Benin, and they had eventually to penetrate inland in order to establish contact with it.

The decision to send an emissary in search of Benin has to be seen against a background of intense African activity inspired by John II who ascended the throne of Portugal in 1481.[2] Thrusting aside the lack of interest in Guinean affairs which had set in since the death of Henry the Navigator, John II immediately embarked upon measures to exploit to the full his monopoly of European trade in these parts of the world, to lay there the foundations of a Portuguese empire, and by further sea-borne and overland exploration to come

---

1 cf. P. C. Lloyd, *The Itsekiri*. London, 1957, and supra p. 13.
2 cf. Parry, *Age of Reconnaissance*, pp. 133–6.

upon the long-sought kingdom of Prester John. The construction of the fortress of São Jorge da Mina, the assumption of the title of Lord of Guinea, the voyages of Diogo Cão to the Congo and Angola, the colonisation of São Tomé and the despatch of envoys to the rulers of the Congo and the western Sudan were all part of the grandiose design. So too was the visit to the hinterland of the 'slave rivers' entrusted to João Afonso d'Aveiro in 1486.

It is unlikely that either d'Aveiro or his superiors possessed much reliable information about the territory he was sent to explore, but it is reasonable to assume that, in the course of several years' slave trading in the rivers, the Portuguese must have learned something about the largest and most powerful state known to the people with whom they were dealing. If the dating of Iginua's establishment among the Itsekiri is at all reliable, the Portuguese could have gleaned some intelligence from that dynastic offshoot of Benin.[1] It is also likely that they gathered information from Edo slaves acquired in the rivers, for they often relied upon knowledge gained from captives when launching into unfamiliar territory. We may suppose, therefore, that in sending d'Aveiro inland the king of Portugal was guided by reports that a considerable kingdom existed there, and that he desired to know more about the ruler, the people, the government, the religion, and the products of that country. Interest in such matters may have been prompted by the needs of the slave trade. With a permanent establishment on the Costa da Mina, the Portuguese presumably required a larger and more constant supply of slaves than in the days of intermittent visits by trading fleets. The ill-organised Ijo and Itsekiri communities would find it difficult to meet this greater demand; hence the attraction of dealing with a large, centralised state. Also a glance at maps of the period will show that in Benin the Portuguese were seemingly approaching nearer than anywhere else in Guinea to the reputed land of Prester John. Expectations therefore grew that some link with the Christian ruler might be established through the interior of Africa. In addition to these considerations, John II was influenced here, as elsewhere in Africa, by a missionary zeal which looked upon rulers as the most efficacious agents of evangelisation, and sought accordingly for the fountainhead of authority. The apparent missionary success

---

1 cf. supra p. 13.

of 1485 in the Congo doubtless strengthened the king's confidence in this royal road to the conversion of the African masses. Finally, a political motive may be discerned in missions such as that undertaken by d'Aveiro: the self-styled Lord of Guinea was anxious to give substance to his title. Papal bulls had laid a legal foundation for it in Europe; the fortress of São Jorge da Mina and settlements in some of the off-shore islands gave it a localised and precarious existence in some parts of Guinea; but it could only become meaningful if recognised, even in the most formal manner, by the rulers of Guinea. Hence the desire to find these rulers, and to establish the position of the king of Portugal as *primus inter pares* among them.

No record of his journey has survived, but it is likely that d'Aveiro, like most subsequent European travellers, went by water to Ughoton, then overland to Benin City. On men accustomed to the small towns of Europe huddled into the narrow confines of their walls, the spaciousness of the 'great city of Benin'[1] made a powerful impression, and confirmed that here was a state of far greater consequence than the petty chiefdoms which they had hitherto encountered on the coasts of Guinea. The Oba—according to tradition, it was Ozolua who first met the Portuguese—took a lively interest in the strangers, and agreed that the chief of Ughoton should accompany them to Lisbon so that he might learn more about Portugal and its way of life. Visits of this nature were regularly sponsored by the Portuguese government in order to impress African dignitaries with the power and wealth of the homeland, for such qualities were often not conspicuous in the small and unkempt bands that represented it in Africa. The choice of the chief of Ughoton may perhaps be attributed to the importance of his village as the 'port' of Benin, and the one most immediately concerned with the opening of European trade. It may also have been influenced by the chief's relationship to the royal house, signified by the title of *Edaiken* which was otherwise reserved for the heir to the throne.[2] His bearing matched these dignities. 'Their ambassador', wrote the royal chronicler, Ruy de Pina, 'was a man of good speech and natural wisdom.'[3] As for trade, the Oba showed readiness to

---

1 The words are those of Pacheco Pereira, *Esmeraldo*, p. 134.
2 cf. supra p. 13.
3 Ruy de Pina, *Chrónica del Rey Dom João II*. Coimbra, 1950, ch. 24.

permit it not only in slaves, but in other products of interest to the Portuguese. At this time they were seeking in particular a variety of pepper which could compete more satisfactorily with Indian pepper than could the malagetta (*Aframomum malagueta*) which was the only spice they had so far discovered in Guinea.[1] Benin pepper (*Piper guineense*), of which d'Aveiro took samples, proved an admirable substitute, and a trial of the 'tailed pepper' through the Portuguese factory at Antwerp and in other European markets revealed lucrative prospects.[2]

The information gathered from d'Aveiro and the chief of Ughoton on spiritual matters also aroused interest in Portugal. They told about the *Oghene*[3] who exercised some kind of suzerainty over Benin. On the death of an Oba, his successor sent messengers to this overlord bearing valuable gifts; they announced the death of their ruler and asked for the royal insignia in the name of the new Oba. By these same messengers the *Oghene* sent back the emblems consisting of a staff, a headpiece shaped like a Spanish helmet, and a cross which the Oba wore on a chain round his neck. The messengers received similar but smaller crosses which conferred on them a special dignity in Benin after their return from a journey that was estimated to take twenty months. Diligent enquiry also elicited the information that the realm of the *Oghene* lay to the east of Benin.[4] Because John II was seeking eagerly for signs of the Negus, the direction and distance of the *Oghene* from Benin, and above all, the Maltese-type crosses, all pointed to Prester John. The great reverence in which the Edo held the *Oghene*—'like the Pope with us'—and the custom which kept him always concealed by a curtain from the gaze of subjects assured the king that this was a religious figure of no mean significance.

Whereupon, the King and the cosmographers of the kingdom, consulting Ptolemy's general map of Africa and the charts of the coast

1 cf. J. W. Blake, *European Beginnings in West Africa, 1454–1578*. London, 1937, pp. 83–4.
2 Benin pepper acquired the name 'tailed pepper' (*pimenta de rabo*) from the stem that adhered to it.
3 Portuguese writers called him *Ogane*, which may have been an older form of the present-day *Oghene*. cf. supra p. 7.
4 This indication of direction may not be as explicit as is often assumed. cf. Ryder, 'The Ife-Benin relationship', p. 27.

drawn up by his explorers, and considering the distance of two hundred and fifty leagues towards the east where the people of Benin affirmed the state of this Prince Ogane to be, they found that he must be Prester John, for both were concealed behind curtains of silk, and both held the sign of the Cross in great veneration.[1]

These ill-founded calculations inspired John II to despatch Bartolomeu Dias to seek Prester John and India by way of the Cape of Good Hope in August 1487. They also raised hopes of the speedy conversion of Benin, now assumed to be already under the distant influence of a form of Christianity. All in all the first contact with Benin had more than fulfilled Portuguese expectations.

2. The beginning of trade

When the time came for the chief of Ughoton, suitably provided with presents for himself, his wife and the Oba, to return to his country, he was accompanied by a number of officials led by d'Aveiro, whose task it was to establish in Benin a *feitoria* or trading post,[2] the first to appear in Guinea after São Jorge da Mina. By means of this post, the king intended to ensure that the trade of Benin, especially the pepper, passed exclusively through the *Casa da Mina*, a government department created to administer the commerce and possessions of the crown in Guinea.[3] No missionaries joined the party because John II believed that the initiative in religious matters should come from the other side; but to show the Oba the way, 'he sent holy and most catholic admonitions', exhorting him to lead his subjects away from their 'heresies, gross idolatry and fetishes'.[4]

The history of the Portuguese trading post at Ughoton is very obscure. D'Aveiro himself died there—the first known European victim of a place which soon became notorious for the high mortality rate among those serving there.[5] The names of those who

---

1 De Barros, *Asia*, Dec. I, liv. iii, cap. 4.
2 English merchants later used the cognate word 'factory' in the same sense.
3 The *Casa da Mina de Guiné* was established in Lisbon in 1482. It served as a model for the later *Casa da India* in Lisbon, and the *Casa da la Contratación* of Seville.
4 De Pina, *Chrónica*, cap. 24.
5 Pacheco Pereira, *Esmeraldo*, p. 140. 'All these rivers are very unhealthy because of the fever, which does grievous harm to us whitemen, especially in the winter of this country.'

followed him are unknown, save for Duarte Lopes, who died in Ughoton a few months after his arrival there in 1504,[1] and his successor Bastiam Fernandez, who[2] was probably the last factor, for the post was finally closed in 1506–7. It cannot be assumed, however, that it was manned continuously from 1487 to 1507; in fact there is some evidence to the contrary. De Barros, for example, implies that the post was abandoned during the reign of John II who died in 1495.[3] Pacheco Pereira, who visited Benin on four occasions during the fourteen-nineties, makes no mention of a trading establishment in either Ughoton or Benin City. A further hint that no royal factor resided in Benin at the end of the fifteenth century is contained in a letter written to the king of Portugal by the acting-captain of São Tomé in July 1499.[4] He informed the king that if he were provided with a boat to trade in the 'slave rivers', he could send an adequate number of slaves to the Costa da Mina, so that 'it will not be necessary for Your Majesty's ships to sail down to the slave rivers, unless it be for pepper'. It would seem, therefore, that the post at Ughoton had a chequered, discontinuous existence. The reasons are not far to seek. Most of the high hopes the Portuguese government entertained of Benin were quickly disappointed. Trade did not yield the great returns expected of it. Men sent to Ughoton sickened and died with alarming rapidity. In matters of religion the Oba did not respond to Portuguese proddings, and at the end of the century Pacheco Pereira was complaining that 'the manner of life of these people is full of abuses, fetishes and idolatry'. From the Benin point of view it is evident that the arrival of the Portuguese, though it aroused interest, was only a marginal development, insufficient to bring about any major change in the economic pursuits or way of life of the people.

The failure of Portugal to draw Benin into its political and

---

1 A.T.T. *Núcleo Antigo, maço* 166. This document contains many references to goods which the *Casa da Mina* sent to Lopes.
2 A.T.T. *Livro das Ilhas*, 192r–v.
3 De Barros, *Asia*, Dec. I, liv. iii, cap. 3. After stating that the officials were withdrawn, he continues, 'However, for a considerable time afterwards, both during the life of Dom João and of Dom Manuel, this sale of slaves continued from Beny to Mina.' Too much reliance should not be placed on his chronology with regard to early Portuguese activity in Guinea.
4 A.T.T. *Corpo Cronológico*, I, *maço* 2, no. 128, 30 July 1499.

commercial orbit can more clearly be understood by examining the detail of the trade between them. It must first of all be emphasised that Benin did not control all trade in the 'slave rivers'; those parts where the Portuguese had traded before 1486 lay outside the Benin sphere of influence and remained largely independent of it in following years. Conversely, the Portuguese crown was not the sole European trading interest in the area, though no other could operate there without its licence. Important concessions permitting Portuguese subjects and others to trade in the 'slave rivers' were granted from time to time. The first of them antedates d'Aveiro's visit to Benin. It took the form of a privilege granted to the pioneer settlers of São Tomé in 1485; by it they were free to trade in the 'five slave rivers' except in those commodities reserved exclusively to the crown.[1] In the event this colonisation project came to nothing, but a similar privilege was given to the settlers who did occupy the island in 1493.[2] By the following year they had begun to send their ships to the rivers in search of slaves, thus inaugurating a commerce which continued with little interruption until well into the nineteenth century. Another interest created before the Portuguese had visited Benin came into existence in 1486 when the trade of the 'slave rivers' was leased to a Florentine merchant named Bartolomeo Marchione.[3] Since Marchione retained the lease until 1495, it must be presumed that the Benin trade which opened in 1487 under direct royal control was not held to conflict with the Italian's contract—a supposition which is strengthened by the renewal of the lease in the early years of the sixteenth century when it was held by Fernão de Loronha.[4] In practice it is very unlikely that these diverse interests—crown, settlers and lessees—could be adequately distinguished and prevented from clashing in a region so remote from even the most nominal supervision by the

---

1 A.T.T. *Livro da Ilhas*, f. 109v–111v. 16 Dec. 1485.
2 ibid. f. 105v. 11 Dec. 1493.
3 J. W. Blake, *Europeans in West Africa, 1450–1560.* 2 vols. Hakluyt Society, London, 1942, I, p. 106. Marchione paid 1,100 milreis per annum for the lease. He lived in Lisbon and furnished letters of credit for Pero de Covilham and Afonso de Paiva when they set out on their Ethiopian mission in 1487.
4 Blake, *Europeans in West Africa*, II, p. 198. De Loronha paid 1,600 milreis per annum; this increase over the rent paid by Marchione indicates that the value of the concession had not lessened.

Portuguese government, and where the local rulers were ready to trade with all parties, supposing that they could distinguish one from another. All three interests wanted slaves from Benin and the rivers. The Ijo and the Itsekiri, as well as the Edo of Benin, managed to supply them, partly by selling the criminals and outcasts of their own society, partly by drawing upon existing slave markets in the interior,[1] and partly by disposing of war captives. Ozolua's numerous campaigns must have swollen the number of prisoners available for sale in this period, but there is no reason to suppose that his policy of conquest was in any way prompted by the opening of the European slave trade. Many of the slaves were carried to São Jorge da Mina to be bartered for gold at a great profit.[2] Yet the number involved was not very large, because demand for slaves in this quarter was governed by the supply of gold which, though subject to considerable seasonal fluctuation, showed little overall increase from one year to another. Over a period of 28 months (August 1504 to January 1507) the factor at São Jorge received a total of 440 slaves, almost all of whom must have come from the slave rivers. This figure may be accepted as a fair measure of the average volume of this branch of the slave traffic in which the Portuguese played the role of middlemen between African sellers and purchasers. Different considerations governed the trade with São Tomé, where the slaves were required as a labour force in an island lacking an indigenous population. Agriculture, building, domestic service all depended upon a large importation of slaves from the mainland. To meet the initial needs of the colony of young Jews, Portuguese settlers and exiles sent to São Tomé in 1493, and to encourage further voluntary settlement, John II had given the captain of the island a licence to import 1,080 slaves from the 'slave rivers' over a period of five years. By July 1499 about 920 of this number had been landed.[3] In addition to these, the occasional slave

---

1 Pacheco Pereira mentions that slaves were obtained from the 'Opuu', a people of the interior. Possibly this is a reference to the Ibo.

2 Blake, *Europeans in West Africa.*, Vol. I, p. 107. Pacheco Pereira estimated that trade on the Costa da Mina yielded the crown a profit of 500 per cent. (*Esmeraldo*, p. 124.)

3 A. Brásio, *Monumenta Missionaria Africana: Africa Ocidental*, vol. I. Lisbon, 1952, p. 175.

was presented to prominent inhabitants of São Tomé as a gift from the Oba of Benin.[1] When the neighbouring island of Príncipe was colonised by the Portuguese in 1500, it too depended for labour upon imported slaves, and received trading privileges in the 'slave rivers' similar to those enjoyed by São Tomé.[2] A third destination for slaves from Benin was the slave market of Lisbon, where they were brought for sale by agents of the *Casa da Mina* and private contractors. Most of these passed into employment in the households of the Portuguese and other European aristocracy, for it rapidly became the fashion to possess Negro domestic servants. A survey of Lisbon in 1554 revealed no less than 9,500 slaves—many of them, of course, were of Moorish origin—in a total population of 100,000.[3] But the market for slaves in western Europe was a rather restricted one, and not especially profitable; the *Casa da Mina* found that a slave sold in Lisbon yielded only half the profit of one sold to the gold merchants at São Jorge. Thus, bearing in mind the possible markets, it can be seen that there was a limit to the number of slaves that could profitably be acquired by the Portuguese crown in any one year. During the existence of the trading post at Ughoton that limit appears to have fluctuated around a figure of 500 a year, and of this number no more than half, and probably fewer, came from

---

1 The Oba also made gifts of slaves to officials at São Jorge. He sent five to Fernão Lopes Correa (Captain of the Mina, 1495-9), and three to the factor Gil Matoso. (A.T.T. *Núcleo Antigo*, *maço* 186, ff. 3r and 14v.) Especially interesting is the case of the slave which the Oba presented to Dom Francisco, a baptised Congolese chief, who must have received the gift in São Tomé. (A.T.T. *Corpo Cronológico* III, *maço* 1, no. 34. 24 April 1499.) The Portuguese records contain a number of other hints of some contact between the kingdoms of Benin and Congo. In a letter to John III of Portugal (25 August 1526), the king of the Congo complained of people from Cacheu and Benin who were causing trouble in his land. (Brasio, *Monumenta*, vol. I, p. 479.) In 1541 came a further Congolese complaint that Benin slaves and freemen were participating in disturbances provoked by a Portuguese adventurer. (A.T.T. *Corpo Cronológico* I, *maço* 69, no. 72.) The culprits could have been Edo taken to the Congo via São Tomé by Portuguese, but there can be no certainty that they had come from Benin, because the name tended to be applied indiscriminately to all Africans from the coast adjoining Benin.

2 A.T.T. *Livro das Ilhas*, ff. 39v-40r. 20 August 1500.

3 C. Rodrigues de Oliveira, *Summario em que brevemente se contem algumas cousas (assi ecclesiasticas como seculares) que ha na Cidade de Lisboa.* Lisbon, 1554.

Benin if the total of 227 slaves bought there by the royal factor over a period of twenty months is at all representative of the normal volume of trade.[1] The slave trade, therefore, though a necessary adjunct to the gold trade, could not, so far as the Portuguese government was concerned, provide a basis for any very substantial dealings with Benin.

Slaves, it is true, were not Benin's only contribution to the conduct of the gold trade. The Portuguese quickly discovered that certain varieties of stone beads available in Benin and the Forcados River could be exchanged for gold on the Costa da Mina, so they began to buy them in large quantities. Most of the beads were fashioned from a blue stone veined with red: the Portuguese called them *coris*.[2] Others, some yellow[3] and some grey, had still greater value as objects of barter, and were treated by the Portuguese as semi-precious stones. All these beads must have reached Benin and the rivers through trade with the interior, and possibly from a source which also had links with the Costa da Mina, for it seems likely that they were known there prior to the Portuguese period. In his twenty months' management of the Ughoton post, Bastiam Fernandez bought 33,382 *coris*, 900 of the yellow beads and 162 of the grey. One other item from Benin which figured among the goods the Portuguese bartered on the Costa da Mina was cotton cloth. They bought it also to clothe their slaves, and to make awnings for ships. Pacheco Pereira mentions a trade in cloth in the Forcados River, while Fernandez bought 1,816 cloths described in his accounts as 'muslin'.

Ivory, though highly valued in Europe, played a surprisingly small part at this time in trade between Benin and the Portuguese. According to Pacheco Pereira, plenty of tusks were available in

---

1 A.T.T. *Livro das Ilhas*, f. 192r-v. 20 April 1512. Quittance issued to Bastiam Fernandez in respect of his office as factor in Benin over a period of 1 year 8 months 12 days following the death of Duarte Lopes.

2 This appears to be a name of Costa da Mina origin. Describing the trade done with merchants at S. Jorge da Mina, Pacheco Pereira wrote that 'certain blue beads which they call "coris" ' were much esteemed by them. (*Esmeraldo*, p. 124.) Despite the large numbers traded, these beads have still not been identified with any certainty; in modern Ghana the name 'akory' is applied to any bead of some value and antiquity. cf. R. Mauny, 'Akori beads'. *Journal of the Historical Society of Nigeria*, vol. I, no. 3. Dec. 1958.

3 Yellow beads known as *ekan* may still be found in Benin.

Benin, many of them coming from the 'Opuu' region, yet Fernandez acquired only 128 in twenty months. It is still more surprising to find that in the year ending in September 1505, the *Casa da Mina* in Lisbon recorded the receipt of only six tusks, all of which came from Benin.[1] Private traders may have been buying ivory on a much greater scale,[2] but it clearly did not figure prominently in the commercial activities of the crown.

The economic viability of the Ughoton post rested, therefore, upon a satisfactory development of the pepper trade, which was sternly forbidden to all but the royal factors. Ships from São Tomé and Príncipe might buy pepper in the rivers, but the inhabitants were required to sell to royal factors all that they did not consume themselves. Royal monopoly may have been equally strict on the Benin side of the pepper trade; later in the century, at least, the Oba permitted none but his own agents to sell pepper to Europeans. Some degree of centralised control may indeed have been necessary in order to organise an adequate supply of pepper, for it had to be gathered from a large area in the Benin, Urhobo and 'Opuu' countries, then transported to the Portuguese ships lying at Ughoton. How much pepper changed hands is difficult to estimate because so little information has survived. Between 1498 and 1505, the Portuguese factor at Antwerp received 75 quintals of Benin pepper annually,[3] in addition to which an unknown amount was consumed in Portugal and distributed through other markets. Bastiam Fernandez bought only 414¾ bushels, but this figure is not a good indicator of the normal volume of purchases because during his twenty months at Ughoton the decree forbidding Portuguese subjects to buy Benin pepper came into operation. The motives which prompted the decree of 1506 may be appreciated by comparing the 75 quintals of Benin pepper sent to Antwerp in 1504 with the 2,000 quintals that came from India in the same year.[4] When such

---

1 A.T.T. *Núcleo Antigo, maço* 166, f. 468r.
2 e.g. in 1505 Fernão de Loronha, Alvaro Pimentel and Duarte Tristão paid 143,097 reis to the *Casa da Mina* in respect of freight charges and crew wages for a ship which had carried a cargo of ivory and pepper from Benin on their account. (ibid.)
3 Blake, *European Beginnings*, p. 85.
4 H. van der Wee, *The Growth of the Antwerp Market and the European Economy*, vol. II. The Hague, 1963, p. 126.

great quantities began to flow from the East, it ceased to be profitable for the Portuguese crown to exploit the relatively minute supply from Benin, nor would it allow its subjects to compete with its monopoly of the Indian product by a private trade in Benin pepper. Thus, the commerce upon which the profitability of the Ughoton post had rested was deliberately proscribed, and soon afterwards the factor was finally withdrawn.

The abandonment of Ughoton did not mean the end of Portuguese trade with Benin, though the government of Portugal henceforth took little direct interest in it. Two or three caravels continued to be sent each year from São Jorge da Mina in search of slaves,[1] and, more important, the island of São Tomé, entering upon the heyday of its sugar fortunes, demanded an increasing supply of slave labour. Private interests also continued to lease trading rights from the crown. In fact, most indications point to a quickening of trade between Benin and the Europeans in the two decades following the withdrawal of the royal factor from Ughoton.

Benin reaction to these first twenty years of contact with an alien people and culture is poorly documented both in European records and in Benin tradition. Besides the chief of Ughoton who visited Portugal, a small number of Edo saw something of the Portuguese way of life when they visited São Jorge da Mina or São Tomé as interpreters or agents of the Oba. A few of these became Christians. Many saw only the small parties of white men who came to Benin City or Ughoton. The artists of Benin observed the newcomers and their accoutrements with great accuracy, as many of their works still testify. Indeed, the most obvious result of the Portuguese arrival upon the scene must have been the appearance in Benin of many articles previously unknown there. A large proportion of the goods acquired from the Portuguese reflected the preferences of the Oba and court chiefs who controlled European trade, and much of what they received was probably consumed within their own households. However, the household of an important chief—above all the royal palace—was a large and complex organisation, so that trade goods might find their way into many hands, at least within the capital.

A few surviving quittances and accounts from the post at Ughoton

---

[1] So unpopular was this voyage with ships' crews that extra payments had to be made to those who undertook it. A.T.T. *Núcleo Antigo, maço* 166, ff. 108v–111v.

give some idea of the nature and quantity of the merchandise that the Portuguese brought to Benin. During his twenty months as factor Bastiam Fernandez, for example, received manillas, cloth, beads and caps, besides a number of articles evidently meant for the use of the establishment. Manillas, of which he had 12,750, were mostly expended on slaves. In Pacheco Pereira's time a slave had cost between 12 and 15 manillas, but that price moved steadily upwards to reach 57 manillas in 1517.[1] Benin had also shifted its preference for copper manillas in the earlier years of the trade to those made of brass, though 7,991 of the copper variety were sent to Ughoton as late as 1505.[2] An increased use of brass in *cire perdue* casting may have influenced the change, and it is perhaps significant that tradition credits Oba Esigie with the improvement of brass-casting in Benin at a time when the metal would have become available in quantities sufficient to permit experimentation and continuous production.[3]

The amount of cloth supplied to Fernandez was relatively small, and seems to have been consumed mainly in customary presents to Benin chiefs, interpreters, and other officials who administered trade with the Europeans. It comprised 128 yards of coloured cloth, 52 yards of linen, 16 yards of fustian, 31 yards of a cloth known as *studilha*, and 22 yards of Indian Cambay cloth. Coral and glass beads were imported in large quantities, amounting, for the twenty months in question, to 44⅜ ounces of barrel-shaped coral beads (the most valuable variety), 33,844 pieces of small coral, 97 strings of glass beads, 28,969 loose glass beads, two strings of red beads fashioned from bone, and 84 large enamelled ones. The headgear, consisting of 37 caps dyed in grain and 12 coloured hats, was clearly destined for the adornment of chiefs; likewise the 32 horse-tails which the *Casa da Mina* had purchased especially for the Benin trade in the time of Duarte Lopes.[4] Dapper explained in the following century that horse-tails were symbols of authority.[5]

---

1 A.T.T. *Corpo Cronológico* I, *maço* 22, no. 70. 24 August 1517. This was the price in large manillas; the price of a slave in a smaller manilla, known as the Flemish manilla, varied from 80 to 90.

2 A.T.T. *Núcleo Antigo, maço* 166, f. 369r.   3 cf. Egharevba, *A Short History*, p. 30.   4 A.T.T. *Núcleo Antigo, maço* 166, f. 35v.

5 Dapper, *Naukeurige Beschrijvinge*, p. 127. In the seventeenth century the tails adorned the caps of war chiefs.

Apart from such regular items of trade, the occasional article of a more unusual or luxurious nature was despatched as a gift to the Oba. The chief of Ughoton had brought him 'a rich present of such things as he would greatly prize'[1] on his return from Portugal, but we do not know what these were. A present delivered in the name of King Manuel in 1505 consisted of a caparisoned horse, a necklace of Indian beads, a piece of printed chintz from Cambay, a *marlota* (a short, close-fitting cloak with hood attached) of orange taffeta and white satin, six linen shirts, and a shirt of blue Indian silk.[2] Such gifts no doubt helped to establish the convention that only the Oba might wear silk.[3] The three officials principally concerned with European trade also received presents, but they were limited to linen shirts. One of them is described by the Portuguese as the Oba's chief counsellor, another as his *veador*—this was the chief who directly supervised trade—and the third was the chief of Ughoton.

It is worthy of note that many of the finer articles among the gifts and merchandise were of Indian manufacture, and that such items continued to figure prominently among the goods brought to Benin by the Portuguese and other European traders. One would like to know whether they exerted any influence upon local taste and design. But perhaps the most striking thing about these trade goods and presents is that almost all could serve only for personal ornamentation; strictly utilitarian articles were conspicuously absent. Possibly there was no demand for them among those who controlled the trade; possibly the Portuguese were conscientiously observing papal prohibitions on the sale of arms and iron to non-Christians.[4] Whatever the explanation, it is evident that none of these things was vital to the strength or survival of Benin. Consequently that state could regard its trade with the Portuguese with a high degree of indifference.

---

1 De Pina, *Chrónica*, cap. 24.
2 A.T.T. *Núcleo Antigo, maço* 166, ff. 23r, 24r, 35v, 37r, 63v, 317v, 326r.
3 cf. H. L. Roth, *Great Benin: its customs, art and horrors.* Halifax, 1903, p. 83.
4 They were armed with a dispensation, if they chose to use it. The bull *Eximia devotionis affectus* (13 Sept. 1496) permitted Dom Manuel to send forbidden commodities to Guinea. A.T.T. *Bulario, maço* 16, no. 24.

3. The island trade and the first mission

After the withdrawal of the royal factor from Ughoton, the islands of São Tomé and Príncipe became the main bases for Portuguese trade with the 'slave rivers'. The islanders were already accustomed to the intricacies of navigation and commerce on the coast, and had among them an acclimatised population able to man the trading ships without the loss of life suffered by newcomers from Europe. São Tomé's traffic with the rivers had begun in 1494 using the three vessels, each of about thirty tons, which belonged to Alvaro de Caminha, the first captain of the island.[1] Other officials and wealthy settlers soon acquired their own boats, and after 1500 the number was further increased by those of Antonio Carneiro, the royal secretary to whom King Manuel had granted the island of Príncipe. This growth in local shipping soon led to suggestions from island interests that all trade with the rivers might be confided to them in return for an undertaking to supply the Costa da Mina and Portugal with all the slaves they needed. A proposal of this kind, made in 1499 by the acting-captain of São Tomé, has already been mentioned.[2] The new captain, Fernão de Mello, who took up his office in 1500, signed with the king of Portugal a contract embodying the same arrangement, but with most of the benefit going to the captain. His contract stipulated that de Mello should receive from the *Casa da Mina* 16,000 manillas to be used 'for the barter of slaves and pepper in the rivers of the said island'—that is to say, the 'slave rivers'.[3] Later he received another 1,877 manillas from the royal factor at Ughoton, as well as a quantity of fetters and irons for slaves. It may be inferred, therefore, that the contract envisaged a form of joint enterprise, with de Mello contributing ships and crews, and the crown supplying merchandise. Contemporaries believed that de Mello waxed rich on the profits.[4] The manner in which the

---

1 A.T.T. *Corpo Cronológico* I, *maço* 2, no. 130. 30 July 1499. Given the ravages of the climate and marine animals on the timbers, and the shortage of skilled men and materials for thorough repairs, the life of a boat in the islands did not usually exceed five years.

2 cf. supra p. 33.

3 Blake, *Europeans in West Africa*, vol. I, pp. 111–12. Quittance for Fernão de Mello, 9 Dec. 1510.

4 Gonçalo Pires, a seaman who had several times visited São Tomé, told Valentim Fernandes in Dec. 1506 that de Mello might have made a profit of

contract described de Mello's sphere of operations, and the fact that a royal factor still resided at Ughoton, makes it improbable that the contract applied to Benin; but with the closing of the Ughoton post, pressure mounted for the grant of a similar contract in this area. Representations from the islanders were reinforced by the inconveniences involved in relying upon ships sailing directly between São Jorge da Mina and Benin for a regular supply of slaves. In August 1513, the captain of the Mina wrote to King Manuel to explain that he was unable to send the amount of gold demanded by the *Casa da Mina* because he lacked goods with which to buy gold. Above all, São Jorge was totally unprovided with slaves, for which it still depended entirely upon the 'slave rivers'. That year a caravel had taken five months over a voyage to Benin, whereas, the captain argued, such a voyage ought to take at most two and a half months. He attributed the delay to the bad faith of the Oba in not supplying slaves promptly, and reasoned that, in these circumstances, at least four caravels would need to be permanently engaged in the Benin trade in order to ensure an adequate supply of slaves.[1] Some of this exculpatory argument has to be discounted. São Jorge did not rely exclusively upon Benin for its slaves;[2] the experience of later voyages proves that two and a half months was a minimum, rather than a maximum, time for a round trip to the Benin River.[3] On the other hand, the captain's allegations would seem to support our argument that the Oba paid only casual attention to the slave trade. Moreover, what the Portuguese, rightly or wrongly, regarded as unjustified delays provoked friction and sometimes incidents, as happened in 1514 when a cannon was seized from a royal caravel lying in the Benin River.[4] It was in these circumstances that King Manuel decided in 1514 to grant a four-year lease of the Benin trade to

---

10,000 cruzados in a year had he exploited his contract to the full. He was using two 30-ton boats built in the island. Valentim Fernandes, *Description de la côte occidentale d'Afrique*. Bissau, 1951, p. 132.

1 A.T.T. *Corpo Cronológico* I, *maço* 13, no. 48. 19 August 1513.
2 cf. supra p. 36–7.
3 A.T.T. *Corpo Cronológico* I, *maço* 20, no. 19. 8 April 1516. In this letter written to Antonio Carneiro from Príncipe, his factor explains that ships sent from that island to Benin usually spent four months on a round voyage.
4 A.T.T. *Corpo Cronológico* II, *maço* 46, no. 165. 29 April 1514.

Antonio Carneiro, the lord of Príncipe, with the provision that Carneiro should supply all the slaves needed for the gold trade.[1]

Príncipe thus became for a few years the principal base for Portuguese trade with Benin. Carneiro's factor in the island employed three ships in regular voyages to the Benin and Forcados Rivers; many of the crew were Negroes. Royal caravels, and sometimes Carneiro's ships, transported the slaves from Príncipe to São Jorge, where the secretary kept another factor to watch over his interests, and receive the third of the sale price of each slave which belonged to him under the terms of the contract. To safeguard for Carneiro what was evidently a limited supply of slaves, and to prevent the price being forced up, the king had stipulated that the inhabitants of São Tomé might trade in the Benin River only under licence from the lessee. São Tomé looked upon this restriction of a hitherto lucrative trade with jaundiced eye, especially since it was imposed when the island was enjoying an economic boom based upon a rapidly expanding sugar industry that absorbed large numbers of slaves. The Oba too was not disposed to favour this kind of regulation: he desired to sell his slaves and produce on the best terms available, whoever might offer them, and it is likely that he had in previous years been making better bargains with São Tomé ships than with those from São Jorge and Príncipe, with the result that the latter had been delayed in completing their cargoes. Accordingly, both the Oba and the São Tomé traders continued their earlier practices, though the latter had to resort to subterfuges. In 1516 the captain of one of Carneiro's ships found a São Tomé vessel of, so he asserted, 100 tons in the Benin River holding a licence for a vessel of only 40 tons. The merchants aboard this interloper had given the Oba and his *veador* (on this occasion specifically identified as the *Osodin*) presents valued at more than fifty slaves, whereupon the Oba had ordered all markets to be opened for them. This meant that they were able to buy whatever they pleased. Carneiro's captain vainly protested, and on his departure was summoned before the

---

1 cf. A.T.T. *Corpo Cronológico* I, *maço* 20, no. 127. 19 Nov. 1516. The contract appears to have been awarded first to Jorge de Mello, then revoked. On 8 April 1514 the government paid him 80,000 reis on account of the Benin farm. (A.T.T. *Corpo Cronológico* I, *maço* 15, no. 19.)

Osodin, then governing Benin City in the Oba's absence, to be warned not to return empty-handed, having seen the value of the presents brought by the interlopers.[1] In the following year, the factor in Príncipe complained to Carneiro that competition from São Tomé ships was forcing up prices in Benin.[2] On the other side, the Benin authorities were able to discriminate among the rival Portuguese by opening or closing trade in different commodities according to the prices and presents offered. 'Opening and closing the market' was to remain for centuries a standard Benin device for regulating trade with Europeans, and one suspects that it was practised in local trade long before they appeared.

By 1516 the Oba had added a new refinement to the system by establishing separate 'markets' for male and female slaves. In other words, a merchant wishing to buy slaves of both sexes had to negotiate separate terms for each category, and in practice found it far more difficult to obtain permission to buy males than females. Whether this distinction had been introduced in order to take advantage of a growing demand for male slaves, or to conserve the manpower of the Benin kingdom at a time when incessant warfare was placing heavy strains upon it, cannot be determined. Whatever the original purpose may have been, the restriction on the export of male slaves developed within a few years into a total embargo which persisted until the close of the seventeenth century—striking evidence of Benin's general indifference to the demands and opportunities of the European slave trade. Thus the efforts of the Portuguese government to apportion the Benin trade among various interests was answered by the Oba's determination to trade with whom, and on what terms, he pleased.

Occasional outbursts of violence, such as the seizure of the cannon in 1514, and mounting friction amongst various European interests were the background to an embassy which the Oba despatched to Portugal some time in 1514 to complain to King Manuel about the behaviour of his subjects, and to answer the accusations put forward by the captain of São Jorge and the lord of Príncipe. The other object of

---

1 A.T.T. *Corpo Cronológico* I, *maço* 20, no. 127. Record of the proceedings of the enquiry held in Príncipe to investigate the complaints made by Carneiro's officials.

2 A.T.T. *Corpo Cronológico* I, *maço* 22, no. 70. 24 August 1517.

the mission was to revive the long-abandoned subject of the conversion of the Oba and his people to Christianity, and to link it with
a request for firearms, including cannon. As with so many other
important developments in the relationship between Benin and the
Europeans, we can only surmise the motives which led the Oba to
take this initiative. If we are correct in identifying the Oba as
Ozolua, this was the same ruler who twenty years earlier had rejected a suggestion that he should invite missionaries into his kingdom.[1] It may be that, after long acquaintance with the Portuguese,
many of whom must have spoken to him on the subject, he had
discovered a genuine interest in the alien religion. De Barros,
however, held the opinion that he 'sought the priests rather to
make himself powerful against his neighbours with our favour than
from a desire for baptism'.[2] This explanation seems, on the whole,
the more plausible of the two. At the time he sent his envoys to
Portugal, the Oba found himself hard-pressed by his enemies and
was clearly intent on obtaining firearms, which would have given
him a decided military advantage. He had seen these weapons in the
hands of Portuguese, and had probably heard that they were
supplied to the Christian king of the Congo.[3] Baptism, as the
Portuguese repeatedly stressed to him and to other princes, would
bring him guns as well as grace.

The embassy consisted of two persons whom the Portuguese
called Dom Jorge and Dom Antonio, which may indicate that they
were baptised Christians. To cover their travelling expenses, they
took with them twelve slaves to be sold as need arose; the Oba
gave another four slaves to the captain of the ship in which they
sailed as the price of their passage. Not content with that payment,
the captain seized six of their own slaves, and when Dom Jorge,
the senior envoy, protested, the captain made life miserable for
them by withholding their victuals. After further extortions, they
reached Lisbon in a wretched condition, which was only partially
relieved by a small daily allowance from the king of Portugal.[4] Most

1 cf. Bradbury, 'Chronological problems', pp. 277–80.
2 De Barros, *Asia*. Dec. I, liv. iii, cap. 3.
3 cf. supra p. 36, n. 1.
4 A.T.T. *Cartas Missivas* IV, no. 403. Petition from Dom Jorge to King
Manuel.

of their business they conducted through the secretary Carneiro, whose great personal interest in the Benin trade hastened matters along, so that by November 1514 they were ready to leave.[1] As a parting gift from King Manuel each was given a hood, jerkin and breeches of red cloth, a red cap, and a doublet of camlet.[2] Their mission had, however, met with only moderate success. Missionaries the king readily promised and arranged that they should return to Benin with the envoys, taking with them all the necessary vestments, altar furnishings and books.[3] Arms he refused to send until the Oba should have proved the sincerity of his professed inclination to Christianity. In a letter given to the envoys, Manuel explained his attitude in the following terms:[4]

> ... Therefore, with a very good will we send you the clergy that you have asked for; they bring with them all the things that are needed to instruct you and your people in the knowledge of our faith. And we trust in Our Lord that He will bestow His grace upon you, that you may confess it and be saved in it—for all the things of this world pass away, and those of the other last for ever. We earnestly exhort you to receive the teachings of the Christian faith with that readiness we expect from a very good friend. For when we see that you have embraced the teachings of Christianity like a good and faithful Christian, there will be nothing in our realms with which we shall not be glad to favour you, whether it be arms or cannon and all other weapons of war for use against your enemies; of such things we have a great store, as Dom Jorge your ambassador will inform you. These things we are not sending you now, as he requested, because the law of God forbids it ...

---

1 cf. A.T.T. *Corpo Cronológico* I, *maço* 17, no. 29a. 20 Dec. 1514. A servant of Carneiro named Antonio de Ceiros, who was later the secretary's factor in Príncipe, appears to have looked after the two envoys during their stay in Lisbon.

2 A.T.T. *Corpo Cronológico* I, *maço* 16, no. 118. 21 Nov. 1514.

3 In December 1514, the king ordered three chasubles to be prepared by his wardrobe for the priests going to Benin. One was of purple satin with a centre stripe of black damask; another was made of purple damask with a stripe of green satin; and the third was of camlet with a stripe of Bruges satin. The wardrobe also furnished two albs. (A.T.T. *Corpo Cronológico* I, *maço* 16, no. 117.)

4 A.T.T. *Fragmentos*, *maço* 9. The letter is dated Almeirim, 20 Nov. 1514. A part of it has been torn away.

In the same letter, the king expressed dissatisfaction with the recent trend in commercial relations between his subjects and those of the Oba. He recommended, rather stiffly, that the Oba mend his ways and co-operate with the factors sent by Carneiro to operate his newly granted monopoly.

... We have heard Dom Jorge, your ambassador, in all that he has said to us on your behalf. We were much pleased with his coming to us, so that from him we might learn of the goodwill which you profess touching our service. And we have received much pleasure from all that he has told us of your goodwill. Be assured that, because of our constant desire to further your interests, you may command and make use of all that is ours as though it were your own. For no king, either in Guinea, India or any other more distant part, has ever, God be praised, had cause to regret our friendship; rather they have sought and seek to increase it, as we to preserve it with them by the favours and good services which we do them. It will please us to do the like for you, if in our interests you act as befits a king who is our friend, and such we believe you to be, though in past years we have been otherwise informed and have seen effects to the contrary ...

We earnestly recommend that you order your markets to be opened and trade to be carried on freely, and in the manner in which it was always conducted; also that you order trade to be carried on freely with his [sc. Carneiro's] ships, and in as proper a manner as we expect from you and your friendship. We shall give you much thanks for it. Nor will anything but good and profit follow for you and your country by acting thus. Our aforesaid secretary, being a person very close to our service, will always represent your interests to us, as we have entrusted and recommended them to him.

The Oba replied promptly to this letter through another envoy styled Pero Barroso in Portuguese documents; he was an Edo, and probably one of the *faladors* or interpreters employed in trade with the Portuguese, for it was in this capacity that he returned to Benin on one of Carneiro's ships in 1516.[1] Reaching Lisbon in the autumn

---

1 A.T.T. *Corpo Cronológico.* I, *maço* 20, no. 127. He had probably taken his name from a Portuguese Pero Barroso who served as an official in São Jorge da Mina c. 1502. (*Corpo Cronológico.* I, *maço* 8, no. 45.) cf. the career of Fernão de Vella, an Edo slave who, after serving as an interpreter on ships trading between São Jorge and Benin, was appointed to reside in Benin with the royal factor in the same capacity. Having served three years, he was given his freedom, and returned to São Jorge in 1509 with an Edo wife and twelve slaves of his own. (*Corpo Cronológico.* I, *maço* 8, no. 72.)

of 1515, he soon found himself, like his predecessors, without funds and was obliged to petition the king for clothing and money.[1] He too received a suit of clothes made of red cloth—a colour which had become the badge of rank in Benin.[2] Unfortunately no record has survived of the letter which, it may be presumed, Barroso took back to the Oba; but we have some knowledge of another letter that he carried to a Portuguese named Duarte Pires. This man was living in Benin together with João Sobrinho, who hailed from Príncipe, and a converted Edo named Gregorio Lourenço who had formerly been a servant in one of the islands and now acted as interpreter for Pires and Sobrinho. Since these two had connections with Príncipe, it is possible that they were in Benin to look after Carneiro's interests. They were certainly in close attendance upon the Oba, assisting him in military affairs, and perhaps giving him occasional support with their own firearms,[3] prototype white mercenaries, in fact. Early in 1516 the master of one of Carneiro's ships had seen these 'white men who are with the Oba at the war' when he visited the Oba in his camp.[4] In October 1516, when Pires replied to the letter from King Manuel, he wrote that he and his companions were again accompanying the Oba on a campaign.[5] Judging by the reply, the king's letter had instructed Pires to make proposals to the Oba about weapons, and to further the work of the missionaries. Pires reported that he had duly obeyed these orders and had received from the Oba fulsome assurances of his esteem for King Manuel and of his goodwill towards the missionaries.

Some progress had indeed been made. When they reached Benin in August 1515, the priests had found the Oba engaged in war some distance from the capital, but he immediately sent for

---

1 A.T.T. *Gavetas* XV, *maço* 1, no. 49. Petition from Pero Barroso to the king, n.d.
2 A.T.T. *Corpo Cronológico* I, *maço* 19, no. 62, 20 Dec. 1515.
3 cf. Bradbury, 'Chronological problems', p. 279. 'There is at Benin City a ward known as Iwoki whose members had, among other functions, that of looking after the Oba's guns and cannon. The Iwoki date their foundation to Esigie's reign and some claim to be descended from Europeans called Ava and Uti. Ava and Uti are said, on one occasion, to have protected the Oba by standing with guns, one on each side of him.'
4 A.T.T. *Corpo Cronológico* I, *maço* 20, no. 127.
5 A.T.T. *Corpo Cronológico* I, *maço* 20, no. 18. Translation in T. Hodgkin, *Nigerian Perspectives*. London, 1960, p. 99.

them, and they remained in his camp, together with Pires and Sobrinho, and enjoying every mark of favour until he returned to Benin City in August 1516. The question of conversion was put aside during the campaign, 'because he needed leisure for so deep a mystery as this', but once in his capital, the Oba sent one of his own sons with those of some chiefs to be baptised and taught to read by the missionaries. Reading lessons—probably using catechisms in Portuguese[1]—progressed very satisfactorily, according to Pires. The Oba also gave orders that a church should be built in Benin City. Whether any work was done, much less completed, is open to doubt, for although Benin tradition insists that Roman Catholic churches were built in the city, and even the sites are indicated with some precision, there is no documentary or archaeological evidence to show that churches existed there.[2] The rains would have made it difficult to begin building before October 1516 when the Oba again departed to resume the war, taking Pires, and possibly the priests, with him.

A letter from the captain of Príncipe to Carneiro implies that the Oba died late in 1516 or early in 1517,[3] and presumably during the campaign he had begun in October 1516 with the hope of bringing the war to an end in that dry season. The only Oba of this period whose death is traditionally associated with war is Ozolua. Benin and Ishan oral histories agree that at the time of his death in the Uromi war he had become very unpopular with his subjects, and in particular with his war-weary soldiers who brought about his death.[4] Too close an association with the person and policies of an unloved

---

1 cf. the thousand *cartinhas* or reading books which King Manuel ordered to be prepared in 1514 as a present for Prester John. (A. Baião's preface to his edition of the *Décadas* of J. de Barros. Lisbon, 1945, vol. I, p. xlvi.)

2 cf. Egharevba, *A Short History*, p. 28. '. . . churches were built at Ogbelaka, Idumwerie and Akpakpava (Ikpoba Road), the last named being the "Holy Cross Cathedral". The residence of the Fathers was situated between the present Roman Catholic School and John Holt's store. They had another in Idunmwen-Ebo, and the missionary cemetery was where the Government School now stands.' Some of these sites may be associated with later missionary activity.

3 A.T.T. *Corpo Cronológico* I, *maço* 22, no. 69. 24 August 1517. The letter states that the throne of Benin is occupied by a youth under the guardianship of two chiefs.

4 Egharevba, *A Short History*, p. 26. C. G. Okojie, *Ishan Native Laws and Customs*. Yaba, n.d., pp. 223–4. cf. supra p. 12.

ruler might explain the subsequent failure of the mission. His successor, who appears to have been the baptised son, was still a boy, so effective control of government passed into the hands of *Osodin* and *Uwangue*, at that time the most powerful of the palace chiefs. The late Oba's autocratic manner in imposing baptism on their sons may have antagonised these and other important men who now had an opportunity to put an end to such innovations. The fate of the mission could also have been affected by the re-affirmation of traditional religious belief implicit in the funeral ceremonies of an Oba and the installation of his successor; these brought the young, newly baptised prince back inexorably to the religion of his people and his ancestors.[1]

Nothing more is known about the missionaries after Pires' letter. However, there is reason to believe that they must either have died or left Benin shortly after the Oba's death, because on 30 May 1517 the vicar of São Tomé, Father Diogo Bello, with three other priests arrived in Príncipe looking for a ship to take them to Benin where, they declared, they hoped to convert the young Oba.[2] They would hardly have undertaken this task had the earlier mission been still in Benin. Father Bello and his companions arranged to sail to Benin at the end of August 1517, but whether they did so is not known. Even if this second party of missionaries reached Benin, they met with no recorded success; nor for another twenty years did the Portuguese make any further attempt to convert the Oba and his people. Such Christian influence as persisted in Benin during the interval was confined to a handful of free Edo and slaves who had been converted while in the service of the Portuguese. For example, Gregorio Lourenço, the companion of Duarte Pires, still adhered in some measure to his new religion; in 1526 he gave a female slave as alms to the church of São Tomé.[3] The books of ships trading to Benin also mention a Dom Antonio who may have

---

1 I owe this suggestion to Dr. R. E. Bradbury. The funeral ceremonies of a ruler of Benin were described by a Portuguese pilot c. 1560, apparently from information gathered in São Tomé; they may, therefore, have been those witnessed in 1517. The account, first published by Ramusio, appears in translation in Blake, *Europeans in West Africa*, vol. I, pp. 150–1.

2 A.T.T. *Corpo Cronológico* I, *maço* 22, no. 69. With the priests was a Jeanes Clerigo who had come to São Tomé from Benin.

3 A.T.T. *Corpo Cronológico* II, *maço* 151, no. 69.

been a Christian and, like Gregorio Lourenço, an interpreter.[1] But without the aid of priests or church, their Christianity must have been of a most nominal kind.

Because the mission had failed, the Portuguese supplied no firearms to Benin. On the contrary, they took stringent precautions to prevent arms smuggling from the islands and the theft of weapons from vessels lying in the rivers.[2] On the whole these measures were successful; so the great achievements of Benin armies in the sixteenth century owed nothing to the use of firearms.[3]

Carneiro meanwhile was reaping little benefit from the king's exhortations to the Oba on behalf of his trading interests, for São Tomé ships continued to flout his monopoly with the open connivance of the Benin authorities. Nevertheless, considerable numbers of slaves were carried from Benin to Príncipe throughout the four years of his contract. One ship arrived with 280 slaves in 1516,[4] another with 182 slaves in 1517.[5] Remembering that three ships were employed in this traffic, and that a round voyage lasted, on an average, four months, it may safely be assumed that Carneiro's agents were transporting well over one thousand slaves annually from Benin to Príncipe. Only about half of these were sent to São Jorge da Mina,[6] for the African merchants there refused to buy any slave suffering from a physical defect or skin blemish. Those of an imperfect physique were disposed of either in the islands or in Portugal.

The clandestine nature of the unlicensed traffic from São Tomé makes it difficult to estimate its volume, but it was clearly substantial. The interloper that caused Carneiro's agent so much trouble in 1516 was reckoned to have bought more than 400 slaves. Between them, therefore, licensed and unlicensed traders were acquiring a

---

1 A.T.T. *Corpo Cronológico* II, *maço* 149, no. 29. In 1522 both men received 20 yards of cloth for services rendered to a Portuguese ship trading with Benin.
2 e.g. ibid. Instructions to the ship's master on the custody of arms while in the Benin River.
3 cf. infra p. 68.
4 A.T.T. *Corpo Cronológico* I, *maço* 20, no. 19.
5 A.T.T. *Corpo Cronológico* I, *maço* 22, no. 70.
6 e.g. of the cargo brought to Príncipe in August 1517, 90 slaves were sent to São Jorge. The royal factor there carefully scrutinised the slaves and returned those in whom he detected any imperfections. Those that were sold fetched an average of half a mark of gold apiece.

substantially greater number of slaves than in previous years. This increasing Portuguese demand was partly met by an inflow of captives taken during the campaigns of 1515 and 1516, but it nonetheless brought about a marked increase in prices. With São Tomé traders leading the way, the price of a slave had risen in 1517 to an average of 57 manillas.[1] An ever-increasing supply of manillas combined with demand for slaves to keep prices moving upwards; whereas the factor Fernandez had received 12,750 manillas in twenty months, one of Carneiro's ships carried 13,000 manillas to Benin in a single voyage.

Trade in ivory likewise grew apace and became fiercely competitive. In December 1514, Carneiro's factor informed him that 385 tusks weighing 10,520 pounds had been sold in Lisbon at the rate of 13 cruzados a hundredweight. In August 1517 the master of the secretary's ship *Oliveira*, having orders to buy as much ivory as possible, reached Príncipe from Benin with 187 tusks which had cost 1,623 manillas. The largest tusk in this cargo—a fine specimen weighing 80 pounds—cost 45 manillas, and the factor was beginning to doubt whether trade could be profitable on such terms.[2] Meanwhile the São Tomé ships also were carrying away large consignments of ivory; the interloper of 1516 was alleged, no doubt with much exaggeration, to have bought some 800 tusks weighing 9,600 pounds. In later centuries elephant hunters constituted a special class in Benin, with an organisation resembling that of other trades and skills devoted to the service of the Oba, and it is possible that they acquired their importance at this time when the palace needed to secure a large and regular supply of ivory for its Portuguese customers. Elephants were killed with poisoned darts or arrows.[3]

4. The resumption of royal trade

His profits squeezed between rising prices, the demands of the Oba, and interloping from São Tomé, Carneiro allowed his lease of the Benin trade to expire in 1518. It then fell to the bid of the triumphant

1 cf. supra p. 40.
2 A.T.T. *Corpo Cronológico*. I, *maço* 22, no. 70.
3 cf. Roth, *Great Benin*, p. 144. Bradbury, *The Benin Kingdom*, p. 25.

São Tomé interests. However they did not long enjoy the concession, because their failure to deliver to São Jorge the number of slaves stipulated in the contract faced the Portuguese government with a situation that threatened to undermine the gold trade. Lisbon accordingly resolved to revert to the pre-1514 policy of engaging directly in the slave trade, with the important modification that São Tomé was henceforth to be the base for the crown's operations. Experience and the spectacular profits of São Tomé merchants had demonstrated the peculiar advantages that island enjoyed as a base for trade with the mainland, advantages which it was now hoped to use for the benefit of the crown. A royal factor based in the island would be able to employ its acclimatised seamen to gather slaves from any convenient market on the coast between Benin and the Congo. Moreover, São Tomé had become a focal point of shipping routes thanks to the development of Portuguese trade with the Congo and the importance of its own sugar industry, so that the transport of slaves to either the Costa da Mina or to Portugal presented few difficulties.[1]

Instructions reorganising trade on these lines were issued in February 1519 to come into operation at the end of that year.[2] That its principal function was to engage in the slave trade is made clear by the official designation—*nosso trato dos espravos da Ilha de Sam Tomé* (our slave trade in the island of São Tomé)—but the

---

[1] In March 1518 the king of Portugal had likewise announced the revocation of all trade leases in the Cape Verde region of the mainland, and his intention of conducting all trade directly through crown officials. A.T.T. *Corpo Cronológico* III, *maço* 6, no. 96.

[2] A.T.T. *Livro de registo de leis e regimentos de El Rei Dom Manoel*, ff. 83–88v, 92. *Regimentos* of 8 and 28 Feb. 1519. In these instructions the officials appointed to manage the trade on behalf of the crown are told to do their best to reduce the salaries paid to ships' crews by the lessees of the Benin trade, viz.: for a pilot, 6 slaves p.a.; for a master, 4 slaves p.a.; for a sailor, 3 slaves p.a.; and for a ship's boy, 2 slaves p.a.; each of these was permitted to send his slaves to be sold in Portugal. Crown officials were also to endeavour to bring down the price of slaves whether paid in manillas, cloth, coral, or any other merchandise. Any slave who proved particularly suited to the work of the royal estates on the island might be kept there as an overseer. The factor at São Jorge was to keep them informed of his requirements in slaves, beads, cloth, etc., and as an incentive to keep him supplied, the São Tomé officials were to receive 1 per cent of the proceeds from the sale of all slaves and goods which they sent to the Costa da Mina.

factor in charge had orders not to neglect any other commodities suitable for barter on the Costa da Mina, among which were specifically mentioned *coris*, grey beads, 'muslin' and Benin cloth. For the European market he was to buy ivory and camwood—a wood valued for its dye which had first been brought from Benin by Carneiro's ships. Care was to be taken that no slave cost more than 40 manillas, and that those bought at this price were young and healthy. Rather than pay more than 40 manillas, officials should buy no slaves at all. By a show of firmness King Manuel believed he could force prices below the level reached in the second decade of the century, but he seriously weakened his position by permitting the São Tomé contractors to continue their trade as a supplement to that of the crown.

Besides dealing with such matters as prices, the instructions given to royal factors in São Tomé contained detailed regulations on the treatment and disposal of slaves. Immediately a slave had been purchased, a cross was branded on his or her right arm to mark him as the property of the king of Portugal, and he was to be kept under close guard aboard the ship while it lay in the Benin River. When the cargo had been completed, the ship sailed directly to São Tomé where slaves could be employed on the royal plantations until the best of them were shipped to the Costa da Mina and the rest to Portugal. Unless suited for employment as an overseer on the plantations, no slave was to be kept long in the island, for fear that he might run away to join the growing number of fugitives who already constituted a serious menace to Portuguese authority. Hence the royal sugar plantations relied upon a continuous flow of slaves from the mainland. After their brief sojourn in these transit-cum-labour camps, some were transported to the Costa da Mina in small local vessels which occasionally called at the slave rivers for further trade on their return voyage to São Tomé. Those destined for Portugal were carried in the larger ocean-going ships which called at the island on their homeward voyage from São Jorge to take aboard slaves and sugar.

Ships' books recording the sailing and trading of those small vessels (mostly of no more than fifty tons burthen) that plied between São Tomé and Benin give a fairly clear picture of the manner in which Portuguese and Edo conducted their trade in this period. A typical voyage was that of the *São Miguel*.[1] Under the command of Machim Fernandes, who combined the functions of master and pilot, the ship left São Tomé in April 1522. The instructions given to Fernandes by the royal factor stressed that he must not pay more than 50 manillas for the best slaves—efforts to reduce the price to 40 manillas had soon been abandoned—failing which the cargo of linen, coloured cloth, coral, glass beads and cowries was to be bartered for *coris*, yellow and grey beads, ivory and camwood. Trade in all other commodities was specifically forbidden. In order that adequate watch might be kept over slaves aboard the ship, no more than two of the crew should be allowed ashore at any one time in order to sell the goods they carried on their own account. Each member of the crew might bring back a duty-free allowance of palm oil—two jars for a seaman, three for the pilot and ship's clerk—but for all their other purchases they had to deliver one quarter, in kind or in value, to an official known as the *recebedor dos quartos de beny* who resided in São Tomé. The pilot was warned to keep good watch over all arms in the ship, 'so that they do not fall into the hands of the negroes'. On the return voyage the *São Miguel* was not to stop or put a boat ashore at any river or island, lest the crew seize such opportunities for smuggling and illegal trade.

The *São Miguel* took almost a month to reach Ughoton, thanks to an unusually stubborn struggle with contrary winds. Immediately upon arrival at the port on 16 May 1522, the pilot and clerk went to Benin City where they paid their compliments to the Oba, and delivered the presents customarily given before trade began. On this occasion the presents consisted of 20 ounces of coral, four Indian caps, and ten and a half yards of red satin for the Oba; 20 yards of cloth apiece for *Osodin* and 'Ruquuru'[2] (described as the *veadores* in charge of European trade); and 10 yards for Gregorio Lourenço and a Dom Antonio[3] who were probably being remunerated for their services as interpreters. The chief of Ughoton (in the

---

1 A.T.T. *Corpo Cronológico*. II, *maço* 149, no. 29. This document is the ship's book of the *São Miguel* for the Benin voyage of 1522. Appendix I.

2 Other documents of this period indicate that *Osodin* and *Uwangue* were the chiefs in charge of European trade, and since 'Ruquuru' does not correspond to any known Benin title, it is likely to have been a personal name of the *Uwangue*.

3 Probably the junior member of the embassy sent to Portugal in 1514.

ship's book he is called 'Rife') received 20 yards of cloth, and 4 yards were given to the person who 'according to custom asks the king of Benin for slaves in the palace'. Not all these presents and payments would have been made before the opening of trade. References to the yard measure of cloth as the *'vara acustumada'* suggest that it was by this time accepted in Benin as a standard unit of value; from it are derived the *pano*, *pagne*, *paan* and *pawn* of later centuries.[1]

A house in Benin City rented by the pilot for 10 manillas served as a store to which the ship's cargo was carried from Ughoton by hired porters paid at the rate of one manilla a head-load for 38 loads of manillas, 10 of cowries, seven of cloth and two of glass beads. As trade progressed 80 loads of ivory passed in the opposite direction and four parties of slaves were transferred to Ughoton under the supervision of officials provided by the Oba. As a further precaution against escape, each slave was manacled and the whole party bound together by one long chain. The ship carried only one of these chains, so on the arrival of each party at Ughoton it had to be taken back to Benin City by a porter. Several references to customary payments made during the course of his trade in Benin City give the impression that Fernandes was following precedents well established by 1522, and that other traders had likewise conducted their trade in Benin City. Indeed it is possible that the former royal factor in Benin had been stationed in Benin City rather than Ughoton, though the latter place had always to be used for the loading and unloading of cargoes. Among these customary payments was the one manilla a day which Fernandes gave for the yam, wood and water supplied to his party. Custom also required that, when his cargo was complete, he should ask the Oba for the services of two officials who accompanied him to Ughoton in order to organise a supply of yams to feed the slaves during the voyage to São Tomé. For this provisioning, which occupied the officials for no less than thirty-seven days, each was remunerated at the customary rate of one manilla a day. By the time he was ready to sail, Fernandes had bought yams to the value of 828 manillas and

---

1 *Pano* is Portuguese for cloth. It is likely that the Edo word for cloth—*ukpon*—comes from the same source.

8,000 cowries, as well as palm oil worth 35 manillas. At any other time of the year it would not have taken so long to provision a small ship, but he was buying in August, just before the beginning of the yam harvest, when stocks were at their lowest; and at this date alternative foodstuffs were not available. Another expenditure worth noting was the 26 manillas given for fibre mats which served as awnings for the deck and as beds for the slaves.

On 25 August the pilot and clerk took their leave of the Oba who, the ship's book noted, made no return for their presents. The following day they left for Ughoton, and on 27 August 1522 the *São Miguel* began its homeward journey. But before putting to sea Fernandes called at the village of Oere on the main Benin River in order to take on board the slaves from another royal ship which, after completing its trade in the Forcados River, had run into heavy seas off Cape Fermoso and been driven back, leaking badly, into the Benin River. The clerk of this ship had then gone to Benin City to ask Fernandes to take over its cargo on the grounds that it was unfit to put to sea.[1] The riverside port of Oere where the transfer of cargo took place had been known to the Portuguese since at least 1516, and had become a frequent stopping place for ships bound either for Ughoton or for the Forcados River by way of the creek route from the Benin River. Although no place of that name exists today, Portuguese references seem to locate it somewhere near the junction of the Benin River and Nana Creek. The name almost certainly derives from *Iwere* and affords evidence of Itsekiri settlement in the river at a point where they were able to gain a footing in European trade. In all probability the Itsekiri had been attracted here in the second decade of the sixteenth century by the increasing volume of Portuguese shipping, the competition between various Portuguese interests, and by the restrictions which Benin began to place on the sale of male slaves. Taking advantage of their strategic position, the mobility of their canoe fleets, and a centralised, autocratic system of government modelled on that of Benin,[2] the

---

1 A.T.T. *Corpo Cronológico* II, *maço* 102, no. 20. Ship's book of the *Santa Maria da Conceição*. Translated in A. F. C. Ryder, 'An early Portuguese trading voyage to the Forcados River'. *Journal of the Historical Society of Nigeria*, vol. I, no. 4, 1959.
2 cf. supra pp. 13 and 28.

Itsekiris were soon to become serious rivals of the Edo kingdom for European trade, and eventually the absolute masters of the Benin River. In 1522, however, Oere still lived in some dependence upon Benin—a status perhaps derived from the establishment of a branch of the Benin dynasty among the Itsekiri.[1]

In rather less than three weeks after leaving the Benin River, the *São Miguel* reached São Tomé with a total of more than two hundred slaves. Five had died on the voyage and been cast into the sea after witnesses had testified in a written statement that the brand mark on their arms showed them to be slaves of the king. Only one had died while the *São Miguel* lay at Ughoton. Of the whole cargo of 83 slaves bought by Machim Fernandes only two were males—and it is quite possible that these were acquired outside the Oba's territory—despite a whole month spent in vain attempts to have a market opened for male slaves. The 81 females, mostly between ten and twenty years of age, were purchased in Benin City between 25 June and 8 August at the rate of one, two or three a day. Two of them went to the hospital and church of São Tomé, for the king of Portugal had decreed that every vessel trading to the coast from the island must bring back two slaves whose sale would provide funds for the upkeep of these institutions.[2] Seventeen other slaves represented the pay due to the officers and crew of the *São Miguel*, or slaves which they had bought with their own merchandise. The remaining 64 belonged to the crown. Two of these royal slaves had been bought for 24 yards of cloth each, and eight others for strings of glass beads, the price varying from 46 to 50 strings. Like the cloth length, the string of beads had become a standard unit of value. Another seventeen slaves had been exchanged for manillas

---

1 In the ship's book of the *Santa Maria*, Oere is described as 'a port of Benin'. The Oba may also have exercised some authority in the Forcados River. The São Tomé interlopers were allegedly told by him in 1516 that if Carneiro made it impossible for them to send a ship into the Benin River, arrangements could be made to send slaves and other commodities to the Forcados.

2 King Manuel ordered that the vicar of São Tomé be given six slaves a year for his own subsistence and the maintenance of the church of Santa Maria. (A.T.T. *Corpo Cronológico* I, *maço* 19, no. 131. 29 Feb. 1516.) The hospital of the island was founded in 1504 with an annual assignment of six slaves. (A.T.T. *Misticos*, liv. 2, f. 208v. 3 May 1504.) These arrangements seem, therefore, to have been based on the assumption that six ships would make slave-trading voyages to the coast each year.

—all at the fixed maximum of 50 manillas, apart from a young girl aged 10 and an 'old' slave of 24, both of whom fetched 45 manillas.[1] The other 37 slaves had been paid for in cowries, commonly known to the Portuguese as *buzeos da India*, though in the São Tomé trade they often gave them the Edo name *igos*, a word whose meaning nowadays extends to money in general. Pacheco Pereira gave some valuable information about shell currencies in West Africa at the opening of the sixteenth century:

> There are two small islands ... called the *Ilhas das Cabras* which are very close to the mainland and are inhabited by negroes under the rule of Manicongo ... in these islands the negroes gather certain small shells, no larger than pine kernels in their husks, and these they call *zimbos*. In the land of Manicongo these serve for money: they give fifty of them for a chicken, three hundred are worth a goat, and other things in proportion ... And in the country of Benin ... they use for money certain shells somewhat larger than the *zimbos* of Manicongo; these shells are called *iguou* in Benin, and everything is bought with them, and the more a man has of them, the richer he is.[2]

Clearly then the Portuguese did not introduce the shell currency to Benin, and the *igos* used there in the pre-Portuguese era were of different origin to the Congolese shell currency. Since there is no local source of such shells, and since the Portuguese were able to dispose of Maldive cowries as the equivalent of *igos*, there is a possibility that the earlier currency shells of Benin had also originated in the Indian Ocean and reached Benin by exchange along the trade routes linking east and west Africa.[3] Although aware of the value of this type of shell in Benin before the beginning of the sixteenth century, more than a decade passed before the Portuguese began to bring them from India. The earliest reference to Maldive cowries as a commodity in the Guinea trade occurs in a contract

---

1 Portuguese slave-traders appear to have taken 12 years as the age of puberty, and to have reckoned that a girl thus developed had survived the lethal diseases of childhood.

2 Pacheco Pereira, *Esmeraldo*, bk. iii, ch. 2.

3 A general comparative study of these shell currencies might reveal much about trade routes and cultural contacts in Africa. A similarly general and co-operative approach is needed to elucidate the mysteries that at present surround the bead trade of medieval Africa. The nature, provenance and distribution of *coris* is a case in point.

for the trade of São Tomé signed between King Manuel and Fernão Jorge on 26 March 1515. A clause of the contract stipulates that in each year of its duration Jorge may bring 500 quintals of cowries from India as ballast in the ships of the *carreira da India*, and that these cowries must be used solely for trade with the mainland.[1] Almost certainly this contract marks the first important introduction of Maldive cowries into West Africa by the Portuguese; but the first shipments brought from India for Fernão Jorge can hardly have reached São Tomé until 1517 or 1518, and they were probably not taken to Benin in any quantity until Carneiro's contract had expired. By 1522, however, they had become as important as manillas in Portuguese trade with Benin.

Large numbers of cowries were shipped to Benin in the fifteen-twenties. The *São Miguel* carried ten head-loads in 1522; another ship brought 512,520 shells weighing 15 quintals 96 pounds in 1526.[2] About 1540 de Barros wrote, 'And even to this kingdom of Portugal, in some years as much as two or three thousand quintals are brought by way of ballast; they are then exported to Guinea, and the kingdoms of Benin and Congo, where also they are used for money.' With importations of this magnitude, the cowry began to lose value, but depreciation is unlikely to have gone far by 1522 when for his slaves Fernandes paid an average of seven 'goats' and two or three 'chickens':[3] that is between 6,450 and 6,490 cowries. These transactions reveal incidentally that one small Flemish manilla was at that time equivalent to 130 cowries, and that the manilla could, therefore, serve only for large transactions, while the cowry remained among the Edo the common currency of everyday life.

Besides slaves, the pilot of the *São Miguel* bought 228 tusks of ivory in 50 lots, the largest consisting of eight tusks. At the beginning of his trade the tusks were small, but the average size later increased. He used manillas to pay for 197 tusks, giving 3,845 manillas in all,

---

1 A.H.U. *São Tomé, caixa* 2, 26 March 1515.
2 A.T.T. *Corpo Cronológico* II, *maço* 151, no. 76.
3 Like the Congolese, the Edo counted cowries in units of 'goats' and 'chickens', but with an interesting variation, for whereas in the Congo a 'chicken' represented 50 cowries, in Benin it was only 40; conversely the 'goat', equivalent to 300 cowries in the Congo, amounted to 910 in Benin. It is possible, but on the whole unlikely, that the Portuguese introduced this method of reckoning to Benin.

and 50 for each of the larger pieces. Cloth was given in exchange for the remaining 31 tusks which cost in all 370 'customary yards', the largest being bought for 26 yards. Even allowing for some variation in the size of tusks, the price of ivory had risen sharply since 1517 when Carneiro's ship had acquired 187 tusks for 1,623 manillas. The remainder of the return cargo comprised 1,427 *coris* which the pilot bought in twelve lots, the largest of 194 and the smallest of 30 beads. All the *coris* were paid for with manillas, some at the rate of five and others at the rate of six *coris* to one manilla. From this detail of the trade of one royal ship it is worthy of note that for almost every-thing they bought, and for almost all the services they received, the Portuguese gave either manillas or cowries, the standard currencies of Benin. This trade was conducted, therefore, on a monetary rather than a barter basis. Even the cloth and beads that played a very minor role as media of exchange had been adjusted quantitatively to units that were soon to permit of abstract price and profit calculations. In effect Portuguese trade was adding substantially to the currency stock in Benin, but providing very few articles of consumption.

A relative abundance of documentary evidence for trade between São Tomé and Benin in the fifteen-twenties reveals a continuing evolution in trading practices on both sides, despite constant references to established custom. It is interesting in this respect to compare the voyage of the royal ship *São João* in 1526 with that of the *São Miguel* four years earlier.[1] When the *São João* reached Ughoton in August 1526, the pilot was met by three officials sent there by the Oba; these had to be paid five 'cloths' apiece for un-specified services which had been neither mentioned nor rewarded in 1522. This is also the first reference to the 'cloth' (*pano*) as a standard unit in Benin trade, though in the Forcados River it had been known at least as early as 1522. As used in Benin in 1526 it was a piece of linen two-thirds of a yard in length, and almost certainly equivalent to the earlier 'customary yard', for the pilot of the *São João* gave *Osodin* and *Uwangue* twenty 'cloths' instead of the twenty 'customary yards' they had received from Fernandes. Since it is unlikely that the linen was cut into twenty short lengths

---

1 A.T.T. *Corpo Cronológico* II, *maço* 151, no. 69. The ship's book of the *São João*.

for this purpose, the 'cloth' was already on the way to becoming a notional measure of value. After visiting the Oba and delivering his present (a piece of Holland cloth, a damask hat trimmed with gold thread and a piece of fine cloth dyed in grain), the pilot and clerk settled in Benin City to conduct their trade from a house they rented for ten 'cloths'. Porters brought up 110 loads of manillas (each load containing 100 manillas), 70 loads of cowries weighing altogether 20 quintals, and 10 loads of linen and red cloth. The head-load thus amounted to approximately 30 pounds—a somewhat lighter burden than the 40-pound head-load of 1522.

Most of the *São João*'s cargo was expended on 170 female slaves, five of whom died on the return voyage, while another two were drowned attempting to escape from the ship as it lay in the river. Eighty of these slaves were bought with manillas, almost all of them at the fixed maximum price of 50 manillas. Cowries were used to pay for another 60 slaves who cost approximately one 'goat' above the cowry price of 1522.[1] Considering that the manilla price of slaves remained unchanged and that half the slaves were paid for in that currency, the increased price in cowries presumably reflects a fall in their value as stocks accumulated. During 1526 alone, the Portuguese had unloaded some 36 quintals, or about 1,150,000, of these little shells in Benin. The remaining 30 slaves were bought from the Oba in exchange for all the cloth in the cargo—a transaction which suggests that the ruler had established rights of pre-emption to certain categories of merchandise. He gave 15 slaves for two and a half pieces of red cloth measuring 81 *covados* (60¼ yards), and another 15 for 300 linen 'cloths', which is rather less than the 1522 cloth price. This is the only documented instance of a direct purchase of slaves from the Oba, so we remain in some doubt whether on other occasions they were sold on his behalf or by his subjects; it is possible that any Edo was permitted to sell female slaves. Unlike Fernandes, the pilot of the *São João* made no payment to someone asking the Oba's formal permission to buy slaves, so we may assume that this particular custom or official had disappeared. Instead he had to pay 10 manillas to a chief who

---

1 Earlier in 1526 another royal ship, the *Santa Cruz de Mayo*, had been able to buy slaves rather more cheaply, paying an average of 6,670 cowries for each. (A.T.T. *Corpo Cronológico* II, *maço* 151, no. 76.)

'despatched' the slaves from Benin City to Ughoton, and six to a local blacksmith who made twenty manacles used to secure slaves on their march to the ship. In addition to his slave cargo, the pilot of the *São João* bought 9,620 *coris*. Prices seem to have increased since 1522, for only 3,220 were bought at the former top price of five for one manilla. The remainder cost four for one manilla, which was the price obtaining in 1522 in the Forcados River. Possibly the difference can be attributed to a variation in the quality of *coris*. Ivory, however, had by this time seemingly priced itself entirely out of the market, for the Portuguese bought none in Benin after 1522. An alternative explanation might be that the Oba had forbidden the sale of ivory, as he had that of male slaves.

Depreciation of the cowry currency is further attested by the cost of provisioning the *São João*. To victual his ship the pilot bought yams to a value of 1,600 manillas, as against 828 in 1522 when there were only half the number of slaves; but the yams paid for with cowries cost 89,000 cowries compared with the 8,000 expended on the earlier voyage. Another 55,000 had to be given for yams, wood and water furnished to the slaves in Benin City. Among the provisions appears an interesting item not mentioned earlier; this was *o carousso*, for which the pilot paid 35 manillas.[1]

Other voyages made about this time confirm a narrowing of trade between Benin and the Portuguese to two staple items—slaves and *coris*. Everything else the Portuguese bought in Benin—such as wooden food bowls, manacles, chains, mats and loin-cloths—served only for use in the slave trade. The goods they carried to Benin had become equally restricted in variety; by 1526 only manillas, cowries and linen cloths figured significantly in their cargoes. From the point of view of the Portuguese crown, the loss of the ivory

---

1 The nearest equivalent to this word in modern Portuguese is *caroço*—the stone or hard seed of a fruit. In describing a tree found in Annobon, Valentim Fernandes likened its fruit to an olive without the stone (*coroço*). (*Description*, p. 144.) Possibly palm kernels are meant, for they are mentioned in conjunction with palm oil in the ship's book. There is also some doubt about the identity of the *casoviço* and *emroqueas* which were bought at other times to feed slaves. Guinea pepper (*Xylopia aethiopica*), known to the Edo as *unie* and used as an ingredient in pepper soup, was familiar to the Portuguese of São Tomé in the sixteenth century under the same name. (Blake, *Europeans in West Africa*, p. 152.) Another food-plant familiar in the islands as a food for slaves was the cocoyam. (Fernandes, *Description*, p. 138.)

trade and a growing concentration on slaving made commerce with Benin increasingly unattractive because profits were diminishing. Moreover, with the development of a slave traffic to other parts of the coast—ships from São Tomé were sailing regularly to the Congo, the Rio Real, the Mahin and Forcados Rivers—Benin had lost its former importance as the principal source of slaves for the Costa da Mina. Over the years 1525 to 1527 the royal factor in São Tomé received from the mainland a total of 6,300 slaves;[1] in 1526 Benin supplied only 274, and is unlikely to have accounted for more than one-sixth of the total over the whole period in question. Making due allowance for slaves taken to São Tomé by private merchants, the available evidence suggests that, whereas the total volume of trade from the islands to the mainland had greatly expanded in the fifteen-twenties, that with Benin remained at its former level. The failure of Benin to increase, or even maintain, its share of the West African slave trade can be explained partly by the relatively high prices in Benin; newer slave markets offered slaves much more cheaply. The refusal to sell male slaves, except as a very rare favour, also made Benin an unsatisfactory market in Portuguese eyes, and must lead us to consider the apparent lack of enthusiasm for the slave trade displayed by the rulers of Benin and their principal advisers. Either they had few slaves to sell, which would seem improbable in a period when the kingdom was engaged in constant and successful wars of expansion, or else the services and prestige accruing to the great men of Benin from the possession of many slaves outweighed the value of the manillas and cowries for which they could be exchanged. One can hardly escape the conclusion that the latter consideration had by this time acquired the status of national policy, at least with respect to young, able-bodied male slaves—precisely those that the slave-traders were most anxious to buy.

5. The end of Portuguese monopoly: the second mission

For three years, from 1529 to 1532, the whole of São Tomé's trade with the mainland was farmed to a syndicate of merchants, of whose

---

1 A.T.T. *Corpo Cronológico* II, *maço* 161, no. 91.

operations no record remains. On St. John's day 1532 the crown revoked the farm on the grounds that direct administration would yield a higher revenue, 'and also so that the Mina may be better supplied with slaves'.[1] The syndicate had failed to deliver the five hundred slaves now required every year for the gold trade of the Costa da Mina. Another, though unspecified, reason for ending the farm was a negotiation taking place in Lisbon on the opening of a direct traffic in slaves between West Africa and the Antilles. During the fifteen-twenties a growing number of African slaves had been reaching the Spanish West Indies by way of the Lisbon slave market. Then in 1528 two Flemings, who held a contract to supply slaves to the Spanish islands, opened negotiations with the *Casa da Mina* on a project to transport the slaves directly from West Africa; São Tomé had many claims to be the base for such operations. Agreement had still to be reached in December 1531 when the decision was taken to revoke the farm, but it must have come very soon afterwards, for in November 1532, the *Santo Antonio* (apparently a Portuguese vessel) carried the first cargo of 201 slaves from São Tomé to Santo Domingo and San Juan.[2] Thus began the transatlantic slave trade by the middle passage. In the following year 490 slaves left the island for the Spanish West Indies, and in 1534 the number rose again to 651.

In addition to furnishing the contractors with the slaves required for the transatlantic trade, the royal factor in São Tomé was able to keep the Costa da Mina adequately supplied. In 1532 he sent at least 476 slaves there, and in 1534 the exceptionally large number of 786. At the same time slaves were still going to Portugal: 230 left São Tomé for Lisbon in 1532, and 380 in 1533. How many slaves were absorbed into the labour force of the island we do not know. Altogether the slave trade of São Tomé must have been running at the rate of around 2,000 slaves a year by the middle fifteen-thirties. Information about the Benin share in this trade is entirely lacking, perhaps because of a fortuitous destruction of documents.[3] Considering, however, that the Portuguese government adhered strictly

---

1 A.T.T. *Corpo Cronológico* I, *maço* 48, no. 7.
2 A.T.T. *Corpo Cronológico*. II, *maço* 180, no. 21. 21 Nov. 1532.
3 Most of the records of the *Casa da Mina* were destroyed with the building in the 1755 earthquake. Most of the stray papers that have survived in the

to the maximum price of fifty manillas for a slave, while the Oba continued the prohibition on the export of male slaves, it is very possible that the slave trade with Benin declined to relative insignificance. On the other hand, there may have been a brisker trade in *coris*. The factor at São Jorge took delivery of 19,474 of these beads from São Tomé in 1532, 13,909 in 1533, 46,854 in 1534, and 50,061 in 1535. Benin had always been the principal source of *coris* and may have accounted for much of the increase in their supply, though the Portuguese were in these years intensifying their trade in the Forcados and Mahin Rivers where the beads were also obtainable. Ivory cannot have been of any importance as an article of commerce, if indeed it was traded at all; the factor in São Tomé was able to send only 99 tusks to Lisbon in 1533 and 126 in 1534 from the whole of the coast between the Mahin and Congo Rivers. We do not, of course, know how much private and illicit trade lurked behind this official front. The inhabitants of São Tomé and Príncipe still exercised their rights to sell their own produce to the mainland in return for slaves and commodities required for the domestic economy. They were also engaged in a flourishing but illegal trade in pepper, of which Benin still supplied important quantities despite the vigilance of the royal factor. Nevertheless, one can hardly resist the conclusion that Benin was, by the fifteen-thirties, relatively much less important to Portuguese trade in West Africa than it had been at the beginning of the century.

One of the last Portuguese voyages to Benin during the sixteenth century of which any detail has survived was that begun in January 1535 by the *Santo Antonio*.[1] Twelve barrels of cowries weighing 25 quintals and 10,000 copper and brass manillas accounted for the bulk of the outward cargo, but it included a more varied selection of minor items than had been usual in the previous decade. Among the cloth was a bale of red material measuring 54 yards, a similar bale of blue cloth, 11 yards of green Bruges satin, six pieces of cotton cloth of a kind used by the Moors to make tunics, and 4½ yards of red *vinte e quatreno* (a cloth with 2,400 threads in the warp).

Corpo Cronológico and other collections of the Torre do Tombo appear to owe their existence to the fact that they were, at the time of the disaster, lodged in other government offices, having been originally extracted for legal or accounting purposes.

1 A.T.T. *Corpo Cronológico* II, *maço* 187, no. 18 (2).

The *Santo Antonio* also carried a small quantity of hardware comprising six brass chamber-pots, one large basin, and a large new copper cauldron weighing 106 pounds which had been ordered by the Oba. A barrel of gunpowder weighing one quintal and 500 strings of yellow glass beads completed the cargo. The gunpowder may have been intended for the ship's armament, but its listing among the merchandise suggests that it was to be sold. If this supposition is correct it would imply that, despite the ban imposed by the Portuguese authorities, the Edo had succeeded in acquiring some firearms, probably through smuggling operations from São Tomé. But we shall never know what happened to the gunpowder and the rest of the cargo because the ship foundered on the bar of the Benin River on its homeward voyage.

In the very years that the Portuguese added the transatlantic slave trade as a significant new dimension to their West African commerce, they had to face the first challenge to their monopoly in that sphere since the preliminary struggle with Castile. The threat came from the French whose persistent interloping and piratical activities date from 1530, when the Dieppe merchant Jean Ango obtained a letter of marque against Portuguese shipping.[1] Very soon their operations extended to the Bight of Benin. Two Portuguese ships returning to São Tomé from the Mahin River in 1533 were attacked and plundered by two French vessels,[2] and thenceforward French interloping became a common occurrence. By 1539 at the latest French ships were trading with Benin. Pepper was the main attraction for them, but how much they were buying and to what extent they were ousting the Portuguese from Benin are impossible to estimate since French sources have so far yielded no detailed accounts of these voyages. Nor is anything yet known about French relations with the Edo and the merchandise they offered. Perhaps these are matters destined to remain obscure, for French enterprise in these waters was of a private, small-scale nature that

---

1 cf. Blake, *European Beginnings*, chap. vi. As early as 1526 the French had given the authorities of São Tomé cause for anxiety. In December of that year the *corregedor* of the island ordered artillery to be placed aboard ships returning to Portugal from Goa because a French ship was known to be lurking on the Guinea coast, and it had recently seized a caravel. (A.T.T. *Corpo Cronologico* II, *maço* 137, no. 164.)

2 A.T.T. *Corpo Cronológico* II, *maço* 185, no. 107.

usually left little or no record in the state archives. Benin tradition too has retained no memory of the arrival of the French, or indeed of any Europeans other than the Portuguese. Though the Oba and his chiefs were doubtless aware that they were dealing with Europeans at loggerheads with the Portuguese, their attitude appears to have been that which they had previously adopted towards interlopers from São Tomé: a readiness to trade with all comers. Certain private merchants of São Tomé adopted a similar attitude and made large profits by selling to the French cargoes of Benin pepper which they had smuggled from the mainland.[1] We may assume, therefore, that some Portuguese from the islands continued their private trade with Benin despite French competition and attacks: the slave trade and illicit traffic in pepper justified the risks they took.

At this juncture, when the Benin trade had become relatively unimportant and unprofitable to official trade, the king of Portugal decided to send another band of missionaries to the Oba. Perhaps he hoped to clear away accumulated grudges and turn the tables on French interlopers. More probably his ecclesiastical right hand knew nothing of the doings of its commercial brother. Our knowledge of the 1538 mission rests solely upon a letter which the priests wrote to John III from Benin City[2]. It tells nothing about the antecedents of the mission, but internal evidence implies that the initiative had come on this occasion from Portugal, not from the Oba as in 1515. Three missionaries (two Franciscans and a member of the Order of Christ) were apparently despatched on the orders of John III who also gave instructions that his factor in São Tomé should supply them with provisions while they remained in Benin. On their arrival in Benin City early in 1538 they discovered some traces of Christianity: Gregorio Lourenço was still alive, and the

---

1 cf. A.T.T. *Cartas Missivas* I, no. 96. n.d. 'The French have good reason for coming to these parts, because much pepper is taken from this island to many places. This pepper comes from the rivers and is transhipped into other vessels that sail to the Levant and Flanders. I came to discover that a ship which arrived from Benin transferred a quantity of sacks to another ship that went to the Levant. The factor was requested to conduct an enquiry, as required by His Majesty in his instructions, but he refused.'

2 A.T.T. *Corpo Cronológico* I, *maço* 65, no. 57. Benin City. 30 August 1539. Translated in A. F. C. Ryder, 'The Benin Missions'. *Journal of the Historical Society of Nigeria*, vol. II, no. 2.

Oba held captive a number of African Christians, including some described in the letter as 'kings', and one named Afonso Anes whom he employed in teaching boys to read. Most important of all these relics of Christian endeavour was the Oba himself because he had been, so the priests learned, among the boys baptised by their predecessors in 1516. But their hopes that this youthful brush with Christianity might dispose the Oba to favour their cause seemed doomed from the first audience when a letter of introduction and exhortation from John III was thrown unopened into a box on the left of the throne.[1] Probably nothing more sinister than the ceremonial usage of a non-literate society inspired this gesture, but looking back over a trail of disappointments, the missionaries were inclined to see it as an act of studied malevolence animated by their failure to give presents to the Oba and his principal courtiers. They listed besides many other seeming proofs of hostility. They were lodged, they complained, in a house full of idols and so noisy that they were unable to perform their devotions; guards in constant attendance prevented them from moving freely about the city;[2] Afonso Anes was not permitted to use the booklets of Christian doctrine specially sent for his pupils; and Gregorio Lourenço was unable to have his wives [*sic*] and children baptised because the Oba forbade it. With all allowance made for exaggeration and misapprehension, this second mission obviously never enjoyed the favour shown to the first. Yet, despite all the contrived frustration, the Oba did display some interest in the mission. On his instructions, and presumably at the second audience which followed three months after the first, the three Portuguese solemnly carried a cross and a statue of the Virgin to the foot of the dais on which he sat. After examining these objects carefully and feeling them all over, the Oba ordered them to be placed on the lowest step of the dais; then he permitted the missionaries to expound their doctrine. They

---

1 cf. the experience of the Capuchins in 1651, infra pp. 101–2. The letter was opened and read at the second audience.
2 This restriction may not be evidence of particular distrust of the priests; Dutch merchants visiting Benin City early in the seventeenth century found their movements similarly restrained by these close companions, though they were otherwise welcome. The more wary attitude towards foreigners possibly reflects a change in the character of Benin society, or else a more prying disposition in visitors.

did so in rather minatory fashion, warning the Oba of his 'perilous condition' and denouncing the practice of human sacrifice they had witnessed in his rituals. Their preaching made no impression on the ruler who made it clear that he did not intend to change his religion and refused to receive them again. Undeterred they made several attempts to enter the palace uninvited, only to find the door shut roughly in their faces.

Much of the letter to John III is taken up with personal denunciation of the Oba, to whom the missionaries attributed all their ills. In addition to permitting human sacrifice, he is accused of anointing himself with human blood, making offerings twice a day to the 'enemy of mankind, the devil', persisting in 'idolatries and diabolical invocations', rejoicing in Christian misfortunes, and 'many other superstitions, abominations and errors'. In the throes of failure such accusations are to be expected, and in part they only echo earlier charges, but human sacrifice is reported for the first time as a feature of royal ceremonial in Benin. It may have been practised earlier, yet it is difficult to believe that it could have escaped the notice and condemnation of the Portuguese. Duarte Pacheco Pereira, for example, who noted cannibalism among the Ijo, had nothing to say about human sacrifice in Benin City though he visited the Edo capital on four occasions. Nor is there any hint of such a practice in the letter which King Manuel addressed to the Oba in 1514 when it might well have afforded an additional ground of reproach. There is, therefore, a possibility that it was the baptised Oba who introduced human sacrifice into Benin religious ceremonial as a means of enhancing his divine attributes.

For more than twelve months the three Portuguese remained ineffectually in Benin City, surviving serious illness and gradually parting with their possessions to buy food which was scarce that year after a poor harvest. Supplies sent to them from São Tomé in 1538 had been lost when the ships carrying them were attacked by the French. Another small fleet reached Benin in safety the following year, bringing no provisions for the missionaries, but offering them a means of departure. They accordingly asked the Oba for permission to leave with the ships, and for a reply to the letter they had brought from John III. The Oba refused, telling them that they could not leave until an envoy arrived from Portugal with a letter of recall. Their subsequent importunities he referred to the chiefs responsible for trade who could obviously do nothing but repeat his refusal. Finally they had to reconcile themselves to remaining in Benin, but were able to send a letter in which, after relating the fate of the mission, they appealed to the king for an armed vessel to be sent to their rescue, lest the Oba decide to offer them as a sacrifice to his 'fetish'. In case their own peril might not seem sufficient justification for such trouble and expense, the same vessel might, they added, drive away the French interlopers.

The Oba's insistence that the missionaries should not depart until an ambassador arrived from Portugal with a message recalling them probably arose from the fact that he had already sent, or was about to send, envoys to John III. Their presence in Portugal in 1540 is attested by de Barros,[1] but the purpose of their mission can only be surmised. Almost certainly it was in part concerned with the activities of the three missionaries—perhaps to present the Oba's side of the story before they were freed to deliver their denunciations. Of the result of that embassy, and of the fate of the missionaries, there is no record. De Barros tells only that among the envoys was a man about seventy years of age who wore one of the small brass crosses which the *Oghene* bestowed on those who visited him on the accession of a new Oba.[2] This is the last reference in the written sources to the *Oghene* and to the brass crosses, and another indication that the reign of this Oba may have witnessed a fundamental change in the character of divine kingship in Benin. For more than a century after the failure of this second mission the Portuguese made no further attempt to introduce Christianity into Benin. Instead they turned their attention with some profit towards the emergent kingdom of the Itsekiris.[3]

It is unfortunate that Portuguese and French trade with Benin during the fifteen-forties has left no record, for these were years in which the Edo monarchy, hitherto largely confined to the terra firma beyond the swamp forest, began to impose tribute upon the peoples of the coast as far west as Lagos island.[4] In the missionaries'

1 De Barros, *Asia*, Dec. I, liv. iii, cap. 4.   2 cf. supra p. 31.
3 A. F. C. Ryder, 'Missionary activity in the kingdom of Warri to the early nineteenth century'. *Journal of the Historical Society of Nigeria*, vol. II, no. 1, 1960.
4 cf. supra p. 14.

letter there are some indications that the westward expansion of Benin influence had already begun. They reported that the Oba held prisoner ambassadors sent to him by the rulers of 'Arida and Labida' (Ardra and Labedde), places well to the west of the Lagos lagoon and recently opened to Portuguese trade.[1] Conceivably these little states were already in a tributary relationship to Benin, and had become involved in a dispute with the suzerain similar to that which provoked Orhogbua's campaign in the western coastlands.[2] One may also speculate on the relationship between this Benin march to the sea and the development of European trade, though the general indifference of Obas to the latter would seem to weigh against any direct cause-and-effect explanation. Yet even though the larger impulse may have been dynastic dynamism,[3] it is still possible that this took some direction from the opening of Portuguese trade with places such as Mahin, Ardra and Labedde, perhaps in an effort to ensure that the scope of Benin control extended *pari passu* with the area of Portuguese trading operations.

In the year before Esigie sent his envoys to Lisbon, France and Portugal patched up an agreement on the issues of prize and reprisal that had plagued their relations for a decade.[4] Whether the

---

1 Portuguese contact with Labida began in 1520 when the ruler of the state sent an envoy to Portugal. (A.T.T. *Corpo Cronológico.* II, *maço* 92, no. 93.)

2 cf. Egharevba, *A Short History*, p. 30. Benin tradition attributes the subjugation of the coastal strip to Orhogbua, but the following passage from Egharevba clearly implies that some form of overlordship had been established in the reign of Esigie:
'Some of the towns and villages failed to pay their yearly tribute to him (Orhogbua), so he marched against them, soon after his accession, with a large army. He made his camp (*eko*) on Lagos island, and from there attacked his enemies for many years.'
The identification of the Oba with whom the missionaries clashed in 1538 as Esigie relies mainly upon the report that he had been baptised by the earlier mission; it also agrees with the dates assigned to Esigie in the king-lists of Talbot and Egharevba. The latter's attribution of a missionary education and baptism to Orhogbua rather than Esigie appears to be an inference necessitated by his having pushed the beginning of Esigie's reign back to 1504.

3 cf. supra pp. 12–14. Control over coasts and river mouths would also have given Benin access to supplies of cooking salt obtained both from sea water and from salt-bush. The introduction of 'native salt' to Benin is associated with the reign of Orhogbua.

4 A.T.T. *Gavetas* XV, *maço* 13, no. 16.

Benin embassy resulted in a similar removal of misunderstandings between the Portuguese crown and Benin we do not know; presumably they were at least discussed. But any improvement produced by these efforts of diplomacy was short-lived. Ignoring treaties and protests, French ships continued to frequent the Costa da Mina throughout the fifteen-forties,[1] and doubtless took many a cargo of pepper from Benin. By the early fifteen-fifties there was equally little left of any accommodation between Benin and Portugal. For some unspecified outrage committed in the course of trade, the factor in São Tomé decided in 1553 to prohibit all trade with the kingdom, and urged upon Lisbon the need to punish the Oba before reopening it.[2] A situation was thus created which provides some indication of the importance that the merchants of São Tomé, if not the *Casa da Mina*, attached to Benin. Encouraged by the royal factor, they searched for alternative markets, among them Ijebu,[3] the Popo states, the Cameroons and Corisco. None, they claimed, adequately replaced Benin, and they were soon endeavouring to return there. The principal objection, from the official standpoint, seems to have been the activity of interlopers in the Benin and Forcados Rivers, so in November 1554 an enterprising inhabitant of São Tomé addressed to the king of Portugal a proposal for dealing with the problem.[4] Whenever a ship in the Benin River had news of an interloper, it should slip out through the Forcados River to alert an armed squadron at São Tomé. According to the memorial, between thirty and forty ships sailed every year from Portugal to São Tomé, so there should always be six or seven carrying some armament in the harbour of the island; these would provide the task force to fall upon the interlopers before they could complete their cargo. Such a scheme ignored many practical difficulties, and above all it failed to take into account that the Benin trade was by this time an almost exclusively local interest for which government and private business outside the islands were unprepared to make sacrifices or suffer inconvenience.

1 cf. Blake, *European Beginnings*, pp. 133–4.
2 A.T.T. *Corpo Cronológico* I, maço 90, no. 126. 8 August 1553.
3 Though apparently well known to the Portuguese around the end of the fifteenth century, Ijebu was not frequented by them in the first half of the sixteenth. In 1553 they sent two ships to Ijebu.
4 A.T.T. *Corpo Cronológico* I, maço 94, no. 28.

Within a few years of the writing of this memorial the merchants of São Tomé and Príncipe had overcome their problem, not by driving away the interlopers but by cultivating a new state in the Forcados River. Here a new Oere had grown up at Ale Iwere or Ode Itsekiri, the nucleus and capital of an Itsekiri kingdom ruled by a dynasty descended from Benin.[1] Despite the dynastic bonds, the young state appears to have enjoyed sufficient independence to follow policies very different from those of Benin. It encouraged Portuguese trade, placed no restrictions on the supply of slaves, and accepted Christian missionaries. Before the end of the sixteenth century the rulers of Ode Itsekiri had cemented their special relationship with Portugal by themselves becoming enthusiastic converts to Christianity.[2] A need to attract the European trade on which their wealth and security depended may well have influenced the Itsekiri attitude towards the Portuguese, whose island colonies represented the only assured commercial partners within their reach. But it was a policy which, with the acceptance of Christianity, inevitably strained relations between the Itsekiris and Benin, and led eventually to a struggle for control of the Benin River.

Difficulties with Obas and interlopers cannot alone explain the decay of Portuguese trade with Benin in the second half of the sixteenth century. The French challenge faded by the fifteen-seventies and the more substantial onslaught by the Dutch did not develop until the very end of the century. The withdrawal has, therefore, to be seen as part of the general decline of Portuguese power and commerce in West Africa. These had depended primarily upon the action of a government which now found it more profitable to devote its limited resources to the exploitation of its trade and possessions in the Indies and Brazil. Not only did this shift of interest lead to a run-down of official commerce—especially felt in marginal areas such as Benin—it also undermined the prosperity of the island settlements. Endemic slave revolts, a disease of the sugar canes, and a sack by the French in 1567 added to São Tomé's tale of disaster. Thus private trade too slackened, and the less satisfactory markets, among them Benin, were abandoned.

---

1 cf. P. C. Lloyd, *The Itsekiri*. London, International African Institute, 1957, p. 179.
2 cf. Ryder, 'Missionary activity in the kingdom of Warri'.

Chapter 3
English and Dutch beginnings

1. The English

It happened that the year which brought a rupture in Benin's relations with Portugal produced also the first contact between that kingdom and its eventual conquerors, the English, who were just beginning to join the French as interlopers in West African waters. The voyage to Benin was one of their earliest enterprises in this direction, undertaken when much still depended on the services of renegade Portuguese navigators. On this occasion, a knight of the Portuguese royal household named António Anes Penteado, whom private enemies had forced to flee his own country,[1] agreed with a group of London merchants[2] to captain one of their ships in a venture to Guinea. His fellow captain, Thomas Wyndham, a man of wide experience as seaman and merchant, had shares in the voyage.[3] Their little fleet consisted of *The Lion*, 'a tall ship of 150 tons' which Wyndham commanded, *The Primrose*, and a pinnace called *The Moon*; the two latter vessels were lent by the navy. Among some 140 men who manned these ships were a Portuguese pilot named Francisco Rodrigues, the son of a Lord Mayor of London, and the boy Martin Frobisher. Eager for riches they sailed from Portsmouth in August 1553.

---

1 cf. Blake, *Europeans in West Africa*, vol. II, p. 313, n. 2, and ibid. pp. 283–4 for the efforts of the Portuguese government to lure Penteado home.

2 Sir George Barnes, Sir John Yorck, Mr. Garrard, Francis Lambert (the Lord Mayor of London whose son Nicholas was lost in Benin) and Wyndham. But cf. T. S. Willan, *Studies in Elizabethan Foreign Trade*. Manchester, 1959.

3 cf. R. Tong, 'Captain Thomas Wyndham, Tudor Merchant Adventurer.' *History Today*, vol. VII, no. 4, April 1957. The principal source of information on this voyage is the account published by Richard Eden in *Decades of the newe worlde* (1555). Eden evidently collected his material at first hand from survivors of the voyage, who, as Blake observes (*Europeans in West Africa*, II, p. 255), are likely to have been prejudiced in their judgement of Wyndham, 'that tragical captain'.

Rejecting Penteado's advice that they trade on the Grain or Malagetta Coast, Wyndham insisted on sailing directly to the Gold Coast (the Costa da Mina of the Portuguese) where they secured 150 pounds of gold. Then again ignoring the urgings of Penteado that they should dispose of all their merchandise for gold, Wyndham forced him to pilot the ships to the Benin River. The Portuguese was doubtless anxious to get away as quickly as possible from a region where capture by his own countrymen would have meant short shrift for him. Wyndham was resolved to find the pepper of which Penteado had told him: 'This whoreson Jew hath promised to bring us to such places as are not, or as he cannot bring us unto: but if he do not, I will cut off his eares and naile them to the maste.'[1] Cowed by such threats, Penteado took them on to Benin.

As *The Lion* and *The Primrose* were considerably larger than the small caravels used by the Portuguese in their Benin trade, Wyndham anchored them off the bar of the river, while Penteado and the merchants took the pinnace to Ughoton. Messengers conducted them to Benin City where, in the audience room of the palace, the Oba received them, conversing in the Portuguese he had learned as a child.[2] First Penteado and the English merchants knelt before the Oba who told them to rise and asked why they had come to his country. Learning that they wished to buy pepper, he showed them 30 or 40 hundredweight lying in a storehouse and asked to see their merchandise. His officials then accompanied them to Ughoton to organise the transport of their wares to the capital in the manner already familiar to the Portuguese. Eden's account of the voyage does not specify the nature of the merchandise, but it evidently satisfied the Oba for he undertook to load all three vessels with pepper within thirty days, and was even prepared to grant them credit until the next voyage should their goods not cover the cost of a full cargo. If this was not an unprecedented offer—and it must seem unlikely that the Oba would have granted such a facility for the first time to a people with whom he had never before traded—

---

1 Wyndham's reported jibe at Penteado may indicate that the latter was a *converso*—a converted Jew; *conversos* were prominent in the merchant community of Portugal, but found themselves in some danger from the Inquisition which was often activated by the jealousy of 'old Christian' rivals.

2 By Egharevba's reckoning the Oba in question was Orhogbua. He may have been among the pupils of Afonso Anes.

there existed in the sixteenth century a practice akin to the credit trading or 'trust' of later periods;[1] but the credit was extended by the Edo to Europeans, not vice versa as happened in the later phase. Another noteworthy feature of Benin trade brought out by Eden's account was the active role played by the Oba in negotiating with European merchants.

The bargain struck, messengers were despatched through the kingdom ordering the Oba's subjects to gather pepper and bring it to Benin City, and within the thirty days specified 80 tuns[2] had been produced. Meanwhile fever was beginning to take heavy toll of the crews in the ships lying in the river mouth, with as many as five men dying in one day; so Wyndham sent a message asking Penteado to leave Benin City without further delay, and, on receiving a reply from the Portuguese that he wished to remain until the cargo had been completed, threatened to sail without him. In a final effort to delay the departure Penteado went in person to the ships, only to find Wyndham dead and the survivors in an ugly panic. They refused even to wait until the merchants could be brought from Benin City, and, after sinking *The Lion* because of lack of hands to sail her, forced Penteado to sail with the other two ships. 'Thrust among the boys of the ship, not used like a man, nor yet like an honest boy, but glad to find favour at the cookes hand', in less than a week he too was dead. 'And of sevenscore men came home to Plimmouth scarcely forty, and of them many died.' Of the fate of the merchants left behind we know nothing; Penteado had been able to do no more than write to them with a promise to return as soon as possible.

Despite the harrowing experiences that befell all who took part in the voyage of 1553, profits and prospects were so attractive that another fleet of five vessels sailed for Guinea in the following year. A relative of Wyndham's, Alexander Coles, went to Flanders to buy the necessary merchandise, while the king of Portugal set his spies to work to discover the route the fleet intended to follow. Some of those who had sailed with Wyndham joined these ships and

---

1 cf. infra pp. 130–3.
2 'tunne' in Eden. It is likely that he refers to a measure of capacity, not of weight. On other occasions pepper is known to have been measured in casks and barrels. cf. infra p. 164.

guided them to the places where he had obtained his gold, but on this occasion they kept away from Benin.[1] The prohibition issued by Queen Mary in July 1556 against all voyages by her subjects to 'Guyne, Bynie and the Mina' failed to prevent a steady increase in the number of English expeditions. In April 1559 the governor of São Jorge da Mina reported considerable English activity along the coast every year from July onwards.[2] The Portuguese factor in Flanders informed his government in December 1561 that an English fleet had sailed for the Costa da Mina with the intention of building a fort there.[3] Bad weather forced that fleet to turn back; but in the next year twelve English ships made a successful voyage to the Mina.[4] By this time they had accumulated much experience and information on the commerce and navigation of Guinea, and so could dispense with the services of Portuguese pilots.

Queen Mary's reference to 'Bynie' in the proclamation of 1556 was probably intended to designate the whole of the coast beyond the Costa da Mina, and not the kingdom of Benin alone.[5] Indeed we have no direct evidence that the English returned to Benin during the three decades following Wyndham's ill-fated venture. But in addition to the presumption that so profitable a source of pepper cannot have been ignored, there exists a document based upon the experience of voyages that have left no record. It was written by a certain Randall Shaw, who had himself been to Benin, for the guidance of a Mr. Bingham who intended undertaking a voyage there; the paper is dated 13 May 1582.[6] Shaw recommends that for the sake of the crew's health the ship should not lie outside the bar, but well within the river—he seems to have had Ureju Bay in mind as a suitable anchorage. From there cargo could be carried in ten- or twelve-oared pinnaces to and from Ughoton. 'You have to traffyke with none but with the king himselfe and none other; for he will geve for your commodities pepers.' First the Oba and merchants agreed on the quantity of goods to be given for a bushel

---

1 Eden included an account of this voyage as an appendix to his *Decades*.
2 A.T.T. *Corpo Cronológico* I, maço 103, no. 57. cf. Blake, *European Beginnings* and *Europeans in West Africa*.
3 A.T.T. *Corpo Cronológico* I, maço 105, no. 72.
4 A.T.T. *Corpo Cronológico* I, maço 106, no. 11.
5 cf. supra p. 36, n. 1, for a similarly wide use of 'Benin' by the Portuguese.
6 P.R.O. *State Papers*, 12, 153. Appendix VIII.

or quarter measure of pepper; then the Oba would undertake to provide a full cargo in so many days, according to the burthen of the ship. 'You must agree with the king to bring the pepper so near to the sea as ye can, and procure to have yr pepper so near as you can to be clean, or else ye must procure your selfe to make yt cleane.' From these injunctions one may conclude that the question of who should pay for transporting pepper from Benin City to Ughoton had become a matter for bargaining between the Oba and his customers. So too had the amount of stalk that might be left on the peppers; in any case, Shaw advised his correspondent to take along a garbler to clean it. All trade it would seem was in the Oba's hands, or at least nothing could be sold without his consent, and at this period it appears to have been restricted to pepper. Shaw makes no reference to either slaves or ivory, and besides pepper mentions only something which might be gum copal: 'if you can gett the Balme yt ys a precyous thing'.

A cargo of merchandise for the Benin trade should, according to Shaw, include the following items: a few pieces of brown Rouen canvas; good quality white Rouen canvas; Holland cloth; at least fifteen pounds of artifical Flemish coral (these were tubular beads two-thirds of an inch long which were to be strung into bracelets and necklaces on green, red, and yellow thread, preferably with glass beads of the same colours between each coral—'The estimation of them is much in vallew there'); more artificial coral in nut-shaped beads to be interspersed with artificial pearls; coarse red woollen cloth; red cotton cloth; Calicut cloth; red caps; various kinds of pots and pans; small glasses; belts; knives; saws and hatchets; coats of mail; copper manillas; black horse-tails and small bells. As a present for the Oba, Shaw recommends half a dozen drinking glasses, and three or four mirrors. No quantity of manillas is specified, but they appear to occupy a far less important place than in the period of Portuguese monopoly. As for cowries, the English had at this time no access to the supplies of the Indian Ocean. Manufactured goods therefore played an important part in a Benin cargo. Decorative articles such as cloth, beads, caps and horse-tails had all figured at different times in Portuguese trade, and the first two were still indispensable. What is new and significant in Shaw's list are the utilitarian goods, especially the saws, knives and hatchets, and the coats of mail which were probably used for war rather than adornment.[1] Another piece of advice from Shaw makes it clear that the English had no objection to supplying arms to Benin: 'you may confer with the king to have a trade with him, demanding what commodities he will have out of our countrie to serve for his warres against other kings'. His vagueness on this point, however, would suggest that no traffic in arms had yet developed.

From such a well-conducted venture Shaw held out the prospect of enormous profits: 'you shall by god's helpe have a hundred tonne of pepper for 400 lb of commodities; yf you send sage and wise men that can use the matter well with the king, the next vyadge may be worthe 100,000 lb to you yf you once fawl in trade with the king'. The chief hazard standing in the way of such riches was no longer the Portuguese but disease, so he offered a few hit-and-miss health hints.

> You must be ther the first of december and at the farthest you have not to tarry if it be possible not past the 5 of ffebruarye for saulfegard of your men. The men's drinke must be ther nothing but syder and at any hand lett your men bewarre that they doe not eat any kind of ffruits in the countrye, nor drinke of the water: yf they do, they die for yt. They must be merry and keep them from sleep; and to keep as many cloathes on ther heads as they can.

This preference for confining trade with Benin to the dry season later became common among all Europeans, partly for the supposed benefits to health, but more from the difficulty of crossing the bar once the prevailing winds had veered to the south. The very small craft employed in trade from the Portuguese islands did not suffer from this handicap to anything like the same extent as the deeper-draught vessels sailing from Europe.

Although Shaw's *Instructions* bear witness to some English interest and activity in the Benin trade, they also give the impression that it was not a much frequented branch of commerce. This view is

---

1 Coats of mail may have been in use in Benin as early as the reign of Ozolua. cf. Okojie, *Ishan*, p. 223. '... Ozolua always wore a coat of iron so that all arrows and cutlass blows fall harmless on his body. This used to frighten attackers so much that the legend spread far and wide that Ozolua was invulnerable and that by means of powerful medicines, arrows and cutlasses were meaningless as articles of war against him.'

seemingly confirmed by the report of the chief factor of the *Richard of Arundell* which reached Benin in 1589. Edo officials told this factor, Anthony Ingram, that 'in this king's time no Christians had ever resorted thither to lade pepper'.[1] They clearly intended to imply that the interval had been a long one, and assuming that Oba Ehengbuda was then on the throne, it may have lasted more than ten years.[2] The voyage which ended this long commercial hiatus was undertaken by the London merchants John Newton and John Bird, whose primary interests lay in privateering and, like Wyndham, in the Barbary trade.[3] Their ship, the *Richard of Arundell* of 100 tons, had as its master James Welsh, whose report, with that of the chief factor Ingram, was printed in Hakluyt's account of the voyage.

When the *Richard of Arundell* arrived off the Benin River on 14 February 1589, Welsh found the bar too shallow for his vessel, so he anchored at sea and sent his pinnace and a ship's boat to Ughoton loaded with the cargo of linen and woollen cloth, ironware, copper manillas, glass beads and imitation coral. Ingram describes the trading procedure in some detail. Reaching Ughoton on 20 February, the merchants arranged for messengers to carry news of their arrival to Benin City. Two days later these messengers returned with a palace official (described by the factor as a 'noble man') and 200 carriers to convey them and their goods to the capital, which they reached on 25 February. The Oba was unable to receive them the next day 'by reason of a solemn feast then kept amongst them', so they were met at the palace by 'his Veador, or chief man, that hath the dealing with the Christians: and we conferred with him concerning our trading, who answered us, that we should have all things to our desire both in pepper and Elephants' teeth'. Ivory thus reappears in the records of trade after an absence of sixty years.

---

1 *A voyage to Benin beyond the countrey of Guinea made by Master James Welsh, who set foorth in the yeere 1588*, and *The voiage set forth by M. John Newton, and M. John Bird marchants of London to the kingdome and citie of Benin in Africa, with a ship called the Richard of Arundell, and a pinnesse, in the yere 1588, briefely set downe in this letter following, written by the chiefe Factor in the voyage to the foresaid marchants at the time of the ships first arrivall at Plimouth*, in R. Hakluyt, *The Principal Navigations Voyages Traffiques and Discoveries of the English Nation*. Dent, London, 1927, vol. IV.
2 Egharevba puts Ehengbuda's accession in 1578, Talbot in 1570.
3 Willan, *Elizabethan Foreign Trade*, p. 216 *et passim*.

Although Ingram does not reveal in which language negotiations were conducted, his use of the term *veador* suggests that Portuguese still remained the medium of communication between Benin and European traders of all nations. We can also only surmise that the single *veador* who dealt with Europeans in this period of commercial stagnation may have been the *Uwangue*. The Oba himself, however, still played a personal and decisive part in matters affecting trade, and it was only after Ingram and his companions had been received in audience on 1 March that they were able to complete their bargain with the *veador*.

> The next day we went again to the court, where the foresaid Veadore shewed us one basket of greene pepper, and another of dry in the stalkes: wee desired to have it plucked from the stalkes and made cleane, who answered, that it would aske time, but yet it should be done: and that against another yeere it should be in better readines.

Each day the Oba's subjects brought a little pepper into Benin City until, within a week, 64 serons or bales had been gathered, as well as 28 elephant tusks. But even within so short a time all the Englishmen in the capital had been seized by fever, and when Ingram arrived at Ughoton with his first consignment of pepper, he found the whole crew of the pinnace too ill to work. In three weeks some ten men died, including the captain of the *Richard of Arundell* and two of the principal merchants. 'This sorrowfull accident caused them with such pepper and teeth, as they could find, speedily to returne to the ship', despite promises from the *veador* to hasten the collection of pepper if they would stay longer. Randall Shaw might have pointed out that this voyage had offended both against his precept concerning the season in which Europeans ought to trade in Benin, and also against his advice on diet. Welsh had exchanged some of his merchandise for cowries in order to buy local produce for his crew who drank plentifully of palm wine and ate honey, oranges and plantains, and above all yams which he warmly commended as a substitute for bread or biscuit.[1] If these delicacies affected their health at all, it can only have been for the good.

---

[1] *The Second voyage to Benin, set foorth by Master John Newton, and Master John Bird Marchants of London in the yeere 1590 with a ship called the Richard of Arundell of the burthen of one hundred tunnes, and a small pinnesse; in which voyage Master James Welsh was chiefe Maister*, in Hakluyt, *The Principal Navigations*, vol. IV.

Undeterred by their first experience, Bird and Newton sent James Welsh back to Benin in the *Richard of Arundell* almost immediately.[1] This time disease spared the crew, and the ship was able to lie in the mouth of the river from 10 January until 27 April 1591 while the merchants gathered a cargo of 589 serons of pepper, 150 tusks and 32 barrels of palm oil. Possibly they included small quantitites of the 'cloth made of cotton wooll very curiously woven, and cloth made of the barke of palme trees', samples of which had been gathered on the first voyage. Other products of Benin craftsmen—'pretie fine mats and baskets that they make, and spoones of Elephants teeth very curiously wrought with divers proportions of foules and beasts made upon them'[2]—were bought as curios by officers and men. To complete the generally satisfactory picture of Welsh's second voyage, he had found the Oba extremely ready to trade, the Benin people friendly—'very gentle and loving' was Ingram's description—and no sign of any competition from other nations.[3] Only two obstacles stood between English merchants and the exploitation of the Benin market: these were tropical diseases, which could bring trading to an abrupt and sometimes disastrous end, and the challenge that was soon to be launched by the Dutch.

2. The Dutch

Merchants of Holland and Zealand first began to send their ships to the coast of Guinea in 1593. By the end of the century they had established a trade with Benin to the exclusion of English as well as Portuguese rivals. As early as 1602 there appeared the first of those invaluable works compiled from the observations of Dutch merchants and seamen that have contributed so greatly to our understanding of West African history—the *Beschryvinghe ende Historische Verhael van het Gout Koninckrijck van Gunea* by Pieter de Marees.[4] In his book de Marees included a description of Benin City obtained

---

1 ibid.
2 The manufacture of ivory articles for sale to Europeans may have been introduced into Benin from the Sierra Leone region under Portuguese influence. cf. Ryder, 'A note on Afro-Portuguese ivories'. *Journal of African History*, vol. VI, no. 1, 1965.
3 No Portuguese were encountered nearer than Ardra where the English seized an empty caravel.
4 ed. by S. P. L'Honoré Naber, Linschoten Vereeniging, The Hague, 1909.

from a fellow-countryman, concealed under the initials D.R.,[1] who had visited the Edo capital and lodged in the guest house set apart for European traders on the main thoroughfare that divided the palace from the rest of the city. This account, in contrast to those of earlier visitors, is wholly concerned with the place and people, and neglects to say anything about Dutch trade. However, it is possible to infer from it that the Dutch were already well acquainted with Benin and enjoyed full security for their persons and goods: bodyguards accompanied them wherever they went, and any offence against them was punished by death. On the other hand, they could not wander at will in the city, much less in the palace as Duarte Pires claimed to have done, but only within the limits permitted by their guards.[2]

Another Dutch source reveals that, like the French and English, that nation was first attracted to Benin by pepper; but whereas the former made only few and irregular voyages, the Dutch sent many ships, and quickly put the trade on a regular footing.[3] The Oba undertook to have a given quantity of pepper in readiness against the arrival of the Dutch ships, thus reducing delays and the risk of sickness among their crews. By 1620, and probably much earlier, they were also buying, according to a Portuguese official in São Tomé, ivory, cotton cloths, *coris* and other beads suitable for the Costa da Mina trade.[4] Concerning the merchandise taken to Benin by the Dutch in these early years, only the most meagre information has survived. D.R. mentions the widespread use of Holland linen for clothing by the inhabitants of Benin City. He also remarks that 'our' horses were preferred in Benin to the smaller local breed; which may be taken to imply that the Dutch were in his time importing horses into Benin. This supposition is strengthened by the fact that D.R. himself rode from Ughoton to the city. Yet if

---

1 The evidence for identifying D.R. with Dierick Ruiters is surveyed by K. Ratelband in his introduction to P. van den Broecke, *Reizen naar West Afrika.* Linschoten Vereeniging, The Hague, 1950, pp. LVIII-LX.
2 cf. supra p. 70.
3 cf. *Vertoog van Bewindhebbers en Handelaars op de Westkust van Afrika handel drijvende,* c. 1607, cited by S. P. L'Honoré Naber in P. de Marees, *Beschrivinghe,* p. 232, n. 2.
4 Biblioteca da Ajuda, Lisbon. *codice* 51 viii 25, *Relações do descobrimento da Costa da Guiné,* f. 115.

there was a traffic in horses it cannot have continued for long, because Dierick Ruiters (who is generally considered to have been the D.R. of de Marees) makes no mention of them in his later trade and navigational guide to Guinea, in which he specifies the goods needed for the Benin trade.[1] His list names brass and copper manillas, beads, Silesian cloth, red, yellow and blue kerseys, brandy and wine. All of these had long been familiar items in Benin, with the exception of the last two which appear for the first time. Wine failed to win a permanent place in trade cargoes—Benin had its own palm wine—but brandy had an important future before it.

Until 1621 Dutch enterprise in Guinea was controlled by numerous partnerships and companies; in that year these interests combined to form the chartered West India Company with a twenty-four-year monopoly of all Dutch trade from the Tropic of Cancer to the Cape of Good Hope, and the assurance of military and naval backing from the States General of the United Provinces in its intended assaults upon the tottering Portuguese empire on both shores of the southern Atlantic.[2] Fortune smiled on the company for rather longer than she was wont to favour such enterprises. A foothold secured in Pernambuco in 1630 expanded into a colony with an economy based upon sugar plantations.[3] The next step came in 1637 with an expedition to conquer São Jorge da Mina and the West African slave markets which, for the first time, became of the highest concern to the Dutch as a source of labour for their South American colonies. Another fleet launched from the Brazilian base in 1641 seized Luanda and São Tomé from the Portuguese. Then the tide began to turn. A sharp decline in profits from the Guinea trade after 1645 knocked the supports from under this over-ambitious edifice, with the result that the Portuguese were able to retake São Tomé and Luanda in 1648, and drive the Dutch from Brazil in 1654. By 1674 the West India Company had sunk into such hopeless financial confusion that it had to be wound up

---

1 D. Ruiters, *Toortse der Zee-Vaert* (Flushing, 1623), ed. by S. P. L'Honoré Naber. Linschoten Vereeniging, The Hague, 1913.
2 cf. C. R. Boxer, *The Dutch Sea-borne Empire*. London, 1966. J. K. J. de Jonghe, *De oorsprong van Neerland's bezittingen op de Kust van Guinea*. The Hague, 1871.
3 cf. C. R. Boxer, *The Dutch in Brazil, 1624–1654*. Oxford, 1957.

and replaced by a rather more modest organisation. Of its conquests it retained all the former Portuguese trading places on the Costa da Mina to which it added a number of new establishments. Whether Dutch trade in Guinea was much increased by all this expensive activity is a matter of some doubt. Before the formation of the company, Dutch merchants had, if Portuguese testimony is to be believed, deprived the Portuguese of all trade on the coast between Ardra and the Cameroons, except that in slaves; they were also entering with impunity into the gold markets of the Costa da Mina. Their English rivals, already organised into a chartered Company of Adventurers, were meanwhile succeeding only in making a steady loss from the Guinea trade. Nor did a new enterprise launched by a group of English merchants in 1631 with a thirty-one-year monopoly of trade to 'Guinea, Binney and Angola' fare much better. It may be argued, therefore, that such advantage as the Dutch enjoyed in this region during the seventeenth century derived not from the chartered company form of organisation, but from the general mercantile superiority of the United Provinces over their European rivals.

As far as the Dutch trade with Benin was concerned, the formation of the West India Company seems to have made no great difference, unless indeed there was some falling off. The destruction of most of the Company's records has left a large and lamentable gap in our knowledge of its dealings with Benin during the seventeenth century.[1] Fortunately, however, the loss can partly be made good with the aid of Olfert Dapper's monumental *Naukeurige Beschrijvinge der Afrikaensche Gewesten* (Accurate Description of the Regions of Africa). Published in Amsterdam in 1668, the book drew together the observations of earlier Dutch writers and added to them the detail, especially regarding trade, which Dapper had gathered from his own informants. In his description of Guinea he relied chiefly upon the writings of Pieter de Marees and Samuel Blommaart, once a private merchant in the Guinea trade and later a director of the West India Company, who was able to draw upon

1 A large part of the archives of the first West India Company were sold as waste paper in 1821; more disappeared in a fire in the Department of Marine in 1844. What remains is listed in P. Carson, *Materials for West African history in the archives of Belgium and Holland*. London, Athlone Press, 1962.

personal experience and company records. The material upon which he based his account of Benin does not extend beyond 1644, and refers back in some of its details to the beginning of the century; in the main it would appear to describe things as they were during the first twenty years of the company's existence.[1]

Over that period trading procedures underwent several important modifications. Perhaps the most significant of these was the removal of the trading centre from Benin City to a number of riverside villages, chief among which were Ughoton and Arbo. The former had from the beginning served as the port for European trade with Benin, but the latter was a new settlement on the main Benin River and apparently populated mainly by Ijos,[2] although it was governed in the Oba's name by chiefs from Benin City. Dapper does not reveal which side had taken the initiative in transferring trade to the river; indeed he seems unaware that it had previously been the custom to transact business in the capital. From the Dutch point of view the change offered at least two clear advantages: the onus of transporting goods to and from the waterside now rested upon the Edo, and, more important, they were able to attract traders from areas outside the Benin kingdom. Ijebus, Ijos and Itsekiris[3] all appear to have made their way by canoe into the Benin River to sell their slaves, cotton cloths and *coris* to the Dutch. The extent to which the Oba was able to control this extended traffic can only be surmised. Much presumably depended upon the state of his understanding with the Ijos, for no Benin forces had ventured into the rivers since disaster had overtaken Oba Ehengbuda there at the beginning of the century. For the period to which Dapper refers,

---

1 John Ogilby's *Africa*, London, 1670, is based entirely, and without acknowledgement, upon Dapper. A French translation, *Description de l'Afrique*, appeared in Amsterdam in 1686. Neither French nor English version is wholly reliable.

2 'The Arbo, Arbon, Arebo or Oriboo at which the Dutch opened a factory as an alternative to Gwato in 1644 may have been Arogbo (Arigbo). The present location of Arogbo town is probably too far west of the Benin River to be identified with Arbo, but oral traditions at Arogbo tell of earlier more easterly locations.' Dr. E. J. Alagoa in a paper entitled 'Oral tradition and chronology in the Niger Delta' presented to a seminar at the University of Ibadan, 1967.

3 In 1646 the Dutch West India Company rejected Itsekiri suggestions that it open direct trade with Ode Itsekiri. (A.R. *Oude W.I.C.* 11, nos. 16, 45, 63.)

the presence of Edo governors at Arbo may reasonably be interpreted to mean that Benin suzerainty was still recognised in the river, and that Benin officials were therefore able to exercise some control over the trade there. Further evidence of Benin influence in the river is contained in Dapper's description of the village of Loebo which lay below Arbo. This place was ruled, he reported, by a powerful priest who had inherited from his ancestors certain charms which the Edo believed gave him power to conjure the sea, raise storms and foretell the arrival of ships. On the strength of these impressive and obviously valuable abilities, a past Oba had given the town and all its inhabitants as slaves to the priest's ancestor. This priest was reputed to inspire the greatest awe, even among envoys of the Oba, and tradition in Dapper's time related that former Obas had forbidden him to go near Benin City. Possibly this formidable figure was descended from a scion of the ruling house of Benin endowed with the powers of a priest of Olokun and set to rule over the village.[1] Seeing therefore that Benin still exercised some authority beyond the striking range of its armies, the decentralised form of trade could have been as profitable to the Oba as to the Dutch, for tolls could be raised on a greater volume of traffic. On the other hand, it must be observed that this decentralisation coincided with a marked decline in the effective authority of the Obas, one symptom being their exclusion from commercial negotiations.

On the arrival of a ship at Ughoton, the chief of that town despatched a messenger to inform the Oba, as had been the practice in the sixteenth century. But instead of the Europeans being taken to Benin City, two or three *Iwebo* officials and twenty or thirty traders arrived to deal with them at Ughoton. On occasions when trade was to be conducted at other places on the river, the party of officials and traders commandeered from Ughoton the canoes and rowers needed to transport them where the European ship lay. They were also entitled in the Oba's name to requisition houses for themselves and their goods, and to oblige their hosts to feed them on the first day of their stay without payment. For their first visit

---

1 Loebo may have been the village of Teebu mentioned by Pacheco Pereira in his description of the Benin River. Neither place is mentioned by any other writer.

to the Dutch merchants, the officials wore a dignified dress with strings of beads, described as jasper by Dapper, around their necks. Kneeling they delivered salutations from the Oba, his mother and the three chief counsellors—*Uwangue, Osodin* and *Eribo*—presented some gifts of food in their name, and paid many compliments. Next they enquired after the state of the visitors' country, the progress of its wars and like subjects. Finally, after accepting a drink of spirits, they took ceremonious leave, without once mentioning questions of trade. This formal visit, we may suppose, took the place of that which European visitors had previously paid to the Oba on their arrival. On subsequent days the officials returned in order to fix prices for any goods which had never been traded before; other items remained at the prices previously agreed upon. Keen bargaining ensued, sometimes lasting several weeks, because a price once fixed could not be altered on subsequent occasions. Only when agreement had been reached could the article in question be traded. Thus negotiations over prices still remained in the hands of palace officials. In addition all buying and selling had to be done through them and the traders sent from Benin City, the only exception being that certain local traders were permitted to buy European goods at Arbo for resale in the large market held every three or four days at Ughoton. Dapper's account does not make it clear whether the traders who came from the capital were acting as agents of the Oba, as members of a trading association similar to those which controlled the long-distance trade of Benin in the nineteenth century, or whether they traded on their own account under some form of licence. Whatever the nature of their relationship with the palace, it is probable that the Oba was receiving less of the profit from European trade than in the days when it fell more immediately under his control.

The older forms of regulation came under still greater strain when the Dutch made Arbo the centre of their operations in the Benin area by establishing a resident agent, or *legger*, there. One such official of the West India Company was already busy by 1633 when he was joined by agents of its English rival.[1] Although Dutch

---

1 A.R. *Oude W.I.C.* 11, no. 2. 3 Feb. 1634. As with the earlier Portuguese post at Ughoton, we do not know whether this Dutch establishment at Arbo enjoyed a continuous existence.

pressure or tropical disease forced the latter to withdraw for a space, it returned in force in December 1645 to build a storehouse at the opposite end of the village from the Dutch post. The Council of the West India Company urged their Director at Elmina[1] to counter-action:

> Meanwhile we recommend that you use every endeavour to retain the friendship of the negroes, and employ all imaginable means so that the English may be frustrated in their design and be unable to establish any station in the Benin River at Arbon.[2]

But neither Dutch imagination nor the death of the English master, chief mate and factor could prevent the English from consolidating their position.

From several European points of view Arbo was a more satisfactory trading base than Ughoton. Its position on the main river made it accessible to relatively large ships, whereas Ughoton could not be reached by those of more than fifty tons burthen. We have seen that English ships trading with Benin in the sixteenth century regularly cast anchor in the main river and relied on pinnaces to communicate with Ughoton; it was natural enough that a village should spring up near the anchorage to sell foodstuffs to the ships, and that it should eventually become a centre of trade. Moreover it was a centre more conveniently placed than Ughoton for trade with the non-Edo peoples of the coastal region. Produce from the Benin kingdom continued to pass through Ughoton, and was conveyed to Arbo in yachts and pinnaces.

The volume of trade transacted by the Dutch post at Arbo may be gauged by the fact that it was never manned by more than two junior servants of the West India Company, and never visited by more than two ships in the course of a year. If Dutch reports may be believed, their English rivals did more business, but we have no records of the latter to confirm this. In addition to this company trade, the river was visited by the occasional English interloper; so that at least five or six ships loaded cargoes in the course of a year, and the Dutch were enjoying neither the monopoly nor the abundance of trade on which they had counted. Like others before and

---

1 The ungrammatical name the Dutch gave to São Jorge da Mina.
2 A.R. *Oude W.I.C.* 10. 13 Dec. 1646.

after them the directors of the company had overestimated the commercial potentialities of the Benin region. Their error was compounded by the general decline of the company which set in immediately after the establishment of the Arbo factory. How long the Dutch and English posts managed to survive is not known; as late as 1653 both were still in existence.

Following the opening of the European posts at Arbo, considerations of distance, and the need to provide for a continuous trade with the resident Dutch and English factors, made the procedures described by Dapper unworkable. Officials and traders, instead of travelling from Benin City on the arrival of every ship, began to reside permanently in Arbo and other waterside towns frequented by Europeans. Also they tended to attach themselves to a particular factory, and thus developed into a class of brokers more dependent upon the village in which they lived and the factory or nation they served than upon the Oba of Benin. This change is reflected in a description of the *fiadors* and traders at the end of the seventeenth century as men 'who can speak a miserable sort of Portuguese, which qualifies them to talk with us. This is their only excellency, without which they would be looked on as the very scum of their country-men, and not thought worthy a name among them.'[1] But even though so far removed from the powerful emissaries of royal authority described by Dapper, these officials continued to the end of the century to monopolise European trade. And if the regalian rights of the Oba suffered from these developments, they may not have been equally detrimental to the interests of the palace chiefs who during these years gained an ascendancy in the central government, and with it control over the appointment of village heads and trading officials. In other words, the decentralised system, though so marked a departure from the practice of the sixteenth century, still embodied the principle that no trade might be done save by those who held authority from the Oba or claimed to act on his behalf.

European trade had not only shifted to new centres and acquired new modes of organisation: it had drastically changed in its composition. Slaves figured hardly at all in the cargoes which the Dutch

---

1 Nyendael in Bosman, *A new and accurate description*, p. 434.

took from Benin, even in those years when they were in demand for the Pernambuco colony. Ivory was acquired in large quantities only at the beginning and end of the seventeenth century. Trade in pepper ran a chequered career: one of the most prized and profitable commodities at the beginning of the century, it later declined in importance as the Dutch tightened their grip upon Asian supplies. In 1634 however the West India Company was urging the Oba to have his people plant pepper with a promise that it would buy all they produced.[1] A few years later the Company's council of directors repeatedly ordered its commander in Guinea to see that pepper seedlings were procured in Benin so that a trial might be made of them in the new Brazilian colony.[2] Judging by the absence of pepper in the cargoes shipped from Benin in the sixteen-forties, it would seem that nothing came of the first project; and we hear no more of the second. Thus the old staples of the Benin trade had faded from the scene. In their place stood locally manufactured cotton cloth as the major concern of both Dutch and English merchants.

The flourishing cloth trade of the mid-seventeenth century is of considerable interest because articles of indigenous manufacture had not previously played a role of any significance in Benin's dealings with Europe. Portuguese ships had occasionally carried away a few dozen cloths to cover their slaves; now Dutch and English alike bought them in thousands for resale on other parts of the African coast. In December 1633 the *Beninreyse* reached Fort Nassau (at that time the headquarters of the West India Company in Guinea) with 6,461 pieces of Benin cloth, and had still to leave behind another 6,000 pieces for lack of cargo space. Between 1644 and 1646 the Dutch at Arbo bought at least 16,000 pieces and claimed that their English rivals had bought considerably more. So great an increase in the demand for cloth must have presented many novel problems of organisation to the Africans who supplied it, and may perhaps have influenced the European decision to site factories on the main Benin River where sources of supply other than Benin could be tapped. The Ijebus in particular supplied

---

1 A.R. *Oude W.I.C.* 11, no. 2.
2 A.R. *Oude W.I.C.* 9. 18 Feb. 1642.

large quantities of cloth to Arbo. Benin traders too ranged far afield in search of cloth. According to Dapper, some came from a place named Koffo which he understood to lie one day's journey east of Benin.[1] No existing town lying in that direction bears a name that resembles Koffo, but it is possible that Dapper's informant had misunderstood a reference to Kulfo, once a principal trading centre of the Nupe and renowned for the manufacture of cloth.[2] This identification would accord with the report of a missionary some fifty years later that some of the cloth sold by Benin traders came from 'other kingdoms three hundred or more miles inland'.[3]

Dutch merchants—and presumably their suppliers also—recognised two main varieties of cloth. One kind, known as a 'Benin cloth' to Europeans and *mouponoqua*[4] to the Edo, consisted of four strips sewn together to make a piece approximately three yards by two yards; it was dyed either a plain indigo blue, or in blue and white stripes. Ijebu cloths were of the same size and pattern. The other type of cloth, which the Dutch called *ambasis* or *annebaas*,[5] was made up of only three strips, hence the term *driebants* or three-strip units in which the Dutch reckoned all their cloth purchases. Both types of cloth found a profitable market on the western coast of Africa, the striped variety being bartered for gold on the Costa da Mina, and the plain blue ones for ivory and slaves in Gabon and Angola. Fierce competition in the buying and selling of cloths led to wide fluctuations in prices. Early in 1634, when both Dutch and English were taking very large quantities to the Costa da Mina, supply outran demand, with the result that a *driebant* which had formerly sold for one *engel*[6] fetched only $\frac{3}{4}$ *engel*, and the Dutch

---

1 Dapper, *Naukeurige Beschrijvinge*, p. 127.

2 cf. H. Clapperton, *Journal of a second expedition into the interior*. London, 1829, p. 311. In 'A reconsideration of the Ife-Benin relationship', pp. 27–8, I have suggested that in the Benin context it may be necessary to interpret 'east' as meaning 'inland'.

3 A.S.C. *Scritture Riferite*, vol. II, f. 585. 24 May 1692.

4 Possibly a rendering of the Edo *ukpöoxa*—cotton cloth. cf. supra p. 57, n. 1.

5 The name of a variety of cloth manufactured in Leiden and Haarlem; the cloths obtained in Benin presumably resembled it closely. cf. K. Ratelband, *Vijf Dagregisters van het Kasteel São Jorge da Mina*. The Hague, 1953, p. XCVII.

6 *engel* = $\frac{1}{16}$ gold ounce = 8 *gulden*.

feared the price would fall lower still.[1] The subsequent decline of English activity in the Benin River enabled the West India Company to push the price up again until by 1646 a large Benin cloth sold for four *engels*. Once again the English intervened and offered the same cloth for 2½ *engels*,[2] causing the Dutch director to lament the small profit to be made from the Benin trade.[3] In buying too the English were getting the better of the Dutch. For the larger striped cloths the latter gave three manillas a piece,[4] or one iron bar (weighing 30–1 pounds) for two. What the English paid we do not know, but they seem to have offered either a higher price or more attractive goods. In November 1646 a ship of the Royal African Company arrived at Arbo carrying, in the words of a Dutch skipper, 'a well-chosen cargo' with which it was able to buy up all the best cloth, leaving him with his not-so-well-chosen merchandise at a great disadvantage. The 4,000 pieces of cloth which he managed to carry back to Elmina presented, according to the Director, 'a very sorry sight'.[5]

The Dutch reference to the 'well-chosen' cargo of the English ship calls attention to the great variety of goods that was by this time essential for successful trade with Benin, and indeed with other African states. The cloth, cowries and manillas of the early sixteenth century had been supplemented later in the century by a number of metal tools and utensils, but it was in the seventeenth century—and largely, it would appear, through Dutch enterprise—that a comprehensive range of European merchandise was first offered to the African customer. As a result of this development, trading operations became far more sophisticated than in the previous century. On the Benin side, traders were able to pick and

---

1 A.R. *Oude W.I.C.* 11, no. 2. 3 Feb. 1634. It was in face of this decline in the cloth trade that the Dutch company revived its interest in Benin pepper. cf. supra p. 93.
2 Ratelband, *Vijf Dagregisters*, p. 287. According to the Dutch Director, an English ship sold more than 2,000 pieces at this price late in 1646 so as not to spend a long time on the coast when cloths were in plentiful supply.
3 ibid. p. 284. 31 Dec. 1646.
4 ibid. p. XCVIII. The cost price of the manillas was reckoned at 10 *stuivers*; this figure included a supplement of c. 50 per cent of the cost price in the United Provinces to cover the charges of transport to Guinea, etc. Reckoned in the same manner, the price of an iron bar amounted to 3 *gulden*.
5 Ratelband, *Vijf Dagregisters*, p. 287.

choose among an assortment of goods, and between different qualities and designs. They proved discriminating buyers with a taste for novelty. In 1646, for example, the English did a very good trade at Arbo with a new kind of bead decorated with spirals of white and yellow. The Dutch Director immediately sent home a sample with a request for beads of the same pattern, and he added that the Benin people 'would love some other novelties in bead work'.[1] Stimulated by these importations, fashion and taste in Benin probably changed faster than in any previous age.

A greater variety of goods also entailed the elaborate bargaining over prices which Dapper has described.[2] The Benin merchant may have arrived at his estimation of a fair price by comparing like articles. The European merchant was usually guided by a price-list in which values were expressed in terms of a standard barter unit. In the middle decades of the seventeenth century the headquarters of the West India Company at Elmina provided its employees with the *marktbrief* or price-list assigning a value in gold to each item of merchandise; these prices allowed for a profit margin of between 60 and 70 per cent.[3] A similar list indicated buying prices in terms of the same gold unit. Armed with these lists, the official knew precisely the terms on which he was permitted to trade by the company, and his business was to persuade his African counterparts to accept them; any departure from the *marktbrief* usually earned a severe reprimand. Thus it might happen that when fashion changed or a rival appeared, or when Elmina miscalculated the demand for any item, the factor at Arbo would find himself with unsaleable goods upon his hands and be forced to make do with others. When this happened, the company would sometimes reluctantly agree to a price reduction, but more often it preferred to remove the goods to another part of the coast, knowing that a reduction once granted could not be withdrawn. A further refinement of this barter system arose from the fact that the cost of commodities bought by Europeans varied according to the cost of the articles given in exchange. In the Benin cloth trade, for example, the Dutch gave three manillas

---

1 A.R. *Oude W.I.C.* 11, no. 140. 18 March 1647.
2 cf. supra pp. 89–90.
3 Ratelband, *Vijf Dagregisters*, p. XCIV.

for one large striped cloth, or an iron bar for two pieces. Since the *marktbrief* fixed the price of manillas at 15 *stuivers* and the iron bar at 4 *gulden*,[1] it followed that cloths bartered for iron bars cost the company considerably more than cloths bartered for manillas. It must be presumed that this situation had arisen from a refusal of the Oba's representatives to give more for the iron bars coupled with an insistence that some be offered to them. To meet such problems arising from differential prices both sides evolved a form of composite barter units in which were combined high-cost and low-cost goods. Barter deals involving an assortment of goods became more common and more complicated as the century wore on, forcing the European trader to pay ever greater attention to the selection of his cargo.

Whatever other merchandise might be introduced, manillas still remained the staple trading currency of Benin. Calbeneer, the Dutch factor at Arbo, complained of a shortage of them in 1646 because 'they are necessary here for trade and sustenance'.[2] Cowries, though they continued to serve as the common currency within Benin and were needed by Europeans resident there for minor purchases of foodstuffs,[3] were not imported in quantity because of their high cost price. Towards the end of the seventeenth century the Dutch increased the flow somewhat, but only reluctantly and presumably under pressure. European trade still brought a variety of cloths into Benin. Among them linen held its old pride of place, followed by bedsheets, Indian cottons, and Haarlem cloth decorated with a large flower pattern. Smaller quantities of raised Hessian cloth, *kannekens* (white cotton cloth with a red stripe at one end), ticking, gold and silver brocade, Ypres cloth, kerseys, perpetuanas (a kind of serge), says (a hard-wearing worsted) and red velvet completed the range of textiles saleable in Benin in 1646. Red—the colour associated with high rank—green and blue were the preferred colours. Metal goods too were in constant demand. Besides brass manillas the Dutch

---

1 cf. Ratelband, *Vijf Dagregisters*. pp. CIX and XCVIII for the price of iron bars and manillas.
2 A.R. *Oude W.I.C.* 11, no. 107. 1 June 1646. Dutch manillas were of brass and weighed one-third of a pound.
3 In 1652 some English traders visiting Benin City gave a barrel of cowries to the Spanish missionaries living there. cf. infra p. 104.

sent to Benin brass stew-pans, large and small brass bowls or 'neptunes', copper buckets, pewter ware, lead, cutting knives and bosuns' knives; the knives sold in thousands. The third major category of merchandise consisted of beads of many kinds. The commonest were small coloured glass beads manufactured in Venice and the Netherlands; for a time the Dutch had hopes that they might supplant cowries. As we have seen, novelty played an important part in the bead market, so it is not surprising to find a cargo formula or specification of 1646 listing fourteen different varieties.[1] The absence of coral in this and other lists of trade goods causes some surprise for the Dutch sold it elsewhere in West Africa. It may be that they had priced it beyond what the Oba was willing to pay; it is also possible that the absence of this essentially royal article is another reflection of the monarchy's weakness at this period. Coarse brown earthenware, mirrors, brandy, sarsaparilla[2] and sheepskins complete the specimen cargoes of the mid-seventeenth century, with the exception of one most important new item —iron bars. Iron in a manufactured form had been carried to Benin by Europeans at least since the English voyages of the fifteen-eighties, but it seems to have been the Dutch who introduced the standard iron bar, probably in the sixteen-thirties; by 1644 at the latest it had won a permanent and prominent place in the Benin trade. Thenceforth the Benin blacksmith and craftsman was able to produce on a scale impossible in the earlier days of 'iron hunger'. It is tempting to believe that agriculture too must have benefited from a more abundant supply of basic tools.

---

1 A.R. *Oude W.I.C.* 11, no. 93. 1 April 1646. The main types of bead were the following:
olivetten—glass beads of an olive shape; amber coloured, or white and red striped;
rosados—large round beads, similar to those of a rosary;
quispelgrein—small glass beads in strings, several strings made a *mas* or bundle;
madrigetten—the commonest type of bead; small transparent glass beads in all colours; made in Venice and the northern Netherlands;
margrieten—like *madrigetten*, but larger.
2 Pieces were steeped in brandy and used as a curative for syphilis.

Chapter 4
The Capuchin Missions

1. Spanish missionaries

We know that the Dutch and English factories at Arbo were still in existence in 1652 because in that year they served as a refuge for the survivors of a Capuchin mission to Benin. The renewed impetus to missionary endeavour came not from Portugal, which from 1640 found its energies wholly occupied in the struggle against Spain at home and the Dutch overseas, but from the *Sacra Congregazione di Propaganda Fide* which had been founded in 1622 by the Papacy to direct missionary activity. Inevitably Portugal viewed with some suspicion a body that might encroach upon the crown's ecclesiastical patronage in Guinea, and when Rome refused after 1640 to recognise or have any dealings with the newly independent Portuguese government, there developed, until the reconciliation of 1668, open hostility instead of co-operation between the two powers most interested in the conversion of Benin. Spain did all in its power to foment bad relations between Lisbon and Rome, and tried to derive advantage from the situation by introducing direct Spanish influence into areas where Portugal had hitherto asserted exclusive ecclesiastical authority, hoping thereby to win political and economic as well as spiritual advantage. Spanish designs succeeded so well that in 1648 the *Sacra Congregazione* assigned the Benin mission to the Capuchin Order of the provinces of Valencia and Aragon.[1] The Protestant powers that controlled the seas of Guinea and the trade of Benin took no part in this dispute between Spain and Portugal; nor did they make any attempt whatsoever to propagate their own faith.

---

[1] cf. Ryder, 'The Benin Missions'. Fr. M. de Anguiano, *Misiones Capuchinas en Africa: II. Misiones al Reino de la Zinga, Benin, Arda, Guinea y Sierra Leone*. Madrid, 1957.

The attention of the *Sacra Congregazione* had been drawn to Benin by a French Capuchin, Father Columbin of Nantes, who between 1634 and 1640 had led a French mission in West Africa. During that time he had visited São Tomé where he gathered information about the states of the mainland, and in 1640 he had returned to his home province to seek help in what he proclaimed were promising mission fields. His letter of appeal to the *Sacra Congregazione* gave special prominence to the kingdoms of Benin, Ijebu, Warri and 'Licomin',[1] which he described as:

> . . . parts of Guinea uninhabited by Portuguese. In these kingdoms live a great multitude of people who are truly gentle, civilised, friendly to priests, exemplary in their behaviour, and receptive to all good teaching, so that they lack only the light of the faith, instruction, and an example of true virtue. In the past some Portuguese priests were sent to this kingdom, but because of their bad example they were expelled by the king; now this same king greatly desires to have others, provided they are not Portuguese.[2]

Confusion creeps into this letter with the change of reference from 'these kingdoms' to 'this kingdom': in fact, Father Columbin's information is a jumble of reports from many sources and applicable to no state in particular. Later in the same letter he refers specifically to Benin:

> In this kingdom the people may very easily be led to embrace the Faith, and priests can live here with greater ease than in other parts of Guinea because of the healthy climate, and the fertility of the soil, and because the people are more generous. Their language is simple: it is called the Licomin language and is universally used in these parts, just like Latin in Europe. These people have their pontiffs, priests and other ministers for the performance of their rites. The king is so greatly feared by his subjects that when they but hear his name spoken, they all fall prostrate and adore him with fear and unbelievable reverence. Thus from this it may be imagined that if the king were converted to the Faith, the rest of his subjects would easily be won over.

---

1 The general name applied in this period to the inland Yoruba-speaking peoples. Dapper uses the variant *Ulkami* (*Naukeurige Beschrijvinge*, p. 121).
2 A.S.C. *Scritture Originali*, vol. 83, ff. 379–80.

Another advocate of a Benin mission had been Father Francisco de Pamplona who put his views before the *Sacra Congregazione* in 1646 on his return from the Congo.[1] His principal arguments in favour of the enterprise were the possibility of reaching Benin without reference to Portugal or reliance on São Tomé, and an erroneous belief that the Oba had already been converted to Christianity. In this last particular, which was to be the source of much trouble and confusion, the Spaniard had mistaken the Olu of the Itsekiri for the Oba of Benin.

On the basis of such very imperfect intelligence the *Sacra Congregazione* organised and despatched its mission. Father Angel de Valencia, another veteran of the Congo, was appointed prefect.[2] Of the twelve Spanish Capuchins assigned to him, three died of plague while various authorities in Spain pursued protracted negotiations over their departure. The rest sailed from Cadiz on 12 February 1651 bearing a number of presents and letters for the Oba from the Pope and the *Sacra Congregazione*. Instead of taking the missionaries directly to Benin, as he had promised, their Spanish captain spent over two months trading between Cape Palmas and Takoradi, where another three weeks passed in getting ready a boat that had been specially built in Seville for use in the Benin rivers. Further delay ensued after a brush with the Dutch at Shama that ended with the prefect and one of his companions being taken prisoner to Elmina; but the captain finally decided to take the remaining missionaries to Benin, the captive prefect having meanwhile transferred his authority to Father José de Jijona. All the priests fell sick as they approached the Benin River, and by the time they reached Ughoton some were too ill to travel farther; the vice-prefect therefore decided to go on to Benin City with only one companion. His repeated attempts to obtain an audience of the Oba having proved fruitless, he finally succeeded in winning the ear of an important palace official who promised to hand his letters to the ruler. A few days later the same official told Father José that the Oba had seen the letters and that an audience would not be necessary. Suspecting that he had been deceived, the

---

1 cf. de Anguiano, *Misiones Capuchinas*, p. xv.
2 A.S.C. *Acta Generalia*, vol. 18, ff. 45r, 86v–87r, 95r, 133v–134r.

8

vice-prefect then determined to return to Ughoton to consult his companions.[1]

Shortly afterwards the prefect and the other Capuchin detained by the Dutch rejoined their company at Ughoton, only to see three of them, including Father José, die within the space of six days. Another lay too ill to travel; so the prefect left him in the care of two others, and with the remaining two members of the mission reached Benin City on 10 August 1651. He too encountered stubborn opposition when he sought to meet the Oba, but eventually overcame it and successfully negotiated his way through the 'very odd ceremonial' of the Benin court. Once in the presence of the monarch, Father Angel found him amiable and interested in what he had to say; moreover it transpired that the Oba had never read the letters which Father José had handed to the court official because he returned them to the prefect explaining that there had been no one available to read them. An interpreter with a knowledge of Portuguese was then produced, through whom the prefect managed to convey the contents to the apparent satisfaction of the Oba, for he offered the Capuchins lodgings within the palace so that he might talk with them more conveniently. That offer was never made good, nor did they find it easy to renew contact with the Oba. At their second and, as it proved, final audience they presented gifts to the Oba, the Iy'Oba (the Oba's mother) and the most important chiefs, while the Oba gave them to understand that he would build a church, and provide them with interpreters so that they might explain to him the mysteries of their religion. He even went so far as to indicate a site for the church—perhaps the one selected in 1516 and the place at the present day traditionally associated with the

---

1 The reports submitted to the *Sacra Congregazione* by members of the mission on their return to Europe are to be found in A.S.C. *Scritture Originali*, vol. 249, f. 304 et seq. Two were written by Felipe de Hijar, one being a letter addressed to the nuncio in Madrid (Seville, 2 June 1654), and the second a full report written in Madrid, 25 July 1654. Another undated report was submitted by Alonso de Tolosa. In addition to these reports, there is mention of another by Bartolomeo de Viana which Fr. G. A. Cavazzi da Montecuccolo used in compiling his own account of the Benin mission. (Ref. *Istorica Descrittione de tre Regni Congo, Matamba, et Angola*, Milan, 1690.) The report of the prefect, Father Angel de Valencia, seems not to have survived, but quotations from it appear in Rocca da Cesinale, *Storia delle Missioni*.

religion of Europeans.[1] The Iy'Oba too showed interest in the mission. Much encouraged by these signs of progress, Father Angel summoned his three companions from Ughoton to join in the work of evangelisation.

Yet this promising beginning led only into blank obstruction. For several months the Capuchins sought in vain for a further audience which the chief minister—probably the *Uwangue*—refused to arrange. From what they were told, they believed they had incurred his hostility by offering him too small a present, but we may be certain that his motives were far weightier. He may have been genuinely concerned to defend the established religion; he may have reflected that his own great authority depended upon the Oba's absorption in a round of ritual duties.[2] Whatever his reasons, he exerted himself to keep the ruler and missionaries apart. Twice in the Oba's name he ordered them to return to Ughoton, and twice they ignored him because a brother-in-law of the Oba told them that the minister had acted without authority. In an ingenious attempt to break through this barrier, the prefect presented the Oba, through a courtier, with a chiming clock that worked by weights. The contraption suitably astonished the Oba who, as the prefect had foreseen, soon sent it back with a request to know why it had stopped working. By offering to reveal its secret to the monarch in person Father Angel hoped to meet him once more, but the wary minister saw through the ruse and gave back the clock, saying they would manage without it. Equally strict precautions were taken to prevent the missionaries working among the Oba's subjects. Certain prominent inhabitants of Benin City—relatives of the Oba and members of the court—they evidently managed to see, but they were not permitted to leave the capital to visit other parts of the kingdom, and they could make no progress with the population of the city because they spoke no Edo and the interpreters promised them were never forthcoming. The few Edo who knew Portuguese proved unsuitable as interpreters, perhaps because they had orders to give no assistance,[3] perhaps because knowledge of Portuguese had

---

1 cf. supra p. 50.
2 cf. supra pp. 16–8.
3 Interpreters belonged to the *Iwebo* palace society of which *Uwangue* was the leader.

declined in Benin City since European trade was no longer conducted there. To overcome the language barrier the missionaries set to work to build up an Edo vocabulary, but, before they had progressed far, a chief came to explain that 'the devil had told the Binis of their desire to learn the language and had given warning that anyone who taught them so much as a single word would be beaten to death'.[1] After that they found no more informants. As their hopes diminished, so did their supplies of food and money, and they would have fallen into dismal straits but for the foodstuffs and a barrel of cowries given by some English traders visiting Benin City.

Despite these frustrations and handicaps, the Spaniards managed with clandestine lessons from someone who knew Portuguese to learn enough of the Edo language to make a final effort to confront the Oba. They chose the occasion of a major ceremony involving human sacrifice when it would be possible for them to join the crowds flocking into the palace.[2] Father Felipe de Hijar, whom the prefect chose as his companion for the hazardous enterprise, has left the following description of what occurred.[3]

> The chief men of the city who, the natives say, number more than two thousand, were entering the palace, all wearing the various costumes appropriate to the ceremony. They went in until they filled the four courtyards of the palace, and as it was now one o'clock and the palace was crowded, we entered the first courtyard. Among those who were watching us was a venerable old man who, by his outward appearance, seemed a veritable St. Peter. He made a sign to us that we should follow him. We were amazed because we had never seen him before that moment, and also because the negroes had always taken care that we should not see the sacrifices. In the end we went with the old man from one courtyard to another until we reached the last one where, of

---

1 A.S.C. *Scritture originali*, vol. 249, f. 329.
2 According to de Hijar the incident took place on the first day of Lent. None of the other reports are at all precise as to time, though all give the impression that the mission spent much longer in Benin City than would be the case if de Hijar's dating is correct. The ceremony at the palace might have been a rite in honour of past Obas, but Benin festivals had no fixed dates. (cf. Bradbury, *The Benin Kingdom*, p. 55.)
3 A.S.C. *Scritture Originali*, vol. 249, f. 328 et seq.

his own accord, he told us to stand under the gallery of the courtyard.[1] In the middle of the gallery we found a table on which lay the scimitars[2] that were used to decapitate five men and five animals of every species found in that country. They performed their ceremonies, finished their cries; then the great men began to dance, and the king with them, making a turn of the courtyard so that they caught sight of us. The chief *veedor* sent a message that we should leave, and as we did not wish to obey him, he himself came to us in a great rage to bid us go away. We gave him the same answer as before, then stepped into the middle of the courtyard and began speaking aloud to the king and chiefs of the evil they were doing in making such sacrifices, of the state of perdition in which they stood, that the devil whom they served was deceiving them, and so forth.[3] But we had hardly spoken when those barbarous idolaters rushed furiously upon us and swept us through the courtyard with great violence; they did not stop until they had thrust us out and closed the door. When we tried a second and a third time to re-enter the courtyard with those who were still going in, they prevented us. Finally they drove us out of the palace altogether. Around the gate was gathered a huge crowd who mocked us all the way to our house.

That same evening when it was already night, there came ten negroes, saying they were sent by the king, to order us to leave the city immediately. This upset us greatly for we had set up our altar where we said mass, and we had there many ornaments which we could find no one to carry by night through a wild forest. But it pleased Our Lord to abate their wrath, and they left us for that night, though under guard, so that we might pack up our belongings. In the morning some other negroes came with a false message, saying that the king had summoned us and wished to see us. That it was false became evident when they

---

1 All the courtyards of the palace were surrounded by galleries supported by wooden pillars to which were affixed the brass plaques depicting famous events and personages of Benin history. (cf. Dapper, *Naukeurige Beschrijvinge*, p. 122.)

2 These were probably *ada*, the state sword of the Oba which bears some resemblance to a scimitar.

3 De Aguiano (*Missiones Capuchinas*, p. 227) quotes the account of the mission written by José de Alicante, according to whom the two Capuchins had written down an Edo translation of the following: 'King of Benin, and all who are present, behold how grievously you offend God with these sacrifices that you offer to the devil. See how you condemn yourselves for ever to hell if you will not receive the faith of Jesus Christ which we have come to preach to you.'

took us[1] past the palace and almost outside the city. We thought they were going to kill us in the bush, as they were accustomed to do with other criminals. Seeing that night was approaching and that our companions knew nothing of this villainy, we sent them word that we were held captive by six men. That night the Father Prefect and I spent alone in a hut with those men, and in the morning, shaking the dust from our sandals, we were taken away by those beasts, leaving our three companions in the house in the city. They put us in a hut in the forest four leagues from the city; there we remained suffering hunger and thirst, for they neither wished nor had much to feed us. At the end of four days they took us to the place called Gotto where we were held prisoner throughout Lent until our companions arrived with the baggage. After Whitsun we left that place for another called Arbo which is in the same kingdom.[2] There we stayed five months cared for by four heretics, two of them Dutch and two English, who were trading with the negroes, and though it is true that they bestowed on us this charity, yet we heard elsewhere that they had done us much harm so that we should not remain in that kingdom, and that they might remain there without fear that we should drive them out or interfere with their freedom. . . . Then, seeing that we could achieve nothing there, we determined to leave aboard an English ship that took us to the island of Príncipe which is Portuguese territory.

What befell those left behind in Benin City is described in the report submitted by one of them, Alonso de Tolosa. They suffered great hardship from want of provisions, but not, it would seem, from ill-treatment. They were obviously not kept under close surveillance, for at night they were able to visit the Iy'Oba and the brother-in-law of the Oba who had helped them in the past; and it was through the intercession of these members of the royal family that they finally obtained permission to rejoin their companions at Ughoton. In addition the Iy'Oba gave them some food.[3]

---

1 i.e. the prefect and Felipe de Hijar.
2 De Anguiano (*Misiones Capuchinas*, p. 44) adds that they were rescued from Ughoton by an English and a Dutch trader. While the missionaries were in Arbo, a serious fire broke out and threatened to destroy the whole village. Amid the panic Father Bartolomeo da Viana took up his stand at one end of the village invoking the name of Jesus. The wind providentially changed direction and the fire spread no further, but the Capuchins apparently gained no credit therefrom with the inhabitants.
3 A.S.C. *Scritture Originali*, vol. 249, f. 329.

If the Capuchins had understood aright, both relatives of the Oba had expressed sympathy for them and their mission, and the Oba himself had been friendly on the two occasions when they had met him in formal audience. Of the Benin people too Father Felipe had formed a favourable opinion:[1]

> ... they are wholly illiterate, nevertheless they have many natural gifts: they behave very well, and they know that the Devil is evil and that God is good. But they serve the Devil for the fear they have of him that if they do not do as he bids, he will punish them severely.

So, despite their failure, the Capuchins had not despaired of success and believed that all depended on gaining access to the Oba without relying upon court functionaries or interpreters. It does indeed appear probable that their greatest enemies had been not the Oba but powerful chiefs who controlled the court, and allowed the Oba to see and hear only what they thought fit. Father Felipe hints that these chiefs had in turn been influenced by Dutch and English traders who, like the Portuguese, feared the commercial consequences of Spanish missionary activity. The experiences of the Capuchins also give the impression that a rift existed between the powerful figure of the Oba's mother and some members of the royal family on the one side, and the chiefs who controlled the palace on the other. Between them stood the ruler, by all accounts an ineffectual character whose weakness was encouraged by his courtiers for their own advantage.[2]

> He showed himself [wrote Father Angel de Valencia] well disposed to hear the arguments for our Holy Faith, but he lacks the liberty to follow his laudable inclinations because he is hemmed in on all sides by certain ministers who wholly prevent strangers, and especially Europeans, from approaching him, precisely because of a fear that they might speak to him about religion.[3]

---

1 ibid. f. 328.
2 cf. supra pp. 15–18 for the condition of the Benin monarchy in this period.
3 Ref. Rocco da Cesinale, *Storia delle missioni dei Cappuccini*, III. Rome, 1873, p. 582. cf. Felipe de Hijar, A.S.C. *Scritture Originali*, vol. 249, f. 304: 'This king remains all the year shut up in his palace with four hundred women; and he is held to be a god, for they say that he does not eat. But in truth if he did not eat he would not have such a big stomach. To maintain this fiction and the custom of the country he does not go out of the palace. Also he has a

But if royal authority had fallen so low, it is extremely doubtful whether the missionaries were justified in expecting so much from it, in believing that the Oba could lead his subjects away from their established religion. Their own experience would suggest the very different conclusion that the Oba was held in thrall by a ceremonial religion, apart from which he could exercise but little influence over his people.

In the island of Príncipe the Capuchins heard for the first time about the Christian ruler of the Itsekiris, and of the progress made in that kingdom by Portuguese missionaries. They then realised that in Rome the two states had been confused, and that the Christian inclinations of the Itsekiri monarch had been falsely attributed to the Oba of Benin. Once they understood the true position, the Spaniards tried to reach Ode Itsekiri, for they believed that, besides succouring the Christian community there, a mission based in that kingdom 'would be the best means of converting Benin because the two kingdoms are neighbours, and it would be possible to learn the language of Benin in Ugueri'.[1] But the attempt failed because the governor of São Tomé and Príncipe, although personally well disposed towards the Capuchins, had to treat them

---

negro whom they call the *Veedor Mayor*, who attends him with such assiduity that no one may speak with the king (I refer to foreigners) without this man being present to serve as a second interpreter to the king.' Cavazzi da Montecuccolo (*Descrizione storica*, p. 581) records a tradition current in Benin in the seventeenth century which was used to justify the Oba's seclusion. It referred to a prophecy which foretold that an Oba would be killed by a European, and so, to ward off this danger, foreigners were not permitted to speak with the Oba save as a very special favour. Even then he did not meet them face to face, but listened to them from within a small room which was heavily guarded. Cavazzi had read of this custom in a Dutch book, and received confirmation of it from several Portuguese who knew Benin well. I have been unable to trace the Dutch reference. It is possible that the prophecy in question was one nowadays attributed to Ewuare: 'Ewuare made a remarkable prophecy that one of the Obas of Benin of the Oranmiyan dynasty would be deported and the chiefs would become the rulers of the state' (Egharevba, *A Short History*, p. 18). If so, the palace chiefs had turned it very adroitly to their own advantage.

1 A.S.C. *Scritture Originali*, vol. 249, f. 328. Many varieties in the spelling of Iwere (Itsekiri) appear in European documents. In the twentieth century the English version—Warri—has become the most common, and will be used in future for the kingdom of the Itsekiris. The present town of Warri is, however, a late nineteenth-century foundation.

as subjects of an enemy power and send them under safeguard to Lisbon.[1]

2. Italian missionaries

Although not rich in achievement, the mission had opened the eyes of the *Sacra Congregazione* to its unfortunate confusion of Benin with Warri, and to its error in attempting to go behind the back of the Portuguese government. Father Angel's contention that the first step towards the conversion of Benin must be to secure the firm adherence of the Itsekiris now received full support in Rome. The new mission authorised in June 1655 therefore was designated the 'Mission to Warri and Benin'.[2] And in a bid to secure Portuguese support the new enterprise was entrusted to Italian in place of Spanish Capuchins. Another veteran of the Congo mission, Father Giovanni Francesco de Roma, was appointed to lead it. Further to reassure Portugal the prefect and his twelve companions made their way to Lisbon to seek the blessing of that government and permission to use São Tomé as the base for their activities in Warri and Benin. However, despite these conciliatory gestures, the Portuguese government proved suspicious and would allow only four of the company to depart. Among those turned back was the prefect who handed over his authority, and the letters he carried for the rulers of Benin and Warri, to a Corsican priest, Father Angelo Maria d'Ajaccio. The reduced party went first to São Tomé from where two were finally permitted to visit Warri. But they were never able to put into practice the plan of using the Itsekiri kingdom as a base for missionary work in Benin, because on their return to São Tomé they were arrested and suspended from their mission by the vicar-general of the island. In 1662, like their predecessors, they found themselves under arrest on a ship bound for Lisbon. Resentment among the local clergy at foreign interference in the

---

1 They were soon released by the Portuguese authorities and returned to Spain in May 1654.

2 A.S.C. *Acta Generalia*, vol. 24, f. 221, no. 25, 15 June 1655; f. 440, no. 23, 3 August 1655; vol. 25, f. 55, no. 17, 12 June 1656; f. 63, no. 5, 26 February 1657. Further details of this mission are given in de Anguiano, *Misiones Capuchinas*, pp. 47–8, Cavazzi da Montecuccolo, *Descrizione storica*, pp. 358–9, Rocco da Cesinale, *Storia delle Missioni*, pp. 591–3, and A.H.U. *São Tomé, caixa* 2, Governor of São Tomé to King of Portugal, 13 May 1657.

diocese no doubt helped to bring the mission to this unhappy end; another factor in their downfall was official suspicion that the missionaries had come to spy on the little trade left to Portugal on the West African coast.

Father Angelo Maria did, however, contrive to have delivered the letter which the *Sacra Congregazione* had directed to the Oba; to this he received an encouraging reply, promising to welcome the mission to Benin. So once he and his companions had been cleared in Lisbon of all charges against them, the prefect urged upon the *Sacra Congregazione* the need to follow up his success in Warri and send a new mission to Benin. In October 1663 he asked for at least another four helpers and further letters to the rulers of Benin and Warri, 'so that they may know what report of them has been given to the Holy See and be the more inspired to protect the missionaries'.[1] Eight Capuchins were accordingly appointed to join the mission, but the Portuguese government again became suspicious, refused to grant any passports, and so prevented the Oba's supposed readiness to receive the priests from being put to the test. Whether or why the ruler of Benin had changed his attitude towards missionaries is difficult to determine, for the internal history of Benin at this time is wrapped in obscurity. The elderly Akenzae, who, according to Egharevba, succeeded Ahenzae 'about 1661',[2] might have been one of those princes about the court who had shown favour to the Spanish Capuchins; the hostile minister might have fallen from power. On the other hand, many letters of the kind upon which Father Angelo Maria based his hopes prove to have been written with very little comprehension of the issues involved. Like the treaty-makers of the nineteenth century, missionaries and their agents were often more concerned to obtain formal assent than full understanding from African rulers; and the Spanish Capuchins have left ample testimony to the inadequacy of the translation service available in Benin City. Therefore it would be unwise to assume, on the basis of such a letter, that a mission in 1664 would have fared better than its predecessor.

---

1 A.S.C. *Acta Generalia*, vol. 32, f. 228v, no. 16, 1 October 1663. Ref. also ibid. f. 261, no. 28, 19 November 1663; vol. 33, f. 56, no. 5, 18 March 1664, f. 79, no. 14, 29 April 1664, f. 129, no. 31, 22 September 1664.
2 Egharevba, *A Short History*, p. 36.

Discouraged by Portuguese obstruction, the *Sacra Congregazione* for twenty years made no further attempt to revive the Benin mission. Then in 1683 Giovanni Romano, prefect of the Capuchin mission in Angola, took a new initiative, this time with the blessing of Portugal. He first communicated his project to the Prince Regent of Portugal and had him write a letter of recommendation to the Bishop of São Tomé smoothing the path for a mission.[1] A major handicap that had helped bring earlier missions to grief was thus removed, and the way opened to a period of collaboration between the *Sacra Congregazione* and the crown of Portugal, though the latter still abated none of its claims to patronage.

In June 1684 an Italian Capuchin, Francesco da Monteleone, arrived in São Tomé to establish there a base for a revived mission on the mainland.[2] Difficulties soon gathered around him: the death of the bishop in 1685 threw a heavy burden of pastoral duties upon him, and the prefect of the Angola mission found it impossible to send the help promised. Monteleone had however won the support of the local Portuguese authorities to the extent that both the governor and chapter of São Tomé requested the *Sacra Congregazione* to send him eight Capuchins for the missions to Benin, Warri and Ardra.[3] Rome answered by providing three men and raising the status of the mission to that of a prefecture with Monteleone as prefect; but only one of the three reached São Tomé alive in April 1687, and he died three days later. Another eight arrived in January 1691; three were dead within a few days of disembarking, and by 1693 only three remained alive. Faced with

---

1 A.H.U. *codice* 489, *Registo de oficios para São Tomé e Cabo Verde, 1673–1716.* f. 38r. 20 March 1683.
2 The letters from Father Francesco da Monteleone to the *Sacra Congregazione* reporting on the progress of his mission are to be found in A.S.C. *Scritture Riferite*, vol. I, f. 504, 2 June 1684; f. 565, 20 July 1684; f. 581–5, 20 May 1685: vol. II, f. 110, 28 April 1687; f. 116, 28 October 1685; f. 167, 25 November 1687; ff. 204–5, 8 July 1688; ff. 472–3, 24 April 1691; f. 477, 10 July 1691; ff. 479–80, 25 April 1691; f. 501, 25 July 1691; f. 553, 19 March 1692; ff. 585–6, 24 May 1692; ff. 607–8, 28 August 1692; f. 617, 29 September 1692; vol. III, ff. 37–9, 4 April 1693; f. 80, 18 November 1693; ff. 105–6, 14 June 1694; ff. 109–10, 15 August 1694; ff. 133–4, 20 August 1695. See also *Acta Generalia*, vol. 64, f. 55, no. 27, 20 April 1694; vol. 65, f. 8, no. 16, 11 January 1695.
3 A.S.C. *Scritture Riferite*, vol. I, f. 587, 14 January 1685.

such obstacles, it was not until late in 1689 that Father Monteleone was able to begin his missionary work with a visit to Warri. From there he tried to reach Benin.

> They took me by river to the borders of Benin where there is a power-ful chief who is in rebellion against Warri, and he was to take me on to Benin. But he was afraid that the King of Warri might have his head cut off, as he had done to his father, so he would not let us disembark.[1] When the judges and officials of Benin heard of this, they immediately sent canoes to fetch me and carry me to Benin. But they did not find us because we had returned to Warri without delay.[2]

He did however succeed in making contact with the people of 'Oriboo and Mabbor' whom he was able to visit directly from Ode Itsekiri. A reference by one of Monteleone's subordinates to the prefect's visit to 'a port in the kingdom of Benin where the Portu-guese go to trade'[3] makes it reasonably certain that the places in ques-tion were Arbo and Mobor.[4] He went to these outposts of Benin, again according to the subordinate, 'to determine the manner in which that king was willing to admit our missionaries into his king-dom'; but the few days spent there would have been quite inadequate for any serious negotiations on the matter, and Father Monteleone himself ignores that aspect of his visit to Arbo. Instead he claims that his teaching met with a favourable reception from the people of the villages, and it was presumably from his brief acquaintance with this non-Edo fringe of the Oba's kingdom that he drew his estimate of missionary prospects in Benin:[5]

> I consider the people of Benin kinder, politer, more faithful and more reasonable than the people of Warri. It only needs the king to give the word that they should become Christians and all, all will embrace the faith.

That he had made no progress towards obtaining that word did not

---

1 The manner in which refugees from Warri found protection on the borders of Benin emphasises the breach that had opened between the two states in the course of the sixteenth century. Similar incidents occurred in the eigh-teenth century. cf. Lloyd, *The Itsekiri*, p. 180.
2 A.S.C. *Scritture Riferite*, vol. II, f. 479, 25 April 1691.
3 ibid. f. 475, 24 April 1691.
4 cf. infra p. 126.
5 A.S.C. *Scritture Riferite*, vol. II, f. 479.

in the least dampen the prefect's enthusiasm, and he returned to
São Tomé determined to organise missions to Benin and Warri.
He first intended that two priests should go to each kingdom, but
the plan miscarried owing to the refusal of the vice-prefect, Giuseppe-
Maria da Busseto, to undertake the Benin mission on the grounds
that the Oba had not been baptised. As vice-prefect he preferred,
and claimed the right, to go to Warri where he could be certain of a
friendly reception from a baptised ruler.[1] Monteleone took the
view that Busseto, as the senior member of the mission, must go to
Benin; otherwise the Oba would take offence. The Oba would be
equally offended, he argued, if the vice-prefect visited Warri before
Benin, because relations between the two states were very strained:
'they are not exchanging ambassadors, and the people of Warri
cannot go to Great Benin, but only to two areas called Oriboo and
Mabor which are far from Benin; everywhere else they are resort-
ing to arms'.[2] The vice-prefect would not yield, so, rather than
prejudice the future of the mission, Monteleone decided to send
no one to Benin until the opportunity came for him to lead a
mission there in person. In the meantime he sent a letter to the Oba
by the captain of a Portuguese ship that carried missionaries to
Warri in August 1691.[3] By the same ship the Oba replied that he

---

1 Putting his own point of view, the vice-prefect argued: 'The kingdom of
Benin is completely heathen, and has never (as the Father Prefect admits)
asked for us priests, either by letter or by messenger sent for that purpose . . .'
(ibid. f. 475.)
2 ibid. f. 479.
3 A deposition from the captain, Lourenço Pinto, was sent to the *Sacra Congregazione* by Father Monteleone. A summary in A.S.C. *Acta Generalia*, vol.
64, f. 55, no. 27, 20 April 1694, gives a few interesting details about Benin
City.
'According to the testimony of this captain, Great Benin, where the king
resides, is larger than Lisbon; all the streets run straight and as far as
the eye can see. The houses are large, especially that of the king which is
richly decorated and has fine columns. The city is wealthy and industrious. It
is so well governed that theft is unknown and the people live in such security
that they have no doors to their houses.
'The artisans have their places carefully allocated in the squares which are
divided up in such a manner that in one square he counted altogether one
hundred and twenty goldsmiths' workshops, all working continuously.'
Pinto presumably mistook the brassworkers for goldsmiths. The civil war
had obviously not yet wrought the devastation which was so apparent in the
capital six years later.

would gladly receive Christian priests, and that he was especially anxious to meet Father Monteleone; he would give a house and all necessary provisions to any missionaries who might come. Although friendly, the letter remained non-committal on the central issue of the monarch's conversion and hardly justified Monteleone's gloss upon it which ran: 'the king of Great Benin has taken counsel with all his chiefs and has sent a message that I should go to his kingdom, for they will accept what is preached to them'.[1] For some time his eagerness to turn this presumptive opportunity to account was frustrated by a lack of helpers that was not overcome until late in 1694 or early 1695 when another body of Capuchins set foot in São Tomé. On 8 September 1695 Father Monteleone realised his long-cherished wish and at last set sail for Benin; but he never saw the Oba, for he fell mortally ill at Ughoton and died there in mid-November of that same year.

It is not known whether the prefect's companions perserved with the mission to Benin after his death; if they did nothing was achieved, and in a report to the *Sacra Congregazione* written in September 1696 the vice-prefect held out no hope of progress in the kingdom.[2]

> In the kingdom of Benin no good can be done for the moment, since it has been almost destroyed by the wars which have been waged among those negroes: for more than seven years they have been destroying each other. If peace is restored I shall not fail to do everything possible for the service of God and the salvation of those poor souls.

Whether, as in 1515, there was any connection between the Oba's supposed willingness to receive missionaries and his military difficulties must remain a matter for conjecture. It is certainly unlikely that a desire to acquire firearms had influenced his attitude towards Father Monteleone because in the sixteen-nineties the Protestant Dutch had begun selling guns to Benin in the normal course of trade. Nevertheless it is possible that questions of religion were involved in the civil war. It is remarkable, for example, that no

---

1 A.S.C. *Scritture Riferite*, vol. III, f. 105, 14 June 1694.
2 A.S.C. *Scritture Riferite*, vol. III, ff. 137–8, 4 September 1696.

mention of human sacrifice occurs in Nyendael's generally un-flattering description of Benin. Still more significantly, he writes that in May 1702 he attended the 'coral feast' (*ugie-ivie*)[1] but says nothing about human sacrifice which in later years, at least, was a central feature of that ceremony. If human sacrifice had indeed been eliminated from the royal rituals, this was a radical departure from earlier practice which must have borne some relation to the issues of the civil war. Nor can one ignore the parallel which the Oba could have drawn between his own struggle with a rebellious chief and the similar situation that had faced the ruler of the Itsekiris a few years earlier. Rightly or wrongly the Olus of Warri regarded their special relationship with Portugal and the Roman Catholic church as a source of power and prestige among their subjects and neighbours; an Oba *in extremis* might have grasped for the same support.

A little further light falls on this question during the final phase of missionary activity which began in 1709 with a visit to Benin by the new Capuchin prefect of the São Tomé mission, Father Cipriano da Napoli. According to Francesco da Collevecchio, one of the priests who accompanied the prefect, the Oba showed no interest whatsoever in the mission:[2]

> ... after we had been there many days, the king and his chiefs would not in any manner receive missionaries; the king would not even give the prefect an audience. So realising the impossibility of doing any good there, the prefect left in the ship that had brought him, together with the brothers.

Since this report to the *Sacra Congregazione* bears the signatures of four Capuchins who were with the prefect, it may be accepted as reliable. Within a year, however, the Oba wrote letters to the Pope, the *Sacra Congregazione* and the Procurator-General of the Capuchin Order, all of which reveal an astonishing change of front. That addressed to the Pope is the most substantial of the three.[3]

---

1 Bosman, *A new and accurate description*, p. 465.
2 A.S.C. *Scritture Riferite*, vol. III, f. 475, 20 January 1710.
3 The letter, written in Latin, is printed in Michael a Tugio, *Bullarium Ordinis FF. Praedicatorum*, tom. VII. Rome, 1729, pp. 232–3.

Blessed Father,

Today, thanks be to God, I acknowledge myself the most humble son of Your Holiness whom I revere as the Vicar of Christ, and whose Holy Blessing I reverently and earnestly ask. In myself and in all my subjects there dwells a desire to embrace the Faith of Christ, a desire which has long been burning within us, as in the time of my father who was of the same mind, thanks to the edifying example set us in past years by some Italian Capuchins who passed through this kingdom on their way to the kingdom of Warri. That our conversion was not accomplished at that time did not arise from any lack of care or preaching by the said Fathers but from the wars which were raging throughout my kingdom. So when the Prefect, Father Cypriano a Napoli, who in the past year worked among us to that end, found that the difficulties caused by the war had been removed, he returned to the island of São Tomé filled with a firm hope in God that neither his labours nor our desires should be wanting of their effect. Now the Divine Mercy has deigned to shine upon us, for the aforesaid Prefect has sent us two Fathers whom we have received cordially; both I and my chiefs have taken them to our hearts and follow their counsels. Moreover I have given orders that they should be assigned a site for a church and a house suitable for their abode and for other Fathers who may be summoned here in future. These have been given them by a public deed of gift, so that they may use them freely, dwell there and labour in the worship of God. But considering the vast extent of my kingdom, a greater number of workers is needed for the labour of the Gospel. Therefore, with the utmost devotion, I pray that Your Holiness may deign to send more priests for the furtherance of so holy a work, and be assured that I for my part will see that everything needful is provided which concerns the worship of God and the needs of their own persons. By this same occasion I submit myself in obedience to Holy Mother Church and to Your Holiness whom I acknowledge as head of the Church and lord of this my kingdom. May God prosper Your Holiness whose sacred feet I kiss with all reverence. In the Kingdom of Benin, 2 November 1710.

the unworthy and humble son etc.,
Obba, King of Benin

Neither the Oba nor any of his subjects could have written this letter; most probably it is the work of the two Capuchins to whom it refers, and it might be dismissed as a fabrication designed to boost the prestige of their mission and order did there not exist confirmatory evidence to support some points of substance. A letter from the Portuguese Secretary of State Diogo de Mendonça Corte Real to the Capuchin superior reports that the Oba has also written to the king of Portugal announcing the reception into his kingdom of the Capuchin mission and asking for more priests; the king, through his secretary of state, urges the superior to meet this request, and if necessary ask Rome to provide the Capuchins of Portugal with the men needed.[1] There also exists circumstantial evidence concerning the grant of land to the mission. On 19 April 1712 the Portuguese Council for Overseas Affairs wrote in the name of the king to the governor of São Tomé as follows:[2]

> Father Sipriano de Napoles Prefect of the Capuchin missionaries in that island has informed me in a letter of 28 April of the past year, that he has sent two priests of the mission to the kingdom of Benin where they were so well received by the king and his chiefs that he at once ordered them to be given houses and a site for building a church. This same king has assured me of the same in a letter which he wrote to me, and he appears inclined to accept the Catholic faith. Because in his letter he gives the impression that he has received the said priests in the name of the *Sacra Congregazione*, I order you to obtain all the necessary information concerning the manner in which the said Fathers accept and settle the grant to them of this site, and report your findings to me.

That same day the Council wrote also to the prefect ordering that, if the land had been accepted in the name of the *Sacra Congregazione*, 'you will immediately tear it [i.e. the deed] up and see that another is made in which it shall be stated that it is accepted in my name ... because it is for me alone to send missionaries to that kingdom, as I am the lawful patron'.[3] Father Cipriano replied on 19 January 1713 that he had instructed the superior of the Benin mission to destroy the offending document and obtain another couched in the terms demanded by the king of Portugal.[4] Still further evidence is provided by the Capuchin Father Filippo Calvello who returned to Italy from São Tomé in 1713 and reported

---

1 Tugio, *Bullarium*, p. 233, 15 March 1714.
2 A.H.U. *codice* 489, f. 236r.
3 ibid.
4 ibid. f. 243r.

that the Oba had received the two missionaries courteously and given them a house.[1]

There is, then, good reason to believe that in 1710 a Capuchin mission was established in Benin City with a degree of support from the Oba such as no other had enjoyed since 1515. Unless some missionary journey has completely escaped record, the visit to Benin by a group of Italian Capuchins on their way to Warri mentioned in the Oba's letter can only refer to the ill-fated adventure of Father Monteleone. The letter would also seem to imply that the signatory's father was reigning at the time of that visit; if so, he was probably the ruler who in the preceding years had exchanged messages with Monteleone inviting a mission to Benin. He would also be the Oba whom Nyendael met, and whose rituals were apparently not accompanied by human sacrifice. These circumstances and references to civil war in a number of European documents are not easily reconciled with Benin tradition which retains no clear memory of a major civil war at this time. It does however record a large-scale rebellion of the chiefs and people against the Oba Ewuakpe around the end of the seventeenth century.[2] Again on the evidence of the letter, the Oba of the civil war/rebellion period must have died some time between Nyendael's last visit to Benin in the early months of 1702 and the time the letter was written in 1710.[3] The extraordinary contrast between the reception given to the missionaries in 1709 and 1710 furnishes some reason for fixing the change of ruler within that year, which would accord reasonably well with the traditional dating of Ewuakpe's death.[4] King-lists agree that Ewuakpe was succeeded by his son Ozuere who may, therefore, have been the Oba who welcomed the Capuchins and gave them land on which to build. Of Ozuere, Egharevba gives the following account:[5]

---

1 A.S.C. *Scritture Riferite*, vol. IV, f. 30.
2 cf. Egharevba, *A Short History*, pp. 38–40. Egharevba dates Ewuakpe's accession to 'about 1700'. Talbot, *Peoples of Southern Nigeria* (London, 1926), vol. I, ch. 4, puts it back to 1685. If Monteleone's visit and the civil war fell within his reign, Ewuakpe could not have ascended the throne later than 1690. cf. supra pp. 18–9.
3 cf. Bradbury, 'Chronological problems', p. 274.
4 1712 according to Egharevba; 1715 according to Talbot.
5 *A Short History*, p. 40.

After the death of Ewuakpe, his second son was made Oba with the title
Ozuere. Ozuere usurped the throne in spite of the law which Ewuakpe
had made that only the eldest son of the Oba should be the heir and
successor. Ozuere's claim was supported by Iyase Ode and there was
civil war which lasted many weeks. At last Ozuere was utterly defeated
and took refuge at the court of his maternal uncle, Ejima of Okeluhen,
and from there went to Uhen where he was eventually killed by a
thunderbolt. Ozuere reigned for one year.

So brief and troubled a reign may provide the explanation for the
welcome given to the mission, and for its subsequent collapse which
was reported to the *Sacra Congregazione* in 1719 when one of the
two Capuchins who had taken part in it returned to Italy. Father
Celestino d'Aspra stated that he and his companion had spent three
years in Benin and failed to make any progress because the people
'were most obstinate in their errors, and they worship the devil:
but there are some who would follow the Holy Faith, were it not
that the king will not give them permission and freedom to profess
it'.[1] The debacle would be more intelligible if the Oba reigning in
1710 had been supplanted by a ruler hostile to him and his policies.
As historians we must bewail Father Celestino's failure to make a
fuller report on events in Benin during these critical years.

The period during which the two Capuchins were living in Benin
City corresponded with a hiatus in Dutch trade and an effort to
increase Luso-Brazilian trade with Benin, as well as with a period
of internal upheaval. About 1709, when the Dutch stopped visiting
the Benin River, the Capuchin prefect in São Tomé was suggesting
to the king of Portugal that a ship belonging to his subjects should
visit Benin every year, so that it might carry provisions to missionaries and, at the same time, collect a profitable cargo of ivory.[2]
Since most Portuguese trade on the West African coast was by this
time conducted from Brazil,[3] the matter was referred to the governor
of Brazil for discussion with the merchants of Bahia, the centre of
the West African trade, on the understanding that the government

---

1 A.S.C. *Scritture Riferite*, vol. IV, f. 320, 3 July 1724.
2 A.H.U. *Consultas da Baia, codice* 253, f. 103r–v.
3 cf. Ryder, 'Re-establishment of Portuguese factories on the Costa da Mina to
the mid-eighteenth century'. *Journal of the Historical Society of Nigeria*, vol. I,
no. 3, 1958.

would be prepared to make fiscal concessions in order to establish a regular commerce. Three merchants expressed interest in the undertaking on condition that they were given the privileges already enjoyed by the inhabitants of São Tomé and Príncipe, and that the trade included slaves as well as ivory. After Treasury approval had been obtained, the Council for Overseas Affairs was able to advise acceptance of the merchants' proposal:[1]

> ... and although it is thought that there may be some reduction in royal duties, these should be sacrificed in the interest of propagating the Catholic faith in this kingdom of Benin, and also to assist the needs of commerce, and the importation of more slaves into Bahia where they are very necessary for labour on the plantations and the cultivation of those lands ...

But this convenient reconciliation of commerce with conscience was not effected until December 1714, by which time the Capuchins had already abandoned Benin, and the Dutch had resumed their trading.

With the departure of Father Celestino and his companion in 1713, the activity of Christian missions in Benin came to an end, and was not revived until after the British occupation. For some years Capuchin prefects in São Tomé continued to hope that new opportunities might arise. One of them, Father Illuminato di Poggitello, set out for Benin, probably in 1748, on a report that the Oba was ready to welcome a priest. The report proved true, but the royal messengers who met Father Illuminato on the borders of Benin territory also made it clear that he would have to undertake the enterprise at his own expense. Hampered by sciatica and lack of provisions, Father Illuminato thought it more prudent to turn towards Ode Itsekiri.[2] With this episode Benin disappears from the records of the *Sacra Congregazione*.

That Christianity failed in the space of three hundred years to establish itself in Benin can hardly be a matter of surprise. The missions sent there were woefully inadequate in numbers—most mustered no more than two or three clergy. Moreover these few were ill-prepared for their task, having little understanding of the

---

1 A.H.U. *Consultas da Baia, codice* 253, f. 103r-v.
2 A.S.C. *Scritture Riferite*, vol. V, f. 177-8, 28 May 1749.

complex religious system they were trying to displace, and no command of the Edo language, so that they were reduced to reliance upon interpreters who could put their arguments only in crude and misleading terms. Lack of communication with their base in São Tomé and very indifferent material support from the Portuguese authorities aggravated their shortcomings, for they were thereby deprived of the visible moral backing of their co-religionists; the presence of Dutch and English merchants they regarded only as a threat and an embarrassment. Above all, conversion to Christianity involved for a people such as the Edo not only the adoption of a new set of religious beliefs and practices, but a social revolution entailed in the abandonment of polygamy. To effect such a change the missionaries needed the full support of the secular power—to that extent they were justified in concentrating their attention upon the Oba; but in Benin that power was not cast in the post-Reformation European mould of royal absolutism to which they were accustomed. Only a major internal crisis, disrupting the established system, might offer an opening through which the missionaries, backed by the presence or promise of European arms, could effectively form an alliance with native authority. Such a situation arose in the Congo early in the sixteenth century; there seemed a possibility that it might be repeated in Benin in 1515 and again in 1710, but on both occasions the missionaries and their temporary local backers received little or no material support from Europe and were defeated.

By the beginning of the eighteenth century, Rome and its servants had perhaps a better understanding of the task that faced them in Benin than they had possessed fifty years earlier; inevitably that knowledge brought disillusionment. In 1650 the way ahead had seemed clear and hopeful. Writing from Seville while waiting to embark for Benin, Father Angel de Valencia had given full rein to his optimism:[1]

> . . . we have received great news from a man who has come from Benin where he spent six months. He never tires of praising that country, the great number of its people, the kindness of the inhabitants, their politeness and affability. . . . all agree on the great goodness of the

---

1 A.S.C. *Scritture Originalis*, vol. 249, ff. 19–20, 21 June 1650.

people and their readiness to receive the true faith. The absence of this light is due to the lack of ministers of the gospel to teach it. So great is the tyranny that the devil exercises over them that he obliges them, at certain times of the year to offer up some of their children ... and because of the great evils which they suffer from him they say that they worship him and make sacrifices, and that he answers them through his idols. They are aware that there is a true God, but because he is so good that he does them no harm, they do not fear him—so they say— as they do the devil; nor do they bother to pay respect to him and offer him sacrifices. The truth is that they do not worship him because there is no one to bring them to know him and save them from the tyranny of so cruel an enemy. These and many other good tidings that we have received from the kingdom of Benin have greatly encouraged these missionaries.

So narrow and distorted a view of Edo religious belief saw it as founded only on ignorance and fear, and was wholly oblivious of its positive role as the binding force which held society together, which assured the individual of his position in the visible and invisible world through his relation with ancestral spirits on the one hand, and with the spirits of nature on the other. The religious ceremonial of the Oba performed like functions for the people as a whole. Years of intermittent contact with Benin never gave the missionaries a true insight into the religion they were observing and attacking, but it brought at last a realisation that the attachment of the Edo to their own religion did not arise solely from ignorance of any other faith. When Father Celestino reported to the *Sacra Congregazione* the failure of his mission, he returned—probably unwittingly—to the theme of Father Angel, but in a very different mood:[1]

... no good can be done there, for those people are most obstinate in

---

1 A.S.C. *Acta Generalia*, vol. 89, f. 16, no. 29, 9 January 1719. In their repeated references to an Edo belief in a creator God and a Devil missionaries had in mind the Edo gods *Osa* or *Osanobua* (the high god and creator of the world) and *Esu* (a god employed by other gods to trouble men). *Osa*, a god remote from the affairs of men, had few shrines and priests, whereas every house had its image of *Esu* for propitiatory purposes. By confining their attention to these two deities the missionaries were able to interpret Edo religion in terms of their Christian model, but only at the price of fundamental misunderstanding.

their errors; and though they admit that there is a God who is the creator of all, they say that the true God is the god of the white Christians and that theirs is the Devil, whom they worship because he is evil and wicked but tells them what they want to know, and also because by so doing he harms them less.

Another report, submitted in 1707, made reference to the obstacle presented by polygamy:[1]

... the people are negroes and pagans; in most respects they are good-natured, but because of the aforementioned vice of polygamy the missionaries have made no progress there, though they are otherwise welcomed and well regarded by these same people.

It was no accident that this more realistic, but pessimistic, reappraisal of the situation coincided with the virtual extinction of the fire kindled in the Roman Catholic church by the counter-reformation. More concerned to hold their ground than to dissipate their diminished energies on seemingly fruitless ventures, Rome and the Portuguese patron quietly abandoned the missionary enterprise in Benin.

---

1 A.S.C. *Acta Generalia*, vol. 77, f. 448, no. 24, 5 December 1707.

Chapter 5
The Dutch at Ughoton

1. Trade in the main river (1650–1700)

Destruction among the records of the Dutch West India Companies and the English African Companies has left us very ill-informed about European trade with Benin in the second half of the seventeenth century. We do not know, for example, how long the rival factories continued to function in Arbo after the departure of the Spanish Capuchins in 1652; the Anglo-Dutch war (1651–4) added to bitter local rivalry may well have put an end to both. But Arbo continued for several decades to be the main centre for European trade in the Benin River, and from time to time both Dutch and English resurrected their trading posts. Arbo was almost certainly the site of the factory whose establishment was reported by the reformed Company of Royal Adventurers into Africa in January 1665,[1] and of the 'thatcht house and about five men' which the Royal African Company (chartered in 1672) was maintaining in the Benin River about 1690.[2] Nyendael, writing in 1702, affirmed that Dutch as well as English companies had several years earlier had factories at Arbo, and that the English factory had since fallen into ruin 'and their factors and brokers are incorporated with ours'.[3] Despite the implication in this statement that the Dutch factory was still in existence when Nyendael wrote, the records of the West India Company prove the contrary, so the probable meaning is that the English having ceased to trade in the Benin River by the end of the seventeenth century, the local traders who had previously done business with them had turned instead to the Dutch. Missionary archives show that the Portuguese too traded

1 E. Donnan (ed.) *Documents illustrative of the history of the slave trade to America*, vol. I. Washington, 1930, p. 89.
2 W. Wilkinson, *Systema Africanum*. London, 1690.
3 Bosman, *A new and accurate description*, p. 431.

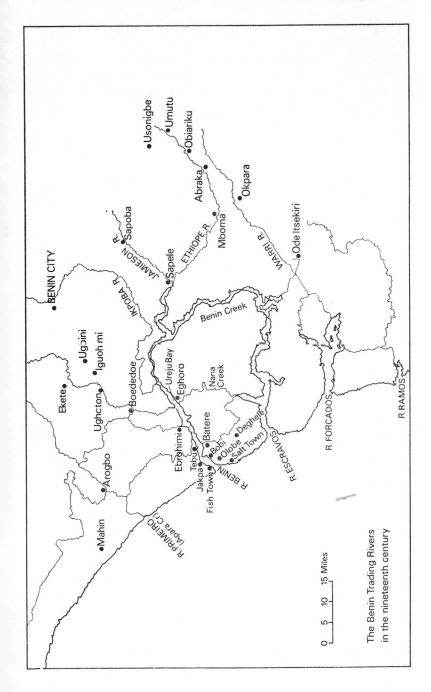

The Benin Trading Rivers
in the nineteenth century

at Arbo towards the end of the seventeenth century,[1] but they kept no factory there.

Nyendael tells an interesting story about another abandoned trading post at a village on the Benin River named *Meiborg*. Though Nyendael thought the name must be derived from that of a Dutch official, it may more plausibly be identified as *Mabbor* which Father Monteleone visited in 1689.[2] Not long after that visit there occurred an event which demonstrated that the Oba's power could still extend with decisive effect to these river settlements, even if it could not regulate their routine affairs. Beeldsnyder, the man in charge of the West India Company's factory in the village, made himself hated by the people for his brutality.

> Besides which, he cast a lascivious eye on one of the negro governor's wives, which he ravished, and thereby so enraged her injured husband, that he resolved to take his utmost satisfaction of Beeldsnyder, and came against him with a party of armed men, designing to have his life.[3]

Although the factor escaped this summary vengeance by fleeing aboard a ship, he later died of wounds received in the pursuit. Without waiting for any enquiry, the Director-General of the Company

> immediately sent a ship reinforced with Elmina soldiers to Benin, with strict orders to take the utmost revenge for the murder or massacre, as it was termed. These soldiers so rigorously executed, or perhaps stretched their commission, that they killed, or took prisoners, every person of the village that could not make their escape.

Not content with such punishment, the Oba then summoned the chief of the village to Benin City and 'caused him and his whole race, to the third and fourth generation, to be cut to pieces . . . and their houses were razed to the ground with strict orders that they should never be rebuilt'.

At the beginning of the century, D.R. had reported that any subject of the Oba who inflicted the least injury on a foreigner was punished with death.[4] If the purpose of that custom was to ensure

---

1 cf. supra p. 112.
2 ibid.
3 Bosman, *A new and accurate description*, pp. 431–3.
4 De Marees, *Beschryvinge ende Historische Verhael*, p. 240.

the flow of trade, it achieved its objective on this occasion, for Nyendael, while deploring Dutch and Edo severity, had to admit that 'we finding the King so zealously interested for us, have ever since continued our trade there' (sc. with Benin). The Oba's reprisal against *Meiborg*—which had the effect of obliterating the trading port—might also be interpreted as a step towards reasserting his control over subjects who had taken advantage of the removal of European trade to the main river to claim an unwelcome degree of independence.[1] As long as trade went smoothly he might have hesitated to take action for fear of driving away European trade, or else encouraging the people of the river to break away from Benin with European support, as the Itsekiri appear to have done in the previous century. But a situation which saw the Dutch—currently the most important European trading power—at loggerheads with one of these river villages and appealing to Benin for support, offered an excellent opportunity to deal a heavy blow at these over-independent subjects. Finally, it must be remembered that this incident occurred about the time that aggressive measures by the court against the town chiefs of Benin City drove a large part of the capital's population into open rebellion:[2] at a time, that is to say, of acute crisis for monarchical authority. In this larger political context the destruction of *Meiborg* can be understood as one manifestation of a determined effort to re-establish the fallen authority of the Benin throne.

Impressed by the Oba's vigorous championship of their interests, the West India Company began in the sixteen-nineties to trade more intensively in the Ughoton Creek. Ughoton itself benefited from the diversion of trade away from the lower river, but it had long been apparent that it could not alone satisfy European demand —still less at a time when its hinterland was restricted and disrupted by civil war. To overcome the deficiencies of Ughoton the West India Company traded also at the nearby village of Boededoe, a settlement of some fifty houses (built in the Arbo, not the Edo,

---

1 Arbo and Mabbor continued to trade with the Itsekiris despite the state of war which elsewhere existed between Benin and Warri. cf. supra p. 113.
2 cf. supra p. 19.

style)[1] standing about one mile inside the Ovenama Creek. With its largely non-Edo population gathered on the fringe of Benin suzerainty for the purpose of trade with Europeans, Boededoe resembled the trading ports on the lower river, and like them it was governed in the name of the Oba by a headman assisted by a council of chiefs. The merchandise it supplied to the Dutch came, apparently, from the Yoruba areas to the westwards with which it communicated through a maze of creeks.

By the end of the seventeenth century the Dutch Company was sending one or two yachts each year from Elmina to these riverside ports—Arbo, Ughoton, Boededoe—controlled in varying degrees by the Oba. But it had no factory in Benin territory and rejected a request that it should replace the one destroyed at *Meiborg*. Commenting on that proposal, which was made by some unspecified peoples of the river in 1696, the Director-General argued that the company could only consider a new establishment if it were possible —and he thought it was not—to build a fort near the river mouth to exclude all other Europeans. The directors of the company, though not thinking in terms of such militant monopoly, still stipulated that any new factory must be so sited as to tap the trade of the neighbouring rivers.[2] They were in effect reaffirming the principle which had directed the choice of Arbo as a factory site sixty years earlier, and which made unlikely a return to a trade conducted exclusively with the Edo kingdom.

In his report on the proposed factory the Director-General had not specified which competitors he wished to drive away from the river. Neither the English nor the French seem to have been trading there at the end of the seventeenth century, but he may have feared their return.[3] The stray Spanish vessel may have entered the river, as in the middle of the century. The Portuguese of São Tomé and Príncipe, driven out by the Dutch in the first half of the century,

---

1 Nyendael describes them as 'built with reed and leaves'. (Bosman, *A New and Accurate Descrpition*, p. 430.)

2 A.R. *N.W.I.C.* vol. 54, *Minuuit brieven naar de Kust van Guinea*. Middelburgh, 5 October 1697.

3 cf. '*Relation du Sieur Du Casse (1687–88)*' in P. Roussier, *L'Etablissement d'Issiny, 1687–1702*. Paris, 1935. At the moment there is no evidence of any French trade with Benin in the seventeenth century, but investigations in the French archives may well reveal a certain amount of small-scale enterprise.

were certainly reappearing in some force towards its end. The Capuchins on São Tomé were often able to communicate with Benin by means of ships sailing to the river where they traded in slaves, ivory and cloth.[1] And on both occasions that Nyendael visited the river—in 1699 and 1702—he found two Portuguese vessels trading there. A Frenchman who visited Príncipe in 1698 provides some information about this Portuguese trade.[2] On the island was an establishment belonging to a company which held a contract to supply slaves to the Spanish West Indies, and which maintained a trade with Benin and Calabar using four or five boats of fifty or sixty tons. Other islanders unconnected with the company were trading profitably in wax, ivory and cloth from the rivers, the nature of which gave their small boats a great advantage over the larger vessels employed by other nations.

Thanks to Nyendael's description of Benin, we have a reasonably clear picture of trading procedures at the end of the century. Some details remain obscure: for example, we do not know whether a messenger informed the Oba of the arrival of every ship, or whether the ship's officers were obliged to visit him. Nyendael himself had an audience with the Oba, but he may have sought this from curiosity rather than necessity. In any event, the details of business were settled with the *fiadors* and *mercadors* who had taken up residence in the river ports earlier in the century, and of whom Nyendael had a rather poor opinion. However, they still bore the rank of royal officials which raised them in status and privileges above the common people—a rank signified by a string of beads 'of pale red coctile earth or stone, and very well glazed, and very like speckled red marble'.[3] This string, bestowed on them by the Oba, 'they are obliged to wear continually about their necks, without ever daring to put it off on any account whatever. For if they are so unhappy as to lose it, or carelessly suffer it to be stolen, they are ipso facto irreprievably condemned to die . . .'[4] To these men and

---

1 A.S.C. *Scritture Riferite*, vol. II, f. 585. Father Monteleone to *Sacra Congregazione*, 24 May 1692.
2 '*Relation du Chevalier Damon*' (*1698*) in P. Roussier, *L'Etablissement d'Issiny*, p. 85.
3 Bosman, *A New and Accurate Description*, p. 437.
4 ibid. p. 436.

to the chief of the town where trade was to be conducted the Europeans paid 'some sorts of customs'[1]—the equivalent of the cloth that the Portuguese had once given to the chief of Ughoton and the officials responsible for trade. Each ship also paid 'customs' to the Oba and his chief counsellors, but of a modest value, for all the 'customs' taken together did not, according to Nyendael, 'amount to above six pounds sterling, for which we become entirely free to trade'.[2] The duties imposed on European trade had not, therefore, risen appreciably since the sixteenth century.

Nyendael is none too precise in his description of the functions of *fiadors* and *mercadors*, or 'factors and trustees . . . the last of which are here but a sort of brokers'.[3] Having a smattering of Portuguese (still the lingua franca of European commerce), they acted as agents in all trading negotiations and transactions. The *fiadors* or factors, it may be assumed, continued to act for the Oba in greeting traders and bargaining over prices. The function of the *mercadors* or brokers is more obscure; they appear to have acted as licensed commission agents rather than as traders on their own account, for if Nyendael observed correctly, the regulations which had once prevented the generality of the Edo from trading with Europeans no longer applied with the old rigour. It was the practice of the free-born Edo, he wrote, 'to loiter about whole days, till they hear of any ships being come into the river, upon which they go thither to trade with what goods they have in store'.[4] As the trading agent the broker was a key figure in the working of the trust or credit system which arose with the rapid growth of the local cloth trade during the middle period of the seventeenth century. The history of 'trust' is obscure. We have seen the Oba offering credit to Englishmen in the previous century.[5] By the middle of the seventeenth century the Dutch had introduced 'trust' into their slave trade with Ardra, and the Portuguese had adopted a similar practice with the Itsekiris. On the other hand, the West India Company refused trust to the Itsekiris in the sixteen-forties, and there is no evidence that they had extended it to Benin at that date. Before the end of the century, however, it was firmly established there—at least in the purchase of cloths. Father

---

1 ibid. p. 434. 2 ibid. p. 461. 3 ibid. p. 431.
4 Bosman, *A new and accurate description*, p. 462.
5 cf. supra p. 78.

Monteleone explained that 'the cloths are not found ready made, but they [i.e. African traders] take goods on credit, and with these goods they have the cloth made in five or, at the most, six months'.[1] Which nation—Portuguese, Dutch or English—had introduced the practice we do not know, but once extended by one, the others had perforce to offer similar facilities. From the cloth trade trust soon moved into other branches of commerce, especially those which, like cloth, entailed long-distance traffic with the interior. Ivory, for example, was commonly traded in this manner by the early eighteenth century.[2]

Goods might be given on trust to the chiefs of the river ports and to the *fiadors*, but most of the credit evidently went into the hands of the *mercadors* or brokers who dealt in turn with traders from Benin City and the interior. From the European point of view the system had little to recommend it, except that it probably increased the supply of cloth and ivory. Its drawbacks were several and serious. Ships had to spend longer in the river to complete their cargoes: 'trade in Benin and Oere takes many months, in contrast to all other places on this coast of Guinea where on the spot exchange is the custom; in Benin, on the contrary, the custom is to give goods on credit for six months'.[3] The mortality rate among crews rose correspondingly: on both his visits to the Benin River Nyendael lost half his crew; and this was not considered unusual. Both Father Montelone and Nyendael agreed that despite the delays a Benin trader could generally be relied upon to meet his obligations:

> ... this commerce, which consists in slaves, ivory and various kinds of cotton cloth, is very slow: the cloths are not found ready made, but they take goods on credit, and with these goods they have the cloths made in five or, at the most, six months ... then, although they are heathens and unknown, they faithfully deliver the cloth to the captain of the ship.[4]

---

1 A.S.C. *Scritture Riferite*, vol. 2, f. 585, 24 May 1692.
2 Early in the nineteenth century, a European visiting Benin noted that much ivory sold there was obtained from the Igala country, seventeen days' journey to the north-east. *Royal Gold Coast Gazette*, no. 1, vol. I, 25 March 1823.
3 Father Francesco da Monteleone, A.S.C. *Scritture Riferite*, vol. 2, f. 553, 19 March 1692.
4 ibid., f. 585, 24 May 1692.

... at our arrival here, we are obliged to trust them with goods to make 'panes' or cloths of; for the payment of which we frequently stay so long, that by reason of the advancement of the season, the consumption of our provisions, and the sickness or mortality of our men, we are obliged to depart without our goods: but on the other hand, the next time we come hither, we are sure to be honestly paid the whole.[1]

But quarrels over credit inevitably arose—sometimes with disastrous consequences for individuals or whole communities. Nyendael relates one such incident which occurred at Boededoe about 1700.[2] A Portuguese ship

was obliged to stay a month or two after me in order to get in his debts; which coming in very slowly, the captain resolved to cause a fiador, that was his greatest debtor, to be arrested in his ship; but when he attempted it, the other resisted, and endeavoured to escape; and during the scuffle with the sailors, the pilot caught hold of his chain of coral, broke it in pieces and threw it overboard, which so dispirited the fiador, that he let go his hold and surrendered himself immediately. But sometime after finding the pilot asleep, and having gotten a blunderbuss he shot him through the head. ... The Portuguese did not venture to punish him, but delivered him to the governor of the place who despatched him to the king; and the bark departing, his majesty committed him to close prison, in order to punish him very severely in the presence of the next Portuguese that should come hither. This very year[3] I saw the negro; and just upon my departure two Portuguese ships came with orders to demand justice for their murdered pilot.

A few years later the Dutch burned Arbo itself in a dispute over trust. We have no contemporary account of the affair, but the Director-General at Elmina made reference to it in 1715 as an illustration of the unsatisfactory nature of credit trading.[4]

---

1 David van Nyendael in Bosman, *A new and accurate description*, pp. 433–4.
2 Bosman, *A new and accurate description*, pp. 436–7.
3 i.e. 1702.
4 A.R. *Bezittingen ter Kuste van Guinea*, vol. 825. *Instructie voor den Commies Revixit van Naerssen waer naer hy zig in zyn te doen voyagie met het scheepje Commany na Rio de Benyn, Gabon en Caap de Lopes sal hebben te regulieten*, Elmina, 16 May 1715. Art. 7.

... contrary to the practice observed throughout the world, we were obliged to give out a great quantity of goods on credit, and these were sent off inland for the purchase of ivory which could not be had otherwise. This practice gave rise to many difficulties and tricks, as happened some time ago when the village of Arbo was burned for failure to pay for the goods given out on trust.

Such disasters and objections notwithstanding, trust proved ineradicable and remained a normal part of trading until the end of the nineteenth century.

The details of trade not contained in Nyendael's invaluable account of Benin may be extracted from the archives of the West India Company, which are relatively complete for the period between the sixteen-nineties and the seventeen-thirties. In the nineties ships based at Elmina were making extensive round voyages that took them to the Benin River as their first port of call before sailing south as far as Gabon or Cape Lope Gonçalvez, and thence to the Grain Coast. The accounts made up at the conclusion of these voyages rarely distinguished the purchases made at different markets on the coast, so that it is impossible to ascertain precisely the nature and quantity of cargo acquired in the Benin River. However, ivory stands out unmistakably as the most important commodity sought by the Dutch in these Bight voyages, and we may be certain that much came from Benin. The yacht *Nagtegaal*, for example, collected 13,785 pounds of ivory tusks, 2,222 pounds of small tusks (the Dutch called them *scrivilios*),[1] 20 aums of palm oil, 558 pounds of wax and 11,415 pounds of peppers in the course of a voyage lasting from June 1696 to February 1697.[2] On a further expedition to the Bights between March and November 1697, the captain of the *Nagtegaal* bought nothing but ivory to a total of 11,396 pounds of tusks and 5,967 pounds of *scrivilios*.[3] Only in the following voyage of this vessel made in 1698 do Benin cloths appear among the cargo, and then only to the very modest tune of 285 pieces.[4] A decline in their trading value from the mid-century price

1 The instructions given to van Naerssen in 1715 stipulated that 'tusks should preferably weigh three to a hundredredweight'. The name *scrivilios* was applied to tusks weighing less than 14 pounds.
2 A.R. *N.W.I.C.* vol. 97, f. 205r.
3 ibid. f. 207r.
4 ibid. f. 211r.

of four guilders to three guilders apiece offers some explanation for their virtual disappearance from Dutch cargoes: so too does the evidence of strong Portuguese competition in this branch of trade contained in Father Monteleone's letters.

Calculated as the difference between the market value of the commodities purchased and expenditure on merchandise, crew salaries and provisions, the profit from the three voyages of the *Nagtegaal* mentioned above amounted to 5,207, 4,217 and 1,579 guilders respectively. For the first two voyages this represents a profit of rather less than 50 per cent, and 25 per cent for the last. A voyage to the Benin River alone by the snow *Johanna Maria* showed a rather better return, even though the vessel had to lie in the river from October 1698 until March 1699;[1] the return cargo, consisting of 6,127 pounds of tusks, 1,998 pounds of *scrivilios* and 200 cloths, showed a profit of 2,504 guilders for an expenditure of 5,225 guilders.[2] It is therefore difficult to understand why the Director-General should have declared, on the completion of this voyage, that the Benin trade was unprofitable.[3] Possibly his judgement was influenced by the devastating casualties among the crew: seven of the fifteen men aboard the *Johanna Maria* died in the Benin River. Nevertheless the experiment was repeated in 1699 when the snow brought back a larger cargo of ivory and would, in the opinion of the Director-General, have done better still but for sickness among the officers.

For several years thereafter the West India Company continued to send small vessels directly to Benin, while larger ships sometimes visited the river in the course of voyages into the Bight of Biafra. They bought only ivory, cloth having fallen out of favour again after its brief reappearance in 1698; but so important had the ivory trade become that in April 1704 the chief clerk of the *Opmeer* was instructed to discuss with the governor and chiefs of Arbo the possibility of reopening the factory in that town. It is noteworthy that the

---

1 David van Nyendael probably paid his first visit to Benin on this occasion.
2 A.R. *N.W.I.C.* vol. 97, ff. 212v–213r. It must be remembered that the market price of the Company's goods included a supplement of 50 per cent on the cost price. cf. supra p. 95, n. 4.
3 A.R. *N.W.I.C.* vol. 97, f. 7v. 1 March 1699; f. 60v. 8 May 1699; f. 147r-v. 15 April 1700. J. van Sevenhuysen to the Council of the West India Company.

Dutch did not find it necessary to negotiate with the Oba,[1] and were able—apparently without any direct reference to him—to reach agreement upon the factory with the chiefs of Arbo. Here is the first of many signs that Benin had, quite suddenly, lost control of the river below Ughoton, and that the chiefs of villages such as Arbo and Boededoe were no longer men appointed from Benin City, but the leaders of independent communities. Only a few years earlier the situation had been very different; when Nyendael visited Arbo he found it governed in the name of the Oba, and saw several corpses there waiting to be carried to Benin City for burial in their native land. At Boededoe a 'viceroy' governed for the Oba to whom was reserved jurisdiction in all criminal cases and matters of importance: the cases of *Meiborg* and of the *fiador* who shot the Portuguese captain demonstrated the substance of the Oba's power. Neither European records nor Benin tradition offer any explanation for this sudden and dramatic disappearance of Benin control over the territory between Ughoton and the coast; indeed they take no account of it. The prolonged civil war could have played its part in undermining the Oba's authority, especially if—as is likely in view of the *Meiborg* incident[2]—the sympathies of the river peoples lay with the rebels. As to when the *débâcle* occurred, we may place it with some certainty between Nyendael's departure from the river at the end of 1702 and the Dutch dealings with Arbo in 1704. And if it be objected that details of the latter are not sufficiently complete to justify such a conclusion, that objection cannot be brought against

---

1 A.R. *Bezittingen*, vol. 234, 1 April 1704. Instructions for the chief clerk Louis Isaac Bardet.

'Art. 4. From there [Ardra] set course for the Rio Benin, and on arrival there the steersman commandant is to sail into the river with the utmost caution and go up to the place known as Arrebo where he is to begin to open trade in ivory and *scrivilios*. And should experience show that the inhabitants are doing their best to detain him there for two months or more, he is hereby expressly ordered not to stay there longer than five or six weeks. During that time he must not fail to do everything in his power to encourage and promote trade.

'Art. 5. And since the Company had a factory there for more than 10 or 12 years with the object of promoting trade in the Bights and rivers more intensively, the chief clerk Bardet is hereby expressly ordered to enquire of the chief and other important men whether it could be re-established.'

2 cf. the independent attitude being adopted by the people of Arbo and Mabbor as early as Monteleone's visit.

the circumstances surrounding the negotiations of 1715 between the Dutch company and the Oba which make it perfectly clear that Benin had lost all control over Arbo and Boededoe.[1] Far-reaching effects were to follow from the collapse of Benin authority over the river, for it created a vacuum which the river communities were unable to fill despite the efforts of Arbo and Boededoe to develop as petty trading states. Not until the days of intensive palm-oil commerce in the nineteenth century was the Benin River able to support powerful, semi-independent merchant states similar to those which flourished earlier in the eastern part of the Niger delta. Instead the way was opened for Itsekiri expansion and domination, and for the gradual isolation of Benin from the main currents of European trade and influence.

The re-established factory at Arbo enjoyed but a brief existence. A factor named Jan van der Venne arrived in January 1705 with an under-clerk, a surgeon and a soldier to staff it.[2] The inhabitants, according to Director-General Willem de la Palma who was responsible for the enterprise, expressed great satisfaction.[3] Immediately afterwards, however, a new Director-General, Pieter Nuyts, eager to demonstrate his energy and originality, began to overturn all the dispositions made by his predecessor—behaviour only too common among the chief officers of the West India Company in the eighteenth century, and often attended with unfortunate results. Among his targets was the Arbo factory which he attacked by having the Council at Elmina, who would rarely venture to cross swords with the Director-General, resolve in November 1705 that van der Venne be called upon to decide whether the Company would profit from the factory, or whether it would suffice to have three ships visiting the river each year to conduct their own ivory trade.[4] Assuming that the factor's reaction was motivated solely by commercial considerations—and this is a considerable assumption—prospects were indeed

1 Ref. infra p. 141.
2 A.R. *N.W.I.C.* vol. 98, f. 417. Muster roll, 31 August 1705.
3 ibid. f. 323v. W. de la Palma to Council of Ten, 5 Sept. 1705.
4 A.R. *N.W.I.C.* vol. 98, f. 603. *Extract uyt de resolutie genoomen by den Oppercoopman President en Raaden in datum Maandag den 2 November 1705.* *N.W.I.C.* vol. 1287' P. Nuyts to Council of Ten, 19 April 1706. *N.W.I.C.* vol. 55, 23 July 1706. The Council of Ten replied leaving the decision on the factory to the Director-General.

bleak, for he not only abandoned the factory forthwith, but also convinced the Director-General's council that not three but one voyage a year would suffice to carry away the ivory and wax available in the Benin River.[1]

Once again, therefore, the Dutch reverted to the practice whereby a ship visited the river, gave out goods on credit and waited for the traders to furnish a return cargo from the interior. Results proved satisfactory for a time. One ship reached Elmina in December 1707 with 8,944 pounds of tusks, 4,246 pounds of *scrivilios* and 5,000 pounds of wax.[2] In the following year a Benin voyage yielded 14,400 pounds of tusks, 4,602 pounds of *scrivilios*, 2,602 pounds of wax, and 2,016 cloths,[3] the latter again having come back into favour on the Gold Coast. Then, just when Dutch trade with the Benin River had reached its highest point for many years, it appears to have come to an abrupt halt, and to have ceased altogether until December 1713. The gap could be explained by a fortuitous destruction of documents, but it is more likely to be related to the burning of Arbo in a dispute over trust.[4] The spectacular growth of the ivory trade at the end of the seventeenth century involved giving out more trust and for a longer period as traders were forced to seek their supplies farther afield. At the same time Portuguese from the islands re-entered the Benin River trade as formidable competitors; unhampered by the heavy overhead expenses of the Dutch West India Company, they apparently were able to undercut their rivals in the scramble for ivory as the English had done in the cloth trade earlier in the century. How the company would react to European competition and African delay in discharging debts had been demonstrated by the proposal to build a fort at the mouth of the river and the destruction of *Meiborg*. Arbo fell victim to the same philosophy of force, and with it perished the trading system of which it had for more than sixty years been the hub.

---

1 A.R. *N.W.I.C.* vol. 99, ff. 436v–437r. P. Nuyts and Raad to Council of Ten, 31 May 1707.
2 A.R. *N.W.I.C.* vol. 100, f. 119. P. Nuyts to Council of Ten, 3 December 1707.
3 A.R. *N.W.I.C.* vol. 100, f. 342. P. Nuyts and Council to Council of Ten, 10 March 1709.
4 cf. supra pp. 132–3.

2. Establishment at Ughoton

Benin, one may imagine, did not bewail the fate of Arbo, or the dislocation of trade in the lower river, for here was an opportunity to bring some wealth back to the war-racked kingdom. For its part the West India Company had no desire to forgo the riches of the Benin region, provided that trade could be put upon a footing more satisfactory than that which had led to the *débâcle* at Arbo. Late in 1713, therefore—after an interval of two or three years—the Dutch resumed their Benin voyages by sending a ship to Ughoton with instructions to load a full cargo of ivory and explore the possibilities of buying redwood and gum. Ivory presented no problems, and the ship took away 14,560 pounds.[1] Gum and redwood, however, had not been traded within living memory, and much bargaining was therefore required in order to fix prices. For gum the Dutch captain agreed to an exchange of 761 pounds against 77 pounds of glass beads; a rate which the Director-General considered too expensive.[2] On redwood they failed to reach any conclusion. The next voyage, made towards the end of 1714, produced further disagreement. The chief clerk succeeded only in smuggling a few pieces of redwood on board 'at night and by stealth because it is not supposed to be exported';[3] and he found it impossible to buy any gum at the lower price fixed by the Director-General. So inauspicious a beginning might have ended all prospects of an expanded trade with the Dutch had the Council of the West India Company not stepped in to instruct its Director-General that he should do everything in his

---

1 A.R. *N.W.I.C.* vol. 102, f. 158v. H. Haring and Council to Council of Ten, 4 March 1714. The cargo brought from Benin also included 20 marks of gold. Since no gold had previously been obtained from Benin, and subsequent prospecting proved fruitless, it is possible that this amount was obtained directly or indirectly from Brazilian ships trading with Benin. cf. Ryder, 'Re-establishment of Portuguese factories', p. 158. Gold ornaments were not entirely unknown in Benin. A Dutch factor at Ughoton wrote on 24 March 1717, 'The King also showed me three gold headbands, one of which had a glass stone, one a reddish stone, and the other one was without a stone; and he sent a message requesting me to let him have three of each kind.' (A.R. *Bezittingen*, vol. 84.)
2 A.R. *N.W.I.C.* vol. 102, ff. 275v–276v. H. Haring to Council of Ten, 5 June 1714.
3 ibid.

power to buy gum. The first samples having sold at a great profit in Europe, the Company concluded that it had discovered a sovereign remedy for its declining fortunes, and insisted that it be applied. On the other side the newly-installed Oba Akenzua I had already asked the Dutch to establish a factory on his territory. Thus there appeared to exist a neat equation of interest which the Director-General might set to work by means of a formal treaty or contract such as the Company had been making with the chiefs and peoples of the Gold Coast since the mid-seventeenth century.[1]

Revixit van Naerssen, the Company official who had first drawn attention to Benin gum, was the man chosen to treat with the Oba, on terms specified in great detail in his instructions.[2] Maximum concessions were to be won by emphasising all the disadvantages of the Benin trade: protracted bargaining with the Oba's officials, the trust system, mortality among the Company's servants, and the restricted range of commodities available.

> As we could hardly establish a factory there without over-great expense, and as it is the custom of their people to make a great many promises (as they have frequently done in the past to the officials we have sent) without these producing any practical effect, so it is consequently too risky for us to embark on an undertaking of such importance without greater security.[3]

The security required was spelt out in precise terms. In the first place the Oba 'must give a solemn promise, to be recorded in writing', that he would neither protect nor harbour any runaway slaves belonging to the Company; one such fugitive had recently caused friction between the parties,[4] and van Naerssen had with him twelve Gold Coast slaves to work in the Benin factories. Secondly, the Oba was to have built at his own cost two houses, one at Ughoton and another at Arbo, to serve as factories; 'they must be so constructed as to safeguard the merchandise from fire, thieves and white ants . . . and they must be repaired as often as is necessary'.[5]

---

1 A.R. *N.W.I.C.* no. 12. Contracts and agreements with the natives, 1642–73.
2 A.R. *Bezittingen*, vol. 82, 16 May 1715.
3 A.R. *Bezittingen*, vol. 82. Instructions for van Naerssen, 16 May 1715, art. 10.
4 ibid. art. 12. This article also demanded the return of the runaway slave who had placed himself under the Oba's protection.
5 ibid. art. 13.

The Oba was also to assume responsibility for the swift arrest and punishment of any subject who stole the Company's property. In the likely event of failure to abolish the credit system altogether—though he was to attempt it—van Naerssen was to reach some form of agreement that would make the Oba and the headmen of trading villages sureties for trust given to traders living under their jurisdiction. The other conditions put to the Oba were all concerned with increasing the volume of Dutch trade with Benin.

> The ivory trade to date has not amounted to a quantity which justifies sending many ships there and incurring needless expense; so ... we have considered augmenting the trade with a certain kind of gum and redwood that the Benin people can gather in the forests with little labour and expense, and bring to sell to the resident official at all times.[1]

In truth everything depended on the gum 'which alone will be the cause of success or failure'.[2] To increase the volume of trade it was necessary to persuade the Oba to 'speed up the slow method of trading', so that a ship might carry away a full cargo every three months; only then would the expense of the factories be justified. If Benin would undertake not to delay any ship more than two months in the river, the Company would guarantee to send four every year. Furthermore the ruler of Benin and his chiefs must permit the Dutch to trade in whatever commodities they thought fit, and not insist on the current practice of taking the best merchandise in exchange for cloths which were losing their market along the coast. Finally, van Naerssen was to do his best to persuade the Oba to exclude all other Europeans from the Benin trade.

On 26 August 1715, 'after endless delays and no less expense and labour',[3] an agreement was signed—the first formal treaty between Benin and the Europeans.[4] Many of the conditions set out in the factor's instructions had emerged substantially modified from the prolonged bargaining. While the Oba promised his protection to the goods and servants of the Company, and agreed to exercise his

---

1 ibid. art. 19.
2 ibid. art. 20.
3 A.R. *Bezittingen*, vol. 82. R. van Naerssen to H. Haring, 26 December 1715.
4 Text in A.R. *N.W.I.C.* vol. 122, *Contracten met naturellen*, ff. 74v–76v.

authority when needful for the collection of trust, he refused to abandon his prerogative of selling a number of cloths on credit to every ship.[1] 'They were so obstinate on the question of giving credit for cloth that it proved utterly impossible to make the slightest change in the customs.'[2] Trade in gum and redwood the Oba approved, promising 'to ensure that so constant a quantity of these products shall be brought for sale to the Company's chief official here, that it shall be worthwhile sending three to four ships here from Elmina each year to load the same'.[3] To reduce delays in the turn-round, trade was to continue with the factories whether or not a ship happened to be in the river. But on the important question of granting the Dutch a monopoly of trade the Oba refused to budge from the well-established practice of dealing with all nations, and insisted instead 'that no Portuguese, who may at any time be found in the King's territory, shall be attacked by the Company's ships or servants, since the King, being master of his land, wishes to extend to them, as to all other nations, free access to trade'.[4] Finally, it was agreed that the Oba would build and maintain a factory at Ughoton, and that the Dutch living there should be supplied with provisions 'at the old prices'.[5] Arbo, as the Company had every reason to know, now lay beyond Benin jurisdiction; and it was after the inhabitants of the village, forgetting old grudges, had assured van Naerssen of a flourishing trade in gum, that the Company itself took responsibility for a subsidiary post there. (Van Naerssen had a bamboo storehouse erected, and sent a Dutchman with four slaves to look after it.) When all was concluded, the Oba put his mark on the treaty 'in the presence of all the King's *fiadors* and a chief of the kingdom'.[6]

---

1 Although this privilege is referred to by van Naerssen as one long-established, there is no record of its existence in earlier years and it was probably of quite recent origin.
2 A.R. *Bezittingen*, vol. 82. R. van Naerssen to H. Haring, 26 December 1715.
3 Treaty art. 7.
4 Treaty art. 10. Relations between the Dutch and the Portuguese in Guinea markedly deteriorated at the beginning of the eighteenth century. This article suggests that incidents had occurred in the Benin River. cf. Ryder, 'The re-establishment of Portuguese factories'.
5 Treaty art. 11.
6 The chief so distinguished from his fellows may have been the *Ezomo*—Akenzua's strong right hand.

To stock the new factories van Naerssen had brought with him a cargo of merchandise whose value, as expressed in the price-list, amounted to 44,223¼ pounds of ivory.[1] Ivory had replaced gold as the measure of value in Dutch price-lists for the Benin trade, possibly because ivory was a staple commodity the price of which had already been agreed upon in relation to the regular articles of European merchandise. The exchange value of gum and redwood, on the other hand, still involved van Naerssen in prolonged wrangles with the royal *fiadors* at Ughoton because no price had yet been fixed for redwood, and the Company, anticipating large purchases of gum, was determined to bring the price below that paid for the first two shipments. In the words of his instructions, van Naerssen was to do 'his best to see that the price fixed for the gum is as low as possible, but at the same time high enough to make it worthwhile for the natives to take the trouble of gathering it'.[2] In the end both sides accepted a barrel holding 170 pounds of gum as a standard measure, and valued it as the equivalent of twelve Benin cloths.

By the time he left Benin in October 1715, van Naerssen had purchased 11,176 pounds of tusks, 5,200 pounds of *scrivilios*, 8,600 pounds of gum and 11,200 pounds of redwood.[3] With this impressive cargo he returned to Elmina to report on his mission. Though generally satisfied with the treaty, Director-General Haring had reservations about certain of its clauses, and especially that which guaranteed the right of all nations to trade freely.

> We shall certainly observe the article in the treaty regarding foreign nations as it stands during the residence of the Company's servants there, but we reserve the right of the Company to make further dispositions in that matter, and in course of time to make a new agreement with the King concerning it.[4]

He also had misgivings about allowing the Oba regular trust against

---

1 A.R. *Bezittingen*, vol. 82. *Factura en marctbrieff der Coopmans. te welke zyn geladen in't' scheepje Commany schipper Claas Pietersen waer naer zy den Commies Revixit van Naerssen in't verhandelen der selver in de benin exactelyk sal hebben te reguleeren, actum Elmina 16 May 1715.*

2 Van Naerssen's instructions, art. 24.

3 A.R. *N.W.I.C.* vol. 102, ff. 576v–577v. H. Haring and Council to Council of Ten, 12 April 1716.

4 A.R. *Bezittingen*, vol. 82. H. Haring to F. de Reyke, 11 Jan. 1716.

Benin cloths because arrears under this heading already amounted to the value of one hundred cloths, and he feared that the practice would eventually give rise to serious disputes. As a compromise he instructed de Reyke, van Naerssen's successor, to grant the Oba and chiefs credit to a value of 1,700 cloths on the arrival of every ship, but to deduct from that total any arrears outstanding from previous ships. Equally pregnant with contention were the gum and redwood prices negotiated by van Naerssen. Where his emissary had accepted less than five pounds of gum as equivalent to one of ivory, the Director-General decreed that the equivalence must be seven pounds of gum; for redwood he wanted a price of $12\frac{1}{2}$ pounds of wood to one of ivory; besides which he demanded that the logs be cut longer, thicker and more evenly. These new instructions he sent to Benin by the *Commany* which left Elmina in January 1716 carrying merchandise valued at $25,429\frac{1}{2}$ pounds of ivory, two officials for the factories, and an armchair as a present for the Oba.

Calling at some other Dutch factories on the coast, it took the *Commany* three weeks to reach Ughoton. Five days later de Reyke went to Benin City to deliver the chair and broach the thorny questions of credit and prices. Pleasure over the present did nothing to make the Oba more amenable in these matters:

> The King replied that if I wished to speak of reductions, he would speak of increases, and that he had not the least intention of allowing the agreed total [sc. of cloths] to be reduced. As to the gum, he had intended, instead of a reduction, to demand another six cloths for every barrel.[1]

Here was an Oba very much master of the situation—a ruler reminiscent of those who had governed Benin in the sixteenth century, and very different from the chief-ridden monarchs of the later seventeenth century. In face of his firmness de Reyke had to accept an exchange rate of five pounds of gum against one of ivory, and abandon the Director-General's instruction to pay only half-price for small pieces of gum. 'They have forced me', he wrote, 'to buy one lot of gum with another, otherwise they will no longer trade in it.'[2] Moreover, the Oba's officials ensured that they received the

---

1 ibid. F. de Reyke to H. Haring, 19 March 1716.
2 A.R. *Bezittingen*, vol. 82. F. de Reyke to H. Haring, 19 March 1716.

credit due for cloths before permitting any trade with private merchants. To a certain extent the Company's policy had boomeranged upon it: seeking the commercial advantages of dealing with a powerful ruler, it now had to accept that it could not arbitrarily alter the terms of the bargain it had struck with him.

From cargo lists and inventories of stocks held in the factory at Ughoton, it becomes possible for the first time since the mid-seventeenth century to obtain a picture of the nature and volume of European merchandise traded in Benin. The handing-over inventory prepared by van Naerssen in October 1715 shows that from a stock of more than 2,000 pounds of various beads only a few had been sold,[1] 'because they are frequently brought in by the Portuguese'[2] who sold them below the Dutch price of one pound of beads to $1\frac{1}{2}$ pounds of ivory. Manillas too proved almost unsaleable: a stock held at Ughoton had to be returned to Elmina in 1717 because they could command only a very low exchange value; at least, a rate which the Company was unwilling to accept. In their place came brass and copper pans known as neptunes. These ranged in size from the so-called Spanish neptunes with a diameter of one foot or less, to dishes weighing eight pounds. Of the 4,631 pounds of neptunes that van Naerssen brought to Benin, only 419 pounds remained unsold in October, and the under-clerk who took over the factory asked for another 10,000 pounds. In 1717 trade came virtually to a standstill when the factor exhausted his stock of neptunes and cowries—the other essential, of which van Naerssen had arrived with 3,000 pounds.[3] A great variety of cloth was still in demand, ranging from flower-patterned damask and French silks for the Oba to common white linen cloths which the Dutch sold in very large quantities.[4] Red cloth too retained its long-established popularity. In addition to

---

1 ibid. *Restant der coopmans: welke in de logie tot agathon bevonden zyn te resteren, en op ordre van den Ed. Heer Directeur Generaal H. Haring zyn getransporteert, en overgegeven door den Commies Revixit van Naerssen aen den onder commies Jan Ravens en den adsistent Jacobus de Reyke deese 10 October 1715.*

2 ibid. J. Ravens and F. de Reyke to H. Haring, 10 October 1715.

3 His successor asked for a further 4,000 pounds of cowries in October 1715, and 6,000 pounds in March 1717. (A.R. *Bezittingen*, vol. 82 and 84.)

4 The Dutch called these linen cloths *plathilios*—a corruption of the Portuguese *platilhas*. One cloth was rated at 10 pounds of ivory.

these and other old staples of the Benin trade (iron bars, knives, brandy and rum), the Dutch had introduced some new articles of economic and social significance. Probably the most important was the flintlock gun which they began to sell in small numbers at the end of the seventeenth century. Van Naerssen took with him fifty of these weapons valued at 16 pounds of ivory apiece, as well as 200 pounds of gunpowder and spare flints. Another notable innovation was the sale of tobacco which began to figure in Dutch cargoes at the end of the seventeenth century, although the Portuguese were bringing a certain amount from Brazil rather earlier. Tobacco sold by the West India Company in Guinea had to be bought from the Portuguese, or else taken from them in the guise of a 10 per cent tax levied for the privilege of trading on the coast.[2] The Edo quickly acquired the smoking habit, and van Naerssen was able to dispose of his six rolls of 'Portuguese tobacco' for 48 pounds of ivory each; another eight rolls delivered in 1717 fetched 56 pounds of ivory.

Whatever hesitation Director-General Haring may have felt about his Benin enterprise, Benin had reasonable cause for satisfaction over its new relationship with the Dutch. After a lapse of more than half a century, and despite the loss of suzerainty over the lower river, the main centre of European trade had been brought back into Edo territory on terms favourable to its people. After the long destruction of civil war, prosperity returned—prosperity in which trade played its part. In the words of the Benin chronicler:[3]

> Akenzua I was one of the richest kings that ever sat on the throne of Benin, and because of his wealth was nicknamed 'Akenzua Nisonorho' (Akenzua the rainy sky). Because of the peace and prosperity of his reign he arranged a time of festivity and dancing for the whole nation, and created the title Ine Oyenmwen which means 'merriment'.

3. Trade and conflict

For almost a year after the signing of the treaty relations between Benin and the Dutch remained amicable despite the disagreement over credit and prices. The Oba even backed the Company against

---

1 Ref. infra p. 314.

2 cf. P. Verger, *Bahia and the West Coast Trade (1549–1851)*. Ibadan University Press, 1964, p. 5.

3 Egharevba, *A Short History*, pp. 40–1. But cf. infra p. 150 n. 2.

some Portuguese in a dispute that arose in the middle of 1716 over a cable belonging to the Dutch which had been carried off by a Portuguese ship. Both parties were summoned before the Oba who 'appeared very offended and condemned the Portuguese to pay a fine of three slaves, on condition that we, in accordance with the treaty, left the Portuguese free and unhindered. The King insisted upon this condition, and hoped that such an incident would not occur again, for he would not take it so well another time.'[1]

Against another threat to the Company's trade—that mounted by the Ijos—the Oba's protection proved far less effective. Though Europeans had always viewed the Ijos with some trepidation, they had not previously complained of interference from them. At the end of the seventeenth century, however, the Ijos began to hinder European and local traffic on the Benin River. We do not know the precise reasons for this greater aggressiveness, but it may be relevant to observe that riverside villages, such as Arbo, appear to have included a sizeable Ijo population. The movement of trade back to Ughoton, together with the acts of severity visited upon villages in the main river by Benin and the Dutch Company, must have stimulated unrest among the Ijos who saw their prosperity thus threatened. Itsekiris too were looked upon as rivals for the trade of the river, so the Ijos did their best to keep them away. In a letter written to Father Monteleone in 1692, the Olu of Warri complained that 'matters here are in such a state that everyone is suffering to some extent; the reason is that the Ijos are stopping us from going to Benin, and my subjects are unable to cultivate their farms, which is a great hardship'.[2] Nyendael mentioned the Ijos only in passing:[3]

> These Robbers, or Pyrates, live just at the Mouth of the River, and are called the Pyrates of *Usa*. They are very poor, and live only on Robbery; they sail hence to all Parts of this River, and seize all that lights in their way, whether Men, Beasts or Goods: all which they sell to the first that come hither, for Victuals, with which they are not at all provided.

European trade, however, appears to have suffered no direct interference until the Ijos began molesting traffic between the Dutch

---

1 A.R. *Bezittingen*, vol. 83. M. Heyman to E. Robberts, 4 Sept. 1716.
2 A.S.C. *Scritture Riferite*, vol. 3, f. 38.
3 Bosman, *A new and accurate description*, pp. 427–8.

outpost at Arbo and the main factory at Ughoton. Trade goods and produce were carried backwards and forwards by canoe, sometimes in canoes belonging to the Company and manned by its Gold Coast slaves,[1] sometimes in canoes hired from Arbo and Boededoe, for none were available at Ughoton. In March 1716 two of the former returning to Ughoton from Arbo with gum and ivory were attacked by eight large Ijo canoes, all heavily armed with guns. The attack took place about six miles below Ughoton and ended, after a running fight lasting three or four hours, with one of the canoes in charge of a mulatto being overturned in a hand-to-hand struggle. Most of its cargo of 850 pounds of ivory and 750 pounds of gum was lost in the river; the Ijos made off with the remainder and the captive mulatto. Immediately the news reached Ughoton, the factor de Reyke sent the yacht *Commany* in fruitless pursuit of the assailants, and 'threw into chains four of their countrymen who purely by chance happened to be here with a canoe, all of them being chiefs' sons'.[2] He then tried to deal directly with the offending Ijo settlement, threatening to send his prisoners to Elmina unless the mulatto and the goods were returned. The Director-General, on the other hand, took the view that this was a matter for the Oba of Benin, and called upon him to recover the stolen property and punish the offenders, in accordance with the treaty. In fact there was little or nothing the Oba could do, as the Dutch officials on the spot recognised, for they continued to negotiate directly with the Ijos, and by September 1716 had recovered most of the goods. They seized the occasion to urge these freebooters to turn their energies to the collection of gum, and opined that 'it should be easy to become friends with the Loeverse'[3] (another Dutch name for the Ijos); but these expectations were never fulfilled, and the Ijos were to play an important part in driving the Dutch from the Benin River.

News of the Ijo attack, and still more the Oba's refusal to grant a trade monopoly, stimulated the Council of the West India Company to a new line of action. If Benin insisted on trading with all Europeans, the Company should try to ensure that none but its own ships

---

1 These slaves are described in Dutch documents as *Minas* and *Amabas* (probably Anamabus), both Fante peoples.
2 A.R. *Bezittingen*, vol. 82. J. de Reyke to E. Robberts, 19 March 1716.
3 A.R. *Bezittingen*, vol. 83, M. Heyman to E. Robberts, 4 September 1716.

reached Benin. To that end the Director-General was ordered to investigate the feasibility of building one or two forts near the river mouth. Should the terrain prove unsuitable for such constructions, he was to make the factories themselves defensible, equip them with light cannon and arm all the officials, provided the Oba and chiefs gave their consent.[1] A survey of the river from the mouth as far as Boededoe and Ughoton did in fact reveal that it was impossible to build forts which could command the river with their guns; for there was no firm land at the mouth, and a ship, once inside the river, could by-pass any fort through the innumerable creeks.[2] Less material considerations also weighed against such an undertaking. Dutch officials at Ughoton feared that an attempt to secure a monopoly of trade by force would alienate the Oba, and hence redound to the disadvantage of the Company. The Director-General argued that a fort would immediately attract English attention to Benin, whereas that nation—the Company's most formidable competitor—was not then trading in that river.[3] In face of these difficulties and objections the project was abandoned; nor was anything done to fortify the factories—a measure which must inevitably have aroused opposition from the Oba. But in 1721, when English and French competition was undermining Dutch trade, Director-General Willem Butler did in passing revive the idea of fortifying the river mouth, and ordered fresh studies of possible sites.[4]

While the Company thus failed to strengthen its defences in the Benin River, it was equally unsuccessful in its endeavours to lessen the dangers of attack. Besides giving orders for the building of forts, the Council of the West India Company had instructed its Director-General to publish along the whole Guinea coast a proclamation forbidding the sale of guns and powder in the Benin area. They believed that, since firearms had only recently been introduced in quantity by the Company itself, the stock of weapons held by the inhabitants of that region must still be very small, and that the arms

---

1 A.R. *N.W.I.C.* vol. 55. Council of Ten to E. Robberts and Council, 19 October 1716.
2 A.R. *N.W.I.C.* vol. 103, f. 443. Report on the survey of the river carried out in June 1717.
3 ibid. f. 254r. E. Robberts and Council to Council of Ten, 10 June 1717; ibid. f. 366v. E. Robberts and Council to Council of Ten, 4 March 1718.
4 A.R. *Bezittingen*, vol. 88. W. Butler to J. Munnickhoven, 29 November 1721.

traffic might be halted without difficulty. They were wholly mistaken. In the first place, although the Director-General did issue the proclamation, he did not publish it along the coast from fear that it might come to the notice of the English, who might then seize the opportunity to open a trade in firearms with Benin.[1] And if English intervention was a matter of speculation,[2] the Portuguese were already selling large quantities of arms and powder; so while the Oba insisted that they be allowed to trade unmolested, there was no prospect of the Dutch ban having any effect.[3] Such effect as it did have worked to the disadvantage of the Dutch, because it brought them into conflict with the chief of Boededoe. The Oba, who could obtain arms from the Portuguese, made no fuss about the embargo; but the Dutch monopolised trade at Boededoe, with the result that the chief (usually called Anthony in Dutch documents) had to depend on them for the arms and powder used in his constant skirmishing with the well-armed Itsekiris and Ijos. Fortunately for Anthony, the Dutch in turn relied upon him for the canoes that carried their merchandise on the river and loaded their ships. He was therefore able to bargain:

> He refused us his canoes, saying he would not send his people and canoes without gunpowder and expose them to thieves.[4]

That he did not also demand guns presumably meant that he was already well supplied with them.[5] The Dutch chief clerk soon gave way and let Anthony have one barrel of powder, knowing full well that he would not be able to refuse another when it was demanded. In the event, this surrender put an end to the attempted embargo,

---

1 A.R. *N.W.I.C.* vol. 103, f. 254r. E. Robberts and Council to Council of Ten, 10 June 1717.

2 In March 1717 the Dutch factor at Ughoton reported to the Director-General that a Portuguese ship which had entered the Benin River and then passed through the creeks to Warri had had two English first mates aboard. He believed they had been sent to assess trading prospects in Benin and Warri, but both had died at Ode Itsekiri. (A.R. *Bezittingen*, vol. 84.)

3 cf. Bosman's account of the manner in which competition among Europeans had led to massive imports of firearms on the Gold Coast. *A new and accurate description*, pp. 184–5.

4 A.R. *N.W.I.C.* vol. 103, f. 366v. E. Robberts and Council to Council of Ten, 4 March 1718.

5 In January 1717 the Director-General had presented the chief with one of the flintlocks 'of which I understand he is very fond'. (A.R. *Bezittingen*, vol. 84.)

and supplies of guns and powder were soon flowing again—witness the 24 guns and 600 pounds of powder which a Company ship carried to the Benin River towards the end of that same year.[1]

Chief Anthony's victory in the gunpowder dispute had been hastened because, in addition to their normal dependence on him for canoes, the Dutch were at this moment also forced to rely upon him to feed their men at Ughoton. The year of harmony in Benin-Dutch relations following the signature of the treaty had come to an end over the vexed question of gum prices. Michiel Heyman, chief clerk in succession to de Reyke, had arrived at Ughoton with orders to insist on the lower price which the Director-General had laid down for his predecessor, and which the latter had been compelled to disregard. The *fiadors* refused to accept the reduction, arguing that gum had to be brought from the interior by a roundabout route because 'the war with *are de roy* has closed the roads'.[2] Heyman thought the Edo case reasonable, but the Director-General, under orders from his Council, would not budge; he even went further and instructed Heyman either to buy only pieces of gum weighing at least one pound, or else to pay less for smaller pieces.[3] Here was a situation calling for great tact and patience, and Heyman, like many Europeans in West Africa, was not endowed with those qualities, or even with much business ability. Quite apart from failing to settle the quarrel over gum prices, he had, by the time he died of fever in November 1716, antagonised the Edo in his commercial dealings, scandalised them by his debaucheries, and put the Company's affairs into great confusion. When the second official of the factory reported Heyman's death in Benin City, the Oba 'had nothing to say except that he requested me to be pleased to live with his subjects better than the late chief official had done'.[4] Unfortunately Heyman's misdemeanours were not ended with his death because he

---

1 ibid. Cargo list, 3 October 1717.
2 A.R. *Bezittingen*, vol. 83. M. Heyman to E. Robberts, 4 September 1716. This *are de roy* recalls Nyendael's 'King of the Street' (from Portuguese *rey da rua*) who had led the rebellion against the Oba in the sixteen-nineties. (*A New and Accurate Description*, pp. 466–7.) This and later Dutch references to civil war suggest that the chief was continuing his resistance even though Akenzua was in firm control of the kingdom proper.
3 A.R. *Bezittingen*, vol. 84. E. Robberts to M. Heyman, 19 March 1717.
4 ibid. F. Legrand to E. Robberts, 24 March 1717.

left a large legacy of outstanding credit given for gum, redwood and cloth. His successor, Frederick Legrand, reported in March 1717 that 'even now there is still due 28,390 pounds of gum, 1,997 pieces of cloth, and 14,640 pounds of redwood'.[1] The extension of credit trading to gum and redwood—done wholly against instructions—sowed the seeds of much trouble; in the cloth trade he had, on his own initiative, increased the credit from 1,700 to 1,800 cloths. His concessions were especially unfortunate, from the Company's point of view, in that by Benin custom they created an unchallengeable precedent, as Legrand soon discovered: 'I have further been obliged to give the King an increase of 100 cloths because the late clerk had done so.'[2] In an attempt to reduce the extravagant credit given by Heyman, Legrand determined to suspend all trade at Ughoton until outstanding debts had been cleared, and refused to reopen it, as was customary, when the *Vriesland* arrived from Elmina in January 1717. Meanwhile he pursued a thriving business with Arbo where in the space of a few months the Company bought more than 50,000 pounds of gum. Rather surprisingly he also continued trade at Boededoe despite the fact that its inhabitants were among those most indebted to Heyman; 'boys, penniless negroes, and principally the people of Boededoe'[3] were the traders of no standing to whom the deceased factor had rashly given credit. How then can we explain Legrand's inconsistency in permitting trade with Chief Anthony's people? The ever-present canoe problem must be part of the answer. There is also evidence that Anthony was bidding hard to attract the Dutch away from Ughoton. In 1716 he was promising to supply all the redwood they needed—a proposal which was seriously considered on the grounds that buying from the Oba 'causes too much fuss and is detrimental to the Company'[4]. A little later he took advantage of the stoppage at Ughoton to ask Legrand for a staff engraved with his name, 'as a sign that he is

---

1 ibid.
2 ibid. Any expansion of the cloth trade was unwelcome to the Company at a time when demand for Benin cloths had dwindled on the Gold Coast, and attempts to dispose of them in the Netherlands had met with no success.
3 A.R. *Bezittingen*, vol. 85. R. van Naerssen to E. Robberts, 31 December 1717.
4 A.R. *Bezittingen*, vol. 84. Instructions for van Naerssen, art. 13. 3 October 1717.

captain of the Honourable Company here'.[1] Evidently the Dutch were again wondering whether they might not be better off dealing with petty princelings.

The Oba took the suspension of trade calmly enough; so too did the *fiadors*, only a few of whom made any move to clear their outstanding debts. Legrand thereupon concluded that further pressure was called for, and on 9 April 1717 went to Benin City 'to urge the King very strongly that he should press the debtors to make payment'.[2] In his diary Legrand described the interview that took place on Sunday, 11 April:[3]

> Towards evening a fiador and a falador[4] came for me to take me to the King. When I arrived, after the customary exchange of greetings, I informed him of the reasons for my coming: firstly, that his subjects were still heavily in debt and had paid almost nothing; they had still not even settled with their cloths, and this was the reason I had opened no market. Then he asked me whether I could name those who were in debt. I replied, Yes, for I had brought the debt book with me. So he requested me to name them. Then I read out all their names one by one and how much each was in debt. And when I had finished speaking, the King began to ask the fiadors, faladors and mercadors who were present why they had still not paid their debts, considering it was so long since they had received the goods, and asked whether they thought it honest to take from the white men and not pay back. He said that such a thing had never happened before in his lifetime, and at least twenty white men—Dutch and Portuguese—had come there to trade in his time. Thus he was very angry with his people, and thoroughly agreed with me that I should open no market because of the large debt that was still outstanding.

Despite the Oba's exhortations, only a trickle of gum and cloths came into the factory at Ughoton in the fortnight following the interview. Then on 1 May 1717 a messenger arrived to summon

1 ibid. F. Legrand to E. Robberts, 24 March 1717.
2 A.R. *N.W.I.C.* vol. 103. ff. 435r–440v. Diary of F. Legrand, Thursday, 8 April 1717. Appendix V.
3 ibid. All officials in charge of trading posts were required to keep a diary of which a copy had to be submitted to the Director-General and the Council of Ten. The vast majority of these journals have unfortunately perished. Legrand's journal for the period 25 March–25 August 1717 seems to be the only one to have survived from the Benin factory.
4 i.e. an interpreter.

Legrand back to Benin City. This time the Oba opened the audience by asking

> whether I had noticed on the previous occasion how he had gone for the fiadors and mercadors because they had not paid their debts, and whether I would now open a market for him and the *oome grandes*.[1] Whereupon I replied that since he had spoken so sharply to his people I had still seen very few payments; and therefore I would not open the market, but must first have the payments in full. There the matter rested for the time being, and he asked me to stay there the next day, which, after much hesitation, I promised to do.

This conversation reveals how radically the trading system of Benin had changed in the course of a century. The official character of the *fiadors* had been so eroded that the interests of the Oba and the senior chiefs could now be divorced from theirs. Furthermore the Oba was no longer claiming a personal monopoly in any product that figured in trade with the Europeans; he relied instead on rights of pre-emption. This last development can probably be explained by the great increase in the quantity of products traded—especially cloth and ivory—and the correspondingly larger area from which they had to be gathered; it may be doubted whether the palace possessed the resources to maintain trade on a monopoly basis in such circumstances.

When Legrand returned to the palace on the following day the dispute came to a head.

> Today I went again to the King who once more argued that I should open the market and used threats to that end. He said I must realise that I was in his country where he was master. Whereupon I answered that I would not open the market while so much gum, redwood and cloth was still outstanding: indeed, so long as he and the chiefs had not delivered their cloths, I would give no more additional credit, for such were my orders from the Director-General. Whereupon he said that the General knew nothing about it, and that it was all my fault; and he stuck firmly by his old argument, insisting that the market be opened. When I absolutely refused, he became furious and ordered the natives to sell us no goats, yams etc. nor any other provisions. I

---

1 A corruption of the Portuguese *homens grandes*: literally, 'big men', an expression still widely used in Nigeria. Here it seems to denote the principal palace chiefs.

then said that if he was going to behave in this manner it would not be possible for us to remain here, and that by such actions he was clearly breaking the treaty. But he took little notice of this, and thus we parted from each other.

The Oba's subjects at Ughoton punctually obeyed his order not to sell provisions to the Dutch, and it was at this point that Chief Anthony of Boededoe, a frequent visitor to Ughoton, became doubly indispensable. He was quick to seize the opportunity, as Legrand recorded in his diary:[1]

> The Caboceer Baba[2] came and reported to me that the King had sent two passadors to him to tell him that he should give us no canoes to carry letters and goods to Arebo, also that he should not sell us any goats, yams, oil or any other foodstuffs, or allow his dependants to sell them to us. In reply Baba told the passadors that they should say to the King that he could not and would not do such a thing, but that if we needed canoes or provisions he would supply us with them, for it was his firm intention to live on good terms with us. He brought me a goat, yams and oil as a present; and to please this caboceer, on whose friendship the Honourable Company depends, I presented him with a looking-glass.

For six weeks the deadlock continued, with the Dutch factory living on supplies from Boededoe; in return Anthony received his gunpowder. When another vessel entered the river on 27 May 1717, Legrand persisted in his refusal to open trade at Ughoton, and he kept the ship at Boededoe. Towards the end of June, however, he determined to make another attempt to reach an understanding with the Oba with whom he obtained an audience on the 24th of that month. To Legrand's renewed protestations on the subject of debts which had been outstanding for over a year, the Oba answered 'that every day he was urging these people to pay and that he would again send a passador to tell them that they should come and pay'. When Legrand went on to complain of the Oba's refusal to permit the sale of foodstuffs,

---

1 ibid. Monday, 10 May 1717.
2 Another name for Chief Anthony; from the Portuguese *caboceiro*—a chief—and *Baba*, a common Yoruba expression used in addressing an elder. The use of this name lends support to our earlier contention that Boededoe was not an Edo settlement.

He replied that all would be well if the market were open, but since the market was closed he would not permit the sale of provisions. I said to him that we could not remain here if he would not promise to supply us with foodstuffs. After much talking around this point, he told me he would send for the fiadors to let them know that they might again sell to us.[1]

The Oba also promised to send a *passador* (messenger) to enquire into the theft of some iron bars from the storehouse at Ughoton; but in return he expected concessions from Legrand.

Next he sent to enquire whether I would not now open a market considering that two ships had come and no market had been opened. To this I replied that it would be impossible for me to do so before the debts were settled. Then he sent to tell me that I should open the market which I refused to do, saying that I must first have the payments. He appeared angry again at this and insisted that he would have the market opened, but I refused to agree to it.[2]

But on returning to Ughoton the following day, Legrand had second thoughts.

Today I considered the question more carefully, thinking that if the market remains completely closed it might be very harmful to the Honourable Company, for trade might die off entirely. Also the natives might in future lose the incentive to gather gum. Furthermore, if the King receives no goods, we might, after the departure of the ship, find ourselves and the Company's property in great danger of violent attack.[3]

A messenger was accordingly despatched to inform the Oba that trade would be reopened at Ughoton, but not with those who had uncleared debts; three days later the messenger returned with *fiadors* to open the market. The Oba, it must be presumed, had settled his own debts, so that his brokers were again able to trade freely, but many of the *fiadors* were barred.

Legrand had gained little from the tussle which he had abandoned probably more from fear of violence than from alarm over further damage to trade. Those with large amounts of trust outstanding

1 ibid.
2 ibid.
3 ibid. 25 June 1717.

still did not hasten to discharge their debts, and nothing had been achieved in reducing the price of gum or improving its quality. As far as quantity was concerned, the Company's exhortations to its officials and a proclamation forbidding all private trade in gum[1] had had their effect; despite the increasing distances from which it had to be gathered, gum was being brought to the Dutch factories at the rate of around 150,000 pounds a year. Quality, on the other hand, caused the Company concern from the arrival of the first large gum shipment in the Netherlands, when it fetched far less than antici-pated because of impurities and the small size of many pieces.[2] Directions to buy only large, clear pieces ran into the practical objection that any attempt to do so would bring trade to a standstill. Van Naerssen explained to the Director-General that gum had to be carried in headloads weighing 108 pounds from distances of ten to twelve days' journey in the interior. The maximum price the Com-pany would pay for such a load would be goods to the value of 6 *engels* of gold—say six dozen knives and a swig of brandy; from which amount the factor first deducted sufficient to pay a proportion of the cost of customs and presents to the Oba, chiefs, *mercadors* and *fiadors*; so that the bearer might receive no more than five dozen knives for his headload of gum. In these circumstances it would be impossible, van Naerssen argued, to throw out all small pieces: the trade must either continue as it was, or be dropped altogether. Moreover, he feared that, far from improving, the gum supply would deteriorate, because the gatherers had cut trees so deeply that they would need many years to recover.[3]

4. Efforts to diversify trade

Although the Dutch had certainly not anticipated such a rapid deterioration of the gum trade, they had already made efforts to divers-ify their Benin trade by discovering other products of commercial

---

1 A.R. *N.W.I.C.* vol. 103, ff. 254r. E. Robberts and Council to Council of Ten, 10 June 1717. The proclamation had been issued on 12 March 1717, simultaneously with that which prohibited the sale of guns and gunpowder.
2 A.R. *N.W.I.C.* vol. 55. Council of Ten to W. Butler and Council, 30 Novem-ber 1717.
3 A.R. *N.W.I.C.* vol. 104, ff. 236v–237r. W. Butler to Council of Ten, 27 March 1719.

value, and by extending the area of their operations. Europe had apparently forgotten about Benin pepper, for it needed a report from de Reyke to awaken the Company to the fact that 'a tolerable quantity of pepper grows in Benin',[1] and to set in train further enquiries to discover whether it resembled malagetta or East Indian pepper. The Company had little interest in the former, but was ready to buy 'a good quantity' of the pepper should it resemble the latter; Heyman was also instructed to send some pepper plants to be cultivated at Elmina.[2] Besides investigating pepper,

> . . . during his residence in Benin the Under-Clerk shall on all occasions and by every means possible diligently endeavour to discover what else that region produces that might form the basis of trade. To that end a friendly and amiable acquaintance and manner of speaking with the chiefs and other natives will certainly provide him with the best opportunities. . . . Also he should send us a small sample of everything he may find, no matter how unimportant it may appear to him.[3]

In the course of his voyage to Benin, Heyman was also to explore the entrance to the Lagos River with a view to assessing the prospects of trade in that region.

> And should any natives appear in the neighbourhood or near the mouth of the river, the Under-Clerk and the captain shall try to discover from them what are the tributaries of the river, what is their course, also what countries lie on the banks of or near the river, their situation, what they are called, what things they exchange, whether there might be trade there, and whether ships come there to trade: about these things especially they should make enquiries. But they must be careful not to expose themselves lightly to danger or to disembark on land, for fear that they may be seized by the natives.[4]

An exploration of the river proved impossible.

> . . . the river is shut off by heavens-high breakers, and the land is therefore unapproachable. . . . Since I have been here [sc. Benin] I have

---

1 A.R. *Bezittingen*, vol. 82. F. de Reyke to H. Haring, 19 March 1716.
2 A.R. *Bezittingen*, vol. 83. Instructions for Heyman, 10 June 1716, arts. 23–6. The purpose for which the plants were required was not to be revealed: 'Do not let the natives know of this, but inform them they they are being sent solely as a rarity and as specimens.'
3 ibid. art. 28.
4 ibid. art. 36.

been informed that in order to approach there from Rio Formosa one may make one's way behind the island to Rio Lagos: this is a journey of nine or ten days. I am unable to discover whether it would be deep enough for a ship.[1]

However, Heyman was confident that trade could be extended in many directions from Benin, both among the Ijos and Itsekiris to the east, and among the Yorubas and Ijebus to the west, provided that canoes were available. For it was from the regions to the west that great quantities of gum were being brought to Arbo, whose inhabitants were well acquainted with the country as far west as Jaquin—a journey that took eleven days by canoe. In August 1718 van Naerssen was able to send a letter from Benin to the Dutch factory at Whydah by this route through creeks and lagoons; but passing from hand to hand it took 86 days to arrive![2] Such contact as still existed between Benin and its tributary state on the Lagos lagoon probably depended on this same waterway.

Neither Heyman nor his successors managed to explore the creeks linking the Benin River with Itsekiri and Yoruba territory because they were never able to obtain canoes. The Director-General turned down Heyman's request for a canoe on the grounds that the Mina slaves who would have to man it might cause serious trouble with the local inhabitants through their notoriously unruly behaviour.[3] And even had canoes been available, it is likely that Arbo and Boededoe would have resisted the threat to their middleman position which would have resulted from direct Dutch trade with neighbouring territories to the west. As for country to the eastwards, Legrand believed the Dutch would not be popular in Warri because the Portuguese were well established there,[4] while trade among the Ijos would be dangerous 'because there they are all robbers'.

In his search for natural products to augment commerce in the Benin region, Heyman met with meagre success. Only three *fiadors* knew anything about a 'medicinal gum' to which de Reyke had

---

1 ibid. M. Heyman to E. Robberts, 4 September 1716.
2 A.R. *Bezittingen*, vol. 86. J. Eytzen to W. Butler, Whydah, 10 December 1719.
3 A.R. *Bezittingen*, vol. 84. E. Robberts to M. Heyman, 15 January 1717.
4 ibid. F. Legrand to E. Robberts, 24 March 1717. 'Nay there are even a great many Portuguese Christians there.'

called attention,[1] and Heyman did not think it would be possible to gather more than two or three thousand pounds of it in a year; in the end none was ever bought. Vegetable dye-stuffs seemed to offer better commercial prospects—especially a plant resembling indigo which produced a fast blue dye,[2] and a stem and root which when ground yielded a green dye. Both plants grew abundantly in Benin where they were in common use for dyeing locally-woven cloth. His enquiries about pepper convinced Heyman that it resembled 'the oriental kind'. 'This article', he wrote, 'should prove more satisfactory, for when I enquired about it, in the same way as about the gum, they replied that in three months they would fill ten gum barrels.'[3] Though pepper had long fallen out of European trade, it remained a monopoly of the Oba, and Heyman was unable to give any indication of the price that might be charged for this or any other product because the *fiadors* refused to discuss that question until they had received an assurance that the Dutch intended to buy them in bulk. Samples of these various commodities sent to the Netherlands awakened the interest of the Company which in November 1717 ordered that the Edo be encouraged to grow large quantities, with an assurance that whatever they produced would be bought at an agreed price. The Council of Ten further recommended that the factor in Ughoton should try to establish plantations of profitable crops around the factories, so that supply might hang less upon the efforts of local traders. In addition to investigating these crops, the Company made one more effort to find a profitable outlet for Benin cloth—this time in the European market. The factor was to look into the possibility of having the cloths made larger, and send samples to Europe, together with 6,000 pounds of local cotton yarn.[4] Nothing would come of this project because the looms on which Benin cloths were woven could not produce the

---

1 Could this be the 'balme' recommended by Randall Shaw? cf. supra p. 80.
2 Palisot de Beauvois identified the indigo plant used in Benin as *Indigofera endecaphylla*. (*Flore d'Oware de Benin*, vol. II, Paris, 1807, p. 44.) *Lonchocarpus cyanescens* is also used. Ref. J. M. Dalziel, *The Useful Plants of West Tropical Africa*. London, 1937, pp. 248–9.
3 A.R. *Bezittingen*, vol. 83. M. Heyman to E. Robberts, 4 September 1716.
4 A.R. *N.W.I.C.* vol. 55. Council of Ten to W. Butler and Council, 30 November 1717.

broad, long cloth suited to a European market.

In 1717 most of these difficulties and disappointments still lay in the future, and the Director-General believed that trade might be extended to wider areas and new commodities, that differences with the Oba might be smoothed away, provided a man of tact and experience could be found to take charge of the factory. He therefore gladly accepted a proposal from van Naerssen that he should return to Benin, with de Reyke as his assistant. They left Elmina in October 1717 with instructions to search diligently for new commodities, gather gum from as wide an area as possible, and drive away all foreign ships and Dutch interlopers.[1] To the latter end, van Naerssen was to make another attempt to revise the treaty, failing which he was given authority to capture such ships 'with the aid of the natives or as he shall deem most feasible'. In more practical vein, his instructions sanctioned a gum price of 4½ pounds to one pound of ivory instead of the seven pounds on which the Company had vainly insisted for so long.

Arriving at Ughoton on 25 November 1717, van Naerssen found trade and the factory in a sorry state.

> Prospects for trade have changed entirely since two years ago. I find the negroes disposed to put their foot on the necks of the Company's servants when they are in need, and oblige them to fall in entirely with their illegal demands. The factory is not at all of the kind required for the proper protection and housing of the Company's property and servants, nor as had been shown to them previously by the Under-Clerk de Reyke and myself.[2] I found the storehouse almost entirely bare of merchandise, and the books full of unpaid debts . . . also there were no traders at the factory or anywhere near; nor had any been there for several months.[3]

Van Naerssen's vigorous attempts to improve matters met with some initial success. An interview with the Oba, together with gifts of brandy and cowries to influential chiefs, produced workmen who began to rebuild and enlarge the factory. Within six months they had completed a substantial building which he asserted to be

---

1 A.R. *Bezittingen*, vol. 84. Instructions, 3 October 1717.
2 Earlier in the year Legrand reported that a *fiador* had tried to burn down the storehouse, but had been prevented from doing so by other Edo.
3 A.R. *Bezittingen*, vol. 85. R. van Naerssen to W. Butler, 31 December 1717.

the finest on the coast; presumably it was a structure of the traditional mud-wall type, but it had an upper storey which was used as living quarters, and a quantity of locally-made planks and nails were procured at considerable cost for doors, windows and flooring.[1] The credit situation too improved somewhat, and by the end of the year a large amount of gum outstanding to Heyman and Legrand had been delivered. But when van Naerssen insisted on further payments as a condition of opening trade, he ran into trouble with the Oba who once more cut off food supplies to the factory. Like Legrand he had to depend on Chief Anthony for provisions, and was thereby restrained from pressing Boededoe for settlement of the large debt it had incurred with Heyman. Pressure could indeed have yielded nothing, because the quarrel between Chief Anthony and the Oba had for some months made it impossible for the inhabitants of Boededoe to collect gum. The Company's position grew still more precarious when the heat of that dispute caused an explosion. Exasperated by Chief Anthony's defiance and by his latest boycott-wrecking tactics, the Oba found ready agents of revenge in the Ijo bands that had earlier attacked Dutch canoes. At his instigation, they first threatened to seize any Boededoe canoes hired to the Dutch. Although this warning made Anthony reluctant to send his canoes to Arbo, he continued to supply van Naerssen with food. Whereupon, in January 1718, the Ijos launched a direct attack on Boededoe, forcing Chief Anthony and his followers to flee, while the Dutch were left marooned without canoes, provisions or trade.[2]

Not surprisingly van Naerssen decided that the time had come to make Chief Anthony's and his own peace with the Oba. He interceded in Benin City for the fugitive 'with continuous insistence and gifts';[3] so too did many villages which depended on Boededoe for their trade. Meanwhile the chief, who appears to have taken

---

1 Each plank measuring 5 feet by 9 inches cost 100 cowries; each nail 8–10 cowries, plus the cost of the iron.
2 A.R. *Bezittingen*, vol. 85. R. van Naerssen to W. Butler, 7 January 1718 and 20 March 1718. A Dutch ship lying at Boededoe at the time of the attack soon found itself stranded by a sandbank that formed across the entrance to the creek.
3 A.R. *Bezittingen*, vol. 85. R. van Naerssen to W. Butler, 20 March 1718.

refuge in the creeks to the west of his village, was also busy rallying his supporters. He was joined by two Ijebu and two Ijo chiefs who 'had come out to assist Baba and are completely on his side';[1] presumably their support was directed primarily against the Ijos who had attacked Boededoe, not against the Oba. Nevertheless these various pressures and representations did persuade the Oba to make peace with Anthony in March 1718. The chief had first to acknowledge the suzerainty of Benin—an important step towards reasserting that kingdom's badly mauled authority in the river—then he was formally reinstated at Boededoe by a Benin chief who was 'the fourth in rank after the king'.[2] Later the same chief accompanied Anthony to the Dutch factory at Ughoton where, with van Naerssen, they swore 'a solemn treaty between the three of us of mutual friendship and loyalty towards the Honourable Company'.[3] Thus the Dutch too made their peace with Benin, at the price of dropping all conditions for the opening of trade. To complete the pacification van Naerssen visited Chief Anthony and his Ijebu and Ijo allies at Boededoe, and conferred with them on means of keeping the river free of pirates. Anthony showed his appreciation of Dutch support by presenting the Company with two tusks; but the one who had gained most from the show-down was the Oba who had restored at least the semblance of his authority at Boededoe, and compelled van Naerssen to reopen trade at Ughoton.

For a time the air was cleared, and trade prospered to the extent that during 1719 25,000 pounds of ivory were collected at Ughoton and Arbo; a particularly encouraging result when the Company was coming to rely more and more upon ivory as the sheet-anchor of its Benin establishment. Not that the search for other lucrative products had yet been abandoned. Experiments were made with plantations of tail pepper and cardamom under Dutch supervision at Ughoton, Arbo and Boededoe, but none of the pepper seeds

---

1 ibid.
2 ibid. There was no fixed order of precedence among Benin chiefs, it being within the Oba's prerogative to advance and demote individual titles. Therefore it is impossible to identify this particular chief; but he must have been one of the leading title holders.
3 ibid.

germinated, and the cardamom yielded a poor crop[1]. Still more optimistically, the Company decided to investigate rumours that gold was to be found in Benin, and that it might be had cheaply because it was not valued there. None of the informants in the United Provinces and at Elmina knew the location of these supposed gold deposits, so the Director-General sent van Naerssen six Akim slaves specially chosen for their expertise in gold prospecting and digging. It was a shot in the dark, taken because the gold and slave trade of the Company in Guinea had reached such an ebb that proceeds from it barely covered current expenditure; a providential discovery of cheap gold could transform its affairs. Though openly sceptical, van Naerssen made enquiries in Benin City and among merchants who visited the factories. They could tell him nothing; nor did the digging and panning of the Akim slaves reveal the slightest trace of gold until in March 1719 three of them went with some servants of the Oba to an area where the ruler and his council thought gold might be found. This country, according to van Naerssen, lay two days' journey beyond Benin City and was called *Useea*—possibly it was Uzia in Ishan. There with great labour the slaves gathered a minute amount of gold dust, and a further exploratory mission the following year yielded no better result. Dutch hopes were extinguished; the Oba, on the other hand, may have been impressed for, if van Naerssen understood aright, he immediately began to plot a war with the gold-producing country. War did break out in 1720, but it cannot be assumed that the Oba's principal objective was control of Ishan gold; especially since the struggle dragged on for ten years—long after any prospect of finding gold in worthwhile quantities had vanished. However, it is possible that a dispute over gold prospecting may have inflamed an already delicate situation. Van Naerssen makes it clear that in 1719 the Oba had no authority over *Useea*, a place only a few miles distant from his capital, and in earlier reigns subject to Benin. The civil war had evidently undermined Benin power in that direction as it had in the Benin River; indeed the Ishan area appears to have been the stronghold of the rebel chiefs for many years, and possibly of Ozuere's supporters in the succession war. Seen against this background, the

---

1 A.R. *Bezittingen*, vol. 86. J. de Reyke to W. Butler, 16 June 1719. The cardamom seeds were brought from Axim.

war which broke out in 1720 may be presumed to have arisen from larger causes and objectives than the glimmer of gold brought to light by the Dutch.[1]

Van Naerssen's other efforts to diversify trade proved no more successful than his gold prospecting. Samples of cotton yarn satisfied the Company with respect to quality, but the price—one pound of yarn to one pound of cowries, or the value of one Benin cloth—was considered too high. Negotiations with the Oba in person over the price of pepper foundered on the same obstacle.

> He showed me a 20 lb. powder barrel full of peppers still on their stalks, which I claimed he should have plucked off before filling the barrel; provided that were done, I offered him the value of one Benin cloth for it. As far as I could see there could not have been above 5 or 6 lb. in the barrel, so I believe this would have been a good price. He laughed a little at this and said it was all the same whether I offered that or nothing, and that he did not wish to discuss it further.[2]

Though Chief Anthony at once stepped in with an offer to supply pepper, the factor doubted whether he could do so because his supplies would have to come from Benin territory. After further unsuccessful efforts to bring down the price, the Dutch decided not to buy pepper. Thus, despite much striving and ingenuity, van Naerssen and de Reyke had in two years wrought little improvement in the Company's fortunes. The dispute with the Oba had been ended by giving way on almost every point; the difficulties over gum and cloth remained unresolved; the thorny problem of trust had been avoided; trade was restricted to the same regions and the same commodities as in the past.

5. European rivals and Dutch decline

The Dutch reacted to these disappointments and setbacks by abandoning efforts to diversify their Benin trade, and by concentrating upon the purchase of ivory. Gum had so fallen in value on

---

1 This war may have been a renewal of the fighting against *are de roy* which had been in progress in 1716, and then seemingly died down. But we have no information as to the location of that conflict. cf. supra p. 150.

2 A.R. *Bezittingen*, vol. 86. J. de Reyke to W. Butler, 16 June 1719.

the European market that the factor Jacobus Munnickhoven, who relieved de Reyke in December 1719, had instructions to buy only pieces weighing more than two pounds, which meant, in effect, none at all.[1] Cloth he was to avoid as far as possible, because unsaleable stocks were piling up at Elmina. Even prospects in the ivory trade caused some misgiving as the average size of tusks had so decreased that many weighed no more than half a pound. It is easy, therefore, to imagine Munnickhoven's dismay when, on arriving at Boededoe, he found a French ship of twelve guns trading for slaves and ivory, and learned from its captain that he proposed to return the following year to establish a factory. Immediately he took himself to Benin City and begged the Oba to reserve the ivory trade exclusively for the Dutch company, only to meet with the usual reply that the Oba 'was ready to trade with all nations'. Munnickhoven derived some satisfaction from a slave rising aboard the French ship in which one of the officers was killed and all the slaves drowned while attempting to escape; but the vessel was still able to sail for Martinique on 1 February 1720 with a further 160 slaves and 6,000 pounds of ivory.[2] When it returned to Ughoton in March 1721, it carried away only slaves and established no factory, thus relieving the Dutch of their immediate anxiety.[3] Nevertheless, the French intervention had forced up the price of ivory and caused the general quality to deteriorate still further.

From the time they opened their factories in the Benin area in 1715 the Dutch had nursed anxieties over a possible reappearance of their French and English rivals, and had done their best to forestall them either by agreement with the Oba, or by schemes to fortify the river mouth. Their failure in those endeavours and their fears over the effects of competition reflect the general malaise which was undermining the commercial power of the United Provinces. With the ending of the War of the Spanish Succession,

---

1 ibid. Instructions for J. Munnickhoven, 27 November 1719.
2 A.R. *Bezittingen*, vol. 87. J. Munnickhoven to W. Butler, 18 January 1720; *Bezittingen*, vol. 88. J. Munnickhoven to W. Butler, 20 January 1721. In April 1719 a slave rising on board an English sloop in the Benin River had led to the destruction of the vessel.
3 A.R. *Bezittingen*, vol. 89. J. Munnickhoven to W. Butler, 8 September 1721. The French ship, under Captain Aulard, arrived at Ughoton on 9 March 1721 and left on 4 May bound for Martinique with above 100 slaves.

Dutch overseas trade lay exposed to the full force of English and French competition, while increasing numbers of Dutch interlopers —vessels fitted out by private merchants—infringed the legal monopoly of the West India Company on the Guinea coast. Attempts to drive off these rivals met with no more success on other parts of the coast than they did in Benin, with the result that the Company, burdened with the heavy cost of its establishments, could not compete on equal terms, steadily lost ground, and hardly covered its expenses. As a result, the number of ships despatched from the United Provinces to West Africa began to fall sharply, with serious consequences for out-stations as remote as Ughoton; for the number of coastal vessels kept permanently at Elmina was wholly inadequate for maintaining communication with them. Thus it happened that after the *Bonaventura* sailed from the Benin River in January 1720 no other Dutch ship appeared there until the *Africa* dropped anchor in December 1721. For almost two years Munnickhoven, six other Company employees, and twenty of its slaves were entirely isolated from Elmina, except for one letter which the factor wrote on 20 January 1721 and sent overland to Whydah; it did not reach Elmina until 25 October.[1] He wrote in desperation: by the middle of 1720 he had disposed of all his merchandise and could no longer trade; by the end of 1720 he had bartered all his cowries for food, and had been obliged to borrow more from the Oba in order to feed himself and his companions.

> I have asked the King of Benin to lend me a barrel of cowries, and he told me that he could not spare so many, but only about twenty thousand cowries. Your Honour may be pleased to imagine how long such a small quantity is going to last.[2]

As a last resort he tried to sell some of the stock of ivory and cloth, but failed to do so because the Oba and other merchants of Benin would offer him only half the price he had originally paid them for it. As the months of 1721 passed without any sign of relief, the Oba made further loans of cowries to the stranded Dutchmen, and with a

---

1 A.R. *Bezittingen*, vol. 88. J. Munnickhoven to W. Butler, 20 January 1721.
2 ibid. In 1727 a factor stated that it cost 122 pounds of cowries a month to feed the twelve persons then living in the factory. (A.R. *Bezittingen*, vol. 94. J. van der Meer to P. Valckenier, 18 December 1727.)

reasonably good will, so that Munnickhoven afterwards wrote of him: 'I must say that the King of Benin is a good-hearted negro, for he helped me to the last . . .'[1] But he knew that he could not remain indefinitely on this hand-to-mouth basis, so on 8 September 1721 he wrote again to Elmina warning that unless a ship arrived by December, 'we shall be obliged to abandon the factory in Benin and travel overland to Fida; otherwise we must perish here of hunger'.[2] This letter, sent by the overland route, reached Elmina on 7 February 1722, by which time a ship had at last arrived at Ughoton. It came just within the time limit set by Munnickhoven.

On learning of the French slave ship, Director-General Butler had concluded 'that slaves can be bought there without hindrance', and had accordingly resolved to send a ship large enough to carry a substantial slave cargo in addition to the produce accumulated in the factory.[3] He gave Munnickhoven precise directions:[4]

> They must be young and free of all infirmities, and not above 25 to 28 years of age. We have fixed a reasonable price so that you may be able to obtain them quickly: namely, a man at 224 pounds of ivory, and a woman at 160 pounds. You must give the master all the assistance in your power; firstly to obtain as many planks as possible to make beds; next to fill with water all the casks from the brandy, salt and millet; also, in addition to the millet which is in the ship, to obtain as much yam, palm oil etc. as will suffice for the journey here.

He also asked for information: whether Benin could furnish cargoes of between 200 and 250 slaves; how long it would take to supply that number; the price of slaves, and the kind of goods in which it had to be paid; whether sufficient provisions were obtainable for a slave ship; and 'whether the Benin slaves are good or ill-natured, and whether or not they can stand the passage well'.[5]

This sudden awakening of Dutch interest in the Benin slave trade can be explained partly by the flourishing market opened to them by

---

1 A.R. *Bezittingen*, vol. 89. J. Munnickhoven to W. Butler, 2 February 1722.
2 ibid. J. Munnickhoven to W. Butler, 8 September 1721.
3 The ship chosen was the *Africa*, recently arrived from Europe and too large to enter the Benin River. A pinnace ferried goods to and from Ughoton.
4 A.R. *Bezittingen*, vol. 88. W. Butler to J. Munnickhoven, 29 November 1721.
5 ibid.

the return of peace in the Caribbean, and partly by the necessity of fighting off European competition in Benin. The Portuguese had resumed their slave trade in the river about the last decade of the seventeenth century;[1] and at the same time the government of Benin had lifted its long-standing embargo on the sale of male slaves.[2] There can be little doubt that these two developments were connected; and it may well be that they were also related to the outbreak of civil war in Benin, which would have yielded captives whom it would be prudent, as well as profitable, to despatch into permanent exile. The number of slaves bought by the Portuguese was not, however, very large, for they were taken mainly to meet the diminished needs of São Tomé and Príncipe.[3] A proposal to open a direct slave trade from Brazil fell by the wayside.[4] The first Dutch venture in this field—a modest purchase of a dozen slaves in 1714—aroused so little interest at Elmina that the subject was not even raised during the early years of the establishment at Ughoton. But when French and English ships appeared, bought slaves in hundreds, and thereby threatened a radical change in the character of Benin commerce, the West India Company was forced to re-examine its position. Some gentle pressure also developed from the Oba and his military commander, the *Ezomo* Ehennua. The war they began in 1720 was yielding a number of prisoners, the largest share of which went to the ruler and his general, who must have been aware that the sale of only 40 slaves could bring returns as great as that from 10,000 pounds of ivory. Hints were therefore dropped in Dutch ears; on 6 January 1721 a messenger from the Oba informed Munnickhoven that 'his army has routed the viceroy and won much booty in

---

1 cf. supra pp. 128–9.
2 But the right to sell male slaves remained a closely guarded royal prerogative. cf. G. Ockers to P. Valckenier, November 1724: 'no one other than the King may sell male slaves on pain of death'. (*Bezittingen*, vol. 92.) But cf. infra p. 169, n. 2.
3 An undated fragment describing the trade of São Tomé in the first years of the eighteenth century says: 'With these goods [i.e. iron, gunpowder, spirits, cloth] we send to Benin and Calabar to buy negroes who, although less esteemed, are good enough for the purposes of the island; some are also shipped to Brazil where they sell for a lower price than those most highly esteemed, such as the slaves from Ardra.' (A.H.U. *São Tomé, caixa* 3.)
4 cf. supra pp. 119–20.

slaves and ivory'.[1] When the *Africa* arrived, the Oba, confident of imminent and final victory over the 'viceroy', assured the factor that 250–300 slaves, two-thirds of them males, could be supplied within three months. The *Ezomo*, still more confident than his master, offered 300 within two months. 'This captain', remarked Munnickhoven, 'is in a better position to trade than the King himself.'[2]

Neither his instructions nor these promises succeeded in arousing Munnickhoven to enthusiasm over the projected slave trade. He cast doubts on the quality of Benin slaves: 'As far as I have been able to judge, the Benin negroes and slaves are very obstinate when they are sold to whitemen,[3] but once they are on board and out of sight of land, they become very dejected and in too poor health for the voyage.'[4] The French ship, he warned, had lost half its slaves on the voyage to Martinique. Another difficulty, familiar in the sixteenth century, was that provisions could not easily be obtained in Benin, especially in the quantities needed for a transatlantic voyage. His decisive argument, however, was the inability of Benin to supply the slaves quickly. Ships sent from Elmina usually had instructions not to delay more than one month in the river for fear that they might find it impossible to put to sea at the onset of the rainy season when southerly winds made it difficult to cross the bar; should this happen,

---

1 A.R. *Bezittingen*, vol. 88. J. Munnickhoven to W. Butler, 20 January 1721. The reference to the Oba's opponent as the 'viceroy' strengthens the supposition that this war was a continuation or development of the earlier struggle against the *are de roy*. cf. supra p. 164, n. 1.

2 A.R. *Bezittingen*, vol. 89. J. Munnickhoven to W. Butler, 2 February 1722. This is the earliest reference to the greatly enhanced power and prestige of the *Ezomo* which, founded upon his services in war, was to overshadow that of all other Benin chiefs in the eighteenth century. Apparently he had already established his right to share the royal monopoly in the sale of male slaves, as he later enjoyed the otherwise exclusively royal right to possess brass castings in his shrines.

3 Munnickhoven doubtless based his judgement upon what he had learned from the captain of the French slave ship, and upon his knowledge of the recent slave risings aboard French and English vessels. The late eighteenth-century Liverpool slave captain Hugh Crow had a rather different opinion of Benin slaves: 'They are the most orderly and well behaved of all the blacks.' (*Memoirs*, London, 1830, p. 201.) However, Captain Crow had little personal experience of slave-trading in Benin; also it is possible that slaves sold in Benin in his day were of different origin to those sold earlier in the century. The latter are likely to have been war captives taken in the Ishan region.

4 A.R. *Bezittingen*, vol. 89. J. Munnickhoven to W. Butler, 2 Feb. 1722.

the consequent enforced stay of several months could consume all the profit of an otherwise successful voyage. To permit the ship to depart within the stipulated time, the factor was expected to have accumulated a return cargo which could be loaded without delay. But slaves did not fit into such a pattern because Benin could not supply a full cargo in less than two or three months, and it was physically impossible to hold a large number of them at the factory in anticipation of the arrival of a ship. Feeding them, possibly for months on end, would have proved very expensive and put the Company still more in the power of its provisioners; preventing their escape would, as later experience demonstrated, have been impossible. By playing upon the time factor, Munnickhoven was able to send the *Africa* away without any slaves. He explained to the Director-General that, before he could buy slaves or open a general market, he was obliged by custom to await delivery of the Oba's cloths; and by the time that transaction had been completed the *Africa* had already overstayed the permitted month. Several years passed before the West India Company again turned its attention to the slave trade in Benin; meanwhile the Oba and the *Ezomo* were able to dispose of their slaves to the French and English.

In November 1722 a new chief factor, Gerrit Ockers, arrived at Ughoton to replace Munnickhoven. With him came two small vessels and a larger ship which was to anchor off the river and carry away the stocks of gum and redwood that now amounted to 33,539 pounds of the former and 161,082 pounds of the latter.[1] How much was removed and how Ockers fared on his arrival in Benin are not known because the letters which he must have written to Elmina between November 1722 and November 1724 have been lost. His report to the Director-General in the latter month shows that relations with Benin had once more deteriorated badly in face of the Edo refusal to pay higher prices for Dutch goods.

> The natives here so carefully regulated trade at the time the factory was established that it is now impossible to move them to pay more for the merchandise. For if I tell them that the merchandise now costs more, they answer me that it does not concern them, that they agreed to trade on those terms at the time, and that they will now continue to

---

1 A.R. *Bezittingen*, vol. 90. Instructions for Ockers, 10 November 1722.

trade in the same manner. They say too that they would rather do no trade than be forced to abandon their old rights and customs.[1]

Ockers and many other Dutch factors had to admit that the Benin stand was not one of pure unreason, and that the Dutch case for higher prices was weakened by the readiness of their French and English rivals to sell their goods more cheaply. In September 1724, for example, Edo determination to insist on the old prices was stiffened by the arrival at Ughoton of an English ship which began to buy slaves, ivory and redwood at twice the price the Dutch factor was permitted to pay. In other words, Dutch goods were already twice as expensive as those offered by other Europeans. Competition threatened to become still more severe when the English captain told the Oba that he had been sent from the headquarters of the Royal African Company at Cabo Corso to investigate the possibility of setting up an English factory in Benin. This news brought Ockers in haste to Benin City where, in return for a promise from the Oba that no ivory or redwood would be sold to the English ship, he had to agree on a return to the old prices.

Earlier in the year the Dutch had suffered a severe setback when Chief Anthony, 'the only person around Ughoton who has canoes and canoemen',[2] was once more attacked and driven from Boededoe —this time for good. Although Ockers does not identify the attackers, a number of details in his report point to the Ijos. He mentions, for example, that he had lent the chief two half-pounder cannons for his defence, and that these had been lost to the attackers; he also complained that the fighting had made it impossible to trade with Arbo. Had the Oba been openly implicated in the affair, it is almost certain that this would have been reflected in Ockers' reporting of it and in his subsequent actions, e.g. to recover the cannon. Yet it is not unlikely that he had at least countenanced an action which rid him of a trading rival and an insubordinate vassal. The Dutch on the other hand had lost a reliable, if canny, supporter and agent; and the destruction of Boededoe meant the closing of a centre through which had flowed produce from the Yoruba areas to the west as well as from Arbo and the lower Benin River. Restricted henceforth

---

1 A.R. *Bezittingen*, vol. 92. G. Ockers to P. Valckenier, November 1724.
2 ibid.

more closely to Ughoton, they became more subject to pressure from Benin, and had little hope of expanding or diversifying their commerce. As for the loss of Chief Anthony's canoes, demand soon produced a supply in the shape of 'a certain negro named Baba who maintains himself on the water'[1] at Ughoton. From this man— probably the chief of a small Ijo waterside settlement—the Dutch were able to hire canoes. At one time they even contemplated enlisting him in the repair and defence of the factory.[2]

Treaty arrangements with the Oba for the maintenance of the factory had broken down. When Arnauldt Bambergh took it over from Ockers in September 1725, he found the storehouse roofless and 'full of holes and cracks, some of them big enough for a man to walk through'.[3] The personnel living there in a state of semi-permanent drunkenness were hardly in better shape. Nor was trade, thanks to an English and a Portuguese ship doing brisk business at Ughoton, and another Portuguese at Arbo.[4] Because the Oba was occupied with the new yam (*agwe*) festival,[5] Bambergh was unable to do anything towards improving this state of affairs until the end of October when he and Ockers visited Benin City to deliver the presents customarily offered by a new factor. And then, although they were politely received first by the three principal chiefs of the palace and then by the Oba, they failed to make any progress over the vital matter of prices.

---

1 A.R. *Bezittingen*, vol. 97. W. van Essen to J. Pranger, 13 April 1731.
2 ibid. cf. infra pp. 188-9.
3 A.R. *Bezittingen*, vol. 93. A. Bambergh to P. Valckenier, 11 December 1725.
4 The Portuguese ship trading at Arbo foundered with the loss of all the slaves on board when trying to leave the river.
5 The Oba informed Bambergh that this ceremony obliged him to remain secluded for seven days. Landolphe describes the new yam ceremony as one of the three or four main Edo festivals in the eighteenth century. It took place at the time of the yam harvest, and was preceded by several days of fasting. The Oba opened the festival by receiving offerings of new yam, then followed eight days of dancing and celebration. (*Memoires du Capitaine Landolphe, rédigés sur son manuscrit par J. S. Quesné*, 2 vols. Paris, 1823. vol. I, p. 56.)
Either Landolphe or his editor erred in assigning the festival to the months of June and July. Yams are harvested from mid-September to November, so that the *agwe* festival would normally take place in September or October. In 1725 it came as late as the third week of October. cf. infra p. 219.

With all the foreign ships that come here every day, the King and his chiefs are very uppish, and one has to give them what they ask for their goods otherwise they keep them for another ship.[1]

Far from lowering prices, the Oba demanded that the Dutch pay more for Benin cloths. Bambergh resisted successfully on that point, but at the cost of having to agree to continue trade in redwood which the Company was anxious to bring to an end because the wood had lost its value in Europe, and 50,000 pounds of it already lay rotting at Ughoton. The only concession the Oba would make here was that the Dutch need only buy redwood to the value of one cask of cowries,[2] half a cask of neptunes, and half a cask of *plathilios*: in Bambergh's estimation some 20,000 pounds of redwood. As with the obligatory number of cloths, this minimum quantity of redwood had to be purchased from the agents of the Oba and the principal chiefs on the arrival of every ship before other trade might begin. Also by this time it was established that the cloths had to be paid for in cowries. Since the Dutch had little use for either the cloth or the redwood, they looked upon these expenditures (amounting to 732 pounds of cowries for each vessel) as a form of 'customs' payment by which they acquired the right to trade.[3]

Eight months after this unpromising beginning Bambergh died at Ughoton. According to the regulations of the Company, the official next in rank should have assumed command in his place, but that person—one of those whom Bambergh had accused of drunkenness —refused to accept the responsibility, and attempted to pass it to the next in order of seniority. This man, Peter Pistorius, made his consent conditional on the Oba's approval, so he went to Benin to explain the situation in the factory.

Thereupon the King declared that he recognised no other merchant than myself, and he said: My fiadors will make the palaver with you, On the 27 May he again sent for me and proclaimed me merchant here. and I promised to accept. For his part he undertook to settle all the

---

1 A.R. *Bezittingen*, vol. 93. A. Bambergh to P. Valckenier, 11 December 1731.
2 Cowries were packed in casks holding 366 pounds; such a cask was reckoned as the equivalent of 260 Benin cloths. (A.R. *Bezittingen*, vol. 91. J. van der Meer to J. Pranger, 12 November 1729.)
3 Ships continued, of course, to pay the 'customs' proper which had risen very little during the seventeenth century.

debts of the Under-Clerk Bambergh, and gave me his word on this. On the 28th I left for Agathon accompanied by four passadoors in order to inform the gentlemen of the King's wishes.[1]

This is the first recorded instance of the Oba's direct interference in the internal affairs of the factory; and though he intervened at the request of the Dutch, the incident suggests a change in his attitude towards the factory which was matched by a growing sense of insecurity among the Dutchmen living there. The feeling appears to have stemmed ultimately from the knowledge that their strength on the West African coast was fast waning, while that of their rivals grew. The Benin factories, which had always been distant outposts, began to seem dangerously isolated. In the factory at Ughoton, now visited only once a year by the ship from Elmina, the sense of isolation was heightened by the knowledge that the post was virtually defenceless. Factory buildings were no longer kept in a good state of repair; partly through the indifference of the factors, and partly through the reluctance of the Oba to supply labour and materials for repair work unless first given a substantial present. Usable firearms were always in short supply: in December 1727 the factory could muster no more than six good flintlocks. What the Dutch feared was not violence from the Oba or his subjects;[2] apart from brushes with thieves trying to break into the storehouse, they lived peacefully with the Edo. The threat came, they believed, from the Ijos, or rather that hostile group of them which had driven Chief Anthony from Boededoe and subsequently forced the Dutch to abandon Arbo. An attempt by Pistorius to reopen trade in the lower river furnished further proof of their enmity. In 1727 he placed two Dutchmen and four slaves in Arbo, and they succeeded in beating off an Ijo attempt to dislodge them with some loss to their attackers. Soon afterwards, however, one of the Dutchmen was waylaid and killed while travelling by canoe from Arbo to Ughoton,[3] and there were fears that the main factory would be assaulted as soon as the

1 A.R. *Bezittingen*, vol. 94. P. Pistorius to R. Norre, 6 December 1726.
2 The Obas of Benin never took it upon themselves to interfere in the affairs of factories, and to make and unmake factors in the manner familiar in Dahomey.
3 A.R. *Bezittingen*, vol. 94. J. van der Meer to R. Norre, 18 December 1727. 'According to reports he was cut into a thousand pieces and his head was offered to their idol.'

annual ship had left. Thoroughly alarmed, the factor had the Company's slaves throw up an earthen wall around the storehouse, while he wrote to the Director-General asking for seven cannon and fifty flintlocks to arm a larger body of slaves which he wished to buy and train as a defence force.[1] Benin apparently had no forces of its own at hand to defend Ughoton. Though certainly exaggerated, these fears of attack and massacre by river marauders were to persist as long as the Dutch remained at Ughoton.

The Itsekiris too gave the Dutch some anxiety. Attracted by the growth of the slave trade, they were beginning to frequent the lower river again, and occasionally came to do business with the factory at Ughoton. All went well until late in 1726 when a party of Itsekiris killed an African crew member of the ship from Elmina. Pistorius retaliated by clapping in irons an Itsekiri trader who had been in the company of those responsible for the murder. Then the Oba stepped in to demand that the man be handed to him for trial, and threatened, in case of refusal, to stop all trade with the Dutch. 'After some time he sent him back stating that he had found him guilty, but that he would execute no justice on him until he had informed the King of Owerry.'[2] The Dutch factor, however, was convinced that the Oba merely wished to procrastinate until the ship had sailed, when the factor would either have to release the prisoner or face war with the Itsekiris. 'The Oweryze and the Osonze are birds of a feather', he commented.[3]

The most serious consequence of these brushes with the Ijos and Itsekiris was that the Dutch had to abandon Arbo and their trade in the main river, and confine themselves henceforth to such products as could be obtained in or through the Benin kingdom. Unfortunately these were few. They wished to buy only ivory, and moderate quantities of palm oil and soap for consumption or resale within West Africa. Redwood they were determined to eliminate, despite the agreement of 1726; in 1728 the factor accordingly received strict instructions to buy no more. There ensued a struggle of familiar pattern: the factor refused to buy redwood and demanded a higher price for neptunes; the Oba cut off provisions and refused

---

1 ibid.
2 ibid.
3 ibid. Osonze = Ijos.

to sell ivory. After holding out for two months, the factor had to capitulate. Neptunes remained at the old price, and by 1732 70,000 pounds of unwanted redwood lay in store at Ughoton.

Only a few months after the Dutch defeat over redwood, another conflict blew up over some slaves which the Oba insisted they must buy. Since the abortive attempt to open a slave trade in 1721 the West India Company had ignored this branch of commerce, and Benin had not attempted to draw them into it. Yet in 1730 the Oba pressed the factor to buy some prisoners taken in his never-ending civil war,[1] and threatened to stop all trade when the Dutchman tried to refuse.[2] The motives behind the forced sale are difficult to discern. Perhaps the Oba was concerned at a falling off in the slave trade at Ughoton. French vessels rarely came there, and the Portuguese were increasingly gathering their cargoes from Ijos and Itsekiris in the lower river; in the last months of 1730 three Portuguese ships visited Ode Itsekiri, but none went to Benin. On the other hand, English ships were still calling regularly at Ughoton and buying many slaves, 'with the result', the Dutch factor noted, 'that they [sc. the Edo] regard our merchandise with the greatest scorn, apart from the pans and some few other wares'.[3] The Oba too was fond of asserting that he could trade with the English and Portuguese on much better terms than with the Dutch. The most plausible explanation of the incident would therefore seem to be that the Oba faced an immediate and awkward shortage of goods or cowries, and that he had no ivory available for a quick sale.

Once the slaves had been foisted upon him the factor faced the problem of what to do with them. The ship then lying at Ughoton was too heavily laden to carry them, so they had to be put under the guard of the Company's slaves, with the prospect of having to wait a year before they could be despatched. Within a few weeks more than twenty-five had escaped, and though quickly recaptured by the Oba's men, they were not returned to the Dutch; some were

---

1 There is good reason to believe that this was the same war whose end had been predicted as long ago as 1721. cf. supra pp. 168-9. In May 1726, Pistorius was told that the Oba could not attend to him immediately because 'he had still so many palavers to settle in connection with his war'. (A.R. *Bezittingen*, vol. 94. P. Pistorius to R. Norre, 6 December 1726.)

2 A.R. *Bezittingen*, vol. 97. W. van Essen to J. Pranger, 15 April 1731.

3 A.R. *Bezittingen*, vol. 97. W. van Essen to J. Pranger, 15 April 1731.

beheaded, and others sold to English and Portuguese traders. To complicate the situation still further, when the factor tried to punish the guards whose negligence had led to the escape, they too ran away.

> Before I could lay hands on them, eleven men, one woman and an infant took flight and placed themselves under the King's protection. He handed them over to Assema the Captain of War. As soon as I heard of this affair, I immediately had the King informed of it and claimed these slaves in accordance with the third article of the treaty signed between him and the Honourable Company. In reply he sent to say that he would do his best to get hold of them, and that they should be returned to me. I know well enough that these are fine words, for in my opinion this business has been brewing a long time. Therefore it occurred to me that I might recover them with presents, but so far all my endeavours and efforts in this affair have been in vain.[1]

The *Ezomo* appeared to be, in van Essen's eyes, the principal obstacle to the recovery of the slaves.

> His impudent words have plainly shown that he has not the least respect for the Honourable Company. He will no longer give any acknowledgement to their Lordships or their servants, declaring roundly that he can trade much better with the English and Portuguese.[2]

Plainly the *Ezomo* had become a great power in Benin; he enjoyed many privileges otherwise reserved to the Oba alone,[3] and, though Captain of War, could trade freely with Europeans—a privilege strictly denied to those who held similar office in the seventeenth century.[4] It is possible that in this affair of the Company's slaves he had acted on his own initiative, knowing that the Oba, who depended on his military services, could not afford to cross him. But the Oba

---

1 ibid.
2 ibid.
3 cf. supra p. 169 n. 2.
4 cf. Dapper, *Naukeurige Beschrijvinge*, p. 125. '*Want het is den genen, die tot den oorlogh verordent zijn, geheel en al verboden met de blanken te handelen, ja, derven in hunne loosjes niet komen, veel min eenige Europische Waren van hen kopen; maer zijn gehouden dezelve ten dierste van de gemelde Fiadoren en Koopluiden te koopen. In tegendeel vermagh geen Koopman en Fiadoor iet zich onder-winden, 't geen den oorlogh betreft.*'

himself had two years earlier laid claims to a certain degree of juris-diction over these slaves. One of them had killed an Edo and then committed suicide; the Oba had stepped in to claim the property of the dead slave, 'on the grounds that, since the slaves live in his country, they are bound by its customs, so that on their deaths all their goods fall to him'.[1] After much argument, the factor had been obliged to pay the Oba compensation for both the dead men.

Van Essen's attempts to recover the runaways by presents and persuasion did not please his superiors. Director-General Jacob Pranger ordered him to demand that the Oba honour his treaty obligations:

> But in case he makes no satisfactory reply, we order you to tell him in our name and without mincing words, that we shall break up the factory, and, further, that we shall certainly find means of obtaining satisfaction for past wrongs.[2]

The Oba's reply proved satisfactory enough, for he assured van Essen that the slaves would be returned before the ship that had brought the Director-General's message left Ughoton. But for the fulfilment of that promise he referred the factor to his Captain of War who told him that, although he knew the fugitives' whereabouts, recovering them would be a very expensive business. When van Essen subsequently discovered that they were living in one of the *Ezomo*'s villages,[3] he naturally came to the conclusion that he was being hoodwinked, and that the slaves would never be recovered unless the Company was prepared to buy them back. For that reason, and also because he was finding it increasingly difficult to trade against English and Portuguese competition, van Essen recom-mended that the factory be abandoned, and a punitive force sent to Benin. The Director-General and his Council heartily concurred.[4]

---

1 A.R. *Bezittingen*, vol. 94. J. van der Meer to R. Norre, 18 December 1727. The factor had the slave's body 'hung up by the legs' as a warning to others.
2 A.R. *Bezittingen*, vol. 96. J. Pranger to W. van Essen, 24 November 1731.
3 A.R. *Bezittingen*, vol. 98. W. van Essen to J. Pranger, 22 February 1732. The factor was informed that the slaves were living in a village named *Iggie*— probably *igue*, the general name for a bush village.
4 A.R. *N.W.I.C.* vol. 284. J. Pranger and Council to Council of Ten, 14 December 1732.

6. We're here because we're here

Talk of abandoning the factory came soon after a revision of the Company's charter, brought into force in 1730, had abolished its monopoly east of Apa and Badagry. The Director-General fully expected independent Dutch traders to flock in and join the English and Portuguese in undercutting the Company. Even without them, he wrote to the Council of Ten, 'Benin is now in such a deplorable state that the meagre cargoes sent from there no longer cover the cost of our establishment'.[1] To support his argument he pointed to the cargo of 10,000 pounds of ivory brought from Benin in 1731 instead of the anticipated 15,000 pounds. A few years earlier such a quantity would not have been considered unsatisfactory, but with only one ship making the Benin voyage each year larger cargoes were needed to meet the running costs of the factory. Manifestly the Company was in no shape to carry out its threat of an expedition 'to bring this tyrant to reason', but Director-General Pranger was not deterred from presenting the Oba with an ultimatum which he fully anticipated would be rejected. Van Essen was to demand full satisfaction for the damage done to the Company by the Edo—presumably a reference to the *Ezomo*'s hand in the affair of the fugitive slaves—and a revision of the treaty releasing the Company from its obligation to buy gum and redwood, and to send at least two ships each year. In face of a refusal to comply with all or any of these conditions, the factor was to put all the Company's servants and property in the ship and return to Elmina; 'but not before you have first given the King to understand that the Company will assuredly find means in its own time to revenge past insults and breaches of faith'.[2]

If van Essen may be believed, he delivered this stern message word for word and received a surprisingly conciliatory reply.[3] The Oba, he reported, had promised to do everything in his power towards recovering the slaves, and had meanwhile, as an earnest of good intentions, taken in hand the repair of the storehouse at Ughoton. Even the *Ezomo* had given assurances that the slaves should be returned within a month, and was preparing an armed

---

1 ibid.
2 A.R. *Bezittingen*, vol. 98. J. Pranger to W. van Essen, 4 November 1732.
3 A.R. *Bezittingen*, vol. 99. W. van Essen to J. Pranger, 3 March 1733.

expedition to round them up. Such undertakings might well have been given since it was not to the advantage of Benin that the Dutch should cease trading. On the other hand one may doubt whether van Essen ever made any determined effort to carry out his instructions. He did not raise the question of gum and redwood, and justified his silence on the grounds that the Company's obligations had been tacitly abrogated, neither commodity having been purchased for the past four years. And he did not, in the end, recover any of the slaves. His failure in these circumstances to abandon the factory he attributed to a lack of slaves for the work of dismantling it, and to the impossibility of doing it with hired local labour. Constant ill-health, which led to his death at Ughoton on 5 December 1733, doubtless contributed to van Essen's lack of energy and irresolution. These also owed much to his extreme inefficiency and the entanglements of illicit trading. An investigation after his death revealed that he had kept neither the proper account books nor the journal required by Company regulations; a poor disciplinarian, he had lost all control of his Gold Coast servants.[1] His mulatto concubine, Anna Maria of Accra, had been the effective manager of the Company's slaves and trade. His fellow officials were also deeply involved in illicit trade, as indeed were most of the Company's servants on the Guinea coast. Falling in with a practice whereby factors in the out-stations received credit from senior officials at Elmina to trade on their behalf, van Essen had arrived at Ughoton already in debt to a certain Jan Elet, which debt he had promised to discharge by sending Elet ivory and beads. On top of this Elet had given him a quantity of knives and salt for sale in Benin; but the salt proved unsaleable because 'a lot of salt comes here from Ommega'.[2] Being unable to deliver any ivory or beads, van Essen had done no more than send Elet a present of Benin soap, a long list of saleable goods, many promises for the future, and a suggestion

---

1 A.R. *Bezittingen*, vol. 100. A. van Pothoven to J. Pranger, 24 February 1734. ibid. P. Pieter to J. Pranger, 20 February 1734. ibid. W. Hoog to J. Pranger, 20 May 1734. These are all letters written to acquaint the Director-General with van Essen's death and the state of affairs at Ughoton.

2 A.R. *N.W.I.C.* vol. 113, f. 468r-v. W. van Essen to J. Elet, 15 April 1731; f. 513r-v. A. van Pothoven to J. Elet, 24 February 1734. *Ommega* may be Omakou. Hoog noted that much salt came to Benin from *Coeramis*, i.e. Curamo—the Lagos lagoon area.

that he might buy some slaves. Considerable ability would have been needed at the best of times to handle these undercover trans-actions; combined with the confusion that reigned in official busi-ness, they overwhelmed van Essen and probably contributed to his decision to remain in Benin rather than face the upheaval and probings that would have come with departure.

The factor's death created a situation similar to that which had arisen in 1726. Following that precedent, his subordinates informed the Oba who at once sent two messengers and an interpreter to Ughoton. These emissaries not only gave formal recognition to the next senior official, as on the previous occasion, but also proceeded to count the neptunes in the storehouse. None of the Dutchmen present contested their right to do this, and the reasons for their action were not explained in any of the letters written to the Director-General. Possibly the Oba knew of the disorder in the late factor's accounts and the general indiscipline that prevailed in the factory, and intended by taking an inventory to safeguard the Company's property. There is certainly nothing to show that he was exploiting the situation to his own advantage, and yet a precedent had been set for further intervention in the affairs of the factory.

When Willem Hoog, the replacement for van Essen, reached Ughoton in April 1734, he found the Company's trade and buildings in a state of dissolution, and the two surviving Dutchmen critically ill. In the absence of account books, he had to accept a statement from the dead factor's concubine as a basis for collecting outstanding debts.[1] But these debts were of small significance compared with the great issue of the lost slaves whom his instructions urged him to pursue with the utmost vigour, and to deliver no presents to the Oba nor open any trade until they were returned. Probably the Oba felt uneasily aware that he had not heard the last of the slaves, for he sent two *fiadors* with horses to escort Hoog on his first visit to Benin City[2] and welcomed him warmly at the palace. When the inevitable

---

1 A.R. *Bezittingen*, vol. 100. W. Hoog to J. Pranger, 20 May 1734. The mulatto woman later went to Apa with some slaves and other property of van Essen. There she was seized with all her goods and imprisoned in Elmina castle as security for van Essen's debts to the Company.

2 This is the first reference to a European riding to Benin City since D.R. (cf. supra p. 85.) In 1778 Landolphe was offered the choice between a hammock and a horse; he chose the former.

question arose, the Oba asserted that the slaves had 'fled to his enemy'.[1] Hoog countered with the claim that in the absence of its own slaves the Company was incurring impossibly heavy charges on hired labourers, and suggested that the Oba supply him with free labour until his own slaves were returned. But the Oba refused to admit any responsibility or blame for loss of the slaves, and consequently denied any obligation to replace them. Deadlock and a prolonged cessation of trade might have followed but for the arrival of an English barque and barquentine trading for slaves and ivory. In order to keep the vital ivory trade out of rival hands, Hoog was forced to deliver the presents, and even consider increasing them. In return he secured an order to Benin merchants that they should clear their debts and sell all their ivory to the Dutch, for the factor confessed frankly to the Oba that he could not compete with the English in an open market. As for the slaves, he had to rest content with vague and obviously empty promises of further efforts to recapture them.

Before long Hoog was foundering in the same difficulties as his predecessor: he too was burdened with unsuccessful illicit enterprise as an agent of the undaunted Elet;[2] he made little progress in recovering trust given by van Essen; his official trade languished, and he found that, contrary to assurances, ivory was being sold to the English. When he protested against what he regarded as a breach of the bargain lately concluded, the Oba explained that although he could order his subjects to offer their ivory to the Dutch, he could not oblige them to sell it unless Hoog could give goods and prices that compared with those of the English; and this, he maintained, Hoog had failed to do.[3] How the factor coped with the situation is not known, because before he was able to make another report to Elmina he fell victim in dramatic fashion to its frustrations. On 30 December 1734, the Dutch chief factor at Apa wrote to the Director-General:

I understand from a chief of the Benin River that Commandant Hoog

---

1 A.R. *Bezittingen*, vol. 100. W. Hoog to J. Pranger, 20 May 1734.
2 A.R. *N.W.I.C.* vol. 113, f. 520r-v. W. Hoog to J. Elet, 19 May 1734.
3 Among the goods demanded by the Edo, but not available in the Dutch factory, were red and yellow perpetuanas, round red pipe-coral, large neptunes, light silks and beads.

has been made prisoner in Benin. The reason would seem to be that he went to the King in Great Benin to collect some debts, and when in the presence of the King some dispute arose, he pulled out a pistol intending, it is said, to shoot the King. But he failed to do that, and instead shot down one of the most important chiefs. So they have seized him and put him in irons.[1]

Hoog's death appears in the Company records under the date 18 January 1735 without any indication of the manner in which he died;[2] a letter from the man who eventually replaced him implies that he met a violent end.[3]

The extraordinary fate of its Benin factor fell upon the West India Company in a crucial year when it lost the remnant of its West African monopoly. Two years earlier the Dahomians had driven it from the important slave market at Jaquin.[4] Faced with this steady reversal of fortune, the Company had resolved to decentralise its organisation by creating an autonomous trading area that extended from Apa to Benin; beginning in 1735 all its operations within that zone came under the control of the chief factor at Apa, Hendrik Hertog, who answered for them to the Director-General. Had trade been flourishing, such a measure might have proved workable and beneficial; in a period of decline it merely lessened the attention given to the needs of the Benin establishment. Hertog, himself starved of men and supplies at Apa, could spare no one to replace Hoog,[5] and the Director-General now felt no direct responsibility for the distant out-station. Thus almost two years passed before a new chief factor arrived in Ughoton. In the middle of 1735, however, Hertog did manage to despatch a small vessel with a few trade goods for the two Dutchmen marooned there. The instructions sent with these goods stressed the need to reach a new understanding with the Oba.

Neither side could pretend that the 1715 treaty had been a success: few of its provisions had ever been observed; disputes had repeatedly

---

1 A.R. *N.W.I.C.* vol. 284. Director-General Overbeke and Council to Council of Ten, 7 May 1735.
2 A.R. *N.W.I.C.* vol. 110, f. 874. *Lyste der overleedene Bediendens.*
3 A.R. *Bezittingen*, vol. 102. A. Raems to H. Hertog, 8 December 1736.
4 cf. Ryder, 'Re-establishment of Portuguese factories', p. 165.
5 A.R. *N.W.I.C.* vol. 284. H. Hertog to the Amsterdam Chamber, 29 August 1735. In this letter Hertog requests men for service in the Benin factory.

brought trade to a standstill and roused tempers—finally to the point of murder. As most of the quarrels had arisen over debts incurred by Benin traders, the Company's officials believed that a fundamental cause of conflict might be removed by ending the system of credit trading, and an agreement to this effect formed one of the principal points of a new treaty signed in Benin City on 1 June 1735.[1] The slate was first to be wiped clean by a discharge of all debts contracted with the late Hoog—longer-standing debts, one assumes, were tacitly written off along with the fugitive slaves. Once Hoog's trust had been accounted for, van Marken—the senior of the two Dutchmen at Ughoton—promised to unload the boat sent from Apa, pay the old customs and reopen trade, on the understanding that for the future all transactions should be on a non-credit basis. Other clauses dealt with the number of ships the Dutch were to send to Benin. Experience had shown that it was neither possible nor profitable to send the two per annum promised in 1715; moreover the recent reorganisation of the Company made it likely that in future the Ughoton factory would have to rely mainly upon small boats sent from Apa through the creeks, rather than on sea-going vessels. The Oba accordingly agreed that five or six small boats might come each year by the inland route, and that in the event of one boat making several such trips it should be liable to pay the customs only once in a year. Both parties recognised that Dutch trade would continue on a much smaller scale than that envisaged in 1715, so in order to safeguard the Oba and *fiadors* against loss, they were to be informed immediately on the arrival of any vessel, and given first option on its cargo. A guarantee of mutual support in the event of hostile acts against either party was presumably intended above all to secure the Dutch from Ijo aggression. The contentious trade in gum and redwood was suspended pending further orders from Elmina or Apa. In the absence of any reference to the equally vexed question of cloths, we may suppose that the Oba had insisted on retaining his existing privileges in respect of that commodity: subsequent references to cloths owed by the Oba and *fiadors* and to cloth shipments appear to confirm this supposition. The treaty was signed for the Company by Jan van Marken; on the Benin side the

1 A.R. *N.W.I.C.* vol. 488, ff. 157r–158r. Text of the treaty.

Oba's mark was followed by those of the *Ezomo, Uwangue, Osodin, Eribo,* 'Bassanje' (*Obasoyen?*), 'Uninne' (*Ine?*) and 'Pewde de reo'.[1]

Though the treaty had stipulated that the Company should staff the factory within three months with an adequate complement of officials, a year passed before Hertog managed to send a new factor. The delay arose partly from shortage of personnel, and partly from his preoccupation with the transfer of his headquarters from Apa to Badagry in the early months of 1736. But at length, on 4 June 1736, the *Elmina Galley* left Badagry bound for Benin with a chief factor, Abram Raems, and presents for the Oba, his principal chiefs and the Olu of the Itsekiris.[2] After a severe battering from storms which spoiled some of the cargo and at one time drove the ship back to Jaquin, Raems arrived in the Benin River on 24 June. His first impressions of the factory were inauspicious:

> When I reached the warehouse I found it buried in fetishes and other filth, and the walls fallen down in so many places that there were more than twenty-five exits and entrances. It reminded me of Jerusalem laid waste. The door was in pieces, so when the time came to close it in the evening, the loose planks were just propped against the opening. But truly, Your Honour, if the decrepit condition of the outside made me unhappy, I had still more reason to be so when I came to the living quarters and found the staircase broken, so that I could not get upstairs except with the help of the negroes. Having got upstairs, I confess in all sincerity that I nearly lost all heart, for the ceiling threatened to fall on my head, the walls were so black that the room resembled a ship's galley rather than a living room, and they were covered with dirt instead of whitewash—looking more like a pigsty than a human dwelling. As for the floor, it seemed to me that no broom had touched it for the past year.[3]

He was further disheartened to find that only one fellow-countryman remained alive, and that provisions were unobtainable at Ughoton; to find yams for the ship Raems had to send as far afield as Arbo. Added to the knowledge of his predecessor's fate, this depressing

1 The text of the treaty describes all these chiefs as *hommes grandes*. The titles of *Obasoyen* and *Ine* were both created by Akenzua I. 'Pewde de reo' bears no recognisable resemblance to any Edo title, but by analogy with earlier European references to 'street kings' (*re da rua*) it might be a town title.
2 A.R. *Bezittingen*, vol. 102. H. Hertog to M. F. de Bordes, 18 October 1736.
3 ibid. A. Raems to H. Hertog, 22 October 1736.

introduction to life in Benin helped to turn him into a jittery melancholic.

Dutch trading prospects offered little cheer. Hopes of establishing friendly relations with the Itsekiris and persuading them to resume trade at Ughoton foundered when Raems discovered that the ruler of Warri had recently fought against Benin and then been driven out of his country by his own subjects, who 'are his greatest enemies and have forsaken him, and will never at any time allow him to return there'.[1] The disgrace of the Olu, for whom Raems had brought presents, had not, however, put an end to hostilities between Benin and Warri, and the factor found that no Itsekiri would venture into the Benin River, much less to Ughoton to sell ivory. The present intended for the Olu went instead to the *Ezomo*, on whose pre-eminent authority Raems set great store. His first visit to Benin City began with a call upon the war captain.

> Following the old custom[2] I went first to the Captain of War where I was received with the utmost politeness, and he promised to help me in everything in which I might have need of him. ... This Captain has great authority here and does most of the governing of the kingdom.[3]

In particular, Raems hoped that something would come of the *Ezomo*'s promise to use his influence to end hostilities with Warri. The handsome reception concluded, the *Ezomo*'s servants took the factor to a house set apart for European merchants. His account of his audience with the Oba on the following morning is worth repeating because Raems had an eye for detail and a facility of pen not found in his predecessors.

> Arriving at the palace, I found some mats laid on the ground a few paces from the place where the throne stands. The interpreters told me to sit down on them, but I refused and called for a chair, which I

---

1 A.R. *Bezittingen*, vol. 102. A. Raems to H. Hertog, 22 October 1736. The Edo-Itsekiri war mentioned by Raems must have been fought late in 1735 or early 1736, and it is likely that the fugitive Olu was the one who ascended the throne c. 1733 and abandoned the strongly pro-Christian policy of his predecessor. cf. Ryder, 'Missionary activity in the Kingdom of Warri', pp. 19–20.

2 In fact the custom had been established barely ten years.

3 A.R. *Bezittingen*, vol. 102. A. Raems to H. Hertog, 22 October 1736.

had expressly brought for that purpose, to be put there, and I sat on that ... in a little while the King came and sat on his so-called throne, and after he had received the usual compliments from all his chief courtiers, the interpreters approached the *homme grandes* to inform them of my arrival. They in turn repeated this to the King, who thereupon had someone ask me what I had to say.[1] I answered that I had been sent by Your Honour and had brought a valuable present for the King, but had been ordered by Your Honour not to deliver it before I had spoken to him personally ... I did this to get rid of the mistrust of Europeans caused by the affair with Under-Clerk Hoog, for since that time no white man can boast of ever having seen the King, much less of having spoken to him. Whereupon the King had someone tell me that on that day his fetish did not allow him to let a white man come so near him, but that he would send for me again. Then he rose and left. When I also rose to leave, I was surrounded by all the *homme grandes* who came to tell me in His Majesty's name that I should not go before I had taken a meal with them, which the King had prepared for me. They led me to another room where I was grandly entertained after their manner.[2]

Such hospitality may have been customary, although no other Dutch factor mentions it. Raems certainly believed that he was being shown special favour; some years later he asserted that the Oba had also made him an *homme grande*—possibly referring to honorary membership of the *Iwebo* palace association.[3] The Oba's affability continued the next day when he received the present from Raems, shook him by the hand, and assured him of help and favour; he also made a return for the Dutch present with a cow and an ounce of *conte de terre*.[4] On another occasion the factor witnessed a parade of the Oba's wives, which pleased him far more than the spectacle of

---

1 This reversion to the practice followed in royal audiences during the seventeenth century may have been inspired by Hoog's attack upon the Oba. It was relaxed on the following day, as Raems himself relates.

2 A.R. *Bezittingen*, vol. 102. A. Raems to H. Hertog, 22 October 1736.

3 According to Chief Egharevba (*A Short History*, p. 79), all Europeans were regarded as members of this society which had special responsibilities for trade.

4 Presumably a corruption of the Portuguese *conta da terra*—country beads or local beads: and perhaps the beads known as *coris* in previous centuries. Raems commented sarcastically on the Oba's gift, 'a costly return indeed for so considerable a present, and one which shows clearly the generosity of his Black Majesty'.

the ceremonies performed for the Oba's father (*ugie-erhoba*).[1] Of the latter he gave an uncharacteristically brief account:

> It was indeed a bloody festival for as many as twenty negroes were beheaded and thrown into a very deep pit as sacrifices to the spirit of the deceased.[2]

Once settled at Ughoton Raems contrived to do a fair trade in ivory, sending it by the creek route to Badagry. But it was not long before other matters claimed his attention. In September 1736 an English sloop, forced back into the river by contrary winds, was attacked by night and all the crew killed, save for one man who happened to be ashore. The attackers plundered the ship, then sank it. Incidents of this kind had happened before and Raems' superiors at Elmina and Badagry were not inclined to take any tragic view of it, on the grounds that it was likely to frighten off the English and did no harm to the Dutch.[3] Raems howevei was badly shaken and determined to discover the 'damned rascals' who had done 'this evil deed'. He began to collect information from his own servants and a few confidants among the people of Ughoton—evidence which the Director-General later dismissed as 'the sayings of boys against boys, and therefore not worth a penny'.[4] Some blamed the Ijos who had earlier harassed the Dutch; others hinted that the culprit was that 'Baba of Ughoton' on whom they relied for canoes, and who was believed to have destroyed a Portuguese vessel in similar circumstances some seven years previously.[5] Raems inclined to the latter view which seemed to confirm a distrust of this chieftain already conceived on other grounds. When he arrived at Ughoton, Raems had given him and his son a number of presents in order

---

1 cf. Bradbury, *The Benin Kingdom*, p. 55.
2 Mr. Graham Connah has excavated in Benin City a well-shaft fifty-eight feet deep, at the bottom of which lay 'a solid mass of human bones, comprising about thirty individuals who had been thrown in at sometime'. Later examination of the remains revealed that the victims were all young females. The manner of their execution must have resembled that witnessed by Raems. Ref. G. Connah, 'Archaeological Research in Benin City 1961–1964'. *Journal of the Historical Society of Nigeria*, vol. II, no. 4, 1963.
3 A.R. *Bezittingen*, vol. 102. M. F. de Bordes to H. Hertog, 22 January 1737.
4 ibid.
5 These reports strengthen the supposition that this Baba was an Ijo. cf. supra p. 172.

that his canoes might be available to the factory; in addition Baba had received a roll of tobacco which the Director-General wished to exchange for 'fine straw cloths'[1]—presumably a stroke of private trade—some gunpowder and two matchlocks, all of which he had promised to pay for with ivory. When the ivory failed to come in, Raems had refused him further credit.[2]

Still not satisfied that he had got to the bottom of the matter, Raems pursued his enquiries still further and at last concluded that the Oba and the mulatto first mate of the ship which brought him to Ughoton had been accomplices in the attack. The first mate, he believed, had supplied the powder and shot on condition that he should share in the booty and that the lives of the crew be spared.[3] His suspicions against the Oba rested on a story that he had ordered Baba to kill two sailors who had survived the attack and whom the chief had taken into his compound, lest they should one day reveal the plot. Little credence can be given to these charges. So far as is known, no Oba had ever in the past countenanced violence against European traders, and it is impossible to understand why he should instigate an outrage that could only deter English ships from coming to Benin when previously he had done everything to encourage their trade. Raems' belief in the Oba's complicity can probably be explained on grounds similar to those that had led him to a conviction of Baba's guilt. In the letter to Hertog revealing his suspicions, he cited the attack on the English ship as an illustration of the Oba's determination 'to rob and steal everything he can': and by this he meant, 'I find it impossible to obtain payment for what he has bought from me.'[4] A large number of cloths were in fact outstanding from the Oba, the *Ezomo* and other chiefs, yet at the same time Raems claimed to have accumulated a fine store of ivory and was

---

1 A cloth woven from vegetable fibre, and probably that described by James Welsh in 1591 as 'cloth made of the barke of palme trees'. cf. supra p. 84 and infra p. 207.

2 A.R. *Bezittingen*, vol. 102. A. Raems to H. Hertog, 8 December 1736.

3 It is not inconceivable that the Dutch Company incited the attack, considering its eagerness to eliminate its European competitors and the tenor of the instructions given to van Naerssen in 1717. cf. supra p. 160. Certainly Elmina made every effort to discourage Raems from investigating the affair.

4 A.R. *Bezittingen*, vol. 102. A. Raems to H. Hertog, 8 December 1736. It may be significant that Raems also levied charges of stealing against the first mate.

able to send a fair cargo of ivory and cloths to Badagry in December 1736.[1] We must conclude either that these allegations formed part of an elaborate plan to secure his recall from Benin, or—which on all the evidence is more likely—he was suffering from a nervous breakdown. Eventually the mental stresses under which he laboured overwhelmed him, and at the end of 1737 he fled from Ughoton on an English ship accompanied by his one surviving assistant. They went first to São Tomé, then by another English ship to Cabo Corso, and so to Elmina where they were immediately placed under arrest for deserting their post.[2]

Raems gave his own version of the events leading to his flight in a report to the Director-General soon after his arrival at Elmina, and in a letter to the Council of the Company written following his release from imprisonment two years later.[3] Both letters tell substantially the same story, but they differ very considerably from the version which Hertog pieced together from his own officials, the Oba and Benin River traders who visited Badagry. According to Raems his misfortunes stemmed from the failure of Hertog to supply him with the goods promised the Oba and chiefs of Benin. He had been able to take very little with him in June 1736, so Hertog had promised to send further supplies by the first available English, French or Portuguese ship. When these goods failed to arrive, the Benin traders had laid the blame on him.

> Every day I had to bear the reproaches of the negroes asking, What had I come there to do? and saying that I had deceived them, and that it would be better for them if control of Benin had remained with the Director-General, for then they had been sent at least one ship every year.

---

1 A.R. *N.W.I.C.* vol. 488, f. 216. The cargo manifest of the *Elimina Galley* showed 426 pieces of ivory weighing 5,200 pounds. When checked at Elmina there proved to be 203 pieces weighing 4,952 pounds. The vessel also carried 1,798 cloths in 25 bales.

2 A.R. *Bezittingen*, vol. 103. H. Hertog to M. F. de Bordes, 10 January 1738 and 20 April 1738; ibid. M. F. de Bordes to H. Hertog 9 January 1738. *Bezittingen*, vol. 8. Minutes of a meeting of the Director-General's Council held on 6 March 1738 to consider the desertion of Raems and a similar case at Epe. *N.W.I.C.* vol. 111, ff. 346r–354r. H. Hertog to Council of Ten, 10 January 1738.

3 A.R. *Bezittingen*, vol. 103. A. Raems to M. F. de Bordes, 9 January 1738; *N.W.I.C.* vol. 113, ff. 971r–978r. A. Raems to Council of Ten, 10 June 1741.

Others accused him of coming to prepare for a Dutch attack on Benin—

> because they had heard that by this means the Honourable Company had become master of several lands; also they had heard that Heer Hertog had fought with many kings. . . . Imagine how I felt to hear such things, living in a place that was without the slightest means of defence, and in a house that could be set alight by a tobacco pipe!

His position had, he claimed, become still more unendurable when the time came to pay the 'annual customs' to the Oba, and he had been unable either to deliver them or to open a market.[1] *Fiadors* and interpreters had repeatedly demanded an explanation, and the Oba had finally applied the usual sanction of forbidding all dealings with the factory. For a time Raems had been able to circumvent this embargo, thanks to a friendly Edo who had secretly supplied him with maize and yams, but at length this was brought to light and the man summoned before the Oba, who confiscated all his slaves and goods. Guards were then placed on all approaches to the factory to make the blockade effective.

Only when this point of crisis had been reached did Raems, according to his own account, attempt to approach the Oba directly; even then he sent his assistant to Benin City rather than go there himself. In the capital the assistant was told that if the Dutch did not intend to trade it would be better for them to leave, and that the Edo were thinking of driving them out of the factory in order to hand it over to the English who had recently sent two ships to Benin. On the return journey to Ughoton, the assistant encountered other scaremongers who warned to be on guard because the Ijos intended to plunder the factory and kill the two remaining Dutchmen (three had died in the course of the year) as soon as an English ship then lying at Ughoton had sailed. Five large Ijo canoes were alleged to be prepared for the attack. In his later account Raems did not mention the assistant's visit to Benin City or the Ijo menace, but he lent a new touch of drama to his decision to flee. Late one night the man who had supplied them with food knocked at the door,

---

1 This is the first reference to an annual payment of customs to the Oba in addition to the presents given by a chief factor on arrival and the customs paid by each ship. Raems may be referring to the payment for small boats stipulated in the 1735 treaty.

which gave us no little fright as it seemed our last hour had come. But hearing it was he, I let him in very quietly, whereupon he fell on his knees before me begging me, if I valued my life, to leave with the English ship, for he was perfectly certain that as soon as the ship had left they would settle accounts with us. So I was forced to flee head-long, leaving behind everything in the factory, both my own property as well as a few goods belonging to Heer Hertog.

Hertog, on whom Raems attempted to lay ultimate responsibility for the disaster, put forward a very different version of events. He first heard of the flight from messengers whom the Oba despatched to Badagry at the end of November 1737. Immediately he sent a canoe to Ughoton with two men who found the factory in a deplorable condition, but not plundered; on the contrary, the Company's property was still intact under the care of one of Hertog's slaves, who had gone to Benin with Raems, and two men placed there by the Oba. Allegations of an imminent Ijo attack, and of a Benin plot to deliver the factory to the English, can therefore be dismissed as products of Raems' imagination. After making an inventory of the goods and equipment in the factory, the two Dutchmen visited a new Oba who had ascended the throne a few months earlier.[1] The ruler, the *Ezomo* and the other chiefs all maintained that although Raems' departure had taken them by surprise, it appeared to have been carefully planned. The factor had told them that he intended going aboard the English ship for a day or two and offered to do business for them; the Oba and *Ezomo* had accordingly given him eight slaves to barter, and now complained that they had received nothing in return. They also reported that under cover of night Raems had had most of the ivory and merchandise in the factory carried on board the English ship. In support of their story, the inventory showed a large quantity of ivory to be missing; Raems could have taken it with him, sold it to the English and secreted the proceeds; alternatively, the Edo may have been covering up a certain amount of looting, or failure to pay their debts. When they went on to claim that they had delivered to Raems all the outstanding cloths—although none were found in the factory—there must be a

---

1 Probably the Oba Eresoyen, whose accession Egharevba **dates** to 'about A.D. 1735'. *A Short History*, p. 41.

strong suspicion that they were taking full advantage of the circumstances to wipe out a heavy backlog of debt.[1] But serious accusations against Raems did not come solely from the Edo. A slave belonging to the Company and a number of free Minas living around the factory[2] swore that he had appropriated the property of the Dutchmen who had died at Ughoton, including a large quantity of *conte de terre*. They also told macabre stories of midnight trials and executions of fellow slaves in which the factor was alleged to have taken a full and bloody share, lustily seconded by his 'house women'. Hertog was inclined to discount the more lurid details, though sworn on the most powerful fetish; but even with such allowances, there remained to Raems' charge four proven executions of slaves within the space of a year. As for the dispute between the factor and the Oba which had caused the latter to stop all trade and provisions, Hertog learned from one of his slaves, as well as from a Benin trader who visited Badagry, that it had arisen over the Oba's failure to settle some debts. Losing patience, as he was obviously prone to do, Raems had seized some of the Oba's servants and put them in irons, whereupon the Oba had cut off trade.

While it is impossible to winnow the detailed truth from these conflicting reports and accusations, it must be concluded that Raems' story is improbable and unconvincing. What can be substantiated in his defence is his complaint that he was ill-provided with trade goods. Among the cargo he took with him to Ughoton he mentioned only 1,237 pounds of cowries, 17 long iron bars and 244 short iron bars; if other merchandise was supplied on a similar scale, this was certainly very little compared with the cargoes of former years. Thereafter he had to rely on one or two equally small consignments of goods, and a few canoe-loads sent through the creeks from Badagry. In June 1737 Hertog had to send some coral and a few other items by an English ship because his own coastal boat was no longer serviceable. In the final analysis the flight of

---

1 At the end of 1736 Raems had claimed that the Edo owed him 2,550 cloths.
2 These Minas may have been former slaves of the Company who had managed to purchase their freedom. It is also possible that some at least had settled in Benin of their own free will. Nyendael remarked that Ardra women were noted in Benin for their skill in brewing a maize beer. (Bosman, *A new and accurate description*, p. 459.)

Raems betrayed the growing decrepitude of the West India Company.

For a few years more the Company continued to deny realities. Hertog's men had in December 1737 renewed the treaty of 1735 with the new Oba, intending that the factory should be reoccupied. Hertog for his part assured the Director-General that he would send officials to Ughoton with a party of 'sturdy free Minas' to defend the post. But, he pointed out, such action would be pointless if he were not provided with sufficient and suitable ships to maintain contact with the outpost.[1] Those ships were not forthcoming. Shortly afterwards, on 29 April 1738, Hertog himself was murdered at Badagry, and the Company's affairs east of the Volta River sank into still greater confusion.[2] Hopes that the Dutch would return to Ughoton were also expressed in several messages the Oba sent to Badagry asking them to reoccupy their factory.[3] In July 1740, for example, he informed the official in charge at Badagry—one of the men who had visited Benin City in December 1737—that the factory had fallen down three times, and that he had rebuilt it at his own expense and taken care of all the Company's property.[4] The factor passed this information to the Director-General, adding:

> That same king very humbly begs Your Honour to reopen trade and he undertakes to keep all Englishmen out of Benin; but so long as there are no Dutchmen there he must willy-nilly be friends with the English. Enclosed herewith is a bead or *conte de terre* which the king sends to Your Honour as a sample; he says he has many like it and is ready to trade them.[5]

---

1 A.R. *Bezittingen*, vol. 103. H. Hertog to M. F. de Bordes, 20 April 1738.
2 A.R. *N.W.I.C.* vol. 65, ff. 125–6. M. F. de Bordes to Council of Ten, 26 December 1738. It had been reported in April 1738 that Hertog was at war with the small state of Apa. (ibid. f. 96.)
3 Apart from a wish not to lose Dutch trade, the people of Benin were anxious to have the services of the factory physicians who had saved several lives by their blood-letting and medicines. This point was stressed to the two Dutchmen who went to Benin in December 1737.
4 The remains of the Dutch factory were still visible when Landolphe visited Ughoton in 1786. He was told they were the ruins of a Dutch fort which had been destroyed after all its inhabitants had been massacred!
5 A.R. *Bezittingen*, vol. 105. J. Bronssama to F. Barovius, 7 May 1740, and PS. dated 20 July 1740. For *conte de terre* cf. supra p. 187.

In reply the Director-General wrote a letter which marks the end of Dutch contact with Benin.

> We should very willingly arrange with the King of Benin for the reopening of trade there were it not for our complete lack of ships and the sorry state in which the late Director-General has left the Company's affairs. But, as it is to be hoped that things will not always be like this, you should not turn down the King's proposals, but rather keep on friendly terms with him, and in the meantime find out whether the Company's factory there is really in the condition he pretends.[1]

Even had Dutch trade with Benin not been broken off in so abrupt a manner, it is impossible that it could have continued much longer when the West India Company obviously lacked the resources to maintain it. For many years the factory at Ughoton had been an idle luxury, sustained not by trade but by the inertia of an outworn organisation.

---

1 ibid. F. Barovius to J. Bronssama, 28 February 1741.

Chapter 6
The slave-trade era

1. English and French in the mid-eighteenth century

Numerous references to English ships in the Benin River which occur in the records of the Dutch West India Company make it clear that by the seventeen-thirties English slave-traders predominated among the Europeans visiting the area. Most of these English ships came from Liverpool and belonged to private traders, for the English chartered company, the Royal African Company, had fallen upon the same evil times as its Dutch rival, and it does not appear to have pursued its interest in Benin beyond 1724.[1] Sailing directly from England with merchandise known to be in demand on the Guinea coast, these private merchants suffered none of the handicaps in communications and supplies that beset their shore-based competitors; nor were they saddled with the expense of forts and factories. Hence they were always able to undersell the ill-stocked Dutch factory and win the favour of the Benin authorities.[2] The slaves and a certain amount of ivory bought in Benin they carried directly to the English colonies in the West Indies and North America, sold them there, then loaded their ships with colonial produce to complete the final leg of the triangular voyage.

Very little information about these voyages has survived in English documentary sources for the first half of the eighteenth

---

1 Ref. K. G. Davies, *The Royal African Company*. London, 1957.
2 e.g. A.R. *Bezittingen*, vol. 97. W. van Essen to J. Pranger, 15 April 1731. 'On my arrival here I found an English bark under the command of a Captain Arthur Lane. All his merchandise was very attractive and highly esteemed by the natives, which is the reason why they have paid so little attention to ours and trade has so mightily declined. This is also the reason why these natives are so impudent and rascally for there is no other reasonable explanation to be found.'

century. But from then onwards the Liverpool records begin to fill
in the picture. In 1752, for example, it is known that five ships sailed
from that port for Benin to buy a total of 1,280 slaves.[1] On 28 June
1757, the *Rainbow* under the command of a Captain Harrison, who
was already well acquainted with Benin,[2] entered the river; four and
a half months later it left for Barbados with 261 slaves and 5,400
pounds of ivory. On this voyage the slaves lived up to the reputation
which Munnickhoven had given them by rising and killing several of
the crew, including an interpreter whom the captain seems to have
hired in Benin for the voyage.[3] About the same time a French
squadron seized an English ship leaving the Benin River with 318
slaves.[4] In 1769 the *Cato* carried 210 slaves, 'all of whom have had
the small pox', from Benin to South Carolina. Two ships left
Liverpool in 1771 intending to buy 850 slaves in the river.[5] Taken in
conjunction with the earlier Dutch evidence of English activity,
these stray pieces of information point to a regular trade and help to
explain the tradition that the reigns of the eighteenth-century Obas
Eresoyen and Akengbuda were times of prosperity.

Some difficulty arises, however, in determining how much of this
English trade went to Benin, and how much to centres such as Arbo
and to Itsekiri traders in the main river. Dutch sources make it plain
that English ships gathered some, and occasionally all, of their
cargoes outside the Benin kingdom, and that the growth of the slave
trade was attracting large numbers of Itsekiris into the river. Furthermore, Dutch experience suggests that Benin would have had some
difficulty in furnishing all the slaves needed by these vessels, the
larger of which would have been unable in any case to reach Ughoton. Slaves sold by the Edo in the seventeen-twenties were apparently

---

1 E. Donnan, *Documents illustrative of the history of the slave trade to America*
vol. II. Washington, 1931, pp. 496–8. The totals of slaves given are those
declared by the ships' captains on their departure from Liverpool, not those
actually purchased.
2 In 1752 he commanded the *Africa* on a Benin voyage. (ibid. p. 496.)
3 Donnan, *Documents*, vol. IV. Washington, 1935, p. 370. Capt. J. Harrison
to T. Rumbold & Co., Barbados, 28 February 1758. On this voyage the ship
lost altogether 44 Africans and 28 Europeans.
4 A.H.U. *Brasil: Baia*. Conde dos Arcos to Minister of Overseas Affairs, 10
May 1757.
5 Donnan, *Documents*, vol. IV, p. 429.

the casualties of civil war; similar conflicts later in the century must have yielded further batches of prisoners. Other slaves could have been acquired through the normal course of trade with neighbouring states, but there is no evidence that Benin ever organised a great slave-trading network similar to that which supplied the ports of the eastern delta, or that it ever undertook systematic slave-raiding. That the *Rainbow* had to spend four and a half months collecting 261 slaves indicates that the supply was no more plentiful in the mid-eighteenth than it had been early in the sixteenth century.[1] Other figures relating to the end of the eighteenth century point to the same conclusion. In 1798, for example, English ships were sent to buy a total of 19,450 slaves in the eastern delta against 1,000 in the Benin River,[2] and most of these were acquired from the Itsekiris. Benin either could not or would not become a slave-trading state on the grand scale.

Portuguese activity in the Benin River seems to have declined in the latter part of the eighteenth century. Of 74 ships which entered the harbour of Príncipe between 1760 and 1771 none was bound from Benin; nor did any Portuguese vessel from that river call at São Tomé between 1772 and 1774, though the island was visited by a number of foreign ships coming from Benin in those years.[3] The Captain of São Tomé, writing in March 1772, attributed the falling off in this branch of the slave trade to the high prices being demanded for slaves:

> Today slaves are sold for twice the price that was paid a few years ago, besides which they have increased the customs paid to the King and chiefs of the port where trade is carried on.[4]

For much of our information about European contact with Benin in the latter part of the eighteenth century we therefore have to rely upon the memoirs of the Frenchman J. F. Landolphe[5] which, although detailed and very readable, are not wholly satisfactory as an historical document. In the first place, they were not

1 cf. supra p. 169.
2 Donnan, *Documents*, vol. II, p. 645. Fourteen thousand came from Bonny alone.
3 A.H.U. *São Tomé, caixa* 7.
4 ibid.
5 *Mémoires du Capitaine Landolphe rédigés sur son manuscrit par J. S. Quesné*, 2 vols. Paris, 1823.

written by Landolphe himself, but by a friend who compiled the
account from his notes and reminiscences more than thirty years
after the events described. Secondly, because Landolphe harboured
a grudge against the English who had destroyed his factory in the
Benin River, he was concerned to emphasise, and perhaps exagger-
ate, its flourishing condition before the catastrophe. In matters of
detail he is nonetheless often verifiable and exact; his acquaintance
with the Benin area, extending over thirty years, was an exceptionally
long one for a European; above all his memoirs reveal an uncommon
sympathy with the people among whom he lived and whose manners
he observed.

Landolphe first entered the Benin River in April 1769 as a junior
officer aboard *L'Africaine*, under the command of Captain Desrud.
The ship had come from Nantes, the home port of the triangular
trade between France, Guinea and the French West Indies. In the
course of three month's trading at Ughoton, Desrud embarked 360
slaves and a miscellaneous cargo which included red, blue, violet
and yellow dyewoods, ivory, cloths, gum and palm oil. In return
the French gave fine white cloth of the kind worn by Edo chiefs,
iron bars, guns, gunpowder, swords, pistols, spirits, tobacco, chisels,
razors, mirrors and hats, but none of the cowry and manilla currencies.[1] Following a similar voyage that kept him in the Benin
River from August to November 1771, Landolphe determined to
propose the establishment of a factory at Ughoton where he was
convinced the French might carry on a lucrative trade in slaves and
natural products. He received encouragement from the chief of
Ughoton, the *Edaiken*, who assured him that the French enjoyed
higher esteem in Benin than any other Europeans.[2] To illustrate the
preference given to his countrymen, Landolphe relates that on
anchoring in the main river four leagues below Ughoton his captain
had found an English and a Portuguese ship already there, but
'France enjoying a very marked preponderance over the other
nations of Europe, Desrud had the right to gather his cargo before

1 Landolphe, *Mémoires*, vol. I, pp. 50–1.
2 ibid. p. 51. Landolphe calls the *Edaiken* 'Danikan'. Palisot de Beauvois refers
  to him as the '*chirugien*' of Ughoton. ('Notice sur le peuple de Benin', *Décade
  Philosophique*, no. 12, *année* 9, 1801.) He meant presumably that the chief
  dispensed native medicine.

his two rivals.' If such was the practice, it marked a departure from the long-established custom that all traders should be treated alike, a rule to which the Oba had rigorously adhered even at the height of Dutch power and pressure. Furthermore it was in this same year that two Liverpool ships came to buy 850 slaves in the Benin River, which rather belies Landolphe's assertions of French preponderance, unless other French vessels, of which he makes no mention, were also trading there, or unless the English were not buying their slaves from the Oba. Enthusiasm for his Ughoton project may have led Landolphe, then and later, to see French prospects in too roseate a light.

Not until 1776, after he had passed his captain's examination, was Landolphe able to obtain a hearing for his scheme. He found supporters in the directors of the newly formed *Compagnie de la Guyane* which gave him command of a new ship *La Negresse*, and an appointment as *administrateur en chef* of the proposed factory. Their plan was that he should sail with the equipment and merchandise needed to establish the factory, then send the vessel back to France under his second-in-command for further supplies; from then onwards regular three-monthly shipments of goods were to ensure that trade continued uninterrupted throughout the year.

La Negresse entered the Benin River in February 1778 and was taken upstream as far as a widening in the river known as Ureju Bay, near the entrance to the Ughoton Creek. From there Landolphe had to take the ship's boat to Ughoton. After explaining his intentions to the *Edaiken* and other chiefs of the village, he rented a house to serve as a temporary warehouse and factory. If his estimate of 3,000 for the population was accurate, Ughoton had fully recovered from its decline earlier in the century, but the figure possibly included those who flocked into the village when traders arrived, for another two French visitors who saw it in 1787 put the number of houses at around forty.[1] Three days after their arrival the captain and his lieutenant travelled to Benin City escorted by two royal messengers, 32 porters and 30 men armed with guns. Given the choice between riding a horse and being carried in a sort of portable

---

1 These were two naval officers named Legroing and Balon. Their report on the visit is printed in P. Labarthe, *Voyage à la côte de Guinée*. Paris, 1803, *lettre* xviii.

armchair protected by a sunshade, the Frenchmen chose the latter
and were taken to the capital at a brisk trot which covered the
distance in five hours with only one half-way halt.[1] Before entering
the city, the party stopped at Uzebu so that they might observe the
now firmly established custom of paying respects to the *Ezomo*,
capitaine générale des guerres as Landolphe styles him.[2] The power of
this chief had obviously not declined since the departure of the
Dutch; he was, according to Landolphe's porters, as powerful as the
Oba, and the richest man in Benin, owning more than 10,000 slaves,
none of whom were ever sold; in time of war he could muster fifty
or sixty thousand men. Hyperbolical though these statements may
have been, they illustrate vividly the pre-eminent position which the
Ezomo had attained in the course of the eighteenth century, and
which he did not entirely lose as long as Benin remained independent; a century later Cyril Punch observed that the *Ezomo* was the
only man in Benin, apart from the Oba, permitted to carry an
umbrella.[3] His supposed refusal to sell any of his slaves is also
noteworthy for the light it sheds upon the attitude of powerful Edo
chiefs towards the slave trade: however numerous they might be, a
great man did not sell his slaves. Against these claims it can be
pointed out that an earlier *Ezomo* had offered to sell slaves to the
Dutch; nevertheless it had since become a matter of prestige to
assert that his successor would never do so.

His visit to the *Ezomo* enabled Landolphe to judge the war
captain for himself and see something of his manner of life. Fortunately these impressions are recorded in considerable detail in his
memoirs and, together with the descriptions of his meetings with the
Oba, present us with the most precise picture now available of Benin
ceremonial. Inside the *Ezomo*'s house the Frenchmen were shown

---

1 Landolphe, *Mémoires*, vol. I, pp. 95–6. One must again suspect Landolphe
  of exaggerating. Twenty years later Captain Adams made the same journey
  in a hammock and took two days over it. (J. Adams, *Sketches*, chap. iii).
  Legroing and Balon, who accompanied Landolphe from Ughoton to Benin
  City in 1787, estimated their travelling time at ten hours.
2 Landolphe, *Mémoires*, vol. I, p. 98. He renders the chief's name as 'Jabou',
  obviously confusing it with the name of his village. The personal name of the
  Ezomo whom he met was probably either Odia or Ekenneza—that is, either
  the son or grandson of the *Ezomo* Ehennua who had served Akenzua I.
3 H. L. Roth, *Great Benin: its customs, art and horrors*. Halifax, 1903, p. 94.

into the *owa-igho* (lit. cowry room), a large room the walls of which were encrusted with cowry shells.[1] Here they were subjected to a ceremony which may have been of recent origin, for it is not mentioned by earlier visitors. It consisted of a ritual washing of the visitors' feet in a great brass bowl nine feet in circumference. They were told that they could not meet the *Ezomo* until this had been done, and although they were given no explanation for the ritual, it was doubtless a magical precaution against harmful powers. In the nineteenth century European visitors had to undergo a similar ceremony at Ughoton where it was performed by the priest of *Olokun*. In another long room containing 'several badly executed statues of his ancestors'[2] they finally met the *Ezomo* whom Landolphe described as pleasant and very dignified despite his youth.

From Uzebu the Frenchmen went to the house reserved for European traders; it stood near one of the city gateways[3] and was in the charge of an interpreter. Soon after they had reached it messengers[4] came to inform Landolphe that the Oba would receive him that same night at 11 o'clock—an hour possibly determined by a wish to hold a private discussion rather than a public audience. At the appointed time two messengers and twenty-five men armed with long spears escorted the captain to the palace, their way lit by two

---

1 According to Egharevba (*A Short History*, p. 41) a similar room was constructed for Oba Eresoyen with a floor, as well as the walls, paved with cowries. Such manifestations of wealth may have been common in Benin; four of these rooms still exist.

2 Landolphe, *Mémoires*, vol. I, p. 102. These figures were carved in wood, brass ones being reserved exclusively to the Oba.

3 The European lodging house was probably situated by the gateway that led from Uzebu into the city.

4 Captain James Fawckner (*Narrative*, pp. 82–3) gives a full description of a royal messenger in the early nineteenth century; those of Landolphe's day must have been very similar. 'He was curiously habited, wearing a sort of short petticoat from the waist down to the knees, composed of a cloth very much valued by them, resembling our white bunting. This encircled his loins, and set off like an ancient dame's hooped petticoat; the upper part of the body was naked as well as the legs and feet; his neck was ornamented with strings of red coral. In his hand he held a fan made of leather, to keep off the flies, and protect him from the rays of the sun. His head was quite unprotected, being shaved all over, with the exception of a circular spot on the crown, from which a small tuft was still permitted to grow.'

large palm-oil lamps each with four wicks.[1] Left alone with the
messengers and his young French-speaking Edo interpreter,[2] he
waited half an hour in a large room furnished with an armchair
until the Oba appeared accompanied only by two swordbearers
(*emada*). This Oba was almost certainly Akengbuda who, by
Egharevba's reckoning, was crowned about 1750 and reigned for
fifty-four years. Landolphe estimated him to be a youthful, upright
sixty-five, with greying hair, but a face still unlined; his manner he
described in terms similar to those applied to the *Ezomo*. The Oba
evidently believed in personal, even secret, conduct of state affairs,
for he dismissed the messengers and held the interview in the
presence of no one but his two bodyguards. Through the interpreter,
who lay prostrate before the monarch,[3] Landolphe explained his
project of building a factory at Ughoton and a fort at the river
mouth in order to protect French trade. The true purpose of this
fort, like that planned by the Dutch, was doubtless to exclude
European rivals, and in particular the English, the principal foreign
traders of the Benin River. However, such monopolistic motives
could not be openly avowed; instead Landolphe justified the fortification by warning the Oba that war between France and England
was imminent—it came in June 1778—and that it might interfere
with his plans and interrupt trade. At which the Oba is supposed to
have exclaimed against the English ('They are very bad people') and
assured the captain of preferential treatment for the French. The
interview ended with a promise that the royal council would be
assembled the following day to discuss the proposals.

Landolphe spent the next three days paying courtesy calls on the
twenty chiefs[4] who sat on the 'council of commerce'—presumably
the senior members of the *Iwebo* society. The visits followed a set
pattern: accompanied by an escort of thirty armed men, Landolphe
arrived at the chief's house in his hammock; with each one he
exchanged the same polite questions and answers, the same presents,

---

1 There are descriptions and sketches of such lamps in Roth, *Great Benin*, pp.
  120–1.
2 The youth had learned French in the service of Captain Desrud.
3 Palisot de Beauvois also describes this as the posture adopted by the Edo in
  the presence of their Oba.
4 He uses the term *hommes grandes*.

the questions being very similar to those which in the early seven-teenth century *veadors* had put in their first formal meeting with a newly-arrived ship's master.[1] It is noteworthy that in his account of negotiations with the Oba and chiefs Landolphe makes no mention of the three palace chiefs who had for so long been the principal figures in the conduct of European trade. As late as 1725, a Dutch factor visiting Benin City had been received first by these three;[2] *Uwangue, Osodin* and *Eribo* had also followed immediately after the Oba and the *Ezomo* in signing the 1735 treaty with the Dutch West India Company. Landolphe's experience would therefore suggest that they had lost their long-established prominence, and that a significant shift of political power had taken place in Benin.[3] But it must again be emphasised that Landolphe's record of events is not always reliable, and when he elsewhere describes the Benin system of government as based upon three equal councils, each of twenty members, and charged respectively with the oversight of commerce, finance and war, it may be suspected that he is attempting to approximate the structure and functions of the three palace societies to a more familiar European pattern. We may likewise suppose that the sixty *hommes grandes* composing these councils were the holders of *Eghaevo* and *Exaeve* titles who wore as a badge of their rank two necklaces, two anklets and two bracelets of heavy coral.[4] Those whom Landolphe describes as *veadors* and *passadors* (overseers and messengers) belonged, to judge from their single coral necklaces and hair style, to the *uko* rank—the senior untitled grade—of the palace societies.[5] In fact, Landolphe was observing the societies as they had existed since the sixteenth century.

On the day after he had completed his visits, Landolphe met the

---

1 cf. supra p. 89.
2 A.R. *Bezittingen*, vol. 93. A. Bambergh to P. Valckenier, 11 December 1725.
3 Further evidence of a change is provided by the list of customary presents given by Landolphe: the *Ezomo* received goods to the value of 300 cloths, but all *Iwebo* chiefs received the value of 100 cloths, the erstwhile great men apparently getting no more than their fellows. cf. infra p. 210.
4 Landolphe, *Mémoires*, vol. I, p. 113. Fawckner (*Narrative*, p. 71) describes the chiefs of Ughoton as wearing necklaces, bracelets and anklets of coral, but does not state whether they were in single or in double strings.
5 cf. Bradbury, *The Benin Kingdom*, pp. 37-8.

Oba in the full council of titled chiefs which assembled when important questions of policy were to be discussed.[1] Four *veadors* led him through three courtyards of the palace into the council hall, a room sixty feet long with a raised dais at one end on which was placed the throne. Presumably the Oba had already discussed the French requests with this council or with his principal advisers, for in what appears to have been a formal session the council announced its willingness to grant him as much land as he required to build a fortified factory at Ughoton, but had to confess its inability to make similar concessions for a fort at the mouth of the river because that region had fallen under the control of Warri.

Later that same day the captain attended a ceremony meant, or so he surmised, to celebrate the agreement. It took place in a palace courtyard in the presence of the Oba, his chiefs and thousands of his subjects. To the accompaniment of large and small ivory horns and a dozen great drums, two executioners completely masked in long grey robes clubbed a man unconscious and then cut off his head, allowing the blood to flow into a large brass pan so that it might be sprinkled on the royal tombs.[2] Before his death the victim had been told that he was to go to *Olokun*, the deity worshipped by the Edo as the god of wealth and fertility, and of the sea. The association of the *Olokun* cult with European trade lends some colour to Landolphe's supposition that the sacrifice was being made on account of the proposed factory,[3] and perhaps with an intent similar to that which inspired human sacrifices at the mouth of the river and at

---

1 cf. ibid. p. 43 where the functioning of the full council towards the close of the nineteenth century is described:
'For more important matters, such as the promulgation of new laws, the decision to conduct wars, the fixing of the dates of important festivals, the creation of new titles, the raising of special levies, and the taking of ritual measures to prevent epidemics, etc., a full state council was called. This consisted of the *Uzama*, both groups of *Eghaevo*, and, in a subsidiary capacity, the minor ranks of title-holders. When the *Oba* intended to announce an important decision he summoned this council and put his views before it. Each group met separately to discuss its attitude, then a second meeting was called at which the leaders of each group expressed its views.'
cf. the report in the *Royal Gold Coast Gazette*, 1823, which states that a council of *emograns* constituted a judicial body with jurisdiction over all chiefs.
2 Cyril Punch gave a rather similar description of the executioners' robes. Roth, *Great Benin*, p. 57.
3 cf. the powers attributed to the priest of Loebo, supra p. 89.

Ughoton. The former were explained to Adams 'as votive offerings to the sea, to direct vessels to bend their course to this horrid climate'.[1] The sacrifices at Ughoton came to the notice of Captain Fawckner who relates an instance of voluntary self-immolation at this important centre of the *Olokun* cult:

> About the same time I saw a man who had given himself as a sacrifice to the fetish. A procession was formed, in all the splendour peculiar to these occasions, and the man was conducted amid a vast concourse of people to the river. Here, according to the usual custom, they affix weights to the devotee's body, make him drunk, and sink him in the tide.[2]

When, after a sojourn of ten days in Benin City, Landolphe took his leave of the Oba, his reception at the palace was even more cordial than on his arrival. Having dismissed all his attendants save for one *omada*, the Oba invited the Frenchman to sit next to him, and then ordered him to be served with food and drink, including two bottles of port wine and a flagon of rum which the Oba himself poured into a fine crystal glass.[3] Following this liberal refreshment, Landolphe was led into a courtyard that served as a storehouse for the Oba's ivory; it held, in the captain's estimation, more than 3,000 tusks, of which he was invited to choose one as a present. The Oba's right to one tusk from every elephant killed in his kingdom, and an option to buy the other, were the sources of this accumulation that made the ruler of Benin the principal vendor of ivory to Europeans.[4] The captain was also given the choice of a large number of Benin cloths, some woven of cotton and others of 'raffia', stored in another room. The cotton cloths were still of the standard size and colour familiar to Europeans from the seventeenth century—that is, they were made of three strips, each eight feet long, sewn together to

---

1 Adams, *Sketches*, p. 32. Three or four human sacrifices were made annually at the river mouth.
2 Fawckner, *Narrative*, p. 103.
3 The Oba told Landolphe that the port was a present from a Brazilian captain; the rum had been given to him by Captain Chapman of the Liverpool ship *Benin*.
4 In 1787 Legroing (Labarthe, *Voyage*) estimated the Oba's stock of ivory at 1,000 tusks. In 1892 Galway saw 'tremendous stores of ivory' in the palace. (H. L. Galway, 'Journeys in the Benin country, West Africa'. *Geographical Journal*, vol. I, no. 2, 1893, p. 126.)

make a broad cloth; those made of 'raffia' consisted of four strips, eight or nine feet long, of a pale buff colour, and woven almost as fine as silk.[1] According to Landolphe both types of cloth were woven by Benin women on perpendicular looms which were to be found in most houses, but there were other special kinds of cloth that were woven only within the palace for the use of the Oba and his court. Sir Richard Burton described some of the latter as 'fine cotton work, open and decorated with red worsted—a work confined to the ladies of the palace';[2] and Punch saw pieces decorated with life-sized figures that had been worked by the Oba's menservants.[3]

Landolphe and his lieutenant, who had fallen critically ill while in Benin City, travelled back to Ughoton in the same manner as they had journeyed to the capital, except that on this occasion they paused for a meal at the village of Igo. This place, approximately half-way between Benin City and Ughoton, was, and is still, governed by a priest of *Olokun*, the *Ohenolokun*. On arrival at Ughoton the party was met by the three headmen to whom Landolphe gave out twenty bottles of brandy for general consumption. The next morning he paid his escort and carriers with a glass of brandy and six Flemish knives for each man.[4] Later that same day two messengers brought word from the Oba that forty *veadors* would arrive in two days' time to inspect the goods in the cargo, fix their selling price, and determine the 'customs' payable to the ruler and chiefs—a procedure akin to that described by Dapper and Nyendael. The *veadors* duly presented themselves and demanded as a preliminary that each be given a glass of brandy, a pipe and a fathom of tobacco. They then settled down with pipe and drink to evaluate the merchandise displayed to them in large brass pans. The unit of value for this exercise was the *pagne* or 'cloth', a measure that harked back to the Portuguese *pano* or customary yard of the early sixteenth century. Various other standards had subsequently been adopted,

---

1 It is likely that these were the 'fine straw cloths' which the Dutch Director-General had wished to buy in 1736. cf. supra p. 189.
2 R. F. Burton, 'My wanderings in West Africa, by a F.R.G.S.: Parts II and III. The renowned city of Benin'. *Fraser's Magazine*, vol. LXVII, March and April 1865.
3 Roth, *Great Benin*, p. 141. These pieces were over six feet long.
4 Every porter carried a similar knife in a leather sheath. cf. supra p. 98.

among them cowries, manillas and ivory, and at times more than one measure was in use. The difference between the 'cloth' of the eighteenth century and that of the sixteenth appears to be that whereas the latter was notionally based upon a standard piece of European cloth, the later unit referred to the standard Benin cloth. This development probably owed much to the emergence of the Benin cloth as the major item of trade in the seventeenth century, and to the introduction of credit trading. When the 'cloth' became generally accepted among Benin and European traders as the unit for calculating value is difficult to determine. The Dutch, though preferring to use ivory for their reckoning, had occasionally bargained in terms of the 'cloth';[1] it is likely, however, that its common use owed something to the appearance of the Portuguese and English as the chief European trading partners of Benin during the eighteenth century. By Landolphe's time the 'cloth' was well established as the basis for trade reckoning, and it continued to hold that position throughout the following century.

The values assigned to Landolphe's goods were as follows:[2]

1 Cholet kerchief	12 cloths
1 Nîmes silk kerchief	12 ,,
½ piece printed calico—7 ells	7 ,,
1 piece Breton linen—5 ells	4 ,,
1 piece Rouen cotton cloth—6 ells	6 ,,
1 piece white baft—5 ells	6 ,,
1 piece dress Cholet—6 ells	6 ,,
1 piece Nîmes silk satin	6 ,,
1 piece Indian chintz—5 ells	10 ,,
1 roll Brazilian tobacco weighing 80 lb.	20 ,,
1 brass basin 3 feet diameter	7 ,,
1 brass basin 2 feet diameter	4 ,,
1 scrap regulation musket	7 ,,

1 cf. supra p. 164.
2 This list may be compared with another list of goods saleable in the Benin River printed by Labarthe (*Voyage*, letter xviii) and probably based upon information obtained from Lt. Legroing: iron bars, trade hats, pipe coral, royal-blue cloth in pieces of 18 ells, scarlet cloth in pieces of 17 ells, brandy, trade guns, scarlet cloaks with gold lace, cloaks of blue cloth, printed calico in pieces of 12 ells, gingham in pieces of 24 ells, nicanees, pipes, gunpowder, silks, dress material.

1 scrap dragoon's holster pistol	4 cloths
1 regulation sabre	1 ,,
1 barrel of powder—5 lb.	5 ,,
1 bag of lead hunting shot—1 lb.	1 ,,
100 flints	1 ,,
6 Flemish knives with painted *lignum vitae* handles	2 ,,
1 case containing scissors, razor and whetstone	1 ,,
1 common hat edged with red wool	1 ,,
1 barrel brandy—20 pints	8 ,,
1 case of 12 flagons of brandy, each 1.5 pints	8 ,,
1 iron bar, 7 feet long by 3 inches wide	3 ,,
1 necklace of coral at 40 francs a lb.	8 ,,
1 necklace of round coral rosary beads at 60 francs a lb.	8 ,,
1 necklace of 12 small pipe coral beads	5 ,,

Once the price of Landolphe's goods had been determined, attention turned to the prices he was to pay for slaves, a male and female slave being produced for that purpose in the same way that the captain had shown samples of his merchandise. Bargaining began with the *veadors* asking 120 cloths for the man and 100 for the woman; but after long discussion agreement was reached at 100 cloths for a male and 90 for a female. A discharge of muskets at the door of the factory proclaimed that these negotiations were concluded, and that trade might begin. Slaves then began to appear in ones and twos[1]—although on some days he was offered as many as eighteen—until within three months Landolphe had acquired a cargo of 410 slaves. He also claimed to have bought 60,000 pounds of ivory at a rate equivalent to 15–20 sous for tusks weighing more than twenty pounds, and 10 sous a pound for smaller ones. A strong suspicion of exaggeration must attach to this figure which far exceeds any cargo carried by a Portuguese or Dutch vessel, and even the total Dutch purchases over a number of years; 6,000 pounds would be more credible.

Although the price of slaves had increased approximately fourfold since the fifteen-twenties when the Portuguese bought them for between 20 and 24 cloths, it had not risen substantially during the eighteenth century. In 1722 the Dutch had hoped to buy slaves in Benin for the equivalent of 74 cloths for a male and 53 for a female,

---

1 Exactly as had happened in the fifteen-twenties. cf. supra p. 59.

but none were purchased, and the Dutch factor had reported that the English and French were then paying considerably more. The slave prices given by Landolphe also agree fairly well with those that figure in an undated Portuguese document of the eighteenth century.[1] It appears to have been written by an inhabitant of São Tomé who calculated that slaves could be bought in Benin for between 60 and 90 cloths; if 'the presents and other port expenses' were included, the price became 105 cloths for a male and 100 for a female. Slave prices had to be paid in an assortment of goods that varied according to demand and supply, and also the bargaining powers of the merchants on both sides. The list of goods needed for the purchase of one male slave given in the Portuguese document shows that the assortment had come to include the whole range of items carried by a European trader; a merchant who lacked one essential item might find his whole trade ruined.[2] It will be noted that the valuations in this list correspond closely with those negotiated by Landolphe, and differ little from those current in the period of Dutch trade; from which it may be inferred that the prices of European merchandise, like those of slaves, remained relatively stable in Benin during the eighteenth century.

1 piece of good Coromandel, blue	10	cloths
1 Surat coverlet	4	,,
12 pieces of coarse linen with red edging	12	,,
2 bars of lead	1	,,
5 knives	1	,,
1 piece of Indian chintz with flower pattern, 15 yds.	12	,,
12 yards coarse muslin with stripes or spots	12	,,
12 yards East Indian muslin or shirting	12	,,
— glass beads in bright colours	2	,,
3 pounds lead shot	2	,,
3 horn tobacco boxes	1	,,
4 razors	1	,,
4 mirrors	1	,,

1 A.H.U. *São Tomé, caixa* 2. *Vide* Appendix VII.
2 cf. Palisot de Beauvois, *Flore d'Oware et de Benin*, 2 vols. Paris, 1804–7, vol. I, p. 43. The composite barter unit had made its appearance in Benin in the mid-seventeenth century (cf. supra p. 97), and had attained a high level of sophistication by the close of the eighteenth.

16 *alquiers* of fine, white salt	20 cloths
15 pints brandy	4 „
1 iron bar, 14–18 pounds	3 „
4 kerchiefs	4 „
1·5 pounds gunpowder[1]	3 „

Though prices remained steady, 'customs' payments rose sharply in the course of the eighteenth century. Nyendael had dismissed them as 'so inconsiderable that they are hardly worth mentioning'— amounting to no more than 16 *gulden*, or six pounds sterling, for a vessel. Landolphe on the other hand claimed that these dues were very high. They were assessed by the *veadors* according to the size of a vessel, so it has to be borne in mind that the ships engaged by the French and English in the triangular trade were generally much larger than those employed by the Dutch West India Company for the coastal traffic in Guinea. Yet Landolphe's ship *La Negresse*, although a three-master, cannot have been very large if it was able to ascend the river as far as Ureju Bay, and for it he had to pay 'customs' to the following values: to the Oba, 900 cloths; to the *Ezomo*, 300 cloths; to the twenty chiefs of *Iwebo*, 100 cloths apiece; to the forty *veadors*, 20 cloths each; to six interpreters, 20 cloths each; to forty carriers (given the Portuguese-derived name of *carçadors*), 10 cloths each; and 20 cloths each to the three chiefs of Ughoton. In addition to these obligatory payments, Landolphe estimated that he had had to distribute presents to a value of 2,000 cloths, making a total of 15,160 cloths—the equivalent of 150 slaves, or 20 per cent of the value of his cargo. In money terms he estimated the value of a cloth at two francs; some years later Adams put it at an average of 2s. 6d.; so Landolphe disbursed, on this reckoning, almost two thousand pounds in customs and presents. In the Portuguese document this expenditure is averaged among the number of slaves purchased, a factor obviously related closely to the size of the ship. On this basis the writer arrives at a figure of

---

1 Gunpowder is the only item in this list to differ markedly in value from the prices given by Landolphe. It is also the only commodity whose price had increased sharply above the level obtaining during the period of Dutch trade earlier in the eighteenth century; the explanation for this exceptional rise is probably to be found in the increasingly widespread use of firearms at the end of the century.

between 25 and 45 cloths for each slave, depending on the sex and state of health; for Landolphe's 410 slaves a calculation on this basis would give a total of between 10,250 and 18,450 cloths. Thus there exists a reasonable measure of agreement between these two sources which leave no doubt that the 'customs' system in Benin had been revolutionised since the beginning of the century. The chief beneficiaries had been the Oba, the *Ezomo* and the chiefs of *Iwebo*.

2. Landolphe's enterprise in the main river

While gathering his cargo of slaves and ivory, Landolphe had begun clearing a site near the former Dutch factory at Ughoton so that he might build the trading post authorised by the Oba and his council. But before any building had begun, with his ship only two-thirds full[1] and many goods still unsold, he departed precipitately from Ughoton without even taking leave of the Oba. The reason he gives for the sudden abandonment of his plans is the loss of one-third of his crew of ninety through sickness and fear that disease might break out among the slaves. Tropical disease was always a major hazard to European enterprise in Benin, so there is no cause to doubt Landolphe's sincerity when on this and subsequent occasions he used it as an argument against any prolonged stay in the upper reaches of the river. Another motive for his hurried departure may well have been that the wind had changed to the south-west, thus threatening to keep him in the river throughout the rainy season. An attempt to cross the bar on 15 May 1778 proved that he had already delayed too long; *La Negresse* twice grounded, refloated on the incoming tide, and had to re-enter the river. Realising that he had no hope of putting to sea until the return of the seasonal northerly winds, Landolphe determined to spend the rainy season in Ureju Bay where, because it was exposed to the prevailing south-westerlies, he hoped his crew and slaves might be kept healthy. He faced also the formidable problem of feeding them for several months. At this point the Olu of the Itsekiris came to his rescue.

Apart from occasional references in the Dutch West India Company records and in missionary reports, little is known of Itsekiri

---

1 Landolphe claimed that *La Negresse* could have carried up to 600 slaves. *Mémoires*, vol. I, p. 129.

activity in the Benin River before the arrival of Landolphe. The information available, and especially that concerning the Dutch attempt to deliver a present to the Olu in 1736,[1] suggests that they were steadily expanding their trade and influence in the area. Their defeat in the war with Benin in 1735–6 proved only a temporary setback, and by 1778 the Oba's council had to acknowledge that they controlled the lower reaches of the river. The secret of Itsekiri success was their control of the water based on a formidable fleet of war canoes. Thanks to these the Itsekiri war captain, the *Iyatsere*,[2] was able to boast to Landolphe that his people had no fear of war with any neighbour because they fought only on the water where they had sufficient power either to defeat an enemy outright or to overcome him by a blockade. The Frenchman describes the Itsekiri war canoe in some detail. The largest he saw were sixty feet long and ten feet in the beam; they mounted as many as twenty pairs of swivel-guns on cross-beams placed at intervals of five or six feet. Besides this considerable armament, which was probably more effective in terrorising an opponent than in destroying him, the largest canoes could carry over one hundred men armed with guns and sabres, and sometimes a pistol, as well as a complement of forty paddlers.[3] A craft of this kind could cover three leagues in an hour. The Itsekiris also possessed many smaller canoes similarly armed. The Ijos, their principal rivals for the mastery of the Benin River, had equally formidable war canoes, but they lacked the organisation and cohesion of the Itsekiris.

Whether or not the Olu had any knowledge of Landolphe's commercial schemes, he took masterly advantage of the Frenchman's predicament by sending Okorodudu, the *Iyatsere*, to Ureju Bay with 10,000 yams and an offer of as many more as might be required, on credit if need be. Five large, heavily armed Ijo canoes also paid Landolphe a visit and assured him that they had learned from Benin that the ship was under the Oba's protection—an action which

---

1 cf. supra p. 186.
2 Many Itsekiri titles are of Benin origin. In the eighteenth century the *Iyatsere* still performed the military functions that had belonged to his Benin counterpart the *Iyase* in earlier centuries.
3 Landolphe's figures may be exaggerated; the largest canoes seen by his companion Palisot de Beauvois carried sixty men and swivel guns mounted in the prow and stern. (Palisot de Beauvois, *Flore*, vol. II, p. 42.)

strengthens the supposition that the Ijos were the maritime arm of Benin power.[1] Nor did they molest the ship in any way despite Okorodudu's warnings against Ijo perfidy. By the time the returning north-east wind enabled his ship to cross the bar at the end of October 1778, Landolphe's outlook had become strongly pro-Itsekiri. *La Negresse* sailed first to Príncipe to effect some repairs, then to Santo Domingo where the slaves were sold, only fourteen having died despite the long delay in the Benin River. To complete his voyage Landolphe carried back to Nantes a cargo of West Indian coffee and sugar.

He returned again to Benin in 1783 commanding *La Charmante Louise* which M. Brillantois of Nantes had bought and equipped at Middelburg in order that it might sail under the Austrian flag, and so escape attack from British ships. Leaving Middelburg on 15 December 1782 with a crew of sixty-five, the ship is said to have entered the Benin River early in January 1783—a remarkably quick voyage. Landolphe does not mention any dealings with the Itsekiris on his arrival, but appears to have taken his ship directly to Ughoton and exchanged all his merchandise for 390 slaves by the end of April. He is curiously silent upon the details of this visit to Benin, mentioning neither his factory project, nor his relations with the Oba; presumably he had to explain and excuse his neglect to carry out his plans and promises.

Having finished trading, the ship once again failed to clear the bar and had to prepare for another long sojourn in Ureju Bay. Offers of assistance soon began to arrive, the first coming from 'King Bernard' who turned out to be an Itsekiri rebel; not long afterwards the Olu succeeded in capturing and beheading him. The Oba too was not to be left behind; two *veadors* sent by canoe from Ughoton arrived in Ureju Bay on the same day that Okorodudu appeared with a message from the Olu. Landolphe took care that the two parties should not meet, 'for I knew there existed some jealousy between these two peoples, and it was in my interest to procure the protection of both monarchs'.[2] However his preference was clearly

---

1 cf. infra p. 218 and the promise made by the Ijos to send the shipwrecked Captain Fawckner to Benin, despite the efforts of the Olu of Warri to have him and his companions taken to Bobi. (Fawckner, *Narrative*, p. 67.)

2 Landolphe, *Mémoires*, vol. I, p. 305.

for the Itsekiris because he hid Okorodudu where he could overhear the conversation with the *veadors* from whom he requested credit to buy food for his slaves. When the messengers returned a week later with the Oba's reply, Okorodudu, who had arrived the previous day, was already installed aboard the ship. Through his *veadors* the Oba assured Landolphe of all necessary supplies and credit on condition that the ship returned to Ughoton. The difficulty of transporting yams to the lower river may have been the main reason for imposing this condition, but it was one which Landolphe would not accept. He explained his views about the disastrous effect of the Ughoton climate, then courteously dismissed the *veadors* with presents. No sooner had they gone than he accepted Okorodudu's offer to tow the ship to Ode Itsekiri where, the chief claimed, it would be able to await the turn of the wind in comfort and security. Landolphe had never visited the Itsekiri capital, and could have had no idea whether it was more salubrious than Ughoton, yet he readily agreed to entrust his ship to the *Iyatsere* who had forty canoes ready to take it into entirely unknown territory. Here one must suspect that the captain is not telling the whole story, and that some unexplained inducement or fear (such as the threat of an Ijo attack) must have driven him to this decision.

In the event he had no cause to regret his choice. Within four days the canoes had towed his ship without mishap to Ode Itsekiri by way of the Nana Creek,[1] the Escravos River, the Benin Creek and the Warri River—probably the route used by the Portuguese. Once at anchor before the Itsekiri capital, the slaves were sent ashore to be cared for by the inhabitants, while Landolphe and his crew were generously entertained at the Olu's expense. Impressed by this renewed expression of Itsekiri hospitality, the captain decided to revive his factory project, this time with a site in the Itsekiri-controlled region near the mouth of the Benin River in mind. As in Benin, he first broached the subject to the ruler who had to bring the matter before a full council; although Landolphe gives no information about these negotiations, the outcome was favourable. When the time came for the ship to be towed back to the Benin

---

1 It acquired this name in the nineteenth century; Landolphe refers to it as the 'Jabou' (i.e. Ijebu) Creek.

River, the Olu refused all payment for food and lodging given to the crew and slaves, and capped his generosity by presenting Landolphe with a further ten thousand yams for use on the voyage to Santo Domingo. During that voyage more than one hundred slaves died in an outbreak of smallpox.

Immediately on his return to France in October 1784, Landolphe began to drum up support for his Benin River project. He received some assistance from a nephew of the Olu named Boudakan whom he had been asked to take to France; there this member of the Itsekiri royal family made a good impression on Parisian society, including Louis XVI. Landolphe himself drew up the prospectus for his *Compagnie d'Owhere et de Benin* on lines very similar to those envisaged by the defunct *Compagnie de la Guyane*, with the difference that the factory was now to be situated at the mouth of the river instead of Ughoton. Most of the proposals and prospects it dangled before the public were hopelessly unrealistic: the intention, for example, to despatch every three months from France a ship carrying goods to the value of 200,000 francs and forty men to relieve those stationed in the factory; or the visions of a trade amounting to 3,000 slaves a year. The company was nonetheless formed, a royal privilege approved the establishment of a factory,[1] and an *arrêt* of the *Conseil d'Etat* dated 27 May 1786 granted a monopoly of all French trade in the Benin-Itsekiri area for a period of three years. In addition to legislative backing the French government also supplied a four-hundred-ton ship, the *Perou*, to transport stores and equipment to the factory site. Another two small ships—the corvettes *L'Afrique* (70 tons) and *La Petite Charlotte* (40 tons)—were bought by Landolphe for use in the river. All three vessels sailed from Rochefort in July 1786 under Landolphe's command. Among those on board were Boudakan and the naturalist A. M. F. J.

---

1 Instructions given by the French government to the Governor of Senegal in 1785 mentioned the private establishment which the King had authorised M. Brillantois to maintain in the Benin River; it would permit ships to anchor outside the dangerous bar and receive their cargoes from light craft, and it was expected to be successful and profitable. Ref. C. Schefer, *Instructions générales données de 1763 à 1870 aux gouveneurs et ordonnateurs des établissements français en Afrique Occidentale*, 2 vols. Paris, 1921–7, vol. I, p. 133.

Palisot, Baron de Beauvois, who later produced two fine works on the flora and insects of the Benin and Forcados Rivers.[1]

On reaching the river the *Perou* anchored outside the bar, while Landolphe took the corvettes on 21 November 1786 to the Itsekiri village of Bobi in order to confer with the chief whose name he gives as 'Animazan'. From the accounts of both Landolphe and Palisot de Beauvois it is evident that a number of Itsekiri villages had already sprung up near the mouth of the river; Bobi, Salt Town and Eghoro (or New Town as it is styled in most English books) were all in existence by 1786, but it is likely that they were of recent origin. Bobi, for example, according to Itsekiri tradition was founded in the reign of Olu Erejuwa by the *Ologbotsere* of Warri, Eyinmisaren, who may plausibly be identified with Landolphe's Animazan. In the same period the *Otsodi* of the Itsekiri is said to have founded the nearby settlement of Olobe, which may well be Landolphe's Salt Town. The manufacture of salt is indeed the motive nowadays attributed to the chiefs who pioneered these new villages.[2] The interest taken in the French factory by these same senior Itsekiri chiefs demonstrates how much importance they attached to the commercial exploitation of their supremacy in the Benin River.

To the chief of Bobi Landolphe announced the safe return of Boudakan and made a request for permission to build his factory on a site a cannon-shot from that village. The Olu, to whom the chief passed the request, at once gave his consent, so cannon, stores and materials were put ashore, and within eight days the labourers supplied from Bobi had built a house and eight large huts; the French in the meantime saw to the fortifications and the placing of cannon. Having completed these preliminary works, Landolphe went with Boudakan to Ode Itsekiri. With him he took some

---

1 *Flore d'Oware et de Benin*, 2 vols. Paris, 1804–7; *Insectes recueillis en Afrique et en Amerique*. Paris, 1805. Both works are splendidly illustrated. He also wrote, 'Notice sur le peuple de Benin', which was published in *Décades Philosophiques*, no. 12, *année* 9, 1801.

2 Salt continued to be an important product of this area in the nineteenth century. According to Punch, the country around Ebrohimi was highly coveted for the abundance of salt bush found there. The salt was packed into long thin baskets for transport to the interior. 'These long baskets are, or were, the salt measure for trade in Benin.' (Roth, *Great Benin*, p. 143.)

presents for the Olu, including a fully-furnished bed and a stick with a silver knob which, he explained, 'may serve to make known your will, whenever it shall please you to make some request of me'.[1] A similar stick or staff was later presented to Okorodudu in token of his services. Possibly it was these staffs which established the custom followed in the nineteenth century by British consular officials who gave similar symbols of authority to recognised Itsekiri chiefs.

The next move was to visit Benin, for, as the name of his company proclaimed, Landolphe had not intended that by placing his factory at the mouth of the river his trade should be confined to the Itsekiris; rather it was meant, like the earlier posts at Arbo, to serve as a convenient centre for trade with a wide area. He travelled to Ughoton with Palisot de Beauvois and three other Frenchmen in an Itsekiri canoe commanded by Okorodudu—perhaps not the most tactful approach. After a delay of two days during which the *Edaiken* of Ughoton informed the Oba of their arrival, thirty-two porters and the usual two *veadors* came with a present of sheep and yams, and hammocks to carry the travellers to Benin City. Their journey and reception followed the usual course, except that Landolphe gives the impression that the road had been improved since his last visit with shelters and provisions for travellers set out at intervals of two leagues.[2] As before, the Oba received Landolphe privately at 11 o'clock on the evening of his arrival, the only others present being two *emada*, one of whom spoke some English and acted as interpreter. As soon as the captain appeared the Oba began to laugh and express pleasure at his return, but he went on to enquire why the French had built their factory at the river mouth when they had been given land at Ughoton. Landolphe pleaded the unhealthiness of the upper river and promised that a factory should be built at Ughoton with a resident official and an adequate stock of merchandise; as a first step someone should be sent to open trade

---

1 Landolphe, *Mémoires*, vol. II, p. 38. cf. supra p. 151. Staff for Anthony.
2 Dapper mentions large pots of drinking water placed by the Oba's order along the Ughoton–Benin City road 'for the convenience of travellers'. (*Naukeurige Beschrijvinge*, p. 123.) The observations of Legroing and Balon in 1787 confirm Landolphe's remarks concerning the shelters and foodstuffs. (Labarthe, *Voyage*, p. 174.)

immediately he returned to Bobi. These assurances, supported by a present of silks, chintz, muslin and a hat and cloak, appeared to satisfy the Oba, who promised, at Landolphe's request, to send word to 'one of the most powerful Ijo chiefs' that the French should not be molested, with a warning that he would punish anyone injuring them. Although Landolphe mentions no quarrel with or threat from the Ijos, he evidently feared that his close association with the Itsekiris might involve him in the enmity of the two peoples.

It was almost certainly during the course of this visit that Palisot de Beauvois witnessed the celebration of the yam festival (*agwe*) by the Oba and the *Ezomo*; he has left a full account of the proceedings.[1] Both rites followed the same pattern, with those of the *Ezomo*, which had no doubt been modelled upon the palace festival, preceding those of the Oba by a few days. The war captain opened his festival with a procession to the palace in which he was accompanied by several musicians, *veadors* and chiefs, and also by twelve favourite wives wearing hooped petticoat skirts and an abundance of coral round their necks and in their hair; the *Ezomo* wore similar attire and carried his ceremonial sword, the *eben*. After spending more than an hour in the palace, this procession began its return journey to the *Ezomo*'s village Uzebu. Half-way there the chief three times made a staggering motion towards the watching crowds, causing them to scatter, and three times he tossed his *eben* into the air. Palisot de Beauvois, who had followed the procession, was then invited to watch the ceremony which took place inside the *Ezomo*'s house. In the company of some four hundred of the chief's wives he was taken into a courtyard at one end of which stood an altar decorated with two large tusks. The wives ranged themselves on steps on either side of the altar, the *Ezomo* sat in a wooden chair on the right; the *veadors* and some animals destined for sacrifice were placed along the left-hand wall of the court, while a large crowd of onlookers took up their positions at the far end facing the altar. At a signal from the *Ezomo* the ceremony began with a monotonous chant from the people, accompanied by a rubbing of hands. As it ended three men were led in, their hands tied behind their backs and their mouths gagged with a bone; an executioner wearing a red

---

1 In his 'Notice sur le peuple de Benin', pp. 144–6.

loin-cloth forced them to their knees. Then began another chant, after which three *veadors* each took from the *Ezomo* a stick which was hollow at one end; these they thrust three times into a cavity in the middle of the altar, then tapped them three times on the victims' foreheads. Palisot de Beauvois noticed that the doomed men appeared calm, and that each had some defect which made him unsuitable for sale as a slave.[1] These proceedings were followed by a third and longer chant. When it ended the executioner advanced to the middle of the courtyard, raised his sword three times and, at a sign from the *Ezomo*, cut off the three heads which he then displayed to the crowd. These sacrifices preluded the grand climax of the festival—the yam ritual. Taking a newly-harvested yam, the *Ezomo* placed it in a pot and covered it with earth. There ensued more singing and dancing during which some of the chiefs substituted for this pot another containing a much bigger yam that was subsequently uncovered and displayed to the people. The larger the changeling, the brighter the omens for the harvest. The last phase of the festival included a song in which the women joined, and the sacrifice of animals—a bull, a goat, a ram and three cocks—in a manner similar to that followed in the human sacrifices. Some of the flesh was reserved for the *Ezomo*, and the rest distributed to the people. Finally the *femmes des pauvres* came one by one to the altar, knelt, said a short prayer, then placed in the cavity pieces of fruit and vegetable sprinkled with palm wine or spirits. The ceremony of the Oba differed from that of his principal chief mainly in the scale of the sacrifices which for the ruler amounted to fifteen each of men, goats, rams and cocks.

Landolphe's promise to open trade at Ughoton without delay appears not to have been kept; at least he never mentions any such trade. But neither does he give any details of his trade with the Itsekiris, despite the fact that he lived among them for more than five years. The probable explanation for this curious reticence is that things were not going according to plan; so dismally did the *Compagnie d'Owhere et de Benin* fail in its undertakings to send regular supplies of men and goods that in five years only two ships arrived from France, and neither of these brought any replacements

---

1 This observation casts further doubt upon the claim that the *Ezomo* never sold any of his slaves. cf. supra p. 201.

for the large number of factory staff who died of yellow fever within two months of their arrival. Eventually only five of those who had come to Benin on the *Perou* survived their stay in the river and that number included Palisot de Beauvois who was forced by illness to leave after fifteen months. The only reinforcement Landolphe received came from the survivors of a Portuguese vessel wrecked on the bar of the Escravos which it had mistaken for the Benin River; among them was an experienced captain named Olivier (probably Oliveira) who became Landolphe's right-hand man.

Abandoned by his own company, Landolphe was obliged to turn his position to advantage by acting as a middleman or broker for ships of all nations visiting the Benin River. He would buy their cargo on arrival and undertake to provide a return cargo within a given time. Ships were thus able to spare their crews the dangers of a long wait in the river, and to lie outside the bar while the French factory supplied them with water, wood and food at fixed rates, and ferried goods backwards and forwards in its own boats. Landolphe claims that he did much business of this kind with English, Portuguese and Danish ships. In addition he often sent his Portuguese lieutenant with *La Petite Charlotte* to the Gold Coast where he could buy merchandise from European ships trading there. Some independent support for these claims is provided by a report submitted by the master of a São Tomé sloop which visited the Benin River early in 1787.[1] He had observed work in progress on Landolphe's fort, and had been asked by the French to show his passport; he had also seen two large French vessels outside the bar and four small boats employed in carrying slaves and cloth to them. This evidence relates, however, to the earlier and more prosperous days of the establishment, and it is impossible to believe Landolphe's general claim that his trading activities were yielding a profit of as much as 30,000 francs a day—the equivalent, by his own reckoning, of 150 slaves! The only cargo of which he gives any details was that despatched in 1789 by the corvette *L'Afrique* which was lost at sea; it carried, according to Landolphe, fifty wine-barrels of palm oil, 20,000 pounds of ivory, 1,000 cloths, an unspecified quantity of

---

1 A.H.U. *São Tomé, caixa* 10. V. Gomes Ferreira to Minister for Overseas Affairs, 28 April 1787.

gum, and red, yellow, blue and violet dyewoods. For the *Okro* and
the *Boudakan,* the two ships sent by his own company, he supplies
no such information. Other sources, however, reveal that the
Boudakan (300 tons) sailed from Nantes on 26 March 1787, sold 200
slaves in Santo Domingo, and returned to its home port in February
1789; about the *Okro* (80 tons) we know only that it left Nantes on
1 February 1787.[1] There is certainly nothing here to reflect commerce on the grand scale declared by Landolphe.

Some further independent light is shed on the enterprise in the
report submitted by Lt. Legroing following his visit to the Benin
River in May 1787.[2] Because the *Compagnie d'Owhere et de Benin*
was operating under the terms of a royal privilege, the French
Minister of Marine ordered M. le comte de Flotte, commander of
the frigate *Junon,* to visit Landolphe's factory and ensure that the
directors were fulfilling their undertakings. He was also entrusted
with a mission to the Oba of Benin from whom the French government hoped to secure a commercial treaty granting the French sole
trading rights in the Benin River. It is curious that he had no
instructions to negotiate with, or even to visit, the Olu of Warri, in
whose territory the French factory had been built, and who effectively controlled most of the river. Evidently Landolphe had not
succeeded in explaining to Versailles either his intentions or the true
state of affairs in the Benin River.

Junon anchored off the river on 1 May 1787 and was met by one
of Landolphe's corvettes which took ashore twenty-five marines and
the two officers to whom M. de Flotte had delegated his Benin
mission. Some days later Legroing and Balon accompanied by
Landolphe travelled to Ughoton where, by stressing the importance
of their mission, they prevailed upon the *Edaiken* to send a messenger express to Benin City. Two messengers with a hundred
porters arrived the very next day. Legroing noticed that one of the
messengers carried a silver whistle which the Europeans had to
touch, 'pour que nous ne doutassions pas de sa qualité';[3] this form

---

1 P. D. Rinchon, *La traite et l'esclavage des Congolais par les Européens.* Wetteren,
  1929, p. 290. *Boudakan* was owned by Marion and Brillantois, *Okro* by Canel,
  Meslé and Bernard.
2 P. Labarthe, *Voyage,* p. 170 et seq.
3 Labarthe, *Voyage,* p. 173.

of accreditation may have been a comparatively recent innovation, possibly inspired by the same considerations that had led to the introduction of staffs of office among the Itsekiris. They paid the customary visit to the *Ezomo* in the course of which they were permitted to see some of his wives and the shrine of his father which was decorated with eight wooden heads supporting large tusks. Their meeting with the Oba took place, as on Landolphe's previous visits, late at night on the day of their arrival in the capital. Both Landolphe and Legroing have left accounts of the interview which agree that the Oba gave them a cordial welcome and that they then discussed the proposed commercial treaty. Over the question of the interpreter, however, they register an interesting difference. Whereas Landolphe maintains that he had with him a negro who spoke good French, because he thought it prudent not to use his own knowledge of Edo to address the Oba directly, Legroing records that the interpreter spoke only bad English and that they had difficulty in making themselves understood. Such a detail, of small importance in itself, underlines the need for caution in making use of Landolphe's memoirs.

In the afternoon of the following day, 14 May 1787, the Frenchmen were invited to a ceremony which was described by Legroing but not by Landolphe. It would seem to have been the *ugie-ivie*—the festival of the royal coral regalia. With the Oba and his chiefs following in procession all the coral ornaments were carried to a shrine in one of the palace courtyards.[1] Dressed in white the Oba stood on the lowest step of the shrine while the chiefs, the four Frenchmen among them, took up their positions behind him in two parallel lines. A gagged victim was then brought in, made to kneel and killed by a blow on the head. Apparently the head was afterwards severed from the body so that some of the blood might be sprinkled on the coral regalia, and the rest poured on the shrine. An ox and a sheep were sacrificed in the same manner. On a later

---

1 The chief participants in this ceremony were members of the *Iwebo* association for they were the custodians of the royal regalia. In recent times the shrine of Oba Ewuare has been the scene of this ritual, and it is probable that this was also the practice in the eighteenth century because Ewuare is believed to have introduced the coral regalia into Benin. cf. Bradbury, *The Benin Kingdom*, p. 59.

occasion the visitors were permitted to inspect the corals among which they noticed a ceremonial collar formed of between fifteen and twenty strings of beads; collars of this kind figure on many of the Benin brass heads.

Regarding the negotiations for a treaty Landolphe and Legroing are not wholly in agreement. The former states that the subject was discussed at a full council attended by the Frenchmen. His description of proceedings is fairly circumstantial, but the accuracy either of his memory or of his editor may be questioned when he describes the long white beards of the Benin elders! He recounts how the assembly debated the French proposals with great liveliness, and how they decided by a majority against them, many chiefs allegedly recalling unpleasant memories of a similar treaty with the Dutch. Their memories of events fifty years past were, perhaps understandably, not very accurate, for the Dutch had never enjoyed exclusive trading privileges. Legroing on the other hand implies that he did not attend this council, and that he learned its decision from the Oba who reiterated the customary Benin stand on open trade. At the same time the ruler assured them of his favour towards the French and renewed the permission previously given to Landolphe to trade at Ughoton, requesting him to keep Benin well supplied with wine, liqueurs, salt, sugar and good coral—a royal shopping list. Landolphe's complete silence on these matters which so directly concerned him is rather puzzling, unless it arose from embarrassment at his failure to carry on the trade promised both to the Oba and to his company in France.

If his memoirs may be relied upon, Landolphe did not again visit Benin during the five years he spent at Bobi. Considering also that Benin is not mentioned in his admittedly rather vague account of his trading activities in that period, it is probable that he henceforward confined his journeys and trade to the areas under Itsekiri control. One interesting encounter did, however, arise from his earlier visits to Benin. At some unspecified time, but probably in 1787, there arrived at the French factory a group of men lighter in colour and with hair straighter than those he had met on the coast.[1] While in Benin City on a political mission for their ruler they had expressed

---

1 Landolphe, *Mémoires*, vol. II, pp. 85–8.

curiosity about the fort and factory which the Oba had described to them, and had decided to see it for themselves. The only novelty as far as they were concerned proved to be the sight of white men, for they told Landolphe that firearms were manufactured in their own country, and that boats comparable to his corvettes came over a great sea to the city of their king. Between their country and Benin existed a trade in luxury articles which, the Edo claimed, surpassed European goods in both price and quality. Landolphe was told that these men were 'Oyos' who had travelled three months from their own country to reach Benin City. This identification does not however accord very well with their physical appearance, their ability to write and calculate in Arabic, and the pronounced vowel-endings of all the words in their own language; nor would their claim to be able to manufacture firearms seem to indicate that they were Yorubas. In many respects an identification with the Hausas would be more appropriate, though it is quite conceivable that they may have come to Benin through, and even on behalf of, the kingdom of Oyo.[1] Whoever these men were, they afford one of the few glimpses available of Benin's commercial and political relations with the states of the interior which were always more important than its dealings with Europeans.

Another adventure that may have had something to do with Benin befell Landolphe about three years after the establishment of his factory at Bobi. The ruler of Lagos[2] despatched to the Benin River

---

1 cf. El Hage Abd Salam Shabeeny, *An Account of Timbuctoo and Housa*, ed. J. G. Jackson. London, 1820, in Hodgkin, *Nigerian Perspectives*, p. 187. 'Their arms are the same as at Timbuctoo [sc. those of the Hausa]; the muskets, which are matchlocks, are made in the country ... Gunpowder is also manufactured there.' Another clue to the origin of Landolphe's visitors is provided by his interest in the tamarind which, he discovered, grew in their country. Landolphe also mentions that the tamarinds on which he relied for medicinal purposes came to Benin from the Oyo country. The natural habitat of the tamarind lies well to the north of the Niger, but it is possible that it had already been widely diffused farther south.
2 Landolphe refers to him as the 'King of Aunis'. In the eighteenth century many Europeans knew Lagos as Onim, a name which appears in Portuguese documents as early as 1766. cf. P. Verger, 'Notes on some documents in which Lagos is referred to by the name "Onim" and which mention relations between Onim and Brazil'. *Journal of the Historical Society of Nigeria*, vol. I, no. 4, 1959.

some war canoes with the intention—so Okorodudu assured Landolphe—of attacking the factory. So that he might be defended the Frenchman supplied Okorodudu with powder and shot, and that chief then led a fleet of Itsekiri canoes to battle against the intruders. A week later he returned to Bobi having beaten them off and bringing with him four elders taken prisoner in the combat. The story these captives told Landolphe was that the ruler of Lagos had been incited to make the attack by English traders who wished to destroy his factory and take over the site. As Okorodudu had placed their fate in his hands, Landolphe decided to send the four back to Lagos in *La Petite Charlotte*; there his men heard the same story of an English plot that had cost Lagos two hundred men taken prisoner by the Itsekiris and sold into slavery at Calabar.[1] There may have been some foundation for this explanation of the incident, but it has to be remembered that Landolphe's later experiences made him an ardent Anglophobe. Also it is difficult to believe that the people of Lagos would have undertaken such an enterprise solely at the instigation of the English and solely for the benefit of that nation—for one cannot see that Lagos had anything to gain by it. One may indeed wonder whether the Lagos canoes intended to attack the French factory, or whether the Itsekiris had given Landolphe that impression in order to obtain ammunition with which to drive trading rivals out of the river. Lagos at this time was rising into prominence as a major slave-trading port, and might therefore be considered a threat to Itsekiri prosperity. It also, as Landolphe himself was aware, retained strong dynastic links with Benin which had good reason to desire the destruction of Itsekiri power at the mouth of the Benin River. Thus, one may speculate that the Oba might have hoped to see the Lagosians succeed, where the Ijos had failed, in driving the Itsekiris from the river. Admittedly there is no evidence to support such suppositions, yet an uncomfortable air of misrepresentation hangs about the explanation of the affair given by Landolphe.[2]

---

1 It is curious that the Itsekiris sold none of these slaves to Landolphe.
2 cf. the incident recorded in J. B. Losi, *History of Lagos*. Lagos, 1914, p. 19, which he attributes to the reign of Adele, but dates to the end of the eighteenth century. When Adele, according to Lagos custom, tried to take his father's

The destruction of Landolphe's factory in April 1792, for which there exists no testimony other than that of the captain himself, is likewise wrapped in some obscurity. The captains of the two large Liverpool ships that carried out the attack are alleged to have told the captain of a French schooner that they had orders to seize Landolphe dead or alive. Leaving aside the credibility of such an admission to a compatriot of the victim, it may be noted that, apart from the Lagos incident and a quarrel in 1791 with a Liverpool captain over a cargo which Landolphe refused to buy, the latter gives no reason why the English should have harboured such animosity against him; he rather emphasises the many services he had rendered to English ships visiting the Benin River. In revenge for the attack, in which Landolphe claimed to have lost all his wealth and property, Itsekiri canoes seized two English vessels lying in Ureju Bay. Both were burned after Landolphe had refused the one offered to him by the Olu. As a further reprisal the Itsekiri ruler is said to have declared that he would never permit the English to trade in his territory. If he did so resolve, he did not long maintain that posture for Captain Adams received a warm welcome at Ode Itsekiri only a few years later, and his account gives no indication that his fellow-countrymen suffered from any discrimination among the Itsekiris.

3. The last years of the slave trade

After recovering from his injuries, Landolphe was taken to Príncipe by a French captain who had been buying slaves at Ughoton for M. Senat and Company of Bordeaux. From 1791 this firm had maintained an agent in Príncipe to organise a slave trade between the ports of the Niger delta and Brazil. Until the outbreak of the revolutionary wars in Europe put an end to its activities, the

---

remains for burial in Benin City, his brother sent a message to the Itsekiris asking them to intercept the funeral party. An attack was made, supposedly by the Ijos, but within Itsekiri territory. Allowing for a good deal of chronological confusion, it is just possible that this incident is related to that in which Landolphe was involved.

company bought many slaves directly from Benin.[1] English ships too were still acquiring slaves regularly from Benin, though not on the scale of earlier decades; at least, such was the impression gained by John Adams who visited the river some time between the destruction of Landolphe's factory and the close of the century.[2] His observation is supported not only by the few figures available[3] but also, in a rather negative fashion, by the memoirs of European traders frequenting the Guinea coast in this period. Most of them never visited Benin. One of the best known, Captain Crow of Liverpool, entered the river only once in the course of his numerous West African voyages.[4] Adams, who also went only once to Benin,

---

1 cf. A.H.U. *São Tomé, caixa* 11. J. Baptista e Silva, Captain General of São Tomé, to Minister for Overseas Affairs, 20 April 1792. 'I wish to inform Your Excellency that on Quinquagesima Sunday there arrived at the island of Príncipe another three-masted vessel belonging to the French company which has an establishment there; it came from Bordeaux laden with merchandise. Since they had sent their larger vessels to trade on the coast, they chartered one belonging to Gregorio Lucas, an inhabitant of the island, loaded it with merchandise, and sent it to the port of Benin. In that port they have José de Mello Puntoja, an inhabitant of the island and a native of Bahia, with a single-master manned by other natives of the island, and from there he does business with Portuguese captains from Brazil who come to that coast with tobacco in search of slaves. He gives them goods in exchange for tobacco and money, so that he is able to combine these with his own merchandise in the purchase of slaves which he sends to the island of Príncipe.' The arrangement described in this letter is very reminiscent of that in which Landolphe was engaged, and it is likely that the 'port of Benin' was in the Itsekiri-controlled part of the river, rather than at Ughoton. One may again wonder that Landolphe is silent about the activities of this rival French company which must have competed directly with his own.

2 J. Adams, *Sketches taken during ten voyages to Africa, between the years 1786 and 1800; including observations on the country between Cape Palmas and the River Congo; and cursory remarks on the physical and moral character of the inhabitants: with an appendix containing an account of the European trade with the west coast of Africa.* London, n.d. Also *Remarks on the country from Cape Palmas to the River Congo.* London, 1823. His visit must have taken place after the death of Akengbuda who reigned until around the end of the century and who was already an elderly man when Landolphe first met him. The Oba whom Adams saw was only middle-aged. It is probable therefore that the death of Akengbuda, which Egharevba places 'about 1804', needs to be advanced by a few years.

3 cf. supra pp. 197–8.

4 H. Crow, *Memoirs of the late Captain Hugh Crow of Liverpool.* London, 1830. It is significant that Crow's sole visit to the Benin River was made during the course of his first voyage to Africa in 1790–1. 'We proceeded to a place called

attributed this neglect of the river by slave ships to the alarming sickness rate that afflicted vessels anchored there. Ports at the mouths of rivers were reputed healthier than inland places such as Ughoton or Ode Itsekiri. The Benin slave trade suffered from the additional handicap that very large ships could not enter the river, only small ones could reach Ughoton, and once there they had to wait several months to complete their cargoes. Though the occasional São Tomé and Brazilian slaver continued to make its appearance in the Benin River, by the end of the century most of them preferred to gather their cargoes at Lagos. In an indirect manner the Oba may have profited from the rising prosperity of the tributary state which the Governor of Príncipe referred to in 1811 as 'the port of Benin'.[1] He contrived, for example, with the aid of the Ijos and Ijebus, to sell some slaves through Lagos. But there can be little doubt that the European trade which had run briskly in Benin throughout the eighteenth century had, by the first decade of the nineteenth, reached a very low ebb. The last great upsurge of the transatlantic slave trade thus passed the Benin River by in favour of more convenient ports of call.

Adams' observations on trading practices at Benin reveal that these had changed little since Landolphe's time. It was still the custom for masters of vessels to visit the Oba soon after their arrival at Ughoton, to make him a present—in Adams' case a piece of silk damask, scarlet cloth and strings of coral—and discuss business with him. Like his father, the new Oba, Obanosa, took a keen interest in the details of commerce which he discussed for an hour with Adams, lamenting especially the dearth of Brazilian tobacco. On his departure, the Englishman, like earlier French visitors, was presented with a small tusk and a few 'country cloths'.[2] Trading still took place at Ughoton where the Oba maintained a resident *veador* to sell his slaves and ivory; and values continued to be

---

Lagos, with negroes, and thence to Benin.' (p. 34.) He traded between Lagos and Benin for several months, then sailed from Benin to Liverpool with a cargo of ivory and 'other articles' to report the death of all the company's agents on the coast. He does not mention Landolphe's establishment.

1 A.H.U. *codice* 1497, f. 232. 19 April 1811.
2 Crow observed that Benin was famous for the manufacture of 'a beautiful sort of tablecloth'. (*Memoirs*, p. 201.) cf. supra p. 207.

reckoned in cloths—*pawns* in the anglicised form of the word employed by Adams.

The falling off in European trade with the Benin River area probably contributed to a renewed deterioration in relations between Benin and Warri at the beginning of the nineteenth century. In April 1809 the governor of São Tomé reported that war had broken out between the Itsekiris and the Oba of Benin and Onim (Lagos);[1] and when in the following year the Portuguese became involved in a dispute with the Itsekiris over payment for some slaves, the Olu threatened to seize Portuguese ships bound for Lagos.[2] Similar threats were directed against Portuguese trade in the Benin River with the particular objective of keeping it away from Benin. It was anxiety over this situation that led the governor of São Tomé to write to his superiors:

> The King of Oere is not at all pacific, and the position of his port gives him every assurance of success. This warrants the most careful attention of Your Excellency who is well aware that, in order to reach the kingdom of Benin, it is necessary to navigate waters within the territory of Oere, where there are canoes of extraordinary size, many of them mounting artillery and with a considerable number of rowers and warriors.[3]

Itsekiri aggressiveness towards both Benin and the Portuguese seems to have coincided with the accession c. 1809[4] of the Olu Akengbuwa, a man of violent and autocratic ways. His own people too felt his heavy hand. One of the most prominent of his adversaries was the *Uwangue* Uwankun, at one time the governor of New Town and the founder of a new Itsekiri settlement named Jakpa on a creek west of the Benin River.[5] One result of this feud was a

---

1 A.H.U. *codice* 1467, f. 141r. Governor General of São Tomé and Príncipe to Minister of Overseas Affairs, 1 April 1809.

2 ibid. ff. 152v–153v. Governor General of São Tomé and Príncipe to Minister of Overseas Affairs, 31 March 1810.

3 A.H.U. *São Tomé, caixa* 21. Governor General of São Tomé and Príncipe to Conde das Galveas, 25 April 1812.

4 A Portuguese document dated 31 March 1810 (ref. supra n. 2) mentions a letter signed by 'Dom José, Rey de Oere', whereas in 1807 the ruler of Warri had been known to the Portuguese as Dom João. (A.H.U. *codice* 1495, ff. 154r–155v.)

5 cf. Lloyd, *The Itsekiri*, p. 180.

deep and permanent rift among the Itsekiris from which Benin was able to derive some advantage, for the *Uwangue* sought the protection of Oba Osemwede, and his heirs, Diare and Nana, subsequently received investiture from Benin in respect of their possessions on the Benin River. Having taken the Itsekiri chief under his wing, Osemwede continued, according to the Benin version of events, to support him at Jakpa against harassment from the Olu,[1] with the result that the new town became a relatively important centre of European trade to the detriment of rivals that continued to owe allegiance to Akengbuwa.[2] The quarrel reached a climax when the Oba placed a curse upon the Olu and his family with apparently devastating results, for Akengbuwa died 'in agony about a year later, and his heirs who should have been made Olu after him also died in quick succession'.[3]

If European trade in the Benin River had been declining at the end of the eighteenth century, it was not the less profoundly affected by that watershed in West African history—the abolition of the external slave trade. Prohibition of slaving by British ships led to an almost complete cessation of that nation's trade in the river, since its other support—ivory—was not by itself sufficient to sustain it.[4] British warships also began to interfere with Portuguese slavers. Constant complaints of their activities flowed from São Tomé and from Portugal,[5] until in 1815 diplomatic pressure forced the Portuguese government to prohibit its nationals from engaging in the trade north of the equator. Spain followed suit in 1817. Thereafter the clandestine activities of the slavers, harried by British naval squadrons, become difficult to follow. Without any doubt

---

1 Egharevba, *A Short History*, p. 47.
2 'Wacoo's town', i.e. Uwankun's town, is mentioned by E. Bold, *Merchants' and mariners' African guide*, London, 1819, as a place of trade where ships could obtain oil, ivory, pepper, redwood and provisions.
3 Egharevba, *A Short History*, p. 47. It is interesting to note that this ruler of the Itsekiris against whom the Oba turned his 'supernatural' powers was the first of his line since the late sixteenth century to reject completely the teachings of Roman Catholic missionaries. cf. Ryder, 'Missionary Activity', p. 23.
4 The Liverpool merchant Bold (*Merchants' guide*, p. 64) affirmed that since the abolition of the slave trade the Benin River had been completely deserted by British ships.
5 e.g. A.H.U. *codice* 1494 *passim*.

the trade continued on a substantial scale—in certain ports, including Lagos and Bonny, it probably increased after 1815—but all the evidence suggests that in the Benin River it underwent a drastic decline. To the old perils, underlined by a report in the *Royal Gold Coast Gazette* of 1823 that the river was not much frequented by slavers because of the dangerous bar on which four Portuguese vessels had been wrecked in the previous five years,[1] were added new dangers from British cruisers. A ship could not spend too long on the coast gathering a slave cargo without fear of discovery, therefore captains did not favour the Benin River where the turn-round was notoriously slow. Nevertheless some continued to venture there. In 1825 Captain Fawckner met a number of Portuguese slave ships in the river,[2] and it was alleged that in the eighteen-thirties the activities of slave traders had gravely hampered the development of the Liverpool palm-oil trade.[3] The latest recorded incident involving a slave vessel occurred in 1837 when a British naval schooner seized the Portuguese ship *Veloz* in the Benin River, though it is likely that a few others may have slipped in later and avoided capture.

Despite the fact that the slave trade of the Benin River had in its last years been almost entirely in Itsekiri hands, mid-nineteenth-century British observers were firmly convinced that its abolition had brought ruin on Benin. Colour was given to this belief by incidents such as the tirade against British interference with slaving

---

1 *Royal Gold Coast Gazette*, no. 1, vol. I. 25 March 1823. The introduction to the report on Benin reads, 'We are favoured by a friend with the following communication relative to Benin, which we hope may be interesting to our readers, as the intercourse with that part of the coast has been confined for nearly twenty years.'

2 Fawckner, *Narrative*, p. 101.

3 P.R.O. F.O. 84/1031. Campbell to Foreign Office, 4 April 1857. 'About twenty years since some small Liverpool trading vessels entered the Benin River to open a trade in palm oil and other productions. The supercargoes of these vessels found their progress greatly impeded by the presence of slave vessels in the river, for, so long as they remained, the natives paid no attention to the trade in palm oil; means were therefore taken to apprise the British cruisers of slave vessels being in the river, which led to their capture and the total ruin of their undertakings: gradually the slavers withdrew from the river, and the Liverpool vessels were able to get their vessels loaded in reasonable time.'

which Osemwede delivered to an English visitor in 1838,[1] but it rested mainly upon serious misconceptions of Benin's trade in the past. Consul Campbell, for example, declared: 'Benin, therefore, from being a once formidable and dreaded power based on the slave trade, has now dwindled into insignificance.'[2] Following his visit to Benin City in 1862, Sir Richard Burton voiced a similar opinion: 'Though Benin has been ruined, mostly by the suppression of slave export, the king accepts it as a *fait accompli*.'[3] Campbell's error was compounded by a false notion of the relationship between Benin and Warri, for he believed that the latter had been 'the strong arm' of the Oba's power in the Benin River and as far afield as Badagry. These erroneous notions of Benin's role in the Atlantic slave trade are still with us.[4]

Because its economy did not in fact depend upon the slave trade, and thanks to long experience of a heterogeneous commerce with several European nations, Benin might have seemed well-fitted to develop a new pattern of trade as the slavers were gradually driven from the seas. The situation would appear encouraging in that European merchants formerly engaged in slaving were likewise seeking an alternative source of trade. But two major obstacles stood in the way of an Edo commercial renaissance: the first, and perhaps the most important, was Itsekiri control of the river approaches to Benin territory; the second was the familiar problem of finding a natural or manufactured product which could be supplied and marketed in commercial quantities. This latter difficulty was emphasised in a despatch from the Governor of São Tomé written in 1816 in which he discussed the efforts being made by the islanders to develop the traditional staples of Benin trade in place of the officially defunct commerce in slaves. After lamenting the ruin which he believed the abolition of slaving would bring upon

---

1 The visitor was Moffat, a surgeon on a schooner belonging to the Glasgow merchant Robert Jamieson. In company with another surgeon named Smith he paid a visit to Benin City and was received by the Oba. An account of their experiences is to be found in *Journal of the Royal Geographical Society*, vol. II, 1841.
2 P.R.O. F.O. 84/1031. Campbell to Foreign Office, 4 April 1857.
3 Burton, 'My wanderings in West Africa', p. 416.
4 e.g. M. Crowder, *The Story of Nigeria*. London, 1962, p. 73. 'Benin was the most important slave mart, west of the Niger.'

the island, the governor turned to the problem of finding a substitute:

> The Benin trade could be useful to the island, but only to a limited extent. The cloths which may be exported from Benin cannot all be sold in the islands, and in Great Gabon, where most used to be sold, there is now only a little trade in ivory, gum and wood—far too little to justify carrying such merchandise to the kingdom of Brazil. A small number might, however, be sent to Bahia, the only port in which there is some sale for this kind of cloth.
>
> The Colonel of Ordnance in the island of São Tomé sent a schooner of his to Benin and did such a good trade in cloths there that it brought back to the island ten thousand cloths. He sold them, and sent the ship back there again. Another vessel belonging to Dona Maria do Nascimento did likewise. But I can assure Your Excellency that it will take a long time to sell the cargoes of these two ships on their return because there is no market. . . . The cloths of Benin, Warri, Onim and Badagry are an important commodity, but it is not possible to sell a large number of them, and we have no means of exporting the ivory which these places could supply in large quantities.[1]

Bold too stressed the importance of Ijebu cloths bought in the Benin River for ships trading to the south where these cloths still sold in large quantities. The best of such cloths equalled, in his estimation, the finest Manchester products;[2] but, as the governor of São Tomé had foreseen, the cloth trade was to dwindle rather than increase, and most of the buying of that product and of ivory seems to have remained in the hands of local Portuguese traders.[3] Moreover the proportion of this cloth supplied by Benin was probably far smaller than in previous centuries; Ijebu had captured much of the market through outlets at Lagos and Jakpa, as well as by selling directly through Ijebu itself. At the same time, civil wars in Oyo

---

1 A.H.U. *São Tomé, maços* (1816–38), 2 October 1816.
2 Bold, *Merchants' guide*, p. 69.
3 cf. Fawckner, *Narrative*, p. 75. While Fawckner was in the Benin River in 1825 two Portuguese schooners, one from São Tomé and the other from Whydah, arrived to buy cloth and ivory. The schooner from Whydah did some of its trade at Ughoton. Fawckner also noted that the *Ezomo*'s collection of autographs consisted entirely of contributions from Portuguese captains. (ibid. p. 90.)

and Fulani conquests in the Nupe country must have disrupted Benin's traditional sources of supply.[1]

If efforts by both sides to re-establish trade on a basis of cloth and ivory were doomed to frustration, a great future was appearing for the palm-produce trade. Europeans had bought palm oil from the time of their first contact with Benin, but in small quantities such as were required for feeding slaves, or for burning in lamps. Abolition of the slave trade encouraged Liverpool merchants to develop trade in palm produce on a commercial scale because abolition coincided with the growth of an industrial demand for oil in the manufacture of soap and lubricants. Among the earliest accounts of the oil trade is that given by Bold who, while remarking that ivory was still the chief commodity exported from Benin, and that it could be had in large quantities, drew attention to the rich palm-oil resources of the area and noted that oil could be bought in bulk from the Itsekiris of Ode Itsekiri and Jakpa. His description of the method of barter then in operation proves that a certain amount of oil was already being bought in the river, and that prices there were very advantageous to Europeans compared with those paid in Bonny and Calabar where competition was keener. Traders should, he urged, stick firmly to the established prices if commerce in the Benin River was to be worthwhile.[2] Against this price advantage however had to be set the difficulty of bringing ships of large burthen into the river—a handicap from which the ports of the eastern delta did not suffer.[3]

---

1 cf. supra p. 93.
2 Bold, *Merchants' guide*, pp. 60–9. In trade with the Itsekiris two oil measures were used: a four-gallon jar and a three-gallon jar The Olu received 1.5 *pawns* for the large jar and 1 *pawn* for the smaller; his subjects were paid 1 *pawn* for the larger and 2 *pawns* for three of the smaller jars. Taking Adams' valuation of the *pawn* at 2s. 6d. as the basis of calculation, the price of oil therefore varied from 7d. to 11d. a gallon. However, C. J. Gertzel ('Commercial Organisation on the Niger Coast 1852–91'. *Historians in Tropical Africa.* Salisbury, Rhodesia, 1962, p. 294) states that 'In 1825 palm oil could be bought for about 2d. a gallon.'
3 Later in the century insurance companies were charging 1 per cent more for ships crossing the Benin bar than for any other river on the coast. (Burton, 'My wanderings in West Africa', p. 136.) Burton was pessimistic about Benin's economic prospects: 'It is a hopeless task to restore commerce to Benin.' (ibid. p. 409).

At the time Bold and Adams wrote, the palm-oil trade in the Benin River was still largely a thing of the future. When it did develop, the Itsekiris' hold upon the lower reaches of the river would more than counterbalance their dependence upon inland suppliers of oil and ensure for them a prolonged dominance of that trade. But in the meanwhile the Itsekiri economy suffered severely from the decline of the slave trade, and the state came under a strain that broke it to pieces in the middle of the century. A declining income from trade undermined the authority of the Olu and the ruling families, thus producing political tensions of which the flight of the *Uwangue* may have been an early manifestation. Also, because European ships were no longer entering the Forcados River to trade directly with Ode Itsekiri, the centre of Itsekiri economic power had shifted decisively to the new settlements in the Benin River over which the Olu was able to exercise little effective control.[1] Thus it happened that in this crisis of the Itsekiri state and economy growing importance attached to the chiefs of villages such as Bobi, New Town and Jakpa. Bold depicts the governors of the first two—the men who represented the interests of the Olu and collected 'customs' on his behalf—as powerful tyrants who had to be humoured by visiting traders, for a quarrel with them could lead to an attack on a ship. It is difficult to recognise in them the successors of Landolphe's open-handed friends, and one must suspect that the change owed much to economic adversity, signs of which abounded. A correspondent of the *Royal Gold Coast Gazette* wrote in 1823: 'New Town is now nearly in ruins, and a few temporary huts have been erected at Bobee for the convenience of the communication with the shipping in the roadstead.'[2] A letter dated 23 September 1823 from a trader at New Town gives a similar impression:

> The trade of this place is nearly ruined from the villainy of the King of Warree, who has got into debt, and refuses to pay anyone: his

1 When the new settlements were founded the Olu delegated certain of his powers to one of the Itsekiri chiefs who was known to Europeans as the 'captain of the river'. In Landolphe's time this function appears to have been exercised by the *Iyatsere* Okorodudu. Later it passed to the *Uwangue* Uwankun whose rebellion threw the system into confusion from which it never wholly recovered.

2 *Royal Gold Coast Gazette*, 22 November 1823.

governor who regulates the trade here is as great a rogue as his master, and rather promotes his acts of injustice than dissuades him from them. I shall have some trouble to get settled with them, but will do my best to come to an accommodation by fair means.[1]

At the very entrance to the river, the abandoned ruins of Ogheye (Fish Town) bore witness to a spectacular sacrifice made to *Olokun* in March 1818,

in consequence of the king's fetiche-men having persuaded him that this act was necessary in order to appease the deity who had deprived them of their trade. Accordingly, the inhabitants received an immediate notice to carry off their goods and chattels and seek some other abode, after which the huts were separately fired with solemn pomp. A hog and bullock were afterwards thrust into the flames, the blood being sprinkled across the river by the principal chiefs, followed by the credulous natives in their war-canoes, the females uttering cries and singing songs, which it was supposed would be agreeable to this god of the waters.[2]

The European trade of Benin was in still worse plight than that of the Itsekiris in the years following the official abolition of the slave trade. An occasional ship reached Ughoton where 'elephant's teeth, palm oil, hides, skins, cloth of native manufacture, and utensils of various kinds' were bartered for 'European and Indian commodities'.[3] 'Customs' were paid to the Oba in an assortment of goods that, according to Bold, resembled those given to the Olu of Warri; but his income from this source had become small and uncertain compared with the riches of the eighteenth century. Those Edo chiefs who had benefited from European trade likewise found their wealth reduced. Nor was there any prospect of improvement. Adams suggested that New Town would provide the most convenient centre for a palm-oil trade in the Benin River, and that it would be sufficient to send small craft to Ughoton: 'It will be unnecessary to establish a factory at Gatto as was the practice of slave

---

1 ibid.
2 Bold, *Merchants' guide*, p. 64.
3 *Royal Gold Coast Gazette*, March 1823.

ships, unless a competitor has fixed one in that town.'[1] Indeed he thought that the ideal arrangement would be to have a factory at Lagos, 'with ships lying off the Benin bar'. The tide of European trade which had ebbed from Benin showed little sign of returning with the palm-oil flood.

---

1 Adams, *Sketches*, p. 111.

Chapter 7
British encroachment

1. Trade and the flag in the Benin River

Large-scale trading in palm oil came comparatively late to the Benin River, but by the late eighteen-forties the firms of Horsfall, Harrison and Hemingway had factories in the vicinity of Bobi and Jakpa Creek involving an estimated capital of £250,000.[1] In 1856 these companies exported 2,500 tons of oil valued at £112,500,[2] a total not substantially exceeded during the subsequent decade despite the opening in that same year of a mail steamer service, and the establishment in the early eighteen-sixties of another factory by the firm of Stewart and Douglas. Even at this level of production the palm-oil industry dominated the economy of the river and brought about a revolution in its external trade. Equally far-reaching political repercussions attended upon that change, for as British firms controlled most of the export trade, so it was inevitable, in nineteenth-century circumstances, that the British government should take some interest in the affairs of the river. At the same time, it is impossible to speak of a 'British policy towards Benin' in the second half of the century; to a large extent the economic and political situation in the Benin River followed the same pattern as in the other rivers of the Niger delta, and British policy sought always for the highest common factor in a series of complex and individual situations. Since the Benin was only one among several oil rivers, and never the most important, it follows that much of what the British government did there and in the kingdom of Benin was dictated by wider, even extraneous, considerations. It remains true,

---

1 P.R.O. F.O. 84/1002. Campbell to Foreign Office, 24 March 1856. Most of the capital took the form of goods; at least £30,000 had been given out on trust.
2 ibid. cf. Gertzel, 'Commercial Organisation', p. 289 et seq.

however, that from the eighteen-forties the Benin River was an important centre of the palm-oil trade and played its part in involving the British government in the enmeshed problems of protecting and disciplining its subjects and their property involved in that trade. On the other side, the peoples of the region were drawn unwittingly into the larger designs of imperial diplomacy.

Despite the semi-official explorations of Clapperton, the Landers and their successors, supplemented by the coastal probings of the West Africa Squadron, Whitehall remained officially ignorant of the political situation along the oil rivers coast for a suprisingly long time. As late as 1847 a memorandum from the Admiralty to the Foreign Office on the subject of European possessions in West Africa could designate Benin as Portuguese territory, with the illuminating caution that 'it is doubtful whether Portugal actually occupies all these places—Whydah and Benin, for instance, are supposed to be in the possession of the natives'![1] Only two years later Palmerston signalled the end of the attitude typified in this memorandum by appointing John Beecroft as the first British consul for the Bights of Benin and Biafra. Beecroft was a man ideally suited to give the fullest possible expression to the emergent British official interest in that vast area, being an enthusiastic advocate of a 'forward' policy that took the form of forceful interference in the coastal states whenever British interests appeared to demand it. By his actions in Lagos, Bonny and Calabar he set in train what proved to be an irreversible growth of British involvement on this coast, and which led in 1853 to the division of his consular area between a consulate for the new protectorate of Lagos and another for the Bight of Biafra. The Benin River was included under the jurisdiction of the latter authority which Beecroft continued to exercise from his headquarters on Fernando Po.[2]

Although Beecroft and his successors in the consular office were wont to brandish a heavy hand, their authority for long remained anomalous and undefined. Unlike the traditional consul, they were not accredited to any sovereign state, and only nominally did they confine their attention to British citizens and matters of trade. Yet

---

1 P.R.O. F.O. 2/3. Admiralty to Foreign Office, 17 February 1847.
2 cf. K. O. Dike, *Trade and Politics in the Niger Delta, 1830–1885*. Oxford, 1956, chap. VII.

240

the very vagueness of their authority, in a region removed from effective supervision or protest, made them powerful and flexible instruments of a policy which was itself uncertain and only slowly defined. For many years consular authority sat very lightly upon British traders and African rulers in the Benin River, even though the consul's annual visit (not always paid) sometimes resulted in severe punitive action, as happened in 1851 when Beecroft destroyed Bobi, or in 1857 when men from H.M.S. *Bloodhound* attacked settlements in Orogu Creek. Such actions seldom achieved their purpose, but they were eloquent of the official mind upon the problems of the oil rivers and the methods by which they were to be tackled.

Of the impression created in Benin by these consular visitations there is no record. Penetration of British commercial and political influence into the Benin River did not for many years encroach directly upon territory effectively controlled by the Oba. In Lagos, however, the establishment in 1851 of a virtual British protectorate put an end to the authority of the Oba in a state that had hitherto acknowledged the suzerainty of Benin in a variety of ways, including the payment of tribute and the investiture of its rulers and chiefs. Not that the Oba had any immediately effective means of enforcing his will upon Lagos in these matters, but they were not allowed to go by default. Not long before the British occupation Osemwede had sent the *Osodin* and two other chiefs there to demand the tribute, presumably because it had not been delivered at the proper time. They found the town engulfed in a civil war between Akintoye and Kosoko, and it is not clear whether or not they succeeded in their mission.[1] Akintoye, who held the emblems of authority from Osemwede, eventually had to yield to Kosoko, but the latter acknowledged to Beecroft in 1851 that he could not consider himself *de jure* ruler of Lagos without the sanction of Benin, and that this could not be forthcoming so long as Akintoye lived.[2] Beecroft too gave explicit recognition to the Oba's authority in the town when he addressed the following letter to him before the expulsion of Kosoko.[3]

---

1 Egharevba, *A Short History*, pp. 47–8. Egharevba gives 1840 as the date of this mission, but it is more likely to have taken place in 1841.
2 P.R.O. F.O. 84/858. Beecroft to Foreign Office, 26 November 1851.
3 P.R.O. F.O. 84/886. Enclosure in Beecroft to Foreign Office, 31 December 1851.

To the King of Benin,
Greeting.

As Her Majesty's Representative, it is my wish to recall to your recollection the desire of the Queen of England to be friend with *all* Kings and Chiefs of Africa.

In compliance with my Sovereign's wish, Friendship was offered to the present Chief of Lagos, which he refused, and fired on a Flag of Truce. This has placed him at war with England; and I have to inform you that no other King of Lagos will be acknowledged by England, than Akitoye, and knowing your interest in that King, and desire to serve him, I tell you this, that if, *before the end of this month*, Kosoko, the usurper of Lagos does not surrender, and acknowledge his rightful and proper king, Akitoye, and resign the crown in his favour, Lagos will be totally destroyed by fire, and not one house will be left between that and Jabboo. It remains for you to prevent this disaster by assisting Akitoye, whose acknowledgement as King of Lagos will create peace and good-will amongst all parties.

Akitoye is now at Badagry, and has friends at Lagos ready to assist him with yourself.

On your speed in this matter, will be shown your desire or not, of obtaining the Friendship of England.

Given under my hand this 4th day of December 1851,

John Beecroft,

H.B.M. Consul.

Despite Beecroft's seeming readiness to acknowledge the Oba's rights in Lagos, Akintoye seized the opportunity of his restoration under British protection to repudiate his former allegiance. According to Consul Campbell, Akintoye 'on application for the usual tribute, sent the King of Benin's messengers home without anything, telling them that the trade of Lagos was henceforth changed and that he could not afford to pay any more tribute'.[1] No better fortune attended Oba Adolo's attempt in 1860 to reinstate Kosoko who had made his peace with Benin, perhaps by promising to resume payment of the tribute. Adolo sent a message to the new ruler of Lagos, Docemo, informing him of his wish to place Kosoko on the throne. 'King Docemo's reply was that he only recognises the British government now, not as in former times when Lagos was under the King of Benin to whom annually a tribute was paid, and that he

---

1 P.R.O. F.O. 84/1031. Campbell to Foreign Office, 4 April 1857.

requested the King of Benin would not send any more messages relative to the bringing back of Kosoko to Lagos.'[1] British consuls in Lagos obviously approved of this shuffling off of dependence upon Benin because it left British suzerainty unchallenged; and when in 1861 Britain formally annexed Lagos no reference was made to Benin. Nevertheless, though the Obas and chiefs of Lagos might repudiate all dependence on Benin in the face of the British consul, they appear on occasion to have sought the favour of the Oba with presents.[2]

The years which saw the fall of Lagos witnessed also the break-up of the Itsekiri kingdom, chiefly from the effects of the commercial revolution. Because the very existence of the state depended upon it, the Itsekiri kingdom was always far more sensitive than Benin to the vagaries of European trade. It is therefore understandable that the revolutionary switch from slaves to palm oil should have affected the Itsekiris quickly and drastically. Evidence of upheaval is manifest in the dramatic events that followed the death of Olu Akengbuwa on 14 June 1848. He had contrived to hold his state together against the forces of disruption by a generous use of coercion and violence; but even so he had been unable to bring the rebel *Uwangue* to heel. His successors failed altogether to establish their authority: two died on 18 June 1848 and another within two years—all in very suspicious circumstances.[3] Taking advantage of this breakdown at the centre,

---

1 P.R.O. F.O. 84/1115. Hand to Foreign Office, 3 November 1860.
2 cf. P. A. Talbot, *The Peoples of Southern Nigeria*, vol. I. London, 1926, p. 175. 'Lagos itself is stated to have sent tribute on three occasions to Overami.' For this, as for many other statements, Talbot unfortunately cites no authority.
3 cf. supra p. 231.
 P.R.O. F.O. 84/1031. Campbell to Foreign Office, 4 April 1857. 'Some ten years since the King of Warree died, leaving numerous slaves whom he had kept solely for purposes of warfare. The kings of Warree appear generally to have been cruel despots, and that King in particular is remembered for his cruelties. The leading slaves of this king so managed after his death that every successor should have but a short reign, no less than three having died in two years. This so alarmed the heirs to the kingship that none can now be got to assume it; and the leading inhabitants influenced by their superstitious fears have left the town and built themselves towns elsewhere; the soldier slaves of the late king taking advantage of this circumstance have quitted the town and established themselves independent in a creek near to the present English factories, to whom they are most useful agents as traders.'

many inhabitants of Ode Itsekiri migrated to the booming settlements in the Benin River, there to engage in the oil trade and resist all further attempts to impose an Olu.[1] For the remainder of the nineteenth century the Itsekiris were divided into a number of virtually independent groups based upon a 'house' system rather similar to that of Bonny and Calabar, and the bitter political and trading rivalries in which these groups often engaged introduced a new element of disruption into the river.

Events in Ode Itsekiri, unlike those in Lagos, may have caused some satisfaction in Benin. The collapse of the Itsekiri monarchy meant the removal of a powerful and often hostile neighbour. Among the successor houses Benin enjoyed some influence thanks to its special relationship with the family of the *Uwangue* which emerged as the most powerful group in the Benin River. The most famous members of the house, Diare and Nana, became British-appointed governors of the river, paid an annual tribute to the Oba, and, according to Consul Johnston, received investiture from Benin.[2] Their dependent status in relation to Benin probably derived from an agreement concluded by the *Uwangue* when he first put himself under the Oba's protection; it was certainly not, as Johnston believed, derived from their British-conferred governorship of the river. Yet if the break-up of the Itsekiri state conferred some political advantage on Benin, it offered no commercial benefits; far from weakening the Itsekiris' hold upon trade, the events of 1848 led to a more thorough exploitation of the advantage they already enjoyed.

Nor did Osemwede long rejoice over the discomfiture of his Itsekiri rival, for he too died in 1850–1 and Benin itself was plunged into a characteristic succession struggle between his two senior

---

P.R.O. F.O. 2/3. Commander of H.M.S. *Firefly*, 1 March 1849, reporting that he had found the Benin River very disturbed because of the death of the King of Warri on the 14th June, and of his two sons on 18th June 1848.

1 Ode Itsekiri retained its spiritual significance: the bodies of important men continued to be taken there for burial, while for lesser men and women the hair and nails were sent. cf. A. Moloney, 'Notes on Yoruba and the Colony and Protectorate of Lagos, West Africa'. *Proceedings of the Royal Geographical Society*, vol. XII, 1890, p. 606.

2 P.R.O. F.O. 84/1882. *A Report on the British Protectorate of the Oil Rivers*, 1 December 1888.

1. *A Benin warrior chief with attendants; in the corners above, Europeans holding manillas and drinking from flasks.*

2. (a) *A brass box representing part of the Oba's palace. Early European travellers mention brass figures of birds and snakes attached to the roof of the palace. The Europeans with muskets may symbolise the Portuguese who served the Oba in the early sixteenth century.*

(b) *Excavation showing remains of the mud walls of the nineteenth century palace of the Obas. Note the fluting on exterior wall. The floor of a room can be seen beyond the wider wall. Scale : 6 ft. in feet.*

3. *Shrines in the main compound of the present palace. That in the foreground is of the present Oba's father, Oba Eweka II; beyond, that of his grandfather, Oba Ovonramwen and (hidden) great-grandfather. Scale: 1 foot in inches.*

4. *Sixteenth century plaques showing European traders.*

5. (a) *A messenger of the Ogane, wearing a cross* (See p. 31).

(b) *A Benin trader.*

6. *A war captive. A European appears to be covering him with a musket.*

7. (a) *An early seventeenth century representation of a Dutch attack on Portuguese settlements in the bay of the island of Principe, December 1698.*

(b) *A human sacrifice to make the rain cease. The victim was garrotted. From a photograph by Mr. C. Punch, 1891. The fluted and thatched wall, left, may be an outer wall of the palace.*

8. *Oba Ovonramwen, on board the Protectorate yacht* Ivy *on his way to exile in Calabar, 1897.*

sons. Odin-Ovba, the younger of the two, was crowned under the name of Adolo while Beecroft was visiting the Benin River in March 1851.[1] His rival Ogbewekon then fled to Igueben, his mother's town in Ishan, where he rallied his supporters and raised a series of rebellions that kept a large area of Ishan in turmoil until his death in 1880.[2] When Burton visited Benin City in 1862 he was told that the civil war had been in progress since 1854, and that ten thousand men with all the horses in the city had been absent for many years engaged in the fighting. At that time things were not going in Adolo's favour. 'Many of the Benin people, it is said, are now flying to the "Pretender", who if the ministers did not fear for their heads, would soon make himself Obbá.'[3] It was also around the middle of the century that the Nupe launched a series of slave raids into Ishan.[4] Thus, at the very outset of his reign, Adolo's empire and prestige suffered very damaging blows in a number of directions, and it is unlikely that amid so many distractions much attention was paid to British activities.

2. The first consular visit to Benin

We know very little about the extent of Benin's participation in the palm-oil trade in the early years of Adolo's reign. Lack of evidence to the contrary gives the impression that the kingdom remained as much isolated from the coast as it had been in the time of Ose-mwede, for the new English factories were all established at the mouth of the river where the Itsekiris ruled supreme. The first step towards a British paramountcy in that area was taken when a meeting of European and African traders held under the chairmanship of Beecroft on 1 April 1851 elected Diare of Jakpa 'Chief of the Benin

---

1 'The chiefs and ministers preferred the milder and more easily managed man.' Burton, 'My wanderings in West Africa,' p. 415.
   P.R.O. F.O. 84/858. Beecroft to Foreign Office, 26 November 1851.
2 According to Ishan tradition (C. G. Okojie, *Ishan Native Laws and Customs*, pp. 311 and 330) Ogbewekon managed to repulse the forces Adolo sent against him, and remained in Igueben which did not make peace with Benin until after his death. Burton, on the other hand, was told that the pretender had fled from Igueben and taken refuge in Igara.
3 Burton, 'My wanderings in West Africa', p. 415.
4 Okojie, *Ishan Native Laws*, p. 234. The area most affected by these raids was Ugboha in north-eastern Ishan.

River', an office which he retained with one brief intermission until his death in 1870.[1] This appointment was made without any reference to Benin, nor did the Oba receive any portion of the customs dues which Diare was entitled, by virtue of his office, to collect from ships entering the river.[2] Since few vessels, if any, found it necessary to go as far as Ughoton, a once important and expanding source of revenue remained closed to the ruler and chiefs of Benin. It is possible that they were able to compensate in some degree for this loss by taxing the palm-oil trade at the producer stage, for the Itsekiris and Ijos who sold the produce to Europeans depended for their supplies upon the Urhobo country which was still subject to Benin. As the oil trade expanded, an increasing volume of European merchandise must have found its way into the hands of the Urhobo producers, and it is reasonable to assume that some of the wealth flowing into Urhobo country eventually found its way to Benin. One might also have expected that the authorities in Benin would attempt to tap this new-found prosperity by increasing the tribute from the Urhobos, or by placing officials at strategic points to supervise and conduct trade on their behalf: in other words, to have imposed a regime similar to that which had been devised to regulate earlier European trade in the Benin River. However, there is no evidence that they either attempted or managed to do this; tribute from outlying peoples such as the Urhobos seems, like that from Lagos, to have been of a token character not susceptible to substantial increase. Therefore, while further additions to the at present very scanty store of information about Benin-Urhobo relations may in future modify the picture, it seems probable that the Benin kingdom benefited only indirectly and insignificantly from the development of the palm-oil trade in Urhobo country.

Though cut off from commercial and political contact with the British, Benin soon began to occupy a place in their speculations, and a certain attitude towards the state and people begins to emerge

---

1 On 18 February 1858 Campbell replaced Diare by his rival Abrinomy, chief of Batere. He did this at the instance of the European traders who dubbed Diare 'a representative of the old slave trade chiefs'. P.R.O. F.O. 84/1061. Campbell to Foreign Office, 1 March 1858.

2 The chief or governor of the river was entitled to receive 200 *pawns* from each ship: for many years Europeans avoided paying, and Diare apparently made little effort to collect it.

from the early correspondence of consular officials. They draw a picture curiously at variance with that presented by earlier European visitors and chroniclers, most of whom had described a state in which civilisation and the art of government had progressed further than in any other known kingdom of Guinea. Many had also spoken favourably of Edo character and moral standards. Fundamentally the change in attitude between these writers and their Victorian successors must be ascribed to a general shift in the standpoint from which nineteenth-century Europeans viewed and judged other races,[1] to the development, that is, of 'scientific racialism'. With respect to Benin this attitude manifested itself especially in the emphasis given to the practice of ceremonial human sacrifice, which for most visitors overshadowed all else, earning the city such epithets as Golgotha, City of Skulls, and City of Blood. Because European visitors paid so much attention to the sacrificial aspects of Benin ritual, one inevitably gains the impression that human sacrifice was practised on a far greater scale in the nineteenth century than in earlier times; therefore in attempting to arrive at any conclusion in this question care must be taken to allow for a bias in the evidence. On the other hand, there is some reason to believe that a new scale and conception of sacrifice was gaining ground. Moffat and Smith, for example, are the first to draw attention to the use of crucifixion trees which became a common sight later in the century. Among his subjects too Osemwede was credited with a daily recourse to human sacrifice: the chief of Uwepa, perhaps hoping to impress, told members of the 1841 Niger expedition that the Oba sacrificed three men every day—one in the morning, one at noon, and one at night.[2] One need not accept the claim at its face value—indeed it is most unlikely to have been correct—yet it is significant that it was made. The evidence we have also suggests that the sacrifices were intensified during the reign of Adolo, although it must be remembered that the most

---

1 cf. P. D. Curtin, *The Image of Africa—British Ideas and Action 1780–1870.* Wisconsin, 1964, and ' "Scientific" Racism and the British Theory of Empire'. *Journal of the Historical Society of Nigeria*, vol. II, no. 1, 1960.
2 S. Crowther and J. F. Schön, *Journals of the Reverend Frederick Schön and Mr. Samuel Crowther.* London, 1842, p. 107. The Uwepa country lies on the western bank of the Niger opposite Idah.

impressive part of that evidence is provided by Burton who could hardly have been less disposed to sympathise with the values of Edo civilisation. The greater part of his despatch describing his visit to Benin City in August 1862 is devoted to the 'horrors'.[1]

> One of the first objects that met our sight was a negro freshly crucified after the African fashion sitting on a stool with extended arms lashed to a framework of poles. I fear it was in honour of our arrival. We then marched over the space before the King's palace. It was strewed with human skulls and bones like pebbles. Our first visit to the palace showed us the body of a fine young woman fastened to the top of a tree—a Fetish for rain. During the night I heard the voice of the 'Spirit Oro' and next morning we found close to our doors the corpse of a man with broken shin bones and a gashed throat. Walking to the market we remarked a pool of blood where another victim had been slaughtered.

In his account of the visit published in *Fraser's Magazine*, Burton elaborates further on the theme, 'The place has a fume of blood, it stinks of death.' Some of the signs he misinterpreted; for example, the common graveyard on the outskirts of the city where the bodies of criminals and paupers were thrown unburied becomes in his description a sinister 'field of death'. But many of his observations were confirmed by later witnesses. The supposition that Adolo's reign saw human sacrifice practised on an unaccustomed scale is further strengthened by the opinion among British officials in the first years of the following ruler that 'these customs of late seem to have softened and become less savage'.[2] Ovonramwen himself assured Cyril Punch that 'he was sick of it all, but that he could not discontinue the customs of his ancestors'.[3] And if the total of victims lessened in the last years of Benin's independence, the constant round of sacrifice for varied purposes appears to have continued. Punch saw numerous victims offered for rain or dry weather near the palace, pits in the palace courtyards into which decapitated bodies were thrown, and disembowelled corpses stretched across paths which the Oba wished to close to trade. Vice-Consul

---

1 P.R.O. F.O. 84/1176. Burton to Foreign Office, 26 August 1862.
2 P.R.O. F.O. 84/1882. Johnstone, *Report on the British Protectorate*, 1 Dec. 1888.
3 Roth, *Great Benin*, p. 66.

Galway noticed crucifixions on five trees outside and within the palace, 'numerous corpses—some mutilated fearfully—which were strewn about in the most public places', and a number of pits reeking of blood in the compounds of the palace.[1]

The testimony of these various witnesses gives the impression not only that the number of human sacrifices increased in the nineteenth century, but that new forms of sacrifice were introduced. Landolphe records seeing a man convicted of divulging state secrets tied alive to a tree-top, but there is no evidence for the sacrificial use of crucifixion trees earlier than 1838. Again, most pre-nineteenth-century visitors to Benin imply that only men and male animals were sacrificed: Palisot de Beauvois is quite explicit on this point.[2] In the second half of the nineteenth century, however, female sacrifice had become common. Palisot de Beauvois also mentions that the bodies of decapitated sacrificial victims were thrown outside the city walls; in Punch's time many, if not all, were cast into the sacrificial pit (*iyo*) dug in the courtyard dedicated to the Oba's father. Human sacrifices for the purpose of changing the weather and guarding the approaches to Benin City are likewise not mentioned in earlier accounts.[3] Too little is yet known of the internal events in Benin at this time to put these reports into proper perspective and explain these developments. It may be that the Obas and chiefs of the nineteenth century, faced with growing hostile pressure from without and distracted by civil war, had resorted to an increasingly rigorous exercise of their ritual power. The advance of Islam into Oyo, Bida and Idah, the penetration of Christian missions among the southern Yoruba and along the Niger, and the disintegration of the Itsekiri monarchy, left the Oba of Benin

---

1 P.R.O. F.O. 84/2194. Galway's report on his visit to Benin, 30 March 1892. Some of the bodies he saw lying about may have been victims of the influenza epidemic which, he was told, had killed three hundred people in two weeks of February 1892, or perhaps of sacrifices made to end the epidemic.

2 Palisot de Beauvois, 'Notice sur le peuple de Benin'.

3 The late chief Osuma stated that the women sacrificed for the purpose of stopping rain were always Urhobos. The practice of making human sacrifices on 'crucifixion trees' was also known in Agbor during the nineteenth century. F. M. Hensley (*Niger Dawn*, Ilfracombe, 1955, p. 95) saw cotton trees in that town which were used for sacrificing men, and another with two straight branches to which women were fastened to die of thirst.

increasingly isolated as a divine ruler; yet his fetish powers were still widely feared and respected. According to Punch, Ovonramwen claimed 'to give fetish' to all neighbouring states, and even as far afield as Dahomey. Itsekiris and Ijos often paid him a fee to have the sasswood ordeal administered to them by men from the ward of Benin City specially appointed for that purpose.[1] It may be, then, that the loss of territory and political influence further encouraged resort to a terrible elaboration of those supernatural powers upon which the Benin monarchy had been founded.

In so far as relations with Britain were concerned, the reports of human sacrifice singled out Benin for special animadversion among British officials. Campbell set the tone for many subsequent references to the subject when he wrote in 1855: 'There remains only the King of Dahomey and the King of Benin who have not yet concluded treaties with the Queen of England to abolish so cruel and barbarous a custom.'[2] He was also among the first to maintain that the practice of such customs argued a general backwardness in the Edo.

> The people of Jaboo and their neighbours the people of Benin are deeper sunk in barbarism and the observance of superstitious rites, making human sacrifices, etc. than the people of Youraba, and although so many hundreds of Jabous and Benins have been released from slavery and located in Sierra Leone, I am informed not one of these two peoples has been known to have elevated himself by his industry and intelligence beyond the position of a common labourer.[3]

From his visit in 1862 Burton supplied chapter and verse for this point of view which commended itself to an important segment of official thinking and public emotion in Britain. Drunkenness, thieving and indiscipline are the main heads of his attack on the Edo character. Most of the chiefs he met he judged to be inveterate drunkards: the priest of *Olokun* at Ughoton appears permanently drunk in his narrative, the *Ezomo* is tipsy, an Oba's messenger met him 'maudlin drunk', and the chief *fiador* 'begged hard, very hard, for rum'. 'From premier to ultimate slave, these fellows think of

---

1 The sasswood ordeal was often administered at Ughoton.
2 P.R.O. F.O. 84/976. Campbell to J. Dawson, Wesleyan Mission agent at Whydah, 15 October 1855.
3 P.R.O. F.O. 84/1088. Campbell to Foreign Office, 22 March 1859.

nothing but drink and "chop".' Numerous instances of theft or attempted theft are related, including the repeated loss of provisions and the theft of a knife from Burton's pocket by a porter. On this charge he concludes: 'I determined the Beninese to be with the sole exception of the Mpongwe or Gabons the most pilfering race that I had visited on this west coast of Africa.' As for indiscipline, his comment that 'in this half-republican race temporal rulers have little authority' is illustrated by several incidents, and notably the many occasions upon which the leaders of the carrier party had to resort to the whip in order to exact obedience from the porters.

If correct, Burton's estimate of the Edo character would mark a tragic departure from the qualities attributed to that people in earlier times; but he is undoubtedly guilty of exaggeration. No other writer levels such sweeping charges of drunkenness. Petty theft on a considerable scale is certainly attested by several visitors before and after Burton: the Dutch had faced that problem in their factory at Ughoton; Palisot de Beauvois believed that the Edo had no scruples about stealing. Punch gave as his opinion:

> Trade was nearly all carried on by women and they were most dishonest. The lower classes were not such arrant thieves as the Jekri and Ijos. European goods and chattels were under the King's protection and unless by his orders would not be stolen to any great extent.

He had himself lost many small articles when staying in the *Ezomo*'s house. A trader named Brownridge, who spent some years at Ughoton and was never inclined to overpraise the Edo, said only that 'highway robbery is very prevalent, especially of women traders on their way home'.[1] It should also be mentioned that Burton recovered most of his property after carrying off an interpreter as hostage. Perhaps the best answer to Burton's reproach of indiscipline and lack of courtesy is the appraisal of the Edo treatment of strangers given by Punch who had far more experience of it than the castigating knight.

> In my time the Binis seemed to be courteous and hospitable to strangers. The chiefs were dignified and reserved in manner, and even when angry did not as a rule indulge in loud tones or violent gestures. They were

---

1 P.R.O. F.O. 2/102. Brownridge to Moor, 9 November 1896.

very curious when we first visited them. They came in a continual stream from morning till midnight in order to see the white man. All ranks and classes came into the room in which we sat, saluted us gravely, sat down and stared, and then saluting us again got up and left. They did not beg for small presents as most natives do, and if given any trifles expressed their thanks.[1]

From this conflict of evidence it is impossible to conclude that there had been any overall and marked deterioration in Edo standards of behaviour as a result of political adversity or an increased resort to human sacrifice. If some long-standing weaknesses—pilfering below and extortion above, which are in any case noticeable in most human societies—became more pronounced, this may perhaps be ascribed to a changing social balance in the central areas of the Benin kingdom. Repeated and prolonged civil wars were depopulating this region, including Benin City itself, while the rulers continually sought to maintain their power by the creation of new chieftaincy titles. The three Obas Osemwede, Adolo and Ovonramwen between them created at least twenty-five new titles, which was more than the total created in the previous two centuries. When he wrote that the population of Benin City consisted chiefly of nobles, Punch was probably including in their number the lower grades of the palace associations to which most Edo belonged;[2] even so, the support of a rapidly growing body of major title-holders must have told very hardly upon a static or decreasing population of commoners. Increasing competition for wealth and the trappings of nobility may well have led to a situation where chiefs were extortionate and lazy, seldom bothered to visit their villages,[3] but relied upon influence at court to maintain their place in the world; to a situation where a commoner needed to have his wits about him and be none too scrupulous if he was to prosper, or even keep what he had.[4]

However ill-founded they may have been, Burton's opinions on

---

1 Roth, *Great Benin*, p. 45.
2 cf. Bradbury, *The Benin Kingdom*, p. 37 et seq.
3 This was Punch's impression.
4 Brownridge alleged that it was dangerous for a commoner to amass wealth by trade because the Oba or chiefs would bring 'some trumpery charge of witchcraft against him' so that they might seize his property. P.R.O. F.O. 2/102. Brownridge to Moor, 9 November 1896.

Benin and its people gained wide currency in Britain, partly from the reputation of their author, and partly because he was the first British official to visit Benin City and thirty years passed before another made the journey. British consuls before Burton had declared their intention of going to Benin: Beecroft did so in 1851, but became embroiled in a dispute with Bobi; in 1855 Campbell claimed that he had received an invitation from the Oba, but got no farther than the lower river. Burton's visit appears to have been preceded by neither invitation nor correspondence, and has the appearance rather of an excursion prompted by his insatiable desire to visit unusual places and acquire copy for his publications. The full account of the journey published in *Fraser's Magazine* contrasts strangely with the meagre despatch sent to the Foreign Office. At all events the journey was made on Burton's own initiative and on the spur of the moment, and not on Foreign Office instructions.

Burton had gone to the Benin River aboard H.M.S. *Bloodhound* in August 1862 in response to an appeal from an agent named Henry whose factory had been plundered by an Itsekiri chief, Akabwa a grandson of Akengbuwa. After Diare and his chiefs had refused to meet the consul to discuss the complaint, Burton suspended trade, sent to Lagos for instructions, and decided, while waiting for a reply, to visit Ode Itsekiri in order to seek help from the eldest surviving sons of Akengbuwa. The only fruit of that mission was a lively account of the decaying Itsekiri capital,[1] so he next determined to go to Benin City, hoping that the Oba, 'whose "Fetish" is so powerful that the whole river obeys him',[2] might be persuaded to use his influence against the offending Itsekiris. In company with Lt.-Com. Stokes of *Bloodhound*, an army officer and the agent Henry, Burton was rowed to Ughoton and spent the night of 16 August in the house of Kusei, the *Olughoton*.[3] He

---

1 'My wanderings in West Africa, by a F.R.G.S. Part I. The renowned city of Wari.' *Fraser's Magazine*, vol. LXVII, February 1865, pp. 135–57.
2 ibid. Parts II and III, March–April 1865.
3 This chief, Burton was told, was a brother of Osemwede who had been forced to flee from Benin to Lagos over a 'poisoning palaver'; about 1850 he had become involved in some slave-dealing trouble in Lagos, and had then returned to his own country where he had been made priest of *Olokun* and chief of Ughoton. While in Ughoton Burton visited the *Olokun* shrine, but mistook the figures in it for those of the Oba and his consort.

confirms that there were no European factories at Ughoton, and that the village had shrunk to some twenty or thirty houses, mostly in a ruinous condition. Without awaiting a reply to the message sent asking the Oba to receive the party, they set off on foot the following morning, for no hammocks were available in the village. A son of the *Olughoton* and an interpreter led the way.[1] By sunset they were still two hours' march from Benin City and had to camp in the forest. Their slow rate of progress doubtless owed something to the lack of hammocks and experienced porters, and the road itself appears to have deteriorated badly since the days of Landolphe;[2] Burton describes it as 'an occasional tunnel in the bush and a route, or rather rut, which might accommodate a quartette of wheelbarrows in Indian file'. The decline in European trade at Ughoton must have been largely responsible for neglect of the road, but waterpots still stood at intervals for the refreshment of travellers.

On reaching the city they paid the usual courtesy visit to the *Ezomo*, after which they were conducted to a lodging house in the Idembopwa quarter. That same day at 4 p.m. a *fiador* escorted them to the palace in order to deliver their presents of silk, cloth and rum, but on arrival they were told first that the Oba was engaged in sacrifices, and then, after many comings and goings, that he never saw strangers at night. Burton was disinclined to believe this excuse, even though he was apparently unaware of Landolphe's very different experience, and felt certain that none of the messengers had spoken to the Oba. In the end another twenty-four hours passed before they managed to obtain an audience. They spent this time looking around the city where they were permitted to wander at will. Effects of the civil wars were clearly visible in the numerous abandoned and tumbledown buildings that gave the city the appearance of a collection of 'scattered settlements'; the palace too was in a state of dilapidation that may probably be attributed to a breakdown in the customary arrangements for its maintenance. In striking contrast were the houses of the more important chiefs

---

1 Burton styles the interpreter a 'father-boy', which seems to be a corruption of the Portuguese *falador*.
2 The deterioration of the road between Ughoton and Benin City probably set in at the end of the eighteenth century. Both Adams and Fawckner took two days over the journey.

('homograns' Burton calls them) which Mr. Henry visited and found far better kept and furnished than the palace—a further sign of the social and political disequilibrium in the state.

The following day an important eunuch[1] came and went between the consul and the palace until, by threatening to leave at once, Burton managed to get Henry admitted to Adolo who promised a formal audience without further delay. Burton and Stokes then made their way to the palace while the Oba retired to change his dress. He reappeared preceded by some thirty *emada* and ten senior chiefs ('homograns') who stood to the right and left of the throne which was described by Burton as 'a small wooden settle'. Like the *hommes grandes* of Landolphe's day, these chiefs, all of them elderly men, wore a 'crinoline' skirt and the indispensable coral.[2] Of Adolo Burton has left the following thumbnail sketch: 'His complexion is dark, but his aspect is uncommonly intelligent, and the expression of his countenance is mild and good-humoured.' Two interpreters, one from Ughoton and one from Benin City, who addressed the Oba from a kneeling position, completed the assembly.

From Adolo's point of view the main purpose of the audience was to enquire why Europeans were no longer trading at Ughoton, and to this Burton could say nothing other than to recommend that order should first be restored there. Since he nowhere mentions any disorder at Ughoton, it is likely that this remark was intended to bring the conversation round to the state of affairs in the main river. In his earlier interview Henry had raised the matter of the attack on his factory and had obtained a promise that the Oba would send a messenger to the river threatening a stoppage of provisions unless the offenders were given up.[3] Burton pressed the matter no

---

1 This is the first reference to eunuchs in Benin. It is now asserted that they were obtained from the Attah of Idah, and that youths were sometimes sent to Idah to be castrated.

2 The 'crinoline'—a skirt formed by numerous layers of cloth—is still the dress worn by Benin chiefs on ceremonial occasions. Burton noticed that red Mediterranean coral was the variety most highly prized.

3 The Itsekiris depended on the Urhobos for important quantities of food-stuffs, so this threat may indicate that the Oba was able to control trade between the Urhobos and Itsekiris. cf. supra p. 246. An embargo on the supply of food from the Edo kingdom alone could hardly have affected the Itsekiris. Akabwa finally agreed to pay a fine of twenty puncheons of oil for the attack on Henry's factory.

further, even though it was the ostensible reason for his visit; instead he went on to enquire after the papers of the Egyptologist Belzoni who had died at Ughoton in 1823 at the beginning of a journey of exploration.[1] To have recovered them would have put a fine journalistic feather in Burton's cap, but though the Oba promised that a search should be made, they were never produced, probably because they had long since been destroyed. Neither during this audience nor in the brief 'friend palaver' Burton held with the Oba before leaving the city was any mention made of a treaty with Britain. The visit ended on 21 August with a hurried departure that dispensed with a call upon the *Ezomo* and enabled the travellers to spend the night in the house of the *Ohenolokun* at Igo.

The twenty-four-day sojourn of Burton and *Bloodhound* in the Benin River well illustrates the limitations of consular power. A consul had no effective means of coercing the African trader or chief:

> The natives seemed to care little for the suspension of trade: it became painfully evident that they could stand the ordeal better than we could. Indeed, all came to the conclusion that, unless some blow fatal to the prosperity of the river—such as temporarily removing the ships and factories—were struck, the outrages of these barbarians would remain unpunished. . . . No one, however, had authority to enforce so strong though necessary a measure.

Also he had no means of imposing common action upon the European supercargoes engaged in cut-throat competition, and bitterly opposed to any sanctions placed on trade for the benefit of a rival. The only immediate improvement Burton could suggest was to transfer factories from the indefensible shore establishments to moored hulks. The fundamental solution, he believed, lay in the British government adopting a forward policy in West Africa, because only by such means could British trade be developed and the African be lifted from what he had interpreted as despondent barbarism.

---

1 When Fawckner visited Ughoton he found the Italian's grave protected by a roof and a paling; a board placed by it bore the following inscription: 'All travellers are requested to keep up the grave of so great a man as Belzoni.' In Burton's time a local legend had grown up according to which Belzoni had been poisoned by the chief of Ughoton.

3. Retreat into the heartlands

For many years political and economic conditions in the Benin River remained much as Burton had found them. Perhaps the most serious challenge to the *status quo* came from Chanomi, chief of Deghele and a descendant of the royal Itsekiri line through his mother Queen Dolo. In order to undermine the rival families at Jakpa and Ebrohimi, Chanomi led a movement to reopen the Forcados River for the oil trade. The struggle came to a head in 1864–5 when Olomu, chief and founder of Ebrohimi, defeated Chanomi's party in a canoe war and thereby established the commercial supremacy of his own family in the Benin River. That Chanomi was able to succeed his kinsman Diare as Governor of the River when the latter died in 1870 hardly compensated for this setback which further embittered Itsekiri rivalries. The design of developing trade in the Forcados River, on the other hand, went forward despite Chanomi's defeat. Other Itsekiri groups related to the royal family, and smaller European firms aided by the opening of a steamer service between England and West Africa in 1857, were able to establish what Consul Livingstone described as a 'brisk trade' in palm-nut kernels based on Ode Itsekiri.[1] Agents of the older and larger companies (Stuarts, Harrisons and Horsfalls) allied with the *Ologbotsere* and *Uwangue* families to combat this diversion of Urhobo oil from the Benin River as soon as they found themselves undercut by the independent trader James Pinnock. They found backing from the consuls who looked askance at commercial establishments beyond their control and protection, for an Admiralty Station Order prevented warships from visiting Ode Itsekiri. In 1873, therefore, Consul Livingstone approved a decision of the chiefs and agents in the Benin River Court of Equity that European merchants should withdraw from the Ode Itsekiri area and confine themselves henceforth to the Benin River.[2]

In theory the power of the consul was much increased by an Order in Council of 1872 which gave him judicial and administrative

---

1 P.R.O. F.O. 84/1308. Livingstone to Foreign Office, 24 November 1869. Besides the smaller English traders, the Hamburg firm of Bey and Zimmer were active in the Forcados River.

2 cf. Gertzel, 'Commercial Organisation', p. 298.

authority over British and British-protected subjects.[1] In practice he had no means of exercising that authority, apart from the costly gunboat and the ineffective Court of Equity which had been set up in the Benin River in 1866 and received recognition in the Order in Council. The real power in the river after 1865 was Olomu, backed by the most powerful fleet of war canoes seen there since the eighteenth century. With these he subdued the rival Itsekiri 'houses' and gradually extended his monopoly of the oil trade far up-river until he was able to enforce it at the source of supply. Most British agents supported him because they preferred to deal with one man who could guarantee supplies at an agreed price, rather than contend with the uncertainties of a trade disputed among several rival 'houses'. Initial consular disapproval of Olomu's strong-arm tactics was overcome by the persuasiveness and evident ability of his son Nana, and by 1879 his position was so secure that Acting-Consul Easton appointed him Governor of the River in place of his rival Chanomi whom British agents accused of interfering with trade.[2]

The second half of Adolo's reign thus saw European trade confined ever more firmly to the lower Benin River and the dominant Itsekiri middlemen, and hopes of reviving a direct trade through Ughoton became ever more remote. This situation did not, of course, prevent Benin itself from developing a certain amount of trade in European goods with states still farther in the interior, after acquiring them from the Itsekiris in exchange for oil and slaves. In the eighteen-sixties this traffic assumed considerable importance when Benin became one of the principal sources of supply for firearms, powder and ammunition in the wars then being waged in Yorubaland and Ekiti. The vigorous trading associations of Benin City sent weapons and munitions by the Oke Igbo route to Ibadan, also to Ondo and Ife. But the opening of a new route from the coast through Ondo in the early eighteen-seventies offered the warring parties a more direct source of supply that by-passed Benin, and the short-lived arms trade came to an end.

Besides affording a stimulus to Benin commerce, the wars that followed the collapse of Oyo hegemony in northern Yorubaland

---

1 cf. Dike, *Trade and Politics*, pp. 198–202.
2 P.R.O. F.O. 84/1541. Easton to Foreign Office, 18 December 1879.

posed a new threat to the already badly diminished sphere of Benin influence. The area affected was that inhabited by the Ekiti and the north-western Edo groups, which had for centuries been a form of march-land between Benin and Oyo. Ilorin and Ibadan, the principal successor states of Oyo, contended for Ekiti with the advantage falling to Ibadan. By 1872 the Ibadan operations had extended into the territory of Benin's vassal state Akure. Whereas a rebellion in Akure and Ekiti country in the time of Osemwede had called forth a decisive and effective response from Benin, these later invasions produced only a feeble reaction. 'Hundreds of soldiers' are said to have been despatched from Benin,[1] but the burden of the successful defence against Ibadan clearly lay on the people of Akure themselves aided by Ogedengbe and a group of Ijesha refugees. Benin played equally little part in the war which began in 1878 with a general rising in Ekiti and Ilesha against Ibadan domination, except that Adolo took advantage of the general conflict to send the *Ezomo* Osarogiagbon on an expedition which captured several villages in the Ivbiosakon area in 1881. Benin is also said to have resumed its function as a supplier of flintlocks to the Ekiti insurgents.[2] The cease-fire which ended the war in 1886 secured Ekiti independence from Ibadan, but only at the price of extending a virtual British suzerainty over all Yoruba states—a result which was certainly inimical to the interests of Benin. In these same years Nupe-Ilorin incursions were wresting the greater part of Ishan and the northern Edo areas from the informal control that the Oba had once exercised over them.[3] In short, the reign of Adolo saw Benin driven back into the original Edo heartlands.

The threat to the very existence of the kingdom posed by British intervention in the states of southern Nigeria, and seemingly advanced by Burton's visit and advocacy of a forward policy, came no nearer in Adolo's lifetime. It might even appear to have receded,

1 Egharevba, *A Short History*, p. 49.
2 S. Johnson, *The History of the Yorubas*. C.M.S., Lagos, 1921, p. 448.
3 cf. Bradbury, *The Benin Kingdom*, p. 86. The disappearance of horses from Benin may be an indication that the kingdom's communications with the north had been disrupted. cf. H. Galway, 'Nigeria in the nineties'. *Journal of the African Society*, vol. XXIX, no. cxv, April 1930. Burton too had noted the absence of horses in 1862, but was told that they were all engaged in the Ishan fighting.

for no consular official showed any eagerness to pay another visit, and a Parliamentary Select Committee of 1865, far from endorsing consular opinion, recommended that British commitments on the West African coast should be much reduced.[1] In practice this recommendation led to no withdrawals, but it did induce in consuls a caution against any actions which might be interpreted as an open advance. Burton's experience had suggested that Benin could be neither helpful nor harmful to established interests in the Benin River, so for twenty years in word and deed consuls let it lie; for five years before 1884 no consul even entered the river. A few traders, among them Samuel Cheetham and Crawford Clarke, paid visits to Benin City, more it would seem from curiosity than because their trade demanded it.

4. The growth of commercial and consular pressures

By the eighteen-eighties the attitudes and ideas which had triumphed in the Select Committee of 1865 were being abandoned under the pressure of commercial agitation and international rivalry affecting the whole of West Africa. English merchants who had enjoyed a head-start over their competitors in the post-slave-trade era found themselves being overhauled, while British consular officials began to find the representatives of other European nations jogging their elbows or breathing down their necks. In the Benin River German and Dutch firms appeared as 'serious trade competitors' to the hitherto paramount British interest,[2] which in the conditions of economic depression prevailing at home could not offer an effective riposte. Where 'trade' faltered the 'flag' stepped forward in defence of British economic paramountcy.

The long absence of British consuls was broken in 1884 when Consul Hewitt arrived to appoint a successor to Olomu as Governor of the River. The choice of African and European traders, expressed in a meeting held in Hewitt's presence, fell upon the late Governor's

---

1 *Parliamentary Papers* 1865, V (412). *Report of Select Committee on state of British settlements on the West Coast of Africa.*
2 P.R.O. F.O. 84/1882, pp. 58–62. *Minute by Governor Moloney in connection with his visit in April 1888 to the present eastern limits of the Colony of Lagos.*

son, Nana, whom the consul duly installed in office. He then proceeded to give legal form to the assertion of British suzerainty implicit in that act by signing a protection treaty with Nana, Chanomi and the other principal Itsekiri chiefs.¹ British traders in the river hoped that he would consolidate their advantage still further by signing a similar treaty with the Oba of Benin, thus throwing open the trade of that kingdom to merchants ensconced on the coast. To impress upon him the need for such action they claimed that a factory established at Ughoton had had to be abandoned because the Oba had arbitrarily stopped trade.² Though quite prepared to make an official visit to Benin City, Hewitt, unlike Burton, was not prepared to dash outside his area of jurisdiction on his own initiative; instead he applied for permission to visit Benin the following December or January, taking with him presents worth about one hundred pounds.³ When Treasury approval came Hewitt found it impossible to undertake the mission himself, so he delegated it to Vice-Consul Blair who set out from the lower river in May 1885 with a full escort of Hausa troops. On arrival at Ughoton, Blair was seized with fever and succeeded only in getting back as far as Henderson's factory where he died. In October Hewitt reported that a trader named Cheetham had offered to deliver the presents entrusted to Blair, and at the same time attempt to sign a treaty with Adolo,⁴ but neither Cheetham nor any consul made any further effort to reach Benin before the Oba died in 1888. Any urgency which the British government might have attached to the mission in 1885 had perhaps been removed by the Berlin Conference of that year which recognised a British protectorate over the 'Niger Districts', that is, 'the territories on the line of coast between the British Protectorate of Lagos and the right or western bank of

---

1 P.R.O. F.O. 84/1660. Hewitt to Foreign Office, 28 July 1884. When Hewitt and Nana visited the Forcados River in 1888, the Itsekiri towns in that region were persuaded to acknowledge that they too were bound by this treaty.
2 No information exists concerning any European trading post at Ughoton in this period; possibly the reference was to Itsekiri trade.
3 P.R.O. F.O. 84/1939. Hewitt to Foreign Office, 14 September 1884.
4 P.R.O. F.O. 84/1701. Acting-Consul White to Foreign Office, 27 May 1885; Consul-General Hewitt to Foreign Office, 15 June 1885; Consul-General Hewitt to Foreign Office, 14 October 1885.

18

the Rio del Rey'. With Lagos and its hinterland a British colony, and the British hold secured on the coastlands and the Niger, it could be only a question of time before Benin came willingly or unwillingly into a dependent relationship with the new paramount power.[1]

When Adolo died his son Idugbowa succeeded to the throne without the usual civil war, not from lack of a rival and reputedly elder brother, Orokhorho, and his supporting faction, but because he astutely forestalled rebellion. Soon after Idugbowa became Oba with the title Ovonramwen he struck at his opponents, putting to death the chiefs *Eribo*, *Obaraye*, *Obazelu*, *Osia* and large numbers of lesser men on a charge of conspiring against his accession. He also destroyed the large village of Ugbini,[2] presumably because it was against him; and other places possibly shared the same fate, for rumours of massacres reached the factories in the Benin River. Many of his subjects suspected that Ovonramwen had been advised to take these measures by the *Uwangue*[3] who in 1895 fell victim in his turn to a conspiracy headed by *Obaduagbon* and *Erasoyen*, two of the principal suviving chiefs of the *Iwebo* association. Investigations uncovered the plot and a further purge ensued involving the enforced suicide of more *Iwebo* chiefs including these two and several of their accomplices.[4] The trader Punch believed, on the contrary, that the *Uwangue*, *Ezomo* and *Obarisiagbon* had been mixed up with Orokhorho's faction, and that Ovonramwen's chief supporters had been the lower-ranking *ukoba* and the chief eunuch. These two interpretations are not necessarily incompatible, for the composition of factions doubtless changed during the course of the struggle

---

1 The political settlement among European powers did not put an end to their commercial rivalry as evidenced by Governor Moloney's reference to the competition of German and Dutch firms in the Benin River. cf. supra p. 295.
2 P.R.O. F.O. 2/102. Brownridge to Moor, 9 November 1896.
3 cf. Egharevba, *A Short History*, p. 50.
4 The late *Ezomo* Omoruyi informed Dr. Bradbury and myself that the *Iwebo* chiefs denounced the *Uwangue* to Ovonramwen for having incited the British to attack Benin after the deposition of Nana in 1894. The *Uwangue* denied the charge, but did not appear at the *agwe* festival, and when the Oba summoned him with a promise of safe-conduct he was shot down on his way to the palace. Ovonramwen then ordered four *Iwebo* chiefs to commit suicide. Three did so, but *Obaduagbon* refused and was killed by his own sons after he had for some time defied the boycott placed on himself and his family.

between the two brothers; moreover, the bitterness against the *Uwangue* would be all the more understandable if he had deserted Orokhorho's party and used his influence with Ovonramwen to destroy his erstwhile allies. And even though some doubt surrounds these events, it is clear enough that bitter feuds divided the Benin hierarchy, and especially the ranks of the palace chiefs, during the opening years of Ovonramwen's reign. The faction which in former reigns had found an outlet and run its course in civil war was thus diverted into subterranean channels of conspiracy, sedition and murder where they contributed to the final catastrophe.[1]

The swift action against Ovonramwen's opponents in the capital helps to account for the relative quiescence of the provinces at the beginning of his reign. A small punitive expedition sufficed to quell incipient revolt in Akure where the *Deji* had state swords made without the Oba's sanction. Ishan too appears to have lived up to its reputation as an area of endemic disaffection, but in a half-hearted manner.[2] It is also true that Ovonramwen had succeeded to a very reduced patrimony. The Nupe had penetrated far into the Etsakor and Ivbiosakon regions, and had established a slave-raiding base opposite Idah.[3] The ending of the Yoruba wars had seen British influence extended as far as Ondo, while by a proclamation of 5 February 1886 the right bank of the Benin River became the eastern boundary of the Colony of Lagos. To the east the Royal Niger Company was advancing into the western Ibo and north-western Edo areas from its administrative headquarters at Asaba, a town once within the Benin sphere of influence. In June 1888 the Company's agents were negotiating with chiefs in the region of the Forcados and Ramos Rivers, and thus bringing to the fore the problem of a frontier between the Company and the Niger Rivers

---

1 When Punch visited Benin City in the early eighteen-nineties, he found that the *Ezomo* and *Uwangue* were 'objects of suspicion', and that the Oba seemed 'especially anxious for European support and countenance, as he knew well the large party there was against him'. Roth, *Great Benin*, p. 101.

2 In 1892 Galway was told that a Benin force had defeated the Ishans some three years previously. P.R.O. F.O. 2/51. *Report on the Benin District, Oil Rivers Protectorate for the year ending 31 July 1892.*

3 According to E. G. M. Dupigny (*Gazetteer of Nupe Province*. London, 1920, p. 19) the Nupe ruler Abu Bekri raided the Afenmai c. 1885–6, forcing these northern Edo peoples to pay tribute to Bida.

Protectorates.¹ Also in the year of Ovonramwen's accession, Vice-Consul Johnston strengthened British authority in the Benin River by constituting the new 'governing council' which, as in all rivers of the Protectorate, supplanted the largely ineffective Court of Equity.²

To Johnston and his superiors these governing councils marked the first step towards 'a totally different regime politically and legally to that which is now in force', namely an effective British protectorate which was to be extended by treaty to the interior.³ In his Report on the British Protectorate of the Oil Rivers (1 December 1888) he even went so far as to assert that the new Oba of Benin had not only approved the protection treaty signed by Nana in 1884, but 'also considers himself under British protection'. This erroneous notion, which he had probably gained from British traders who visited Benin City in April 1888, usefully supported the important place assigned to Benin in Johnston's vision of British penetration to the interior of West Africa. 'From various points on the Benin River', he wrote, 'towards the western confluents there are well-marked roads leading to the city of Benin, from which centre trade routes diverge to Yorubaland, Borgu and the Niger.' The main obstacle to be overcome was not a benighted Benin (in his report he observed that 'Benin City, since the accession of the new king in the spring of the present year, appears to be more open to European influence than formerly') but the vested interests of the coastal middlemen for whom he had conceived a special aversion exemplified in his treatment of Jaja in the previous year.⁴

Many of Johnston's ideas were taken up by Major C. M. Macdonald, the commissioner appointed by the British government to advise on the future of the Oil Rivers region in that same year of Ovonramwen's accession. Both the Foreign Office and Macdonald interpreted his task to be the determination of the form of government best suited to the area within the recently delimited British sphere of influence. In so far as a choice still lay with the inhabitants,

---

1 The Company denied that Nana's authority, and hence the scope of the 1884 protection treaty, extended to the Forcados and Ramos Rivers.

2 P.R.O. F.O. 84/1881. *Regulation for the constitution of a governing council to manage the local affairs of Benin and the Jekri country, 3 March 1888.*

3 cf. R. Oliver, *Sir Harry Johnston and the Scramble for Africa.* London, 1957, p. 122.

4 cf. Gertzel, 'Commercial organisation', p. 303.

it was confined to one between different forms of British rule, and for all practical purposes to a choice between direct rule and rule by a chartered company. Macdonald's method was to visit each river in turn, sound African and European opinion, then attempt to arrive at a consensus. When he followed that procedure on his visit to the Benin River in April 1889, he found Nana and the Itsekiri traders in favour of 'Queen's Government'. Elsewhere the same choice was made, so his report advocated the establishment of a general protectorate for all the Oil Rivers, with an adequate administration pledged to vigorous social and economic development.[1] These proposals were implemented by appointing Macdonald as Commissioner and Consul-General of the Oil Rivers Protectorate in 1891, and by the extension in 1893 of that protectorate over the hinterland under the new name of the Niger Coast Protectorate.

Although Macdonald had not included the kingdom of Benin within the scope of his enquiries or recommendations, their outcome was bound to affect that state, for Britain had assumed an interest and responsibility which administrative and economic pressures were certain to extend beyond the narrow coastal strip that had so far been the object of attention. Moreover, the establishment of an effective protectorate meant that the days of the coastal middlemen were numbered, and that the barriers which had for so long kept Benin virtually isolated from European influence were beginning to fall.[2]

5. The Protection Treaty of 1892

In 1891 the first steps were taken towards the setting up of a permanent British administration in the Benin River by appointing a vice-consul for the area. At the same time Macdonald proposed

---

1 cf. *Report on the administration of the Niger Coast Protectorate, 1891–4.* C. 7596, H.M.S.O., 1895. Since Macdonald was a determined opponent of the Royal Niger Company, it is hardly conceivable that his findings could have been in favour of chartered company government.
2 Another important factor in the opening of the West African interior to European penetration was the introduction of prophylactic drugs. cf. J. E. Flint, 'The growth of European influence in West Africa in the nineteenth century', in *A Thousand Years of West African History*, ed. J. F. A. Ajayi and I. Espie. Nelson, 1965, p. 368.

that the boundary between the Oil Rivers Protectorate and the Colony of Lagos, fixed at the Benin River in 1886, should be adjusted so that Benin fell wholly within the jurisdiction of the protectorate. His proposal was accepted and the boundary drawn accordingly when the Niger Coast Protectorate came into existence two years later.[1]

The first vice-consul for the Benin River area, Henry Galway, proved a vigorous exponent of Macdonald's ideas; in particular he believed in the necessity of opening a direct trade with the oil-producing areas and looked around to see how this could be done. During his first year, in October 1891, he took a significant step in the desired direction by travelling up-river in a launch hired from Bey and Zimmer to visit the Urhobo oil markets as far as the Abraka district.[2] His purpose was to select a site for the vice-consulate, a barracks and a police post, to urge upon the Urhobos the cultivation of coffee, cocoa and other new cash crops, to investigate the slackness of trade, and, above all, to spread word of the new order that had been established in the river.[3] In the course of his journey Galway passed well beyond the earlier limits of European penetration (he wrote that a few traders had previously tried to reach the markets, but had been turned back by the 'war-like attitude of the natives') and into territory that had for centuries acknowledged the overlordship of the Oba of Benin; and yet when Galway appeared as the representative of a new power claiming paramount authority, it would appear that the Urhobo said nothing about their ties with Benin and gave him the impression that no one

---

1 The Lagos administration did not give up its claims to the Benin area without a struggle. Consul Annesley twice advocated that the whole region be allocated to the Colony. (P.R.O. F.O. 84/2020. Annesley to Foreign Office, 21 May 1890 and 29 October 1890). As late as 13 January 1891, Macdonald himself gave his opinion that Benin must eventually come under Lagos administration because of its geographical situation and the question of slavery. (P.R.O. F.O. 84/2111. Macdonald to Foreign Office, 13 January 1891.) It was in a despatch dated 2 May 1891 that he put forward the immediate claims of the protectorate.

2 At the end of the year he also explored the water connection between the Benin River and Lagos in a canoe lent by Nana. P.R.O. F.O. 84/2194. *Report on the journey from Benin to Lagos by way of the interior creeks, 15 January 1892.* Enclosure in Macdonald to Foreign Office, 9 March 1892.

3 P.R.O. F.O. 84/2111. *Report on a visit to the Sobo and Abrakar markets, 3 November 1891.*

ruler had jurisdiction over the whole area. Indeed it is possible that they were stating the facts of the situation, and that the Oba had lost all control over these riverain Urhobos who had been drawn economically into the Itsekiri orbit.

Unaware of any possible encroachment into the Benin sphere of influence, Galway gained the impression that the prospect of British rule, so far as it was understood, met with general approval among the Urhobos.[1] He made no immediate attempt to exert his authority, apart from ordering an exchange of Urhobo and Itsekiri prisoners at Okpara, and telling all villages to bring their disputes with other tribes before him. Nor did he put the new regime on a legal footing by signing treaties with the local chiefs, because, he believed, the Urhobos would neither understand nor observe them until European influence had been established in their midst.[2] To this end he recommended that the vice-consulate be built at Sapele, which he judged to be the boundary between Itsekiri and Urhobo territory. Above that village he had observed numerous settlements of palm-oil traders and calculated that a vice-consul established there would be able to break Nana's monopoly in that commodity, as well as to encourage the Urhobo to grow other cash crops. His visit had, in fact, strengthened his belief in the need for direct trade, and inclined him still more to brush aside vocal Itsekiri opposition to the double-edged British thrust towards the interior.

Itsekiri concern was being aroused not solely, and perhaps not primarily, by the adventures of the vice-consul. More threatening in their eyes was the new surge forward of European trading posts that began at the end of the eighteen-eighties when foreign competition revived British interest in the Benin River. In 1888 Coxon claimed to have obtained permission to establish a factory near the entrance to the Ughoton Creek from the chief of Akinbodo, and a post must have been set up in Ughoton itself about this time because Punch appears to have been trading there in 1889. A little later two more posts at Sapele anticipated Galway's choice of the place as a suitable centre of British influence. In the Forcados River too the

---

1 He found this attitude of ready acceptance most marked at Uria and Okpara.
2 Nevertheless Galway did sign a treaty with the chiefs of Abraka when he revisited the district in May 1892. The traders Swainson and Punch acted as witnesses.

earlier success of the Benin River interests in checking the European advance[1] was undone when a number of factories were established around Warri; Macdonald found four there in 1889.[2] Trade was jumping ahead of the flag, but the agents of British firms knew that sympathetic consuls were on their heels.

In these circumstances a visit to Benin City seemed a logical sequel to Galway's reconnaissance in the Benin River. Attempts to sign a treaty with the Oba, begun with Blair's ill-fated mission, had again come to nought in 1890 when Annesley made a fruitless journey to the Edo capital. Accompanied by Cyril Punch, the consul had detected several signs of hostility from the time of leaving Ughoton, where they found by the path the remains of a human sacrifice tied between trees and disembowelled,[3] until their arrival in Benin City. 'We did not like our treatment,' Punch remarked, 'and to show we were annoyed refused to enter a house.'[4] Instead they camped in the open. Not surprisingly they returned empty-handed. Galway determined that, for the sake of the prestige of the protectorate, within whose orbit the kingdom lay, the reverse suffered by Annesley must be wiped out by bringing the Oba to acknowledge British claims. He was also inspired to visit Benin by the outcry which traders were raising against a ban which Ovonramwen had placed on the sale of palm kernels following the death of Adolo,[5] and against the restrictions which, in the interest of his monopoly rights, the Oba had placed upon other products such as rubber, gum copal, gum arabic, incense gums and woods. Determined that his mission should succeed, Galway conducted a lengthy preliminary exchange with the Oba by means of messengers, warning that he would make only one attempt to negotiate, and that he would give

---

1 cf. supra p. 257.

2 C. M. Macdonald, *Report by Major Macdonald of his visit as Her Majesty's Commissioner to the Niger and Oil Rivers*. London, H.M.S.O., 1890, p. 38. The factories belonged to Hutton and Osborne, Miller Bros., Pinnock & Co., and Bey and Zimmer.

3 Probably a sacrifice to 'close the path'; i.e. to enforce the trade embargo about which traders were complaining.

4 Roth, *Great Benin*, p. 66.

5 H. L. Galway, 'Journeys in the Benin country, West Africa'. *Geographical Journal*, no. 2, 1893, p. 123. According to Governor Moloney a similar ban had been enforced from 1872-81 because of the death of an Oba.

no presents until a treaty had been signed.[1] In his replies Ovonramwen admitted that he had acted 'foolishly' with Annesley and stated that he was prepared to make a treaty without more delay. With these assurances Galway left for Benin on 21 March 1892 accompanied by a consular agent, the trader Swainson, a medical officer and an interpreter. He took his own servants and about thirty carriers, but no armed escort. At Ughoton, 'now only a small village',[2] they found three messengers already waiting to guide the party, but even so it took three days to reach Benin City, for they covered only eleven miles on the first and nine miles on the second day. Such extraordinarily slow progress may perhaps be explained by Galway's curious admission that 'we regarded the whole thing as a very interesting picnic';[3] alternatively it may have been contrived by the Edo to delay their arrival—royal messengers were continually arriving to confer with the guides.

Further indications that Ovonramwen was playing for time are provided by his actions following Galway's arrival in the city on 23 March. The Vice-Consul first asked for an audience at 7 a.m. the following day, then at the Oba's request changed the time to 8 a.m. When 8 a.m. came Galway was told that the Oba could not see him until later; and so the delays continued until the afternoon of 26 March. The previous day the Vice-Consul had occupied himself visiting the principal chiefs to explain his mission and the meaning of the proposed treaty in very much the same manner as Landolphe had done.[4] They had all expressed their satisfaction, but still did not take him to the Oba as they had promised. On the morning of 26 March he forced the issue by threatening to depart at once and not return as a 'friend'; a number of carriers were sent off to lend colour to the menace. The only immediate result was a request that

---

1 One of the reasons for Annesley's failure, Galway believed, was that he had given the Oba presents on his arrival.
2 H. L. Galway, 'Journeys in the Benin country, West Africa.' *Geographical Journal*, vol. II, no. 2, 1893, p. 128.
3 H. L. Galway, 'Nigeria in the Nineties'. *Journal of the African Society*, vol. XXIX, no. cxv, April 1930.
4 cf. supra p. 203. Galway does not reveal who suggested that he should visit the chiefs, but it is possible that this was considered an indispensable preliminary to any discussion of very important business with the Oba and his council.

he should meet the chiefs once more. Eventually he agreed to confer with 'the three leading men', although he considered them 'a set of intriguing and lying individuals' who were determined to prevent him seeing the Oba. By the afternoon, however, the Oba had announced his readiness and Galway was at the palace. There in an inner courtyard five of the ruler's chief advisers presented compliments in their ruler's name and said that he would be received as soon as the Oba was dressed. Galway afterwards discovered that throughout this exchange Ovonramwen had been concealed behind a curtain to observe his visitor—a proceeding not encountered, or perhaps not discovered, by any previous European visitor. Taken together with Ovonramwen's earlier and later disinclination to meet consular officials, the action might be interpreted as evidence of the mistrust and suspicion which British actions were awakening in Benin.

A further two hours of waiting ensued, with Galway watching a wrestling match staged for his benefit, and the Oba presumably undergoing ritual preparations for the decisive encounter. At last, dressed in his full coral regalia, Ovonramwen took his seat on a dais attended by his chiefs and *emada*, and the Vice-Consul was conducted into the audience chamber. A preliminary difficulty then arose over the interpreter whom Galway judged to be inadequate and afraid of the Oba; he therefore made use of an Akure servant who passed his remarks to the Oba through the principal chief. Once mutual recriminations over hustle and delay were done, the Vice-Consul explained the clauses of the treaty he had brought ready for signature in the standard printed form that was in use throughout the protectorate. Ovonramwen, constantly conferring with his chiefs, seems to have been little concerned with its niceties, but asked many times 'whether it was peace or war'. The menace always implicit in Galway's attitude doubtless contributed to this nervous anxiety; failure to conclude a treaty would clearly entail unspecified unpleasantness. And the Oba had other grounds for disquiet. In 1890 the Oni of Ife had sent warning that his oracle foretold some great calamity in Benin City.[1] During the *ugie-ivie* ceremony in May 1891, a man about to be sacrificed had prophesied

---

1 Egharevba, *A Short History*, p. 50.

that white men would come to 'spoil Ado'. Ovonramwen must also have felt uneasiness over the fear and hatred that his earlier executions had engendered among the chiefs. After many assurances that British intentions were peaceful, the Oba and chiefs agreed to sign the treaty, although Ovonramwen himself refused to touch the pen on the grounds that he was engaged in an important ritual. The 'signing' of the treaty was therefore accomplished by all the chiefs touching the pen after Ovonramwen's name had been written. With the main business completed, Galway broached other undisclosed matters—possibly the hindrances to trade—on which he found the Oba 'most sensible and willing to listen to reason', and still only anxious that there should be no 'war palavers'. To conclude the audience everyone adjourned to another part of the palace for the presentation of the silks and coral brought by the Vice-Consul. Galway saw Ovonramwen once more when he took his leave on 27 March. On this occasion their discussion was concerned wholly with trading matters, and produced promises from the Oba that the Ughoton road should be cleared and widened, and that the embargo on trade in gum copal should be lifted.[1]

Galway's description of Benin City closely resembles that given by Burton. Apart from continuing marks of prosperity in some chiefs' houses, where roof beams were covered with figured metal sheets, the city appeared no more than a 'straggling collection of houses built in clusters here and there in little or no order', and liberally interspersed with ruins. Yet he did not underestimate the power of the Oba who still collected tribute from several states; in importance he ranked Ovonramwen with the king of Dahomey.

In their anxiety to establish that Galway's mission was not a 'war palaver', the ruler of Benin and his chiefs were probably unaware that they had signed away their country's independence.

---

1 The reference to the condition of the Ughoton road may help to explain Galway's exceedingly slow progress to Benin City. The sources for the Vice-Consul's visit to Benin are his official report (P.R.O. F.O. 84/2194, 30 March 1892. Enclosure in Macdonald to Foreign Office, 16 May 1892), his annual report for the year ending 31 July 1892 (P.R.O. F.O. 2/51), and a number of articles: 'Journeys in the Benin country, West Africa'. *Geographical Journal*, vol. I, no. 2, 1893; 'Nigeria in the Nineties'. *Journal of the African Society*, vol. XXIX, no. cxv, April 1930; 'Benin: altars and compounds'. *Ethnologia Cranmorensis*, vol. III, 1938.

Articles IV and V of the treaty obliged the Oba to accept consular guidance in all matters of internal as well as external policy.[1] Article VI threw open trade to all nationalities in all parts of the kingdom; article VII likewise opened Benin to ministers of the Christian religion. One must doubt whether Ovonramwen understood the implications of provisions so wholly at variance with the existing order of state and society. From the British point of view, the signing of the treaty raised the problem of enforcement; the terms of article IX—'This treaty shall come into operation, so far as may be practicable, from the date of its signature'—did little more than underline the difficulty. Galway at that time opposed the use of force, arguing that punitive measures to compel observance of the treaty would only drive the Benin people into the bush and make them 'greater savages than ever'. Macdonald, on the other hand, when forwarding Galway's report to the Foreign Office, commented that he hoped soon to put an end to human sacrifice and that force would probably be necessary. To him the eradication of human sacrifice was the crux of the problem, for he believed that the 'priesthood' was imposing on the Oba a fetish government which was hampering trade and the development of Benin's rich resources.[2]

6. The dispute over trade

As it happened it was not the question of human sacrifice that immediately engaged official attention on Benin, but the charge that the Oba was failing to observe his obligations under article VI. Pressure from commercial interests played some part in forcing that problem upon the Vice-Consul's attention, but probably more important was Treasury insistence that the consular establishment in the protectorate must recoup its expenses from the import duties

---

1 The text of the treaty is printed in Egharevba, *A Short History*, Appendix XIII.
2 P.R.O. F.O. 84/2194. Macdonald to Foreign Office, 16 May 1892. The treaty made no reference to the abolition of human sacrifice, unless it could be understood to come within the scope of article V which bound the Oba to act upon the advice of consular officials 'in matters relating to the administration of justice . . . or in any other matter in relation to peace, order, and good government, and the general progress of civilisation'.

introduced in 1891.[1] Reporting on the Benin district for the first year of vice-consular administration ending on 31 July 1892,[2] Galway declared that trade had been unsatisfactory, amounting to a total value of £139,109 3s. 11d. with a revenue yield of £5,550 7s. od. —in other words a volume of trade not significantly greater than that of the eighteen-fifties. Palm oil and kernels remained the only important exports despite attempts to diversify trade. Ivory Galway considered a potentially valuable commodity, but half the ivory collected in Benin country went by custom to the Oba, and most of what he received he stored. Much of the remainder was used by the Edo, according to Galway, to buy slaves from the Urhobos. The failure of the palm-oil and kernel trade to expand he ascribed, among other reasons, to 'the fetish rule of the king of Benin', by which he meant that most trade commodities were reserved for the Oba by placing a fetish upon them—a practice of great antiquity in Benin. Being thereby obliged to trade only with the Oba's agents for such commodities, the Itsekiri traders of the Benin River had to pay a heavy tax to the ruler of Benin each year. If they failed to pay they were barred from trade and their goods confiscated. Besides exercising this long-established form of royal monopoly, the Oba often stopped trade at different markets for what Galway regarded as 'fetish reasons', though closer investigation would probably have revealed commercial problems at the root of many such stoppages. On the consular interpretation, however, a growth of trade and destruction of the Oba's fetish power went inescapably together.

> The King struck me as being very ready to listen to reason, but he is tied down by fetish custom, and, until the power of the fetish priests is done away with, the trade of the Benin country will continue to be a very doubtful source of profit.[3]

The remedy must, he thought, take time, and might eventually

---

1 P.R.O. F.O. 84/2111, 6 June 1891. Instruction to impose the duties. cf. A. F. Mockler-Ferryman, *British Nigeria*. London, 1902, p. 96. 'The Customs Department was of immense importance, since on it depended the revenue which was to pay for the whole administration.'

2 P.R.O. F.O. 2/51. Though Galway wrote the annual report, H. Haly Hutton had been appointed to succeed him as vice-consul for Benin from 30 June 1892.

3 P.R.O. F.O. 2/51. Annual report for year ending 31 July 1892.

involve a punitive expedition. But though he here veered towards the course first championed by Macdonald, and adopted against Ijebu earlier in the year, Galway took care to point out that such action, 'though it may eventually prove advisable, would paralize trade for a very long period'. Meanwhile he advocated continual 'expostulation'.

In Galway's eyes, one of the most cogent reasons for postponing action against Benin was that the Itsekiri middlemen presented a more immediate problem. Their continual quarrels with Benin and Urhobo oil producers over trust often brought trade to a standstill. One such dispute in July 1891 had led to an attack on an Itsekiri settlement by a large Benin force which carried off about a hundred prisoners and a large quanitity of goods.[1] Another charge against the Itsekiris was that they were endeavouring to hinder the establishment of European factories inland; Galway cited a number of cases of obstruction involving trading posts at Sapele and Ughoton. His further complaint that they were unable to understand European price fluctuations and adjust their own prices in harmony with them revealed that one of the oldest sources of conflict between African and European traders was still very much alive, and that centuries of commercial intercourse had done little to close the gulf between two concepts of price. It is interesting to note that Galway laid no particular blame upon Nana who had been deprived of his office as Governor of the River by Annesley in 1890 for alleged interference with trade; in his opinion, Nana had not tried since then to dominate the river. There were on the other hand many among the European traders and his Itsekiri rivals who saw the chief of Ebrohimi as the villain of the piece.

The establishment of the vice-consulate at Sapele aboard the hulk *Hindoustan* in 1893, and a fall in trade for 1892–3 to £134,337 1s. 7d. hastened the crisis,[2] by rendering the position of the Itsekiri

---

1 Though Ovonramwen denied knowledge of the incident when Galway raised it with him, he did promise to punish the offenders and see that compensation was given.

2 But the year in which the crisis came to a head showed a marked recovery with imports rising by £28,711 10s. 7d. to £84,776 6s. 6d., and exports by £22,139 10s. 4d. to £100,411 16s. 0d. Nana's efforts to strengthen his trading position could not, therefore, be said to have brought commerce in the river to a standstill as many of his enemies alleged.

middlemen still more precarious. Nana, by far the most powerful of the Itsekiri despite his loss of office, reacted strongly to this situation. He tried, according to Egharevba,[1] to prohibit all Itsekiri trade with Benin; in particular he cut off the supply of cooking salt of which he had a virtual monopoly through his control of the salt-bush country around Ebrohimi. In the Urhobo areas his armed retainers were said to have imposed a rigid trade monopoly by marking out a frontier line three miles from the river, and forbidding the Urhobo to pass this line on pain of seizure and enslavement.[2] Incidents between Urhobos and Nana's men multiplied, complaints from rival Itsekiri houses grew in volume until in June 1894 Acting Consul-General Moor visited the Benin River to investigate, and by accident, rather than choice, Nana found himself driven into a conflict with the British authorities that ended with the capture of Ebrohimi by an imposing naval force on 25 September 1894. Nana was a merchant prince whose power and fortune had depended upon a unique combination of geographical advantage with political and military power; the years before his downfall saw this position undermined by advances in technology and medical science that made it possible for the European to trade directly with the interior and introduce there the commercial conventions of industrial Europe. Nana had brought to perfection a system that had become simultaneously anachronistic. His fall warned the lesser Itsekiri princes against imitating his resistance to the advancing forces of European commerce, but it did not lead them to change their methods, so that by the end of the century they and their towns had dwindled to insignificance.[3]

So far as is known, the Oba of Benin took no part in the drama that brought the chief of Ebrohimi to grief, though the latter had continued to pay him an annual tribute, and the issues involved in the conflict threatened him as much as his vassal. The trading practices of Benin, though never inflexible, were still a world away

---

1 Egharevba, *A Short History*, p. 51.
2 P.R.O. F.O. 2/63. Coxon to Pinnock, 1 July 1894.
3 For a description of the main Itsekiri settlements in the lower Benin River in the late eighteen-nineties see C. N. de Cardi, 'A short description of the natives of the Niger Coast Protectorate, with some account of their customs, religion, trade etc.' in M. H. Kingsley, *West African Studies*. London, 1899.

from those envisaged in the 1892 treaty; the very isolation of Benin through much of the nineteenth century had militated against adjustments and innovations that might otherwise have lessened the gulf. As it was, Punch could refer to Dapper's account of those practices as 'excellent' and largely applicable to the conditions of his own day. He found himself 'dealing with a regular spider's web of old customs, and with ways which were no doubt useful in their time, but which in 1889 were an unmitigated nuisance'.[1] Europeans had to visit the Oba before opening trade at Ughoton. 'The King would tell the European traders what was expected of them, and begin with a long list of what was to be given to the various officials'; the latter also continued to expect a courtesy visit from traders. Sums demanded for the right to trade were considerable, and, according to Punch, traders often refused to pay them. When buying commodities of which the Oba had a monopoly, traders had to deal with a class of men who resembled the *fiadors* of old, although that name had apparently dropped out of use. Brownridge describes them in terms reminiscent of Nyendael:

> The Great Parasite of Benin traders are the 'Acurabas'[2] or King's messengers; these are usually men who have been in the King's household as boys and have grown old enough to marry and are therefore sent to look after the various trading centres. The men levy blackmail broadcast, any new articles coming into the country, they bar the sale to anyone but themselves.[3]

Punch's remarks on the same subject tend to confirm the impression that these royal agents were inadequately supervised.

Following the establishment of the Protectorate, the import of arms, ammunition and gunpowder into the river was strictly controlled, so that salt, cloths and gin took their place as the staple articles of trade. Cowries too continued to figure prominently among European imports; Stewart and Douglas brought large quantities from the Malabar coast especially for their Benin trade. Like his ancestors, Ovonramwen showed a preference for silks and coral, but also developed a partiality for sheet brass and Muntz metal which he used, together with large quantities of galvanised

1 Roth, *Great Benin*, p. 136, n. 2.   2 i.e. *uk-oba*, a messenger of the Oba.
3 P.R.O. F.O. 2/102. Brownridge to Moor, 9 November 1896. cf. Bosman, *A new and accurate description*, p. 431.

roofing sheets, in rebuilding and decorating his palace. To acquire these goods Benin depended almost exclusively upon the export of palm oil. European traders, however, were convinced that the kingdom harboured other natural riches and were itching to get at them. In 1896 Miller's agent at Ughoton sent the Consul the following notes on some of these commodities.[1]

> *Rubber.* I know there is plenty of this produced in the country as I had a Cape Coast rubber man with me in Gwatto. I was unable to get it in any quantity, as we could never get the man to go far from the town, he having been twice maltreated when away in the bush.[2]
>
> *Gum Copal.* There is plenty of this article in the country but the natives are debarred from selling it. I have bought quantities of it but only from the King.
>
> *Palm Kernels.* I have also bought these from the King, but only in small quantities. There are tons upon tons of kernels lying rotting in every town, the natives not being allowed to break or sell them, the idea being that when kernels are crushed they give off a noxious gas which is considered injurious to health.
>
> So used are the Benin natives to stoppages of the oil trade that they always keep oil in narrow necked calabashes which they can keep airtight and so keep the oil in good condition for a length of time.

In face of such restrictions and obstacles, Ughoton's revival as a trading centre was short-lived, British firms withdrew their agents, and the centres of trade moving away from the lower river became fixed in the eighteen-nineties at Sapele and Warri. In the eyes of traders and officials, the outstanding characteristics of Benin remained wholesale human sacrifice and an obstructive trading regime.

7. Consul-General Moor's campaign against Benin

Having broken the back of Itsekiri resistance to administrative and commercial advance, Moor was impatient to make a reality of an

---

1 P.R.O. F.O. 2/102. loc. cit.
2 cf. P.R.O. F.O. 2/102. Phillips to Foreign Office, 10 November 1896. 'A Lagos man trading in the Protectorate also went to see the King by the advice of Mr. Moor, chiefly with a view to asking the King to start the "rubber" industry, the country abounding in that product. He made presents to the King to the value of over £30, but the results of his mission have been nil.'

1893 Order in Council that had extended the jurisdiction of the Niger Coast Protectorate over those states of the hinterland which had signed treaties with Britain and did not fall within the Colony of Lagos or the Royal Niger Company Protectorate. The example of Sir Gilbert Carter's spectacular progress through Yorubaland in 1893 may also have spurred him to attempt a similar general settlement in the newly extended and renamed protectorate. Benin presented the readiest and greatest challenge, for it now stood isolated as the last important traditional state surviving in southern Nigeria, and the 1892 treaty remained wholly ineffective.

Immediately after taking Ebrohimi, Moor decided to force the issue in Benin. In messages despatched to the Oba he insisted that the treaty be observed, while he made preparations for a visit to Benin City. To his extreme annoyance, this offensive, designed to exploit the psychological impact of Nana's defeat, came to nothing because his messengers on arrival in the Edo capital found the stage already occupied by Mr. MacTaggart, an official of the Royal Niger Company, who had arrived there with an armed escort. Moor's men returned with what he considered 'an impertinent message' from the Oba, so he called off his visit on the grounds that Protectorate prestige would now demand 'a large expedition' which would require careful organisation.[1] The immediate target of his anger was the Royal Niger Company rather than the Oba, because he believed that the Company had taken advantage of the disturbances in the Benin River to encroach on his jurisdiction. Early in September 1894 MacTaggart, in company with Flint the Agent-General at Akassa, had been busy in the Urhobo country offering to make treaties with the chiefs; in at least one locality—Egoro, a district on the Benin River till then controlled by Nana—they were successful. Moor recognised their activities as a serious challenge, because the revenue collected by the Protectorate in the Benin River would be badly affected if the Company succeeded in its efforts to direct the palm-oil traffic, now freed from Nana's control, to its own stations on the Niger.[2] Protesting vigorously against these incursions into the Protectorate, he asked for a revision of the boundary

---

1 P.R.O. F.O. 2/64. Moor to Foreign Office, 21 October 1894.
2 ibid. Moor to Foreign Office, 10 October 1894.

between Crown and Company territory which as it stood cut off Benin River traders from all markets above Mbona. He argued that all the trade hitherto exploited by Nana and the Itsekiris, as far as Abraka, should continue to come down-river.[1]

MacTaggart's mission to Benin has never been explained. In an apology to Moor he claimed that he had been sent to confirm a treaty signed with the chief of Ado, and that he had been led by mistake to Benin City (Edo). Moor however had information that he had waited for some days at Ogagu (Ogugu?), a village belonging to an important Benin chief, to know whether the Oba would receive him, and continued to nurse a suspicion that the Company had tried to negotiate a treaty with Benin despite the established claims of the Niger Coast Protectorate. Certainly it is difficult to believe that an armed party could have stumbled into Benin City unannounced and unawares.

The manner of the check to his initial plans only made Moor more determined to deal with Benin swiftly and vigorously. By November 1894 he had preparations well under way for a military expedition through which he intended to establish an armed post in the Edo capital. Presumably he meant the operation to be carried out in the coming dry season and did not anticipate serious resistance. Disbelief in the martial qualities of the Edo had been spread by Galway who, from his visit to Benin City, had formed the impression that they were 'far from brave, though more so than their neighbours'. Experience at Ebrohimi did not alter an opinion which was to have tragic consequences. It was not put to the test early in 1895, as Moor had intended, because his superior Macdonald, returning from leave on 5 December 1894, put a stop to military preparations and insisted that 'pacific means' must first be tried. Shortly afterwards Moor himself went to England on leave, and the Brass rising kept Protectorate officials busy until he returned in July 1895. Attempts made during the interval 'to open friendly communication with Benin City' met with no success.[2] Evidence produced at his

---

1 P.R.O. F.O. 2/64. Moor to Foreign Office, 11 October 1894. In 1891 Macdonald had concluded a provisional boundary agreement with the Royal Niger Company whereby the Abraka markets were cut off from the Benin River. The implications of such a boundary were not realised until Galway's journey to the interior markets in the following year.
2 P.R.O. F.O. 2/102. Moor to Foreign Office, 26 December 1896.

trial showed that the fate of Nana had much alarmed Ovonramwen, making him more nervous than ever in his dealings with the British and eager to avoid all contact with them. As Galway wrote in 1896, 'The king has shut himself up since October 1894 and has refused all overtures from the white man.'[1] Among his own subjects too the Oba felt insecure following the murder of the *Uwangue* in 1895 and his subsequent reprisals against the *Iwebo* chiefs. A rebellion in Agbor added to his difficulties. Faced with these threats from without and within, Ovonramwen fell into ever greater reliance upon his fetish powers.

Macdonald's final departure from the Protectorate in August 1895 once again left Moor in command and able to pursue his own line of policy. However, in deference to Macdonald's wishes Vice-Consul Copland-Crawford was instructed to attempt another 'friendly visit' to Benin City early in September 1895. This mission having failed, and having demonstrated to his own satisfaction the futility of such measures, Moor was then ready to denounce them to the Foreign Secretary.

> ... I recommended that force should be employed to open up the country to civilisation and trade and to prevent the horrible human sacrifices and cruelties which were continually taking place therein. The instructions in reply to this were that pacific measures should be employed for a further period before resorting to force.[2]

His appointment as Consul-General in 1896 cleared all local obstacles to Moor's obvious determination to bring Benin to heel within the next year whether by pacific means or by force, but he still faced the problem of obtaining the sanction of the British government for measures which might involve heavy expenditure and large forces. Grounds for action which could be urged in London were not long wanting, for on 2 April 1896 Ovonramwen stopped all trade with the Itsekiris. He did this, says Egharevba, 'on the ground that his people had reported that the Itsekiris were

---

1 ibid. Galway to Foreign Office, 20 October 1896.
   P.R.O. F.O. 2/123. Record of proceedings at the Oba's trial. One of the accused, Obakhavbaye, stated that 'since six years ago that Nana war was fought we heard that whiteman would be coming to Benin City'. cf. supra p. 262, n4.
2 P.R.O. F.O. 2/102. Moor to Foreign Office, 26 December 1896.

cheating them'.[1] British and Itsekiri traders put the blame elsewhere. Brownridge, for example, gave the following account of the situation:

> I may say that the primary cause of the present stoppage of trade is the raising of the price of guns, powder and gin. The King finding that he cannot buy these articles at the price he likes, is now keeping on the stoppage to extort as much money as possible from the Jackries. Stoppages of trade are of common occurrence in Benin, though of much smaller duration; for instance, one market would be stopped at a time and the Jackries trading there made to pay certain monies before trade would be reopened.[2]

Thus each party was accusing the other of extortion, and probably with some justice on either side. As Brownridge admits, this stoppage, although a breach of the 1892 treaty, was not an unusual event. Nor were the Itsekiri traders being entirely truthful when, in a petition presented to the Consul on 13 April 1896, they declared that they were 'wholly dependent for their trade on what comes down from the king's country';[3] much oil must have come from the upper Benin River over which the Oba can have exercised little control after the vice-consulate had been established at Sapele. Moor, however, represented the stoppage as a sign that the policy of peaceful approaches had failed: 'He [i.e. Ovonramwen] refuses all overtures and indeed now only becomes worse the more we attempt to approach him in peace—evidently regarding such courses as signs of fear and weakness.'[4] To strengthen his case, he further complained that the Oba, in breach of article V of the treaty, 'still declines to receive government officers or to allow them to enter his country in any direction peaceably. He punishes severely those of his people who even in outlying districts venture to receive them.'[5] This latter charge was probably based upon the Oba's successful obstruction of Copland-Crawford's attempt to march with an armed

---

1 Egharevba, *A Short History*, p. 51.
2 P.R.O. F.O. 2/102. Brownridge to Moor, 9 November 1896.
3 ibid. Acting Consul-General Phillips to Foreign Office, 16 November 1896. It is possible that the penetration of European trading posts as far as Sapele was compelling the Itsekiris to seek their supplies deeper in the interior, and thus making them more dependent on the markets of the Benin kingdom.
4 P.R.O. F.O. 2/101. Moor to Foreign Office, 6 June 1896.
5 ibid. Moor to Foreign Office, 14 June 1896.

escort from Ughoton to Benin City, and upon some incidents reported by A. D. C. Lecky during a visit to the Kwale country made on the Consul-General's instructions in April 1896.[1] Again, therefore, Moor urged the use of force:

> I consider that if the efforts now being made continue unsuccessful until next dry season, an expeditionary force should be sent about January or February to remove the king and his ju-ju men for the sufferings of the people are terrible. This would of course necessitate the establishment of a post in that country which would serve as a good base for further development.[2]

But an unconvinced Foreign Office still preached caution. The despatch was minuted: 'The King of Benin may have to be dealt with, but it should be set about with care and with a sufficient force, and at our own time'; and Lord Salisbury instructed Moor that he was to persevere with 'pacific means'. The Consul-General's views were also challenged by Major Ewart of the Lagos Colony administration who claimed that he could easily and peaceably have gained access to Benin City had Benin been within the jurisdiction of the colony. In Ewart's opinion, 'patience and presents' would reassure the Oba and persuade him to open up his country, whereas attempts to use force would provoke strong resistance.[3]

However unacceptable and unwelcome such counsels might be, Moor was constrained to make another gesture towards a peaceful settlement. He did so through the Itsekiris; perhaps in order not to hazard the prestige of the Protectorate officials in another failure; perhaps because he thought the whole effort a waste of time. Acting Vice-Consul Locke, District Commissioner of Warri, reported the

---

1 ibid. Lecky to Moor, 28 April 1896. The chiefs of Obiariku, to the east of the Ethiope River, complained to Lecky that Benin people from 'Solugbi' (Usonigbe?) continually interfered with their farms on the other side of the river. Lecky decided to make a treaty with them, 'thinking that the King of Benin would leave them alone when he knew they had one'. At Umutu, where he was told the Oba made annual sacrifices of humans and animals, the chiefs refused to give Lecky any information and declined his present. It was later discovered that they had reported one of his guides to the Oba, and that the man's life was only spared on payment of ten bags of cowries.

2 ibid. Moor to Foreign Office, 14 June 1896.

3 P.R.O. F.O. 2/102. Gallwey (this gentleman changed the spelling of his name from time to time) to Foreign Office, 20 October 1896. Ewart's remarks had been sent to the Protectorate for comment.

result of the mission to Moor in a letter written from Warri on 23 September 1896.[1]

> The free-born Jekris who went as messengers to the King of Benin have returned and with them came two of the King of Benin's messengers. Three markets, namely Boro and Nueme up the Gwato Creek and Gbeque up the Jameson River have been opened some short time but no trading was allowed. The King told the Jekris to send presents to the people at these markets who had been keeping back the trade. Presents were at once forwarded. These three markets, also Gwato and Eketi, are now all opened. The King wants iron to build a house with before opening any more markets. He sends a pistol for which he wants ammunition. He also sends six fans as presents to the Jekri chiefs.
>
> With regards the Jekri's request that the King of Benin should ask for a visit by a Government officer, the King answers that he is afraid, as twice the Government have been in his country, all their men being armed. These occasions were:
>
> I. when Mr. McTaggart of the Royal Niger Company went to Benin via Sapoba.
> II. when Major Crawford went as far as Gwato.
>
> The Jekris explained who Major Crawford and Mr. McTaggart are, also Major Crawford's reason for wishing to go to Benin City to see the King.
>
> Jekri messengers have again gone to Benin City to tell the King that he will get the iron for his house, but ammunition for his pistol is not to be had, also to get him to receive a Government officer. The Jekri chiefs now feel certain that trade will be firmly established.

Such was the situation which Moor left behind him when shortly afterwards he went to Britain on leave. In his absence the Protectorate came under the control of Acting Consul-General Phillips, a young man of limited experience and a staunch supporter of Moor's policies.

8. The massacre and punitive expedition

When Phillips in his new capacity visited the Benin River early in November 1896 he found that all the markets in the Oba's territory had again been closed.

---

1 ibid. Locke to Moor, 23 September 1896.

The King has now asked for a thousand sheets of corrugated iron to build a house with before he will accede to the demands made. The Jekri chiefs promised to give the iron directly the markets were opened, and at the same time asked the King to receive a government officer. His reply was that he was making a big custom to last four months and could not do so until it was over![1]

After conferring with Galway, Locke, the Itsekiri chiefs and British commercial agents, Phillips sent a lengthy despatch to the Foreign Office rehearsing the history of the Protectorate's relations with Benin and concluding that the pacific means advocated by Lord Salisbury had proved completely ineffective. He had accordingly advised the Itsekiris to give no more presents and not to deliver the iron sheets demanded by the Oba. Nor did he intend to carry peaceful measures any further: the removal of Ovonramwen was, he contended, the only possible solution, and he asked for cabled authority to effect it.

> I therefore ask His Lordship's permission to visit Benin City in February next to depose and remove the King of Benin, and to establish a Native Council in his place and take such further steps for the opening up of the country as the occasion may require.[2]

Though he did not anticipate any serious resistance—'there is every reason to believe that they would be glad to get rid of their king'[3]—he would take with him a force of 250 Protectorate troops, 150 Hausas, two seven-pounders, and one maxim, for which 'all calculations as to ammunition, supplies, rations etc. have already been made'.[4] Moor later confirmed that an Intelligence officer had been employed for eighteen months 'preparing all necessary information for the carrying out of offensive operations, and the approaches to Benin City and the country around are now fairly well known, as also the opposition likely to be encountered'.[5] It would appear,

1 P.R.O. F.O. 2/102. Phillips to Foreign Office, 16 November 1896.
2 ibid.
3 ibid.
4 ibid. In a private letter to Sir Clement Hill, Senior Clerk in the African Department of the Foreign Office, Phillips repeated the arguments for action against Benin that he had used in his despatch. He also stressed that the Protectorate needed the extra revenue that would result from the development of trade in Benin country. (ibid. Phillips to Hill, 18 November 1896.)
5 ibid. Moor to Under-Secretary of State, Foreign Office, 26 December 1896.

therefore, that Phillips was hoping to carry through Moor's long–cherished project in his chief's absence. But by the time his despatch reached the Foreign Office Moor was already in London, so the Foreign Secretary referred it to him for comment.

Considering his own past utterances on the subject, the Consul-General could not but support Phillips' argument that humanitarian and economic considerations demanded action against Benin. He likewise favoured a military expedition to depose Ovonramwen by February or March 1897 at the latest, but thought that the force suggested by Phillips needed to be supported by a gunboat and marines. What did not please him was the thought that so important an action might be carried through in his absence:

> ... I have only to add that I have every confidence in Mr. Phillips and the officers now on the Coast, but being fully acquainted with all the circumstances in the past and knowing personally all the intelligence work that has been done, it might be advisable for me to proceed to the Protectorate at once to generally direct the course to be adopted. Should this be thought necessary, I am prepared to start by the next boat.[1]

Despite the hustle, the Foreign Secretary remained unconvinced and, after consultation with the Secretary of State for the Colonies on the question of available troops, he cabled to Phillips on 8 January 1897 that the operation must be 'postponed to another year'. In a despatch written the following day Salisbury explained his decision:

> Whilst it is admitted that a force of four hundred troops would be needed to ensure the success of the expedition, the Colonies of Lagos and the Gold Coast are unable, owing to the present calls on their forces, to afford any assistance to the troops of the Protectorate. These latter are only sufficient to keep order in the Protectorate in normal times, and with the existing spirit of unrest in Brass and New Calabar and the absence of the Niger Company's troops in the north of their territories, it is undesirable for the Protectorate to engage in any operations which can be deferred.[2]

Before either telegram or despatch left London, Phillips had been ambushed and killed on the road between Ughoton and Benin City.

---

1 ibid.
2 P.R.O. F.O. 2/120. Salisbury to Phillips, draft. 9 January 1897.

Following the November meeting with officials, chiefs and traders in the Benin River, Phillips had sent a message to the Oba saying that he intended to return to the river in the new year and would then like to visit Benin City. Whether the purpose of this message was to hide his real intentions, to frighten Ovonramwen, or to leave the door open for a last-minute settlement we do not know. Neither has it been explained why Phillips, having prepared the ground for military action, should suddenly embark on an unprepared and unarmed expedition. Perhaps he anticipated that the military expedition would not be sanctioned and wished at least for the credit of having compelled the Oba to receive him; such a success, in Moor's absence, could have done much for his career.[1] Whatever his motives and objective may have been, his tactics are not open to question: he intended to give Ovonramwen bare notice of his arrival and press on to Benin City whatever objections might be raised.

The messenger sent to inform the Oba that within a few days Phillips would be arriving with eight or nine other white men left Calabar only a little ahead of the Acting Consul-General and his party. On receipt of the news, Ovonramwen resorted to the tactics which had worked well in the past by sending a reply to the effect that he would be ready to welcome Phillips and one Itsekiri chief a month later when the *agwe* festival had been concluded. Too much significance should not be attached to the fact that Phillips' attempted visit coincided with this festival which, although of major importance in the Benin religious calendar, had not in the past been barred to European eyes. Rather it must be borne in mind that Ovonramwen had for some years and at different seasons used the plea of being engaged in religious ceremonials as a means of putting off unwelcome consular visits. On this occasion the Oba's reply failed to produce its usual stalling effect; the urgent warnings of the Itsekiri chief Dogho also failed to deter Phillips, and on 3 January 1897 Benin learned to its consternation that a party of seven

---

1 cf. A. C. Douglas (pseudo. Nemo), *Niger Memories*. Exeter, 1937, p. 35. 'He had only a few months before Moor's return to take over the reins of government and in which to achieve something, and it was reported that he had mentioned in a club late one night that he intended to lead an expedition to visit Benin.'

officials, two British traders and more than two hundred carriers
were assembled at Ughoton. As was revealed by evidence given at
the trial of the Oba and those chiefs accused of complicity in the
attack on the British party, this contingency had been foreseen and
had led to a serious difference of opinion. For Ovonramwen and his
advisers the crucial question was now, as it had been in 1892,
whether the consular visit heralded war. On this point Ovonramwen
might justifiably feel even more nervous than on the previous
occasion. Nana's fate had given clear warning of what was liable to
happen to those who opposed Moor, and it is very possible, in view
of the preparations for an armed expedition spoken of by Moor and
Phillips, that some inkling of the fate designed for him had reached
the ruler of Benin.[1] On the other hand, in the message announcing
his coming Phillips had assured Ovonramwen that his party would
not be armed; he had also, after the meeting with Chief Dogho,
sent back the uniformed Constabulary band in order to divest the
mission of all military appearances. Despite such reassurances, there
appears to have been genuine fear in Benin City that the British
intended to attack. At his trial Chief *Obakhavbaye* gave the following
version of the Oba's reaction:

> We were in this town about five days before the massacre having a big
> play, when we heard that white men were coming with war. The king
> then called the people and told them 'the whiteman is bringing war,
> now if you go you must not fight with them—let them come, and if
> they like they can come and see me and say anything they bring.
> Perhaps they are coming to play, you do not know; you must allow
> them to come, and if it is war we will find out.' The big chiefs hearing
> this said, 'No! the king's word is not good.' So when other people came
> from Gwatto and said that it was true that whitemen were coming, the
> big chiefs called all the people and sent them to go and fight.[2]

When news of these warlike preparations reached the Itsekiris those
at trading settlements within Benin territory hastily packed up and
left, and Chief Dogho warned Phillips of the danger ahead. Of all

---

1 'For three years the king had been expecting war and had men waiting and
watching at Egbini.' Evidence of Agamwoyi, a dependant of Chief *Obaseki*,
at the trial. P.R.O. F.O. 2/123. Proceedings of the trial, enclosed in Moor
to Foreign Office, 18 October 1897.
2 ibid.

the Benin chiefs, only the *Ezomo* is known to have supported the Oba's point of view; against it were ranged the *Iyase*, the war-chief *Ologboshere* and many lesser men including *Obakhavbaye, Obayuwana, Obadesagbon* and *Uso* who directed the attack on the consular party. Up to the last moment, and especially after an inspection of the baggage at Ughoton had shown that Phillips and his companions were not armed, Ovonramwen tried to dissuade the war party, but without success—an ironic commentary on the real power of the supposedly almighty monarch whom the British officials were bent on removing.

The 'massacre' of the British party and its Itsekiri and Kru carriers has been fully described by two survivors, Locke and Boisragon, who managed in the general confusion to hide in the forest, and after five days found their way back to the Ughoton Creek.[1] At the trial of the chiefs held responsible for the attack a number of Edo witnesses and defendants gave their version of events. One of the fullest and most interesting of these is the evidence of Omoregboma who acted as guide to Phillips on the ill-fated march from Ughoton.[2]

> I stayed at Gwatto long time. If any whiteman wanted to come to the king I used to bring him. Ohebó came and met me at Gwatto and told me that the chiefs sent him to say that they had heard that plenty whitemen were coming, and I must send to tell the king what they brought. Ohebó had not come from Benin City yet when the whitemen came and I allowed them a room where they put all their things—so I called Ohebó to look at the things that the whitemen brought. They had neither guns nor swords, the only cutlasses that the carriers had were tied up and put in the launch; I made Ohebó look at them so that he could tell the chiefs what they wanted when he came to Benin City. It was evening so the whitemen slept at Gwatto and in the morning they started for Benin City. I undertook to lead them so I was in front of them. When we reached at a place called Iguohemi the whitemen halted and had some chop. Not long after we left and on the

---

1 Ref. A. Boisragon, *The Benin Massacre*. London, 1897. cf. *Papers relating to the massacre of British officials near Benin, and the consequent punitive expedition, presented to both Houses of Parliament by command of Her Majesty, August 1897*. Cd. 8677. H.M.S.O., London, 1897.

2 Proceedings of the trial. loc. cit. Evidence was given in Edo and translated into English at dictation speed; hence the curious phraseology.

way Herbert Clarke called me and asked whether we could reach Benin City that day. I told him 'No' but we could sleep in the town of Egbini. Herbert Clarke therefore told me to go before them to the town of Egbini and make preparations for the whitemen to sleep there. When I came to the town of Egbini, I was told by the people there that all the people were waiting to fight the whitemen on Benin City Road. Hearing this I proceeded at once on the road to Benin City to tell them not to kill the whitemen. When I reached the place where they had divided the war, I called the people out of the bush and asked them where Ologbosheri was; they told me they had not seen him. I then told them not to kill the whitemen for they were coming to sleep at Egbini, so they must go back and tell the king that it was the same whiteman who had come to see him before that was coming. Then I went on and met Ologbosheri to whom I knelt down and begged that the whitemen were coming and he must not kill them; he must call all the people and send them back to Benin City as the whitemen were bringing nothing but presents to the king. I had scarcely finished talking to Ologbosheri when his boys came and told him that he would be a fool if he followed my advice because the chiefs in Benin City had told them that if they did not kill the whitemen they would themselves be killed. Not long after this I heard firing at my back and the whitemen were being killed. One of them ran to me calling 'Amaregbomo, Amaregbomo', and caught hold of me. When I was coming with that whiteman I met a man called Ekim who told me that the whiteman should not be killed. Then I told him that all the people had been killed with the exception of the one with me. I then left the whiteman with him and told him I was going to bring Herbert Clarke who was also living, when we would bring them all to show the king in Benin City. On my return to the place I did not find Herbert Clarke. Therefore I turned back again to look for Ekim and the whiteman; I met Ekim who told me he had handed the whiteman to Ochudi's boys, one of whom had killed him. ... When I came to Benin City, I went right off to the king and told him that 'I tried all my best to stop the people from killing the whitemen but I could not and all of them had been killed. The only one who did not die, when I left him in search of another one in order to bring them both to you had also been killed.' When the king heard this he got vexed and made a big palaver with all the chiefs and told them he was going to leave the city so that if the whitemen bring another war they could fight for themselves; but they begged him so much that he did not go anywhere. The people who killed the whitemen were turned back to the bush to fight the war that the whitemen would bring.

As Ovonramwen realised, war with Britain was now inevitable and the expected attack came remarkably swiftly. News of Phillips' disaster was first given to the District Commissioner at Sapele by a messenger from Chief Dogho on 7 January 1897 and reached London three days later. While Moor dashed back to the Protectorate, a task force was hastily scratched together by calling on ships from the Cape and Mediterranean squadrons, marines from England and carriers from the Gold Coast and Sierra Leone. In order that the Protectorate forces might also be employed, a detachment of the West India Regiment had to be brought in to take over their garrison duties. By the end of the first week of February some 1,500 men—sailors, marines and Protectorate troops—were assembled for the assault. The main column struck northwards from the region of Sapele; it met spirited resistance the whole way, and was at one time in some danger of having to fall back through lack of water, but by 18 February Benin City was in its hands. A diversionary attack against Ughoton met with still fiercer opposition—possibly because the Benin military leaders had anticipated that the British attack would come from that direction—and no headway was made there.[1]

Ovonramwen remained in his palace until the enemy was at the gates of the city and a chance rocket landed in one of the courtyards. He was then persuaded to leave with most of his chiefs and a number of his wives to seek refuge elsewhere in the kingdom. Much of the population followed his example, so that the British force occupied a city where living beings were few, but where the remains of human sacrifice abounded—a tragic testimony to the means by which the desperate monarch had sought to avert the destruction of his kingdom. Two days after the conquest a great fire swept through Benin City, carrying away in its flames the remains of an epoch.[2]

---

1 For detailed British accounts of the punitive expedition ref. Cd. 8677; R. H. Bacon, *Benin the City of Blood*. London, 1897; G. Rawson, *Life of Admiral Sir Harry Rawson*. London, 1914. Admiral Rawson commanded the expedition. A Benin point of view, though not a contemporary one, is given by E. Akenzua, 'Benin, 1897: a Bini's view'. *Nigeria*, no. 65, June 1960.

2 Fortunately most of the magnificent brass objects belonging to the palace had been gathered together in a place of safety after the fall of the city, and so escaped destruction when parts of the palace were blown up or burned. The

Seizure of the capital did not, contrary to British expectations, bring about an immediate end to Edo resistance. Various incentives and pressures—among them the prospect of serving on the British-created Native Council, and the fear of losing their slaves—induced several chiefs to make their peace with the conquerors within a few weeks of the fall of Benin City, but Ovonramwen, accompanied by some ten chiefs, did not come in to make his submission until 5 August 1897. Dr. F. L. Roth, surgeon to the expeditionary force, witnessed the Oba's arrival and wrote this description of it.[1]

King Overami came into Benin City with a large following, amounting to about 700 or 800 people, all unarmed, headed by messengers with a white flag in front. He was supported in the usual way by chosen men holding him up by each arm. Some twenty of his wives, who accompanied him, were of a very different class from those previously seen. They had fine figures, with their hair worn in the European chignon style of some years ago, really wonderfully done in stuffed rows of hair, the head not having been shaved on top like that of the lower classes, and they wore coral necklaces and ornaments and hair pins galore. About ten chiefs came with him, including Aro[2] a big chief, arriving by the Sapoba Road, not by the water road as was expected. For obvious reasons, all the white men kept out of sight on his arrival. He was preceded by a native band using a sort of reed instrument and took up his abode at the house of Chief Abeseke,[3] a member of the new Native Council established by the Resident. The King's party had a great 'powpow' that night, and kept it up very late. The next day, on the 6th, the king rested after his fatigue, and on the 7th, at 11 a.m. he came down to the Palaver (Court) House, with about 400 of his own 'boys' (men) all of whom were stark naked, as was their custom in the presence of the king. He was also accompanied by about twenty chiefs, including Tosheri the big war chief, besides Eschudi, Aro and Ojomo.[4]

---

majority of these 'bronzes' were treated as spoils of war by the British government which deposited many in the British Museum and sold the remainder. Others were taken away as trophies by members of the expeditionary force. cf. H. Read and O. M. Dalton, *Antiquities from the City of Benin and from other parts of West Africa*. London, 1899.

1 In letters to his brother, H. Ling Roth, who published the account in Appendix III of *Great Benin*. The appendix is reprinted by Egharevba, *A Short History*, chap. xxv.

2 Aro = *Ero*.

3 Abeseke = *Obaseki*.

4 Tosheri = *Iyase*, Eschudi = *Osodin*, Ojomo = *Ezomo*.

The acting Resident (Captain E. P. S. Roupell) was seated at a table at the mouth of a small tent. . . . The king, who is a stout but fine man of considerable intelligence, about forty years of age, was in a very nervous state. The escort of the Resident comprised only eight Houssas, as it was considered advisable not to bring more, for fear of frightening the king and his party. The remainder of the Houssa troops were, therefore, kept under arms inside the stockade, ready in case of emergency to turn out at a moment's notice. The king was simply covered with masses of strings of coral, interspersed with larger pieces, supposed to be worth many pounds. His head dress, which was in the shape of a Leghorn straw hat, was composed wholly of coral of excellent quality, meshed closely together, and must have weighed very heavily on his head, for it was constantly being temporarily removed by an attendant. His wrists up to his elbows were closely covered with coral bangles, so were his ankles. He only wore the usual white cloth of a chief, and underneath, a pair of embroidered and brocaded trousers; he had nothing in the way of a coat, but his breast was completely hidden from view by the coral beads encircling his neck. There was a crowd of some 900 to 1,000 people standing round when the Resident called upon Overami, the King, to make his submission. The king was visibly agitated, and after much consultation with his chiefs, the chief Aro asked that the king might do so in private as he did not like to abase himself before such a crowd. This request was naturally refused by the Resident and then supported by two chiefs who assisted him, the king made obeisance three times in the usual manner, rubbing his forehead on the ground three times. After this, the other ten chiefs who had not previously made obeisance, performed the same homage. The Resident then explained to the king the present political position of the Benin country and informed him that he was deposed. That closed the palaver, the king retiring with his bodyguard of 400 stalwart men to Abeseke's house. Except to get the submission of the king and chiefs, nothing else could be done then, the Resident awaiting the return of the Consul-General, who was expected to arrive at Benin City in from two to three weeks' time, when the big palaver would take place, and when the king and certain chiefs supposed to be guilty would be put on trial for the massacre of Phillips' party. Since the war, the king, it was said, had not sacrificed a single human being.

Moor reached Benin City on 31 August, and on the following day met Ovonramwen face to face for the first time when the trial began. It ended with six chiefs being found guilty of the murder of Phillips and his party; of these one had committed suicide, one had died, one was a boy and was therefore pardoned, and *Ologboshere* remained at large fighting a guerrilla war which was not ended until his capture in May 1899.[1] The remaining two, *Uso* and *Obakhavbaye*, were executed by firing squad on 4 September 1897. Next Moor turned to the problem of the position which the deposed Oba should occupy in the new administrative system. At a meeting held with Ovonramwen and the chiefs on 7 September, he explained that he was prepared to give Ovonramwen the position of a chief in Benin City. 'If he proves himself a wise and suitable man his position as a chief will be a big one and probably the biggest next to the whiteman, but not to work independently of the whiteman and the other chiefs.'[2] No longer would he be able to call upon the services of all the Benin people 'as if they were all his boys', but those villages which were his personal property would be assigned to him for his maintenance, as had been done for other chiefs. He would also have to send away 'these crowds of naked boys that I see around him— they must go to work for their own living and not sit down here'. To give time for these arrangements to be made, and also because the changes 'will no doubt cause some difficulties, owing to the influence which Overami and his people formerly had in this country', Moor proposed to take the Oba with him to Old Calabar and other parts of the Protectorate. He might also be sent to visit Lagos and towns in the Yoruba country. 'When he has seen these places and seen how they are governed and learnt how this country should be properly governed, then he shall come back.' Two chiefs—one from the Native Council and one from among those who had surrendered with the Oba—would accompany him on the tour, together with a number of attendants; and lest his journey be looked upon as a disguised form of banishment, Moor took pains to stress that Ovonramwen was not 'to be removed from his country as Nana was, with no hope of coming back again—he will return to his country when the farms are planted and the crops are grown up

---

1 cf. *Nigeria. Correspondence relating to the Benin Territories expedition, 1899* Cd. 9529. H.M.S.O., London, 1899. After his capture, *Ologboshere* was retried by a court composed of the Consul-General and the Benin Native Council. The court confirmed the verdict of the earlier proceedings, and the chief was executed on 28 June 1899.
2 P.R.O. F.O. 2/123. Moor to Foreign Office, 18 October 1897. Enclosure.

ready to reap'. Finally the Consul-General gave the Oba and chiefs two days to think over what he had proposed, but warned that if anyone tried to flee from the city in the interval his life would be forfeit.

Though he had seemed prepared to accept Moor's proposal, when the morning of 9 September came, Ovonramwen, instead of appearing at the meeting arranged by the Consul-General, went into hiding and was apprehended by a search party that same afternoon. He was then immediately taken before a Consular Court presided over by Moor and sentenced to imprisonment and exile. Why had he hidden? Speaking in his own defence and asking for leniency, Ovonramwen told Moor:[1]

> The first time that I ran away to the bush I said I would not come back, but when the people told me you are a good man I came. Today I was in my house when I saw plenty soldiers coming and going round the house, so I ran away to Ojumo's village only. I did not want to go far away. If I wanted to go far I could have gone.

Dr. Roth's account of events lends some colour to this statement, for it would appear from his letters that, when Ovonramwen did not appear at the time fixed for the meeting, Moor sent an armed detachment of fifty men 'to take the king prisoner, and bring him down'.[2] Was this final unhappy episode another in the long history of misunderstandings between Edo and Europeans over the nature of time and appointments? A little more patience on Moor's part, a little more promptitude from Ovonramwen, and the Oba might have been spared the exile in which he passed the last sixteen years of his life.

So fell the kingdom of Benin and the dynasty that had ruled over it for half a millennium. The dynasty was to return in the person of Ovonramwen's son who was restored to an office and functions similar to those proposed for his father after the latter's death in January 1914. Ovonramwen's grandson still holds the title of Oba in present-day Benin, and British rule has ended barely sixty years after it began. The kingdom has undergone a similar metamorphosis, and after many false starts and experiments seems destined to emerge as the nucleus of a state in the new Federation of Nigeria.

---

1 ibid.   2 Roth, *Great Benin*, appendix III.

Appendix I

Fragment of the ship's book of the *São Miguel* trading to Benin in the year 1522.[1] (A.T.T. *Corpo Cronológico*, II, maço 149, no. 29)

... in the said trade I approve and command that henceforth there shall not be given more than 50 manillas for the best pieces[2] and for others less, as His Majesty has commanded to be put in these instructions for the information of you all, with the penalty that you lose all your goods and salary should you act to the contrary and exceed the said 50 manillas; thus we on his part command and charge you under the said penalties: and should the negroes be unwilling to give you the pieces at the said price, you shall, after spending such time in trade as you shall think fit, return to this island with whatever other things to be had in that country you may have bought; for these things you shall buy and sell at the best prices possible because it is not possible to set fixed prices for them, scil. linen, coloured cloth, coral, glass beads and other merchandise for coris,[3] grey and yellow beads, ivory and redwood; any other things that may be had there, you shall not allow to be bought or traded because they are forbidden by the said Lord, and whosoever does so incurs heavy punishment, as you are aware.

item. You shall not purchase any piece suffering from buboes, or any other sickness, nor any which is dumb, blind or old; you shall rather strive to ensure that they are healthy youngsters as specified in the aforesaid price scale from 50 manillas downwards; and you shall give for them what seems to you to the service of the said Lord; and if you purchase any piece which is sick or has any defect, or any commodity which has no value, you may be certain that it will be set as a deduction against your salary.

item. You will do your trading as quickly and diligently as may be

---

1 cf. Ryder, 'An early Portuguese trading voyage to the Forcados River'. *Journal of the Historical Society of Nigeria*, vol. I, no. 4, pp. 297–9.
2 The word *peça* was commonly used to denote a slave as an item of trade.
3 cf. supra p. 37.

possible, and in such a manner that, by the diligence of each one of you, the ship may not be detained; and if it seems to you that your provisions may run out, supply yourself in good time, so that once your cargo is complete it may not be necessary for you to wait longer.

item. You shall keep good watch aboard the ship on the negroes that you have purchased, so that they do not escape by day or night, for we warn you that, should any escape, either yourself or the one who is to blame for such negligence shall pay for it; thus you shall keep good watch and ensure diligence so that they do not escape or revolt as they may do if there is carelessness.

item. You shall take care not to send any goods out of the ship for trading; you shall conduct your trade as best you may within the ship; should you do otherwise and any ill befall, you shall be responsible for all the loss that may result.

item. You shall not permit anyone to leave the ship by day or night; when it shall be necessary for anyone to go ashore, it shall be by your leave, which you shall not give to more than two; when these have returned to the ship, you may give leave to another two; thus each man may in turn trade as he needs and the ship will be kept safe: to those who go ashore in this manner you shall not allow more time than is necessary for what they have to do; they must return immediately, and should they sleep ashore, they shall lose their wages.

item. Whenever you shall find yourself with another of the King's ships, and it shall have need of anything, an anchor or any other fitting, you shall give it help, because any help which you may give will benefit trade and be to the service of the said Lord; and they will do as much for you should you have need of anything for this ship.

item. If it should happen that another ship arrives while you are trading, you should bring back the pieces it has traded before your departure; and should you find another ship already at that place of trade, you shall give it the pieces which you may have purchased;

should there be two or three ships there, the first to arrive shall leave first with the pieces that the others have purchased, provided that it shall not carry more than is convenient; and so we charge and command you on the part of our lord the King that you observe this without fail under pain of losing your salaries.

item. The pilot may bring back three jars of oil, the clerk an equal number, and each sailor and boy two; if they bring more, a quarter will be taken for our lord the King.

item. The clerk shall keep a book in which he shall enter all the pieces and other things that are traded in the said ship, whether it be on official or private account, with a full and true declaration as directed in detail above; and it shall be stated what the piece or article cost, whether male or female, whether woman or man, and so forth with what it cost.

item. Before you leave this port, you the clerk shall read these instructions to the whole ship's company.

item. You must keep good guard and watch upon the arms that are in this ship, so that they do not come into the hands of the negroes; thus no mischance shall befall.

item. You the clerk shall enter in your book all the merchandise that the pilot receives from the collector,[1] and when in the place of trade you shall enter as expended those things which you shall see expended in the purchase of pieces and other things, and the prices, as declared above.

item. If in the place of trade or during the return voyage any slave of the King should die, he shall not be cast into the sea without it first being ascertained that he is a slave of the King; and the clerk shall make an entry in his book to the effect that on such a day of such a month and year, and in such a port or anchorage, a slave was found dead and cast into the sea in the presence of the pilot and

---

1 The official who received royal taxes and dues in the island of São Tomé.

master and such other members of the crew, and all shall sign the said entry.

item. As soon as you shall, with the help of God, have completed your cargo, you shall leave and come directly to this island, without touching at any other island or land, nor shall you put any boat ashore in any part of this island except off this town and after the factor of the King and his officials have gone aboard, unless you should be in such necessity that by not doing so the cargo would run the risk of being lost; should this happen, the clerk shall make an entry in his book giving such testimony that all that happened in this matter may be truly known; should you do otherwise it is commanded by our lord the King that you lose your property and all your salary. On pain of the said penalty, you shall not permit boats to approach nor anyone to come to the ship until the factor and officials have first been aboard.

item. The clerk shall transcribe these instructions at the beginning of his trading book, and the pilot shall keep the original in his charge so that he may know thereby what he is to do; and the clerk shall observe by means of the transcription that the pilot fulfils these instructions, and require him to do so.

item. The clerk shall keep another book in which he shall enter any expenditure which the pilot may make of the ship's gear and the things that were delivered to him in Portugal, in such a manner that it may be possible to take an accurate account of the pilot for the said gear and things belonging to the ship. Done this 15th day of April of the year one thousand, five hundred and twenty-two.

After this, on the 16th day of the month of April, these instructions of our lord the King given by the factor and officials of our lord the King in the island of São Tomé were made known to the pilot and company of the ship *São Miguel*, and to myself Fernão d'Andrade, clerk for our lord the King, who wrote this.

item. On the 16th day of the month of May we went to speak to

the King of Benin, and we gave him the things we had brought
for him, sc. the letter and twenty ounces of coral   20 ozs.
and four Indian caps   4 caps
and also a piece of red satin measuring 14 *covados*   14 *cov*.^{dos}
The pilot gave the above-mentioned things to the King of Benin
in the presence of me the clerk.

item. On the 25th day of the month of August we finished our
trading in the city of Benin and took our leave of the King of Benin,
and he gave nothing in return for the things we had been ordered to
give him; and we left for Gato [Ughoton] on the 26th day of the
month of August, and on the 27th day of the month of August we
left Gato for Ovyere to take the cargo of another ship. This being
the truth I made this declaration.

Account of the presents that the pilot gave to the *veadores* and to
Gregorio Lorenço, and to Dom Antonio, and to son of Qua, and
to the chief of Gato, and to the one in the palace who according to
custom asked the King of Benin for pieces.

item. The pilot gave to Osody [Osodin] and Ruquuru the customary 40
yards of linen   40 yds.
item. The pilot gave to Gregorio Lorenço and to Dom Antonio the customary
20 yards of linen   20 yds.
item. The pilot gave to Rife[1] and the one who asks for slaves in the palace the
customary 24 yards of linen, sc. 20 to Rife and four to the one who asks
for slaves   24 yds.
                                                                         ────────
                                                                         84

Account of the ivory which was bought with linen.

item. The pilot bought three tusks of ivory for 37 customary yards of linen   37 yds.
item. The pilot bought three tusks of ivory for 30 customary yards of linen   30 yds.
item. The pilot bought four tusks of ivory for 44 customary yards of linen   44 yds.
item. The pilot bought five tusks of ivory for 60 customary yards of linen   60 yds.
item. The pilot bought three tusks of ivory for 57 customary yards of linen   57 yds.
item. The pilot bought four tusks of ivory for 58 customary yards of linen   58 yds.
item. The pilot bought one tusk of ivory for 26 customary yards of linen   26 yds.
item. The pilot bought three tusks of ivory for 25 customary yards of linen   25 yds.
item. The pilot bought five tusks of ivory for 33 customary yards of linen   33 yds.

Account of the pieces which were bought with linen.

item. The pilot bought one female piece aged 18 years more or less for 24
customary yards of linen   24 yds.
item. The pilot bought one female piece aged 17 years more or less for 24
customary yards of linen   24 yds.

1 Possibly *xerife* meaning chief, and hence the chief of Ughoton.

item. On the 26th day of the month of August in the year one thousand, five hundred and twenty-two, in the River of Benin in the port of Gato, we being there at anchor with our cargo, there was found dead a piece which had died of *corromiça*[1] and which belonged to our lord the King; it was cast into the sea in the presence of the pilot and master of the ship *São Miguel*, João Gonzalez sailor of the ship *São Miguel*, and Fernão Dyames, and myself the clerk who testify that I saw the dead body and saw it cast into the sea; in witness to the truth whereof all have signed. Done here this day, the 26th of August.

Machim Fernandes +   João Lourenço ♯   Fernão Dyames ⊕
Joao Gonzalez X[2]

On the seventh day of the month of September in the year one thousand, five hundred and twenty-two, we being under sail in a position off the Forcados River, there died a piece belonging to our lord the King, and it was cast into the sea in the presence of the pilot and master of the ship *São Miguel*, João Gonzalez sailor of the ship *São Miguel*, and João Lopes and myself the clerk who testify that I saw the dead body and saw it cast into the sea; in witness to the truth whereof all have signed. Done here on the seventh day of the month of September.

João Lourenço +   Machim Fernandes †   João Lopes +
João Gonzalez X

I Jorge Mendes, pilot of the ship *Conceição*, affirm that I, on behalf of our lord the King and the factors of our lord the King, requested Machim Fernandes, pilot of the ship *São Miguel*, to give me 30 thousand cowries which I required for a cargo belonging to our lord the King and for the ship; and I Machim Fernandes, seeing that it was for the service of our Lord the King and the benefit of his cargo, and also seeing that Your Honours had commanded it in the instructions which you gave us, accordingly gave them; and I Jorge Mendes affirm this to be true and that I received them from

---

1 A disease of the feet and legs which begins with an infection between the toes and develops into an ulcerous infection of the feet.
2 All the witnesses to the death and burial signed, or rather made their marks, under the entry in the ship's book.

him, and I have therefore given him this acknowledgement for his protection and surety. For the truth of this I have signed here together with the clerk who wrote it. Done on the first day of the month of September in the year [one thousand] five hundred and twenty-two. Do not raise any query in the clearance of this account because it was originally 25 thousand, but after writing this and taking it to him for signature he said that he needed another five thousand cowries, making in all 30 thousand cowries. That this is the truth I have signed thus.

Cristovão Rodrigues   Jorge Mendes

On the 11th day of the month of September in the year one thousand, five hundred and twenty-two, we being 12 leagues off Cape Fermoso bound for the island of Príncipe, while in this position more or less, there died a piece belonging to our lord the King, and it was cast into the sea in the presence of the pilot and master, and João Gonzalez, and João Dyames, sailors of the ship *São Miguel*. In witness to the truth whereof all have signed. Done on the 11th day of the month of September.

João Lourenço +   Machim Fernandes ⊕   João Dyames ‡
João Gonzalez X

Account of the ivory that was bought for manillas.

item.[1] The pilot bought five tusks of ivory for 28 manillas   28 ms.

Account of the pieces that were bought with beads.

item.[2] On the 23rd day of the month of July the pilot bought a female piece
aged 15 years more or less for 47 strings of beads   47 strings

Account of the coris that were bought with manillas.

item.[3] The pilot bought 12 manillas of coris, sc. six for one manilla, amounting
to 72 coris   12 manillas

The total of manillas expended on coris amounted to two hundred and fifty-seven manillas

---

1 There follow forty similar items. In all the pilot bought 189 tusks for 3,750 manillas.
2 Seven similar items are omitted. The eight slaves bought under this heading cost in all 386 strings of beads.
3 Eleven similar items are omitted.

And the total of coris that were purchased amounted to one thousand, four hundred and thirty coris

item. The pilot bought two manillas of osiers.

Account of the pieces that were bought with manillas.

item.[1] On the 25th day of the month of June the pilot bought a female piece aged 16 years more or less for 50 manillas   50 manillas

Account of the pieces that were bought for cowries.

item.[2] On the fourth day of the month of July the pilot bought a female piece aged 19 years more or less for seven goats[3] and three chickens—sc— 7 goats three large and four small   3 chickens

Account of the pieces that were bought on private account with the King's merchandise.

item. The pilot bought one female piece on behalf of Pedro ship's boy in the ship São Miguel

item.[4] The pilot bought one female piece for the hospital[5] for 20 customary yards.

Account of the pieces that the pilot bought on private account with private merchandise.

item. The pilot bought for Fernão Dyames sailor of the ship São Miguel a male piece with his allowances and merchandise for which he owes a quarter and a twentieth to the King   1 piece

item. The pilot bought for Gaspar da Gama, a freedman and ship's boy of the ship São Miguel, a female piece with his allowances and merchandise, for which he owes a quarter and a twentieth to the King   1 piece

item.[6] The pilot bought for Francisco, ship's boy of the ship São Miguel and slave of Jorge Vaz, a female piece with his allowances and the merchandise of the said pilot for which he owes a quarter and a twentieth to the King   1 piece

---

1 Sixteen similar items are omitted. The seventeen slaves bought under this heading cost in all 840 manillas.

2 Twenty-nine similar items are omitted.

3 For these units of the cowry currency *vide* p61. supra.

4 In all five slaves were bought in this manner.

5 The hospital of São Tomé was founded by royal decree in 1504, and it was entitled to receive six slaves each year from the royal factor.

6 In all fourteen slaves were bought in this manner. Each crew member was permitted to take one, on payment of royal dues. Those bought on behalf of the slaves among the crew—there were three of these—would of course belong to the slaves' masters.

Account of the manillas that the pilot expended in the city of Benin, sc. on yams and wood and water according to the custom of Benin.

item. On the 25th day of the month of May the pilot spent six manillas, sc. on yam and wood and water according to custom   6 manillas
item. On the 26th day of the month of July the pilot spent 63 manillas, sc. on yam and wood and water according to custom   63 manillas
item. On the 27th day of the month of August the pilot spent 40 manillas on yam and wood and water according to custom   40 manillas

109

Account of the manillas that he spent on loads, sc. in carrying manillas from the ship to Benin and in bringing ivory from Benin to the ship.

item. The pilot spent 38 manillas, sc. on 38 loads of manillas carried from the ship to Benin   38 manillas
item. The pilot spent 80 manillas, sc. on 80 loads of ivory brought from Benin to the ship   80 manillas

Account of the manillas that the pilot spent, sc. on loads of linen, beads, cowries, and the chain, and on the ambassadors that came to the ship with the pieces from Benin.

item. The pilot spent 27 manillas, sc. 14 manillas that were given to the ambassadors that came from Benin to the ship with the pieces, and seven for seven loads of linen that were carried from the ship to Benin, and four manillas for the four times that the chain was carried from the ship to Benin, and two manillas for two loads of beads that were carried from the ship to Benin   27 manillas
item.[1] The pilot spent five manillas on five loads of cowries that were carried from the ship to Benin   5 manillas

Account of the manillas that the pilot spent in Benin, sc. on oil, and that he gave for the rent of the house.

item. The pilot spent 15 manillas, sc. on oil for the cargo   15 manillas
item. The pilot spent 10 manillas that he gave to rent the trading house in Benin   10 manillas

25

Account of the manillas that the pilot spent in Gato, sc. on yam, oil and mats and *careços*,[2] and that he gave to the ambassadors who came with us to buy yams.

---

1 One similar item is omitted.
2 I have been unable to discover the meaning of this word.

item. The pilot spent 200 manillas on yams for the cargo · · · · 200 manillas
item. The pilot spent 200 manillas on yam for the cargo · · · · 200 manillas
item. The pilot spent 228 manillas on yam for the cargo · · · · 228 manillas
item. The pilot spent 200 manillas on yam for the cargo · · · · 200 manillas

828

item. To the ambassadors that were with us in Gato by order of the King of Benin to buy our yams the pilot gave for the 37 days that they were with us 74 manillas according to the custom of the King of Benin · · · · 74 manillas

item. The pilot bought 35 manillas of oil for the use of the cargo · · · · 35 manillas
item. The pilot bought 26 manillas of mats which were consumed for the awning and the cargo · · · · 26 manillas
item. The pilot bought 10 manillas of *careços* for the cargo · · · · 10 manillas

Account of the cowries that the pilot spent in Gato, sc. on Benin yams, because sugar cane could not be obtained, and for the speedier despatch and benefit of the cargo; to the truth whereof I made this declaration.

item. The pilot spent four thousand cowries on Benin yams · · · · 4,000 cowries
item. The pilot spent four thousand cowries on Benin yams · · · · 4,000 cowries

8,000 cowries

On the sixth day of the month of September were discarded two worn-out mats and two ropes that the pilot had received, sc. the mats were used up on the anchor cables of the ship *São Miguel*, and the ropes on the rigging, and the ropes were made of esparto; the pilot also expended a piece of cloth in which the bale of linen had been wrapped, it was expended sc. in patching the sails; this being the truth I have entered it here in the book as an expenditure.

On the 8th day of the month of September was discarded as worn out a piece of anchor cable which the pilot had received; it was expended sc. on the anchor cables; this being the truth I have entered it here in the book as an expenditure.

On the 8th day of the month of July in the year one thousand, five hundred and twenty-two, Machim Fernandes, pilot of the ship *São Miguel* and myself Cristovão Rodrigues, clerk of the said ship, being in the city of Benin gathering our cargo, there arrived in Benin Francisco Fernandes, clerk of the ship *Santa Maria da Conceição*, who requested the pilot Machim Fernandes on behalf of our lord the King that he should go at once with all speed to take from him the cargo that he had gathered in the Forcados River with the pilot Jorge Mendez, because when they crossed the bar of the Forcados River on the 26th day of the month of June and had sailed as far as Cape Fermoso, their ship had sprung a leak; he said that it had taken in so much water that it would inevitably have gone to the bottom but for the mercy of God which brought them to the Benin River where they put in to Ere. On the 14th day of the month of August the pilot left the city of Benin to perform this task as follows; he could not make an earlier departure from the city of Benin because he had no provisions, nor had he been given an ambassador to buy them; therefore he could not go to take over the cargo any sooner. On the 27th day of the month of August the pilot finished buying the provisions he needed for the cargo, and on the 27th day of the said month we left for Ere to take over the cargo of the ship *Conceiçao* at the request of Jorge Mendez. The pilot took the cargo from him, and once it had been put aboard the ship *São Miguel* Jorge Mendez, pilot of the ship *Conceiçao*, came with Francisco Fernandes, clerk of the said ship *Conceiçao*, and Jorge Mendez said to Machim Fernandes, pilot of the ship *São Miguel*, that he requested that he and the master of the said ship, together with some sailors of the said ship *São Miguel*, should go to see whether or not his ship *Conceiçao* was in a fit state to sail. And the said Jorge Mendez showed him the ship below deck and asked whether or not the ship was in a condition to sail. And the said Jorge Mendez on the 29th day of the month of August took the Gospels and administered an oath to Machim Fernandes, pilot of the ship *São Miguel*, and to João Lourenço, master of the said ship, and to João Dyames and to João Lopes, sailors of the said ship *São Miguel*, of which he drew up a sworn statement with his clerk Francisco Fernandes; the sworn statement remains in the hands of the said Jorge Mendez, and in my hands is a copy of it. The said Jorge Mendez also showed us the leaks that the said ship *Conceiçao* had sprung, for which leaks he took a sworn testimony from the company of the ship *São Miguel*. It being true that all this so happened I Cristovão Rodrigues who wrote this made this entry on the 29th day of the month of August.

On the 8th day of the month of September of the year one thousand, five hundred and twenty-two we being with the ship *São Miguel* in a position 12 leagues at sea off the Ramos River, there died a piece belonging to the cargo of the ship *Conceiçao*; it was cast into the sea in the presence of the pilot and master and João Gonzalez and João Dyames, sailors of the said ship *São Miguel*, and myself the clerk who testify that I saw the dead body and saw it cast into the sea; it was a male; in witness to the truth whereof all have signed. Done here on the 8th day of the month of September.

João Lourenço ‡   Machim Fernandes ⊕   João Dyames *

On the 15th day of the month of September of the year one thousand, five hundred and twenty-two, we being with the ship *São Miguel* in a position more or less between the islands of Príncipe and Corisco, there died two pieces belonging to the cargo of the ship *Conceiçao*, and they were cast into the sea in the presence of the pilot and master of the ship *São Miguel*, and João Lopes and João Gonzalez, sailors of the said ship, and myself the clerk, who testify that I saw the dead bodies and saw them cast into the sea; one of the pieces was male and the other female; in witness to the truth whereof all have signed here. Done on the 15th day of the month of September.

João Lourenço ‡   Machim Fernandes ⊕   João Lopes X
João Gonzalez X

Appendix II

A short account of the things that happened during the mission to Benin 1651–2.[1]

We embarked, nine friars, seven priests and two lay-brothers, in the port of Cadiz on a ship built in Holland for this purpose. Instead of carrying us directly—as we had been promised—it delayed on the coast of Cape Palmas, Malagueta, Cape Layud [Lahou?] and Takoradi for more than two months engaged in trading; and for that same reason we were held up for eighteen or twenty days in the port of Takoradi, while a boat that had been made in Seville for travelling in the Benin rivers was fitted out. Father Angel de Valencia, Prefect of the Mission, thought we should see whether any success might be achieved among the heathen of that port through a Dutch member of the crew. We pointed out to them that they were in subjection to the devil, and that they would all go to hell unless they were converted to the faith of Our Lord Jesus Christ and received baptism and the other sacraments; these and other spiritual matters we expounded to them through the interpreter. These heathen replied that they agreed, and that, from what had been told them, they acknowledged our faith to be good and their own bad; but if we would be willing to stay there to teach them the mysteries of our Holy Faith, they would gladly be baptised and receive the other sacraments. We answered that since we had been sent by the Sacra Congregazione de Propaganda Fide to the kingdom of Benin, we could not remain there, but that we would inform Rome so that they might be helped in their need, and that meanwhile we would baptise the children. They replied that if it was good for the children, they also wanted it for themselves. We answered that we had no opportunity to catechise and teach them the mysteries of our Holy Faith, and that only the infants could be baptised. When the heathens realised that we could not stay there, they had some twenty-two young boys baptised.

---

1 A.P.F. *Scritture Originali*, vol. 249, f. 329–30 and 349–50. Written in Castilian.

About this time, the fiscal of S. Jorge de la Mina de Oro came to the ship saying he had been sent by the General of the Dutch at the Mina to see whether the captains wished to go to Sama, which is a good seaport seven leagues from where we were and where there is a freshwater river, in order to take on water, wood and stores, and to finish the boat; he also said that if the fathers who were aboard the ship wished to go ashore, the General would entertain them well because he was secretly a Catholic.

Having heard this, we decided to go to the port of Sama, where the priests were made much of, and a lot of drink was offered to the captains and sailors—all with the intent of taking our ship by means of a large vessel and two tenders that the Hollanders had there. The trap they had laid failed to work because our captains did not trust them very much, but they seized the Prefect and another Father, and carried them off to the castle of the Mina with a strong escort of soldiers; three friars (one of whom is writing this paper) were kept prisoner in Sama with some others from the ship. The remainder escaped in canoes to the Spanish ship. Seeing what had happened, the Spanish captain gave orders that a tender belonging to the Hollanders should be taken unawares and held until the priests and other prisoners were released. After a few days had passed, the fiscal of the Hollanders came bewailing the fact that he had two chests in the tender, and saying that, if we who were at Sama would see that his chests were returned, he would send us back to our ship. We poor prisoners offered to do our best, and with that he set us free, keeping the Prefect, his companion, and some others from the ship in the castle of the Mina. The Spanish captain would not give back anything until all the prisoners had been returned to him. After waiting some days and exchanging messages each day, the captain saw that the General of the Mina did not wish to return the prisoners, so he determined to carry us directly to Benin. When the General saw that the ship had gone, leaving the friars behind, he said, 'What will these do for me, apart from eating my food?' He then proposed to allow the Prefect to go on to Benin if he wished, and was told that he might thus make good the harm he had done. This General thereupon put the Prefect and his companion on board a ship bound for Benin. As we passed along the coast of Ardra, all the missionaries fell sick, and on arrival at a place in Benin three of the Preaching Fathers died within six days.

The rest of us went to the city of Benin, which is very large and populous, and lies forty leagues from the sea, after we had first waited about four months in another place called Goto, because it was the rainy season. We delivered a message to the King, who gave us an audience, though with some difficulty, and after we had given him some presents. He appeared very friendly and said, according to the interpreters, that he would give us a house for God, and that he would send for interpreters so that we might explain our mission and the mysteries of our holy faith. His mother too showed us much kindness. In this manner we were waiting for six or seven months without being able to speak to the King for lack of an interpreter; and those who understood a little of the Portuguese language were not Christians. The King had a favourite who, as we were told, because we had not given him the present he expected, twice ordered us, in the King's name, to return to the place called Goto, which is where the three priests had died. The brother-in-law of the King told us that the favourite was doing all this on his own authority, without the King having the least knowledge of it. Seeing that this favourite was treating us so badly, many of the heathen took pity on us.

We tried to learn the language of that country by building a vocabulary, but one of the chief men came to tell us how his master the devil had told them that we wished to learn the language, and that anyone who taught us a single word was to be beaten to death. After that no one would teach us anything, whatever promises we might make. With much labour we managed to learn just enough to explain to the King, one day when he was sacrificing many men to the devil, the evil that he was doing and the cruel punishments he would suffer in the next world if he were not converted. When he saw this, the favourite was greatly incensed and had the friars thrown out of the King's palace with great violence; and because they persisted in their admonitions, they were thrust outside and the gates shut upon them. That night, when the sacrifices were ended, they came in great fury upon us, and seizing the Prefect and his companion, carried them off to Goto. The others remained prisoners, suffering greatly from want. Since they had no means of obtaining sustenance, the priests went at night into the city of Benin to inform the King's mother and brother-in-law of their ill-treatment and plight, and to ask that, as they could not speak to the King, they should be permitted to leave and be given a boat to take them to Arbo, where there were Hollanders and Englishmen, so that they might beg these for aid. They took pity on us and because, from lack of interpreters and support from the King of Portugal we were achieving nothing, they gave us as alms enough food of that country to maintain us for several days, and ordered that we be allowed to go to Arbo with the other white men. The reason why these negroes cannot be converted to the faith is, as they said, that they acknowledge themselves to be slaves of their King, and would not dare to become Christians until the King was converted.

Having reached Arbo, the English and Hollanders fed us for four or five months; and when an English ship came to this Arbo place, we asked them to carry us to some other country, which they did with great charitableness. They intended to take us to Cape Lopez, a heathen land, but the wind was contrary and we came to harbour in the island of Príncipe where we were very well received. We spent six months there, converting that whole island into a paradise of spiritual flowers; before it had suffered from having only a single priest. By night and day no songs were heard other than those of the Christian doctrine; spiritual addresses were given every day; masses were well attended; and each day we led an hour of prayer with a reading of a passage from the Passion of Our Saviour for meditation, as was our custom; and three days a week, in the evening, we held a discipline which was attended by practically the whole community from the Governor downwards. Nothing was heard in that island but prayers to God for mercy, and thanksgiving for having sent us there to teach them to be Christians, for they said that previously they had been Christians in name only. By this time the inhabitants were leading such an exemplary life that, when we travelled to Lisbon, there was on the ship a negro from that island who was going to Portugal, and he was teaching the Christian doctrine to Portuguese sailors who had grown up in the city of Lisbon.

The inhabitants of the island, knowing that we had come from Benin, told us that if we had gone to Oery, which borders on Benin, we should have been welcomed with great enthusiasm because they had great need of priests there. For five or six years past those poor people had not seen a single one, and the King had had a wife for five years without being able to marry her for lack of a priest; also many infants had been lost for want of baptism. We were told that in the past they were helped from São Tomé by means of a ship that used to go there every year carrying a priest; during the two or three months that the ship remained in the port, the priest used to baptise and marry. But at present, because there are no more than six priests in São Tomé, and because it is a long time since the bishops of that city and Angola died, almost everyone is suffering in the same manner; the island of Príncipe had been without any priest for a long time, and the one who is now there was for two years unable to make confession to anyone.

In view of this great need, we begged the islanders to allow at least two priests to go to Oery. They replied that they very much regretted that they were unable to do this for fear that the governor of São Tomé would ruin them all if they did such a thing because we had come on behalf of the King of Spain. Don Manuel de Barros, knight of the Order of Christ and Captain-Major of the said island [sc. Príncipe] would, they said, lose his head if he failed to send us to Lisbon to appear before His Most Serene Majesty, Don João the Fourth of Portugal. But in order to see whether the Governor of São Tomé might permit it, he [sc. the Captain of Príncipe] agreed to send us before him so that he might dispose of us as he thought fit. In view of the great good that we had done among the people, he much regretted that he could not keep us in that island.

At this time a ship from Lisbon bound for São Tomé put into the said island, and, seeing that the Captain-Major dared not keep us, the inhabitants realised that we had to leave. For two or three days before our departure, the poor folk were in the utmost distress, crying out, Fathers is it possible you wish to leave us? What are we going to do now? How are we going to carry on what you have taught us? They wept so much that we all could do nothing but weep with them. Thus we took our leave of them. When we arrived in São Tomé, we were very well received by the Governor, Cristovão de Barros, knight of the Order of Christ, and by the chapter, the residents and the city. We explained the matter to him and begged him to do us the favour of sending at least some of us [sc. to Oere]. Father Felipe de Hijar and Father Alonso de Tolosa, to whom the

Governor showed great friendship because they had taken care of him during an illness, made great efforts to win so coveted a prize. The Governor replied that he well knew the need of that King and kingdom which he had been unable to succour with any priest for so long because there were so few, and a great part of the people had to go without confession. It therefore appeared to him that, of the six priests available, only two could be spared to go to relieve them in their necessity. Each of these had been offered a large sum of money and five slaves, but they had shown no concern for those poor people. The priests answered that His Excellency well knew the difficulties that beset the entire kingdom of Portugal and its overseas possessions through not having bishops or priests in those parts, and that, the need being so great, they could not leave the city of São Tomé to go to the kingdom of Oery. Seeing this, the Governor had sent the sacristan of the church of São Tomé to the King [sc. of Oere], because he was a native of Oery, in order to teach them Christian doctrine, and to give them hope that they would soon receive some help.

Some time later, the Governor showed Father Alonso de Tolosa some letters from the King of Oery addressed to His Holiness, in which he asked for selfless priests and gave his obedience to His Holiness. A copy is included with this paper.

Afterwards the Governor said that he was obliged to send us to Lisbon before the King. When we embarked we were given all provisions necessary for the voyage with great generosity. At sea the Prefect fell gravely ill, so as we passed near the island of S. Iago of Cape Verde he asked the captain to allow him to receive the sacraments and die on land; this was granted, and he took Father Alonso de Tolosa with him to serve him. The remainder continued the voyage and soon after reaching Lisbon they were sent to Spain.

Description of the Kingdom of Benin

The Kingdom of Benin is seven degrees above the equator. Its neighbours are on one side the Kingdom of Ardra, on another the Kingdom of Oere, and on others Calabar and Jabo; beyond it one can go to the land of Prester John of the Indies. Beyond the bar, there are great rivers; one of them is called the Rio Fermoso and it divides into others such as the river of Oere, the Salt River, and the Rio de Lagua [Lagos?]. Following the Rio Fermoso, one comes to a place (though there are others on the way) called Arbo where the Hollanders and English have factories. Following the same river for another twenty leagues, one comes upon another large place called Goto which does a lot of trade in the produce of the country at two fairs which are held every week. Here one leaves the river and travels by land for ten leagues, going through thick forest and flat country all the way. Every two leagues there are large clearings where food is sold to travellers, and if one goes a little way from the road, one finds a number of villages. At the end of this road lies a great city where lives the King. It is called Benin, is very extensive, has a good climate and excellent water from a river called Gibel.[1] The city has huge squares in which things are bought and sold. In one of them stands the great palace of the King which has three large courtyards; almost every day ceremonies, sacrifices and worship of the devil take place there. The streets of the city are so broad and straight they they appear to have been drawn perfectly with a level; the walls of the houses are made of a red clay which is so smooth that they seem to be painted or polished; the roofs are covered with palm fronds.

Customs

The people are negroes. The King leaves his palace only once a year. He has three hundred wives. The first to bear a son is served by the others, and the child afterwards becomes the king. In this city the King also gives wives as presents to whom he pleases, after he himself has enjoyed them; and this is regarded as a great favour. Each individual has as many wives as he pleases.

Ceremonies

Before taking a wife, the negro who is to be married has to cover himself completely with a certain white clay, so that he looks like a demon. After going about the city for some days in this livery, he has to wash it off and have his whole head dressed with a white clay paste, giving an effect like Flemish lace. He then goes about the city

---

1 The river from which Benin drew its water is the Ikpoba.

in great state for several days with a number of companions, and afterwards receives his bride from the hand of the King who acts as priest. The woman is fully adorned with coral, brass manillas, glass beads, ivories and cowries. They go to a building which is consecrated to the devil in order to offer him homage and sacrifices with certain ceremonies performed in their own language. Women are obliged to work or trade by buying and selling to support their husbands who idle about the whole day, strolling around, smoking tobacco, and drinking palm wine. If the King makes anyone a chief, the ceremony consists of placing a string of corals round his neck, and thus he becomes a chief. But sons do not inherit this dignity, even though they be the sons of great men, unless the King bestows it on each one personally. These chiefs are masters of the rest of the people, and when speaking to them a man must go down on his knees. So that they may aspire to this greatness, chiefs send their sons to serve the whitemen, for when they have done this service the King is obliged to make them chiefs.

When they go to the King's palace or other places, the chiefs dress themselves like the women of Spain: from the waist down they wear cloths resembling sheets and farthingales. By their side go two negroes who serve them as attendants, and on whose shoulders they rest their arms. They move about with great solemnity, even when on horseback, and especially when they are going to the palace for festivals or sacrifices. It is like the carnival in Europe— he who cuts the most fearful figure is accounted the finest. Each one has a large following and his own band, some playing ivory flutes, others small guitars, others calabashes that have small stones inside, and others drums. Every man whether great or small, and according to his means, has within his house an altar or shrine well adorned with hideous idols, bones, skulls of cows, pigs, monkeys, crocodiles, rotten eggs, and other vile things; they also have some heads, like those of goats, each one of which holds a very large elephant tusk. And there are some holes, in front of which are carved the devil and various other things, according to the devotion of each person. Every day they make sacrifices of cola, which is a bitter fruit, and of palm wine, and some part of all their drink and foodstuff before they begin to eat.

They also have some very large houses, commonly known as the

House of the Devil. It has its own priests, and they regard it with such reverence that when walking past it they keep silence, never daring to speak a word. But in the festivals which they celebrate almost daily, by night and day, they do nothing but shout as they sing and dance.

Common foodstuffs

There is a large root which they call *gnamen*, about the shape of a radish, but very white and excellent to eat, either roasted or boiled or stewed with palm oil. There are also bananas, a little maize,[1] and, as vegetables, certain black and white beans, and pumpkins. There are a few cows, sheep without wool, goats and chickens; but although the negroes are fond of these, they prefer the flesh of horses, dogs and monkeys which they call *macaco* and say excels all other meats. There is also an abundance of fish which they do not like to eat fresh, but rather smoke-dried.

1 'milho turquesco' in the original.

Appendix III

Articles of the agreement concluded between the Honourable General Chartered Dutch West-India Company through me the undermentioned being thereto authorised by special instructions on behalf of the Honourable Heer Hieronimus Haring, Director-General over the North and South coasts of Africa, on the one part, and the King of Great Benin on the other part 1715.[1]

Art. 1

There shall be maintained from this day henceforth a firm and indissoluble friendship and trust between the above-mentioned Company and the said King, and in order that no mischance may be feared in the same, it is hereby stipulated that all former claims on either side (should there be any) shall be considered henceforth nullified, and that no reference shall at any time be made to them, this being particularly understood in the case of the escaped negro named Jan Knip.

2

The King promises to take under his protection the whitemen and slaves which the Company at present thinks fit, and may in the future think fit, to have permanently resident for the promotion of trade here in Benin, so that neither their persons nor goods shall suffer the least injury or hindrance from either the King or any of his subjects, with the sanction that the person who shall dare to give such offence shall be severely punished as an example to others.

3

The King hereby promises, under his own solemn signature, that in future no male or female slave or any other servant of the Company shall be protected and concealed, but that in case any of the same are found missing or fled, he will have them sought for, seized, and securely handed over to the chief official who at the time shall be in charge here on behalf of the Company, so that they may be

---

1 A.R. *N.W.I.C.* vol. 122, *Contracten met naturellen*, ff. 74v–76v.

punished as the occasion shall demand, and the official shall thereby be able to answer for them to the Heer General at Elmina.

4

For the accommodation of the Company's servants, the storage of its effects and the fostering of trade, the King promises that, on the departure of me the undermentioned from this place for Aggeton, he will immediately give orders for the construction of a factory at his own expense in the above-mentioned place named Aggeton, the said building to be so constructed as to serve for the shelter of the goods of the Company's chief official here; likewise the King also undertakes to have any necessary repairs done at his own expense as often as these shall be required.

5

In the event of any of the King's subjects being led by greed to presume to steal some of the Company's goods, or those of the Company's servants, either during this voyage or in the future, whether by violence or by furtive and underhand intrigues, the King promises to answer for it and not only to restore the stolen goods, but in addition severely to punish the culprits and thieves in the presence of the resident chief official of the Company as an example to others.

6

In case it should happen that debts to the Company are incurred, the King shall see that the debtor repays the full value of the goods given on credit at the stipulated time and in such articles as are contracted for, and the King shall undertake to see that the Company's chief official is at all times supported and satisfied in his claims.

7

And since the ivory trade has become much diminished here, and incapable of covering the costs which the Company has been obliged to incur on its account, the Company has ceased to send many ships here; therefore, in the interests of a securer growth of the friendship between the above-mentioned Company and the aforesaid King, it is by these presents stipulated, that the trade here shall be augmented with a certain kind of gum, and redwood, and the King undertakes to ensure that so constant a quantity of these products shall be brought for sale to the Company's chief official here, that it shall be worth while sending three or four ships here from Elmina each year to load the same.

8

Also the King hereby promises that after the departure of a Company's ship trade shall continue steadily and without hindrance, and that in such circumstances the Company's chief official shall be able to buy such kinds of goods and in such quantities as may be reasonable, and as though a Company's ship were present.

9

Since it has not been possible to settle the question of giving credit for cloth on the arrival of a Company's ship, this point is reserved till the arrival of a later ship, so that the final instructions of the Honourable Heer General thereupon may be known.

10

Also it is hereby agreed and established that no Portuguese who may at any time be found in the King's territory shall be attacked by the Company's ships or servants, since the King, being master of his land, wishes to extend to them as to all other nations free access to trade.

11

Finally the King undertakes to give such orders to his people, that the Company's servants resident at Aggeton need suffer no want of foodstuffs (as has happened up to now), but to arrange that all manner of provisions at the old prices shall be brought there, so that the Company's servants, paying no more than the value of the provisions, shall at all times have all they require, or as much as may be procurable.

Thus contracted and determined in good faith, in the presence of all the King's fiadors and a chief of this Kingdom, before me the undersigned and the Assistant Jacobus de Rycke (who, because all the other servants of the Company were sick, was the only one

able to be present) in the royal palace in Great Benin, this 26
August 1715.

this is the mark
of X the King himself
R. van Naarssen

I the undersigned certify
that all the above-mentioned
was agreed upon, having been
present.
Dated as above.
J. de Rycke

Appendix IV

Invoice and price-list of the merchandise loaded in the ship *Commany*, master Claas Pietersen, to which the Clerk Revixit van Naerssen is to adhere strictly when trading with the same in the Benin 1715.[1]

			price	lb. ivory
17 pieces		white salempor—stained	24 lb.	408
42	,,	small blue perpetuanas	$9\frac{1}{7}$	384
7	,,	large ditto of 14 ells	$18\frac{2}{7}$	128
30	,,	broad says	70	2100
50	,,	small red perpetuanas	$9\frac{1}{2}$	$457\frac{1}{4}$
5	,,	large yellow ditto of 34 ells	48	240
29	,,	cambric	16	464
40	,,	French linen	32	1280
100	,,	large annebaas	3	300
200	,,	small ditto	$1\frac{1}{2}$	300
29	,,	king cloths	4	116
76	,,	white bafts each of 6 ells— raised	10	760
250	,,	platilhos	10	2500
50	,,	large unbleached cloths	12	600
25	,,	Irish table-cloths	6	150
44 ells		rough Irish sheets	1	44
102	,,	ditto finer sort $1\frac{3}{4}$ ells broad	2	204
7 pieces		fine East Indian chintz of $14\frac{1}{2}$ ells	40	280
75 ells		red damask 18 ells stained	4	300
100 pieces		bed sheets	4	400
1000	,,	long iron bars	7	7000
1892 lb.		assorted beads	$1\frac{1}{2}$	2838
393	,,	clear glass beads	$1\frac{1}{2}$	$589\frac{1}{2}$
228	,,	element beads	2	456
179	,,	conte cribe	4	716

1 A.R. *Bezittingen ter Kuste van Guinea*, 82.

		price	lb. ivory
40 *mas*[1]	olivet[2] beads, red and white striped	4	160
40 ,,	blue *gitjes*[3]	4	160
260 ,,	red ditto	4	1040
8 ,,	fine coral	300	2400
146 doz.	inlaid knives	4	584
54 ,,	Amersfoort knives	4	216
15 ,,	*dollen*[4]	6	90
100 ,,	bells	16 lb. 10 dz.	160
50 pieces	fine flintlocks with copper mounting	16	800
3031 lb.	large neptunes	$1\frac{3}{5}$	4850
200 ,,	embossed buckets	d°.	320
500 ,,	tin basins and dishes	$1\frac{1}{2}$	750
89 ,,	copper rods	$1\frac{3}{5}$	$142\frac{1}{2}$
600 ,,	gunpowder	$1\frac{1}{2}$	900
400 pieces	flints	2 lb. 100	8
128 kn.	French brandy	2	256
512 ,,	rum	2	1024
6 rolls	Portuguese tobacco to be taken on at Mouree	48	288
1600 lb.	Spanish neptunes	$1\frac{3}{5}$	2560
3000 ,,	cowries to be taken on at Whydah	$1\frac{1}{2}$	4500
		lb.	$44223\frac{1}{4}$

N.B. The above-mentioned Clerk has instructions to purchase as much gum and redwood as possible for the benefit of the Hon. Company.

The tusks should preferably weigh three to a hundredweight, and any weighing less than 14 lb. are to be counted as scrivilios.

Thus given . . . etc.   H. Haring

Elmina 16 May 1715

---

1 When strung, beads were sold by the *mas*—number of strings—and not by weight. I have been unable to discover how many strings or beads made a *mas*.
2 Beads in the shape of an olive.
3 A variety of bead which I have been unable to identify.
4 I have been unable to identify this item.

Appendix V

Journal kept by me Fredrik Legrand at Benin in the Rio Formosa 1717.[1]

Thursday 25 March 1717. Returned here from Boddedoe together with the Caboceer Baba.

Friday 26 d°. Nothing happened except that towards evening I was seized with a severe fever.

Saturday 27 d°. Nothing happened.

Sunday 28 d°. We held the usual service and towards evening received a letter from Mon. Bersan informing me that on his arrival at Arrebo he found the seaman Pieter Abrams very seriously ill and unconscious, so that it was impossible to carry him by canoe to the Hon. Company's ship; therefore he was obliged to keep him there.

Monday 29 d°. Wrote in answer to the above letter that I understood about the seaman and ordered that he should remain there.

Tuesday 30 d°. Nothing happened.

Wednesday 31 d°. Nothing happened.

Thursday 1 April. A fiador came to make some payments in gum and cloths.

Friday 2 d°. Nothing happened.

Saturday 3 d°. Towards midday the Caboceer Baba left here for Boddedoe.

Sunday 4 d°. We held the usual service.

Monday 5 d°. Another fiador came to make payments in gum and cloths.

Tuesday 6 d°. Nothing happened.

Wednesday 7 d°. Nothing happened.

Thursday 8 d°. Made ready to leave for Benin in the morning; since hardly any of the debts have been paid, I intend to press the King very strongly that he should urge the debtors to make payment.

Friday 9 d°. I left for Great Benin.

1 A.R. *N.W.I.C.* vol. 103, ff. 435-40.

Saturday 10 d°. Nothing happened.

Sunday 11 d°. Nothing happened.

Monday 12 d°. The Assistant Commandant returned from Great Benin.[1]

Friday 9 April 1717. Early this morning I left for Great Benin, leaving the physician at Agaton. I arrived towards evening.

Saturday 10 d°. Am unable to obtain audience with the King today because he is holding a feast tonight.

Sunday 11 d°. Towards afternoon a fiador and a falador came for me to take me to the King. When I arrived, after the customary exchange of greetings, I informed him of the reasons for my coming, firstly that his subjects were still heavily in debt and had paid almost nothing; they had still not even settled with their cloths, and this was the reason why I had opened no market. Then he asked me whether I could name those who were in debt. I replied, Yes, for I had brought the debt book with me. So he requested me to name them. Then I read out all their names one by one, and how much each was in debt. And when I had finished speaking the King began to ask the fiadors, faladors and mercadors who were present why they had still not paid their debts, considering it was so long since they had received the goods, and whether they thought it was honest to take from the whitemen and not pay back. He said that such a thing had never happened before in his lifetime, and at least twenty whitemen, Dutch and Portuguese, had come there to trade in his time. Thus he was very angry with his people and thoroughly agreed with me that I should open no market because of the large debt that was still outstanding. He asked me when I intended to return to Agathon, and I told him that I should leave early in the morning. After this I left.

Monday 12 d°. Early this morning I left Great Benin and reached Agathon towards evening.

Tuesday 13 d°. Nothing happened.

---

1 This and the previous two entries refer to the situation at Ughoton. The following entries cover Legrand's trip to Benin City in the same period.

Wednesday 14 d°.   d°.   d°.

Thursday 15 d°. Made a start with transferring the gum to the new store.

Friday 16 April 1717. As above and continued with the other goods; by evening we were through and moved in.

Saturday 17 d°. This morning the seaman Pieter Abrams arrived here very weak and emaciated, bringing a letter from Mons. Bersan. In it he reported that he had suffered another mortal bout of sickness and was still tormented by daily attacks of fever. Also he asked for some goods.

Sunday 18 d°. Towards midday the canoe left with the goods requested. I also ordered the physician to go along with it in order to see how Mons. Bersan was, and I let the seaman go to Arreboe as well so that he could help him.

Monday 19 d°. Nothing happened.

Tuesday 20 d°. As above and I received a few payments in gum.

Wednesday 21 d°. Nothing happened.

Thursday 22 d°. Some payments of cloth were brought in.

Friday 23 d°. Nothing happened.

Saturday 24 d°. The physician returned from Arreboe with the produce collected there: this consists of 900 lb. of ivory, 900 lb. scrivilios, and a quantity of gum. He [sc. Bersan] wrote to me that he is at present feeling rather better.

Sunday 25 d°. We held the usual service.

Monday 26 d°. Nothing happened.

Tuesday 27 d°. As above and I received a certain number of cloths in payment.

Wednesday 28 d°. Nothing happened.

Thursday 29 d°.   d°.   d°.

Friday 30 d°.   d°.   d°.

Saturday 1 May. A passador came from Benin, sent to me by the King. He requested me to come to Benin because the King had something to say to me. I answered that I would go with him in the morning and made ready.

Sunday 2 May. I left for Great Benin.

Monday 3 d°. Nothing happened.

Tuesday 4 d°.   d°.   d°.

Wednesday 5 d°.   d°.   d°.
Thursday 6 d°. I came back again from Great Benin.

Sunday 2 May. Early this morning I left for Great Benin where I arrived towards evening.

Monday 3 d°. I could not obtain an audience with the King today because he had a feast, but he asked me to come and see his feast, which I did. I left him towards evening.

Tuesday 4 d°. Towards evening three fiadors came to fetch me and take me to the King. When I came there he asked me whether I had noticed on the previous occasion how he had gone for the fiadors and mercadors because they had not paid their debts, and whether I would now open a market for him and the *oome grandes* [big men]. Thereupon I replied that since he had spoken so sharply to his people I had still seen very few payments, and therefore I could not open the market, but that I must first have the payments in full. There the matter rested for the time being and he asked me to stay there the next day which, after much hesitation, I promised to do.

Wednesday 5 d°. Today I again went to the King who once more argued that I should open the market, using threats to that end. He said I must realise that I was in his country where he was master. Whereupon I answered that I would not open the market while so much gum, redwood and cloth were still outstanding: indeed, so long as he and the chiefs had not settled their cloths, I could give no further additional credit for such were my orders from the Heer General.

Whereupon he said that the General knew nothing about it, but that it was my fault, and he stuck firmly by his old argument insisting that the market be opened. When I absolutely refused he became furious and ordered the natives to sell us no goats, yams, etc., nor any other provisions. I then said that if he was going to behave in this manner it would not be possible for us to remain here, and that by such actions he was clearly breaking the treaty. But he took little notice of this, and thus we parted from each other.

Thursday 6 May 1717. Today I left Benin and reached Agathon towards evening.

Friday 7 d°. Nothing happened except that I was troubled by fever and several ulcers again broke out on my leg.

Saturday 8 d°. Nothing happened.

Sunday 9 d°. We held the usual service; nothing else happened.

Monday 10 d°. The Caboceer Baba came and reported to me that the King had sent two passadors to him to tell him that he should give us no canoes to carry letters or goods to Arreboe, also that he should not sell us any goats, yams, oil or any other foodstuffs, or allow his dependants to sell them to us. In reply Baba had told the passadors that they should say to the King that he could not and would not do such a thing, but that if we needed canoes or provisions he would supply us with them, for it was his firm intention to live on good terms with us. He brought me a goat, yams and oil as a present, and to please this caboceer on whose friendship the Hon. Company depends, I presented him with a looking-glass. Nothing else happened except that I suffered a severe pain in the mouth together with great swelling of my whole face.

Tuesday 11 d°. Nothing happened except that the Caboceer Baba left again.

Wednesday 12 d°. Nothing happened except that the pain and swelling increased.

Thursday 13 d°. As above.

Friday 14 d°. Nothing happened except that my mouth and cheeks remained as before and the ulcers on my leg worsened.

Saturday 15 d°. Nothing happened.

Sunday 16 d°. As above: we held the usual service.

Monday 17 d°. As above.

Tuesday 18 d°. My mouth began to get better but the pain in the leg worsened.

Wednesday 19 d°. Some fiadors came to pay in cloths.

Thursday 20 d°. Today the physician got some matter and suppuration from my ulcer, cutting away what was affected by gangrene. Under God I hope for a good recovery.

Friday 21 d°. Nothing happened.

Saturday 22 d°. d°. d°.

Sunday 23 d°. We held the usual service.

Monday 24 d°. A fiador came with payments of gum and cloths.

Tuesday 25 d°. Received the produce from Arrebo consisting of a little ivory and scrivilios and 4,000 lb. of gum.

Wednesday 26 d°. Nothing happened except that my mouth and ulcer began to heal.

Thursday 27 d°. Early this morning heard two shots and shortly afterwards there came one of the Caboceer Baba's canoes to inform me that a ship of the Hon. Company had arrived there. Towards evening heard shots at Boddedoe and supposed that the Hon. Company's ship had reached there.

Friday 28 d°. Early this morning the Stuurman Commandant Jacob Huyberts came with the Company's papers which he delivered to me. Whereupon I immediately sent off a letter to Mons. Bersan to let him know that the Hon. Company's vessel *Moure* had arrived at Boddedoe and that he must come up at the first opportunity to go through the Company's papers.

Saturday 29 d°. Made a beginning with unloading the bars.

Sunday 30 d°. We held the usual service and were again busy with the unloading.

Monday 31 d°. As above and Mons. Bersan arrived here; I immediately opened the Company's papers.

Tuesday 1 June. I left towards evening for Boddedoe in order to go with the ship to the river mouth. Unloading finished today.

Wednesday 2 d°. Nothing happened except that Mons. Bersan left again for Arrebo.

Thursday 3 d°. Nothing happened.

Friday 4 d°. Nothing happened.

Saturday 5 d°. d°. d°.

Sunday 6 d°. d°. d°.

Monday 7 d°. I returned here again.

Tuesday 8 d°. The Stuurman Commandant made his vessel ready for loading.

Wednesday 9 d°. Sent six canoes to Arrebo to fetch the ivory, scrivilios and gum.

Thursday 10 d°. Nothing happened.

Friday 11 d°. d°. d°.

Saturday 12 d°. d°. d°.

Sunday 13 d°. We held the usual service.

Monday 14 d°. The canoes returned from Arrebo and brought the

ivory, scrivilios and some gum from there. Understand that the
first mate has come from there seriously ill. Heard a shot about
eleven o'clock.

Tuesday 15 d°. Nothing happened except that in the morning the
Stuurman Commandant came to tell me that his mate had died
yesterday evening.

Wednesday 16 d°. Sent another seven canoes to Arreboe to fetch
gum. Understand that the other mate is sick.

Thursday 17 d°. Received some payment in gum and cloths.

Friday 18 d°. Nothing happened.

Saturday 19 d°.   d°.   d°.

Sunday 20 d°. The canoes returned from Arrebo laden with gum:
also the second mate died at eleven o'clock this evening. Made
ready to leave for Benin in the morning.

Monday 21 d°. I left for Great Benin.

Tuesday 22 d°. Nothing happened.

Wednesday 23 d°.   d°.   d°.

Thursday 24 d°. I came back from Great Benin.

Monday 21 June. I left early this morning for Great Benin and
arrived there towards evening.

Tuesday 22 d°. Could not obtain an audience with the King today
because his chiefs have a feast.

Wednesday 23 d°. Today I could still not gain an audience with the
King, but I was told that I should have an audience with the King
tomorrow morning.

Thursday 24 d°. At daybreak the mercadors came to fetch me to
go to the King. Having arrived there and after an exchange of
greetings, I represented to him that it was very wrong that his
subjects had still not paid their debts since it was a good year
that they had been given trust, and I threatened to report it all to
the Heer General. Whereupon he answered that he was every day
urging these people to pay and that he would again send a
passador to them to tell them that they should come and pay. I
then said that the Heer General would take it very ill that debts
were still outstanding, and further represented that he should
allow the natives to sell us provisions, pointing out that by his
action he had violated the friendship and treaty made with the

Hon. Company. He replied that all would be well if the market were open, but since the market was closed he would not permit the sale of provisions. I said to him that we could not remain here if he would not promise to supply us with foodstuffs. After much talking around this point he told me he would send for the fiadors to let them know that they might again sell to us. Thirdly I told him that fourteen long bars had been stolen from my store at night and that I had spoken to the fiador about this, but that the man had done little about it. So I begged him to see that I recovered my lost goods in accordance with the signed treaty. Whereupon he said that he would despatch a passador to make enquiries everywhere as to who the thief was.

Next he sent to enquire whether I would not now open a market considering that two ships had come and no market had been opened. To this I replied that it would be impossible for me to do so before the debts were settled. Then he sent to tell me that I should open the market, which I refused to do, saying that I must first have the payments. He appeared angry again at this and insisted that he would have the market opened, but I refused to agree to it. Thus we parted from each other and I left for Agathon where I arrived towards evening.

Friday 25 June. Today I considered the question more carefully, thinking that if the market remains completely closed it might be very harmful to the Hon. Company, for trade might die off entirely. Also the natives might in future lose the incentive to gather gum. Further, that if the King receives no goods, we might, after the departure of the ship, find ourselves and the Company's property in great danger of interference by force. I decided therefore to send a passador to the King.

Saturday 26 June. Today I sent a passador to the King to let him know that I would open the market, but that I would give no goods to those who were still in debt until they had paid. I requested him therefore to put pressure on such persons to pay up. I shall wait and see what answer this produces.

Sunday 27 d°. Were busy loading the gum.

Monday 28 d°. The Stuurman Commandant wrote that his boatswain had died; were again busy loading the gum.

Tuesday 29 d°. Today the passador returned with the fiadors to open the market, but they were very displeased that there were so few goods and they requested me to ask the Heer General to supply a large quantity of cowries and basins as well as other goods. I promised to do this. We also loaded some gum.

Wednesday 30 June. Were busy with the opening of the market; loaded some more gum.

Thursday 1 July. As above.

Friday 2 d°. As above and loaded some gum.

Saturday 3 d°. Were still busy with the opening of the market.

Sunday 4 d°. Held the usual service; also the Stuurman Commandant wrote that a seaman had died; loaded some gum.

Monday 5 d°. Were again busy because of the opening of the market.

Tuesday 6 d°. Today came to an end of the opening of the market and loaded some gum.

Wednesday 7 d°. Nothing happened except that I prepared the papers.

Thursday 8 d°. Loaded some gum—which was the last of the gum because the Stuurman Commandant wrote to me that he could load no more.

Friday 9 d°. Were busy making the papers ready so that the hooker might be despatched in the morning.

Saturday 10 d°. This morning I went with the papers to Boddedoe where I delivered to the Stuurman Commandant the papers for His Honour together with his despatch.

Honourable Sir,

Your Honour's humble and obedient servant

Fredrik Le Grand

Appendix VI

Letter from the Dutch factor at Ughoton 1724.[1]

Honourable Sir,

I received the letter which Your Honour sent by the galliot *Juffrouw Rebecca Maria* on 2 September 1724: it was dated the 3 August 1724. I found the accompanying merchandise correct according to the invoice, except that I found the cowries to be 60 lb. short, and some of the goods are moth-eaten. Also I noticed in Your Honour's letter that Your Honour recommends me to be more accurate in my accounts because the Accountant General cannot make them out. This was caused by my severe illness, and I reported this to the Accountant General at the time, asking him, if there were any errors in my accounts, to be so kind as to correct them, for I was then in too poor a state of health to send an accurate account. Your Honour also states in the letter that you cannot understand how trade comes to diminish with a fresh supply of goods. If it were only a question of trade, there was trade enough here at the time, but all the merchandise that was sent here then with the barquentine *St. Jago* was unsaleable, so much so that up to the present not a piece of it has been sold, apart from the knives and cowries. Your Honour will understand that this is through no fault of mine, for I explained the situation to Your Honour at the time.

I also perceive from Your Honour's letter that the master Gerrit Cruys has delivered at Elmina 50 fewer logs of redwood than he received here according to his own signed certificate. I cannot answer for this, for when a master acknowledges receipt of so many goods under his own signature, he must transport the same quantity to the place for which they are destined, otherwise his signature is utterly worthless. In such a way they could make a very good living from the goods if they were inclined to do so. Therefore I cannot

---

1 A.R. *Bezittingen ter Kuste van Guinea*, vol. 92, under 5 Feb. 1725. G. Ockers to Director-General P. Valckenier, Ughoton, ? Nov. 1724.

answer for it, as it appears clearly in his receipt. Likewise I cannot explain how the master Gerrit Cruys comes to have delivered some ivory short in the same manner: the aforesaid master will have to answer for this, as his signed receipt is clear proof that he received it.

The longer trade continues the worse it becomes, and is likely to become still worse because of the high prices in the price-list that General Houtman gave me, and the price-list which the Heer President has sent me is somewhat higher still. And now the price-list that Your Honour has sent me is so much higher again that it is impossible for me to do a good trade for the Company. The reason is that the natives here so carefully regulated the trade at the time the factory was established, that it is now impossible to move them to pay more for the merchandise. For if I tell them that the merchandise now costs more, they answer me that it does not concern them, that they concluded the trade on those terms at the time, and that they will now continue to trade in the same manner. They say too that they would rather do no trade than be forced to abandon their old rights and customs. Also on 4 September a snow belonging to the English Company came to anchor at the Cayman Bank to trade for ivory, scrivilios, redwood and slaves, and anything else it could get. This was very prejudicial to the Hon. Company for the commander of the aforesaid English snow sold his merchandise for only half the price at which it is fixed in my price-list. He bought ivory at the rate of 3 lb. for one engel, and paid 18 to 20 plathilios for a man-slave, redwood likewise. In face of this it is impossible for me to trade. At the time when the Commandant visited the King in Benin, he told him that he had only come here on this occasion in order to see what kind of trade there was and what was in demand here. He would then make a report to Cabo Corso and a factory would be established here in the Benin: should this come to pass, Your Honour may well imagine that trade here will be very bad.

On 5 June 1724 the caboceer Babba was defeated, as Your Honour may see from my diary. This is also a great misfortune for the Company as affecting the loading of ships, for he is the only person around Agathon who has canoes and rowers. My predecessors had lent him two half-pounder cannons and one gun to defend himself, and I left them with him. They have been seized in the war. I hope that Your Honour will take into consideration that they were lent to the advantage of the Company and their loss was caused by war. Therefore I have entered only one cannon in my inventory. Your Honour will be able to see from my diary in what state this place is as regards defence, therefore I beseech Your Honour to furnish me with a few good flintlocks for the defence of this place, likewise with bullets and flints, for there are none here. True there are some flintlocks belonging to the Company here, but not one of them is any good.

My accounts of sales and stocks are sent herewith to Your Honour, and I have no doubt they will be found correct, for my health is now restored, God be praised. I am also sending my previous accounts of sales, together with my other papers referring to this establishment, likewise the invoice of the produce I am now sending: I do not doubt that they will all be found correct. I also enclose herewith a requisition for goods which are badly needed for the ivory trade; also a requisition for tools which are very necessary for this establishment. I most earnestly beseech Your Honour that the requisition for medicines may be met. The two gentlemen you sent—P. Pistorius and G. F. Pels—together with the physician van der Putten, arrived here safely on 3 September 1724. But G. F. Pels died intestate on the night of 4 October 1724: I have sent his estate to the Paymaster-General by this ship.

The physician B. Charles is leaving with this galliot in accordance with Your Honour's orders.

I also humbly beg Your Honour to grant me permission to leave this post, for my health and the poor state of my body will not suffer me to remain here longer. Every day I have attacks of fever, and I suffer from many ulcers on my legs, so I hope Your Honour will grant my request, for I have now been here two years and put up with many hardships. When I was in Benin I had to agree with the King, the chiefs and the veadors to reopen the market on the old footing and in accordance with their old customs, for they would rather do no trade with me than depart from their old customs. I agreed upon this with the King, the chiefs and the veadors, on condition that they promised me not to sell any ivory, scrivilios and redwood to the Englishman. Since Your Honour directed me to look after the interests of the Company, it seemed to me better to do

333

some trade for the Company than to do none, and, as far as possible, to damage the trade of the English snow. And since Your Honour so recommended the interest of the Company to me, I do not doubt that Your Honour will carefully consider putting my price-list back on the old footing, so that I may not be put to any loss, for it was done for the benefit of the Company.

Concerning the references in Your Honour's letters to the trade in male slaves, I have the honour to reply that those who have given Your Honour information about it have strayed far from the truth, for they must know that no one other than the King may sell male slaves on pain of death. Moreover they are extremely dear, for the Portuguese and English are now paying 18 to 20 plathilios for a good man-slave, so that I now have much difficulty in getting them for 14 plathilios.

When I have opened the market here, I shall go in person to Arrebo with some merchandise to see whether I can do any trade there to the profit of the Hon. Company. The war has continually prevented me from sending anyone there, but now the war with Baba is practically over.

I shall end this by wishing Your Honour all the imaginable blessings of Heaven in the new year, and may Heaven bless Your Honour's administration, etc.

(signed) Gerrit Ockers

Agathon, November 1724

N.B. I have kept the chest of the deceased Assistant G. F. Pels here in order to store the Hon. Company's merchandise in it, because it is very badly needed for that purpose.

Appendix VII

Summary for a trading venture set forth from Lisbon for Benin and coming to these islands[1] to hire pilots and sailors suitable for working aboard because they are acclimatised and not so susceptible to the diseases of the river; from that port one may obtain cloths, slaves and some ivory.[2]

For one good slave in Benin	cloths in which one buys	cost of goods in Lisbon	For 200 slaves in Benin	
1 piece good blue Coromandel	10	4$800	200 pieces of Coromandel @ 4$800	960$000
1 Surat cover	4	1$600	200 Surat covers @ 1$600	320$000
12 coarse red sheets @ 370 each	12	4$440	240 coarse red sheets @ $320	76$800
2 bars of lead	1	$320	400 bars of lead @ 160	64$000
5 knives with weighted handles	1	$320	85 dozen knives @ $960	81$600
1 Indian cloth of 15 yds. with attractive flowers	12	4$800	200 pieces coarse muslin @ 4$000	800$000
12 yds. coarse muslin with stripes or spots	12	4$000	200 yards of kannekins or shirting	800$000
12 yds. kannekins or shirting	12	4$000	glass beads coloured of attractive designs, large and small	80$000
glass beads in bright, attractive colours	2	$400	600 lb. lead shot @ 200r.	120$000
3 lb. lead shot	2	$600	600 tobacco boxes @ 80r.	48$000
3 horn tobacco boxes	1	$240	800 razors @ 80r.	64$000
4 razors	1	$320	800 mirrors in gilt paper @ 80r.	64$000
4 mirrors	1	$320	3200 alquiers of salt @ 80r.	256$000
16 alquiers of salt, as white and fine as possible	20	1$280	3000 pints of brandy @ $320	320$000
15 pints brandy	4	1$600	200 iron bars @ 1$000	200$000
1 iron bar, 14–18 lb.	3	1$000	800 gauze sheets @ 240r.	192$000
4 gauze sheets @ 240	4	$960	300 lb. of powder @ 40r.	120$000
1½ lb. gunpowder	3	$640	200 pieces Indian cloth in attractive colours, each 15 yards @ 4$800r.	960$000
value of the slave in cloths	105			
cost of the slave at Lisbon prices		31$640		5,526$400

$ This sign was used to denote one *milreis*.

1 i.e. São Tomé and Príncipe.
2 A.H.U. *São Tomé, caixa* 2.

With the cargo listed above a slave, *peça da India*,[1] should cost one hundred and five cloths; that is for the males, for the females cost up to 100. However, many slaves are bought for between 60 and 80 or 90 cloths, and from this surplus can be taken the dashes (*daixas*) and other expenses of the port. It must also be taken into account that the values in cloths given to the goods above apply on land in the port of Benin, whereas on board a ship anchored in the river it is possible to buy many slaves, *peça da India*, for 100 cloths, and others for prices which can be adjusted according to the calculation that goods which are above valued at 4 cloths will be worth six in the river. All these surpluses will serve to meet the expenses of trading.

The ships that are sent should not draw more than 14 *palmos* when loaded, because the bar has 16 and never more than 18 *palmos* at the highest tides. The worst time for entering is June, July and August, because this is the season of high winds when the bar has little water and is very rough. If the ship is to carry a larger number of slaves, it should have with it a small boat that draws little water and has a deck; this vessel will serve to carry the cargo into the river and keep the ship supplied with water and all it needs so that the ship may remain at anchor outside the bar. A ship can leave this port with slaves for America within four or five months. The small boat may serve more vessels should one wish to send others. The ship should carry at least four pipes of brandy in addition to that noted above in order to have plenty with which to meet port expenses, and also two casks of glass beads of all qualities and attractive designs, as it not only saves a good part of the cargo but can be used to buy cloths which will serve to discharge the duties that have to be paid on the slaves in these islands. In the same manner one may carry additional knives, mirrors, gauze sheets, and also some pieces of ordinary

---

1 A term used to denote a slave aged between fifteen and twenty-five and without any physical defect; such a slave represented the standard for valuation purposes. Thus two *peças* were considered equal to three slaves aged between 8 and 15 or 25 and 35. cf. F. Mauro, *Le Portugal et l'Atlantique au XVIIe siècle, 1570–1670*. S.E.V.P.E.N., 1960, p. 173. Early in the sixteenth century the term *peça* had been applied to all slaves, though the highest prices were always paid for those falling within the later definition of the *peça da India*. It was probably the growth of the transatlantic slave trade that led to the adoption of the slave unit.

gauze which can all be exchanged for cloths, as I have said, with great advantage. Some green and red silks with white flowers that look attractive, of ordinary quality—if these silks are used for buying slaves they are reckoned at 20 trade cloths, which are those one speaks of in purchasing slaves. However, those cloths which are bartered for goods and brandy are double cloths, so called, and their usual value is 800 *reis*. I will therefore now proceed to set out the following calculation, in which I have given their selling price as 640 *reis*.

Cost more or less of goods in Lisbon		Cloths obtained for merchandise and their uses		
			cloths	
200 dozen knives @ 640	128$000	will yield	480	@ 640 307$200
4 pipes of brandy @ 60$00	240$000	do.	1200	,, 768$000
100 dozen paper mirrors @ 64or.	64$000	do.	300	,, 192$000
200 gauze sheets @ 240	48$000	do.	200	,, 128$000
glass beads, stones, agates, artificial coral blue, some granadas and glass beads	200$000	not possible to give fixed rate because it varies with circumstances but will yield at least	1000	,, 640$000
1000 covados of gauze @ 240	240$000	will yield	1000	,, 640$000
600 covados of satin or silk red and green as above @ 70or.	420$000	7 covados for 20 cloths will yield	1700	,, 1,088$000
	1,340$000			3,763$200
Plus the aforementioned cargo	5,526$400	deduct a thousand cloths for additional expenses in the port to be on the safe side		640$000
Total	6,866$400	This balance will amply serve to meet the expenses in these islands.		3,723$000
200 slaves sold in America at 100$000 because they are better than those from Gabon— making allowance for some mortality	20,000$000			
leaving a balance above that arising from the purchase of cloths	13,733$600			

On this basis any businessman who wishes to venture may make his calculations, remembering that the ship will also carry freight from

America to Lisbon. The prices I have given for the goods in respect of cloths are certainly the very least for which they would be sold, and at present they would yield many more cloths because these are times of war and there is no great abundance of merchandise. Salt is an excellent commodity and whatever comes will all be sold at a good profit.

Appendix VIII

Instructions for a voyage to the Benin River and trade there written by Randall Shawe 1582.[1]

Your shipp may ronne within three leagues of the shoare and there may ankor herself till such time that you have been with the King, and might ride there till she were laden, but it is evill for the men, but she may goe 20 leagues up the river and tary there till the time that your lading be readie. Your pinnacies may goe up the river 9 or 10 further leagues to a place called gattoo and then you have 10 leagues to the King, his subjects will convey them hither.

As towching the river you must goe yn at the hether river that goeth to gattoo and you shall ther have 8 or 9 fathom water: the other river ys 4 leagues from that: yt is narrow going yn: you shall know yt by a whit foam that ys upon the water. That river goeth further upp than the other: how high yt ys ere they meet togeather I know not: the other hath more water; but yt ys harder going upp: yf you mysse the on you must take the other.[2]

You have to traffyke with none but with the king himselfe and none other; for he will geve for your commodities pepers. You may take a busshell or a quarter mesure with you and rekon how manye of them doth make a tonne and shew the king the trewth the burthen of the shipp, and he will concure that for your commodities he will lade the shipp in so many dayes.

You must agree with the king to bring the pepper so near to the sea as ye can, and procure to have yr. pepper so near as you can to be clean, or else ye must procure your selfe to make yt cleane.

As towching other commodities ther ys read, yellow, and white coppal [?] and if the king will suffer the grownd to be broken with other commodities: you may confer with the king to have a trade with him, demanding what commodities he will have out of our

1 P.R.O. *State Papers* 12, no. 153. Addressed to E. Cotton for guidance of a relative named Bingham, who was going to Benin.
2 The two rivers referred to are the Benin and the Escravos.

countrie to serve for his warres against other kings: if you can gett the Balme yt ys a precyous thing.

As towching your commodities lynnen cloath ys on of the chefest and other things which I am not able to reherse without my booke.

ffirst of Roan canvas brown.

Roan canvas whit good.

Holland cloth not above 2s 9d unto 14d the eln.

Corrall pfytt in braslette and in braunches not much of yt.

other Corrall in fflaunders some as bigg as a smalle nutt, and so downward de...d round...[1] or both, and to make them in beads.

Other counterfaite Corrall made in beads with some counterfait pearles between everye corrall.

Margaritas of read green and yealow for armes and neckes.

Read cloth. Course broad cloth.

Read cottons.

Read cappes.

Kettells and pannes of sorts.

Belts, knyves and hatchetts.

Shertts of mayle not many.

Sawes great and smawle not many.

Manyles of copper.

horse tayles most blacke.

Some small dauncying bells.

Paynted Calycut cloath that cometh from the indies, to be had in London.

many other things which I have not in memorye.

As towching to all this you may take as little or as much as you shall see cawse according to the burthen of the shipp you will have. You shall by god's helpe have a hundred tonne of pepper for 400 lb of commodities; yf you send sage and wise men that can use the matter well with the king, the next vyadge may be worthe 100,000 lb to you yf you once fawll in trade with the king, and he may and will gather you together against your next returne 3 or 400 tonne of yt peradventure. They must have much conference on many matters with the king abowt the next voyadge as by instructions you have to give them after that they do gre to deal with the king in all things.

---

1 Manuscript illegible.

The victualls.

good Bisquett. ⎫
good wyne. ⎬ according to the number of your men
good oyle and vinaicre. ⎭
great abundance of cyder.
Rice.
Stockfishe.
Butter.
Beefe.
honnye.
pork in pyckle.
Aquavita.
garlicke.
other dry fishe without salt.
Backon in flythchs.
pesen and beanes.

You must be ther the first of december and at the farthest you have not to tarry if it be possible not past the 5 of ffebruarye for saulfegard of your men. The men's drinke must be ther nothing but syder and at any hand lett your men bewarre that they doe not eat any kind of ffruits in the countrye, nor drinke of the water: yf they do, they dic for yt. They must be merry and keep them from sleep; and to keep as many cloathes on ther heads as they can. And ther everie morning between 4 and 5 heads of garlicke and a pynt of sacke: your pynnaces must be as great as may be, but they must roe with 10 or 12 owers a peece to gett up the ryvers: they must take ther owne victualls with them. But you shall fynde henes and other kinds of fleesh ther, the which they may eat of, but nothing ells in the countrye as afore written. And thus I have not to enlardge your worship no farther for want of my bookes; but consyder of these small things that I have written. I have writt to my wiffe if it be possible to send them to you. And thus I pray you pardon my ende and simple writinge. I wryte in hast and thus my humble commendations to the gentlewoman your wife and the rest of the gentlemen in your house and the lord blesse us and keep us all.

Yours to command as your owne,

Randall Shawe

There is in flaundres a commodytie that you caule correll, yt is counterfaict, yt is Blewe and is aboute this longe ———, and some longer, and is as bygg as the tagge of a point. gett at the least xv lb of it, and putt it uppon grene, read and yellowe lase and make a braslett of it. Some of a handfull longe, some of a foote longe, and some half a yard longe. And yf you can gett any glasse beads of read, yellow and grene; and betwene every corrall putt one of the beads of glasse. The estimation of them is much in vallew there. You had need of wyse men in this voyadge that may have and use all good government, or else you overthrowe your voyadge. Take a feawe drinkynge glasses with you, but 6, and lett them be of dyvers sortes: and 3 or 4 looking glasses of christall for the kinge, and some small flaunders glasses of 2d or 3d the pece. More I am not able to wryte, but as before, for want of my bookes. I humbly thank your worship for your gentleness and cortesy showed me, prayinge god to send you as prosperous a voyadge as I wishe to this our voyadge: and this to the good gentlewoman your wyfe my hertie comendations: from the house the 8th daye of Maye 1582. There dwelleth one at Rattless beyond London his name is William Rose, if you can gett him to goe, he hath byne uppon the coste, and in one of the Rivers, you maye showe hym I wysht hym unto you.

Yours to command,

Randall Shawe

P.S. Amonge all other things that I wrote you, I had forgott one thing very necessary, you must procure to have in your voyadge a garblar and that he must think uppon and not forgett it, and that he must take his vans with him, both great fans and small, to make clean the pepper that you may bring it clean home. And going thitherwards beware at any hand that they do not overshutt nor shott past the place. If they do the corrant of the water will not suffer them to sett it agayne in a long time. And as I have written you, let your men governe themselves ther. They might so governe themselves there, that your shipp might ride still ther tyll you be lade. And ware this you must do which is the principall matter, that as your shipp is there, you must have long pekes that will reatche to the kele of your shipp, and that you must make shift to have her cleane three tymes a week under water, or ells the worms will destroy her; this must nedes be done. And this I leave to truble you. Beseching god to send you a prosperous voyadge.

The House the 13th of Maye 1582.

Yours to command as your owne,

Randall Shawe

Appendix IX

Report on visit to Ubini (Benin City) the capital of the Benin country by H. M. Gallwey 1892.[1]

I left my Vice-Consulate on the morning of the 21st March 1892, my object being to visit Ubini the capital of the Benin country, and to see the King with a view to concluding a Treaty between him and Her Majesty the Queen of England.

All previous efforts in this direction have been futile—the last attempt having been made by Consul Annesley in 1890—Consul Annesley presented the King with a number of valuable presents, but was unable to persuade him to sign a Treaty.

Knowing of this, and of previous failures, I corresponded with the King, by messenger, for some time before I started to visit him.

In these messages I endeavoured to make it plain to him what the object of my visit was—and that should I be unsuccessful, I would on no account make a second attempt—and further, that I would make no presents until a Treaty was concluded—and that I expected him to see me the day following my arrival in his capital.

I received replies to all my messages to the effect that the King would be very willing to make a Treaty, and that he knew he had acted foolishly in his treatment of Consul Annesley, and that he would see me, if I wished it, directly I arrived.

I therefore fixed upon the 21st March as the day of starting.

My party consisted of my Consular Agent Mr. H. H. Hutton, Mr. J. A. Swainson, a trader, who knows the country, and does a fair trade with the Benin people; and Dr. Hanley, the Medical Officer in charge here. As I expected to be away for 8 or 10 days, I found I had to take about 40 carriers, but took no escort.

On the first day I reached Gwato, by launch—slept there for the night—and started through the forest the following day for Ubini.

We marched 16 miles that day, sleeping at Egoru, a small village —and reached Ubini the following day about noon, a distance of

---

1 P.R.O. F.O. 84/2194. Enclosure in Consul-General C. M. Macdonald to Marquess of Salisbury, Old Calabar, 16 May 1892.

9 miles—making the total distance from Gwato 25 miles—This I measured by a Pedometer.

The direction was generally ENE and my aneroid showed an altitude of 320 feet above the sea. Having no chronometer, I was unable to fix the exact position of the place: but hope to do so at some future date.

On arrival I was conducted to the house the King had ordered for the accommodation of myself and party—a house was also told off for my carriers: for the latter accommodation I had to pay. I immediately sent my 'service' to the King and said I would like to see him the following morning at 7 a.m.

The King sent back his 'service', and asked me to make it later— I said I could not make it later than 8.

Accordingly he promised to send his messenger for me at that hour.

The next morning, the 24th, on arrival at the King's residence, I was informed that the King could not see me till later—and to make a long story short, I did not see him until the afternoon of the 26th. His messages which kept coming to me all day, were a series of lies and excuses.

I fancy he is afraid of doing anything without the full concurrence of his big men. On the 25th I had an interview with all the leading men of the place and fully explained to them the object of my visit, and also what a treaty was, and what it meant. They were fully satisfied, or said they were, at my suggestions generally: and promised to conduct me to the King that morning. However, as I stated before, they did not do so. The following day I determined to bring matters to a crisis—and so sent word to the King that I was leaving that day, and had no intention of returning any more—i.e. as a friend—and to complete the ruse, I sent off a number of carriers with baggage that was not required—telling them to wait at Egoru for me.

The King immediately sent and begged me not to be 'vexed'— and that if I would see his big men once more, they would bring me straight to him. I said I would on no account see them again, as they had already told me enough lies. Eventually after receiving several begging messages, I consented to see the 3 leading men.

They asked me to wait till the sun went down that day, as it was too hot for me to go out during the day, and asked me not to be 'vexed'. I said far from being 'vexed', I was amused—and although it might be too hot to see the King, it was not too hot for me to return to Gwato. I then dismissed them. Finally, two of the leading men came and said the King was ready to receive me. I told them I would think about it, and in the meantime told them to wait—I kept them waiting some time, and eventually about 2 p.m. I went to the King's residence, accompanied by Mr. Hutton, Mr. Swainson, and Dr. Hanley.

After a half-hour's wait I was taken up to a curtain, and after a few minutes waiting, the five chief advisers of the King came forward and gave me the King's 'service' in due form—I returned the compliment—and the King sent me his 'service' a second time and said he would be ready to see me as soon as he was dressed. It appears the King was behind this curtain, as he wished to see me before he decided whether to receive me or not!

The process of dressing took nearly 2 hours—and I was then conducted to the King. He was surrounded by all his chief men and 'boys'—the latter wearing no clothing of any description.

There were about 500 people in all.

The King's dress was composed entirely of coral—with a large coral head-piece—and he sat on a throne resembling a big drum with a linen cover on it—his right arm supported by a pedestal—and his left arm by an attendant.

I first gave him 'service', and told him that I considered he had treated me very badly—and the that 'whiteman' did not understand such customs. He complained of my having hurried him.

The rest of the 'palaver' was most satisfactory—the King and chief men being more than anxious to sign the 'Book', as they called it. Owing to the King being in the middle of celebrating some big fetish custom, he explained to me that he could not touch the pen—but that all his big men would do so, and that it would be the same as if touched by him, provided his name was written. I found the interpreter that I took up with me was, owing to his fear of the King, useless—but fortunately, my man Agaie, proved a most efficient interpreter. He fully explained each Article of the Treaty, as propounded by me, in the Acure tongue (a country bordering on Benin)—this was passed on to the King's chief adviser, who passed it on to the King.

Eventually the king signed the Treaty in full, and I gave him one copy—it having been signed in triplicate.

The signing was witnessed by the three whitemen with me.

I then had a talk with the King on several matters—and I found him most sensible, and willing to listen to reason. He laid great stress upon the fact that there should be no 'war palavers'—I informed him that as long as he kept to the terms of the treaty, that the Queen of England would always be his friend.

I then presented the King with some presents, and, after giving him 'service', went away.

I did not leave the town until the morning of the 28th—reaching Gwato on the 29th and my Vice-Consulate the following day.

I received every assistance from Mr. Hutton my Consular Agent, and I am indebted to Mr. Swainson for his excellent arrangements for supplies, carriers, and messengers. Fortunately the professional services of the Doctor were not required.

The day following the signing of the Treaty, the King said he would widen and clear the road to Gwato—which at present is a single track.

He also took the 'fetish', which had always existed, off gum copal, in which the country abounds, and gave orders for it to be collected.

I feel certain that the Treaty will prove most beneficial towards the future welfare of this particular country.

At present the whole Benin country is, and has been for hundreds of years, steeped in Fetish. The Town of Ubini might well be called 'The City of Skulls'—I saw no less than four crucified victims during my few days there in addition to numerous corpses—some mutilated fearfully—which were strewn about in the most public places. The rule appears to be one of Terror, and one can only hope that this Treaty may be the foundation of a new order of things throughout the vast territory ruled over by the King of Benin.

This King, it would appear, does not pay tribute to any state, but receives tribute from a dozen or more surrounding states.

The Town of Ubini is not very populous, judging from the little I saw during my few days there: though I daresay in the days when the Portuguese traded there, up to about 1859, when the slave traffic was in full swing, that the population of the place was much larger.

It can hardly be expected that any great change in the Fetish rule of the country can take place at once, but, in time, I trust a great change for the good will be the result of these negotiations.

H. M. Gallwey

Dep. Com. and Vice-Consul

H.B.M.'s Vice-Consulate
Benin
30th March 1892

Bibliography

MANUSCRIPT SOURCES

I. Portugal[1]

Archivo Nacional da Torre do Tombo, Lisbon.
Corpo Cronológico. Many documents in this collection are useful for the study of Portuguese relations with Benin. All belong to the sixteenth century.
Gavetas xv.
Cartas Missivas, maço 4.
Leitura Nova, vol. 36.
Archivo Histórico Ultramarino, Lisbon.
São Tomé e Príncipe, caixas 1–21, *maços* 1–13.
Codices, nos. 253, 1467, 1494, 1495, 1496.

II. Netherlands[2]

Algemeen Rijksarchief, The Hague.
Archief van de Nederlandische Bezittingen ter Kuste van Guinea, vols. 8, 65, 82, 83, 84, 85, 86, 87, 88, 89, 90, 92, 93, 94, 95, 96, 97, 98, 99, 100, 102, 103, 105, 234, 238, 1287.
Archief van de Eerste (Oude) West Indische Compagnie, vols. 9, 10, 11.
Archief van de Tweede (Nieuwe) West Indische Compagnie, vols. 54, 55, 97, 98, 99, 100, 102, 103, 104, 105, 106, 109, 110, 111, 113, 122, 284, 488.

III. Italy[3]

Archives of the Propaganda Fide, Rome.
Acta Sacrae Congregationis de Propaganda Fide, vols. 17, 18, 19, 23, 24, 25, 32, 33, 59, 64, 77, 79, 81, 82, 83, 84, 89.

---

1 cf. A. F. C. Ryder, *Materials for West African history in Portuguese archives.* University of London, Athlone Press, 1965.
2 cf. Patricia Carson, *Materials for West African history in the archives o, Belgium and Holland.* University of London, Athlone Press, 1962.
3 cf. Richard Gray and David Chambers, *Materials for West African history in Italian archives.* University of London, Athlone Press, 1965.

Scritture Originali Riferite nelle Congregazioni Generali, vols. 97, 249, 255.

Scritture Riferite nei Congressi, vols. I, II, III, IV, V.

IV. England

Public Record Office, London.

State Papers, vol. 12.

Foreign Office 2, vols. 3, 9, 11, 51, 63, 64, 100, 101, 102, 120, 122.

Foreign Office 84, vols. 858, 886, 976, 1002, 1031, 1061, 1088, 1115, 1176, 1201, 1290, 1308, 1326, 1343, 1375, 1455, 1487, 1541, 1569, 1634, 1660, 1701, 1749, 1881, 1882, 1939, 2020, 2111, 2194.

PRINTED SOURCES

ADAMS, J. *Sketches taken during ten voyages to Africa between the years 1786 and 1800; including observations on the country between Cape Palmas and the River Congo; and cursory remarks on the physical and moral character of the Inhabitants: with an appendix containing an account of the European trade with the west coast of Africa.* London, n.d.

— *Remarks on the country extending from Cape Palmas to the River Congo.* London, 1823.

AKENZUA, E. 'Benin, 1897: a Bini's view.' *Nigeria*, no. 65, June 1960.

ALLEN, W. and THOMSON, T. R. H. *Narrative of the expedition to the River Niger in 1841.* 2 vols. London, 1848.

ARMSTRONG, R. G. *The study of West African languages.* Ibadan, 1964.

AUCHTERLONIE, T. B. and PINNOCK, J. 'The City of Benin.' *Transactions of the Liverpool Geographical Society*, vol. VI, 1898.

BACON, R. H. *Benin the City of Blood.* London, 1897.

BAIKIE, W. B. *Narrative of an exploring voyage up the Rivers Kwo'ra and Bi'nue in 1854.* London, 1856.

BANE, M. J. *Catholic Pioneers in West Africa.* Dublin, 1956.

BARBOT, J. *A description of the coasts of north and south Guinea.* London, 1732.

BARROS, J. DE *Da Asia.* Lisbon, 1552, ed. H. Cidade, Lisbon, 1945.

BEAUVOIS, A. M. F. J. PALISOT DE. *Flore d'Oware et de Benin.* 2 vols. Paris, 1804–7.

— *Insectes recueillis en Afrique et en Amérique.* Paris, 1805.

BEAUVOIS, A. M. F. J. PALISOT DE. 'Notice sur le peuple de Benin.' *Décade Philosophique*, no. 12, *année* 9, 1801.

BEECROFT, J. 'On Benin and the upper course of the River Quorra or Niger.' *Journal of the Royal Geographical Society*, vol. II, 1841.

BEVERLEY, W. H. *Military report on Southern Nigeria*. H.M.S.O., London, 1908.

BLAKE, J. W. *European Beginnings in West Africa*. London, 1937.

— *Europeans in West Africa, 1450–1560*. 2 vols. Hakluyt Society, London, 1942.

BOISRAGON, A. *The Benin Massacre*. London, 1897.

BOLD, E. *Merchants' and mariners' African guide*. London, 1819.

BOSMAN, W. *Nauwkeurige Beschryvinge van de Guinese Gout-T and-en Slavekust*. Utrecht, 1704.

— *A new and accurate description of the coast of Guinea, divided into the Gold, the Slave, and the Ivory Coasts. Written originally in Dutch by William Bosman, chief factor for the Dutch at the castle of St. George d'Elmina, and now faithfully done into English*. London, 1705.

BOUCHAUD, J. 'Les Portugais dans la Baie de Biafra au XVIième siècle.' *Africa*, vol. XVI, no. 4, Oct. 1946.

BOWEN, T. J. *Adventures and missionary labors in several countries in the interior of Africa, from 1849 to 1856*. Charleston, 1857.

BOXER, C. R. *The Dutch Sea-borne Empire, 1600–1800*. London, 1965.

BRADBURY, R. E. and LLOYD, P. C. *The Benin Kingdom and the Edo-speaking peoples of south-western Nigeria, together with a section on the Itsekiri*. London, 1957.

BRADBURY, R. E. 'Comparative ethnography in Benin and the Yoruba.' *The Historian in Tropical Africa*, ed. J. Vansina. Oxford, 1964.

— 'Chronological problems in the study of Benin history.' *Journal of the Historical Society of Nigeria*, vol. I, no. 4, Dec. 1959.

BRÁSIO, A. *Monumenta Missionária Africana: Africa Ocidental*. 6 vols. Lisbon, 1952–6.

BRAUN, S. *Schiffarten*, 1624, ed. S. P. L'Honoré Naber. Linschoten Vereeniging, The Hague, 1913.

BRITISH GOVERNMENT. *Papers relating to the massacre of British officials near Benin, and the consequent punitive expedition, presented to* both Houses of Parliament by command of Her Majesty, *August 1897*. Cd. 8677. H.M.S.O., London, 1897.

— *Nigeria. Correspondence relating to the Benin territories expedition, 1899*. Cd. 9529. H.M.S.O., London, 1899.

BROECKE, P. VAN DEN. *Reizen naar West Afrika*, ed. K. Ratelband. Linschoten Vereeniging, The Hague, 1950.

BURDO, A. *The Niger and the Benueh*. London, 1880.

BURTON, R. F. *Wanderings in West Africa*. 2 vols. London, 1863.

— 'My wanderings in West Africa, by a F.R.G.S. Part I. The renowned city of Wari.' *Fraser's Magazine*, vol. LXVII, Feb. 1865.

— 'My wanderings in West Africa, by a F.R.G.S. Part II. The renowned city of Benin.' ibid., March 1865. contd. ibid., April 1865.

BUTCHER, H. L. M. 'Four Edo fables.' *Africa*, vol. X, no. 3, July 1937.

CARSON, P. *Materials for West African history in the archives of Belgium and Holland*. London, 1962.

CAVAZZI DA MONTECUCCOLO, G. A. *Istorica descrittione de' tre regni Congo, Matamba, et Angola situati nell'Etiopia inferiore occidentale e delle missioni apostoliche esercitatevi da religiosi capuccini*, ed. P. Fortunato Alamandini. Milan, 1690.

CLAPPERTON, H. *Journal of a second expedition into the interior*. London, 1829.

CONNAH, G. 'New light on the Benin City walls.' *Journal of the Historical Society of Nigeria*, vol. III, no. 4, 1967.

— 'Archaeological research in Benin City, 1961–4.' *Journal of the Historical Society of Nigeria*, vol. II, no. 4, 1963.

CROW, H. *Memoirs of the late Captain Hugh Crow of Liverpool*. London, 1830.

CROWTHER, S. and TAYLOR, J. C. *The Gospel on the banks of the Niger*. London, 1859.

CURTIN, P. D. *The Image of Africa—British Ideas and Action 1780–1870*. University of Wisconsin, 1964.

— ' "Scientific" racism and the British theory of empire.' *Journal of the Historical Society of Nigeria*, vol. II, no. 1, 1960.

DALZIEL, J. M. *The Useful Plants of West Tropical Africa*. London, 1937

DAPPER, O. *Naukeurige Beschrijvinge der Afrikaensche Gewesten*. Amsterdam, 1668. 2nd ed. 1676.

DAPPER, O. *Description de l'Afrique.* Amsterdam, 1686.

DARK, P. C. *Benin Art.* London, 1960.

DAVIES, K. G. *The Royal African Company.* London, 1957.

D'AVEZAC-MACAYA, M. 'Notice sur le peuple des Yebous en Afrique.' *Mémoires de la Société Ethnologique,* vol. 2, 1845.

DE ANGUIANO, M. *Misiones Capuchinos en Africa: II. Misiones al reino de la Zinga, Benin, Arda, Guinea y Sierra Leone.* Madrid, 1957.

DE JONGHE, J. K. *De oorsprong van Neerlands bezittingen op de kust van Guinea.* The Hague, 1871.

DE JONGHE, F. and SIMAR, T. *Archives Congolaises.* Fasc. I. Brussels, 1919.

DE LA FOSSE, E. 'Voyage à la côte occidentale d'Afrique, en Portugal, et en Espagne (1479–1480)', ed. R. Foulché-Delbosc. *Revue Hispanique,* 1897.

DE MAREES, P. *Beschryvinge ende Historische Verhael van het Gout-Koninkrijk van Guinea,* ed. S. P. L'Honoré Naber. Linschoten Vereeniging, The Hague, 1909.

DE PINA, R. *Chronica del Rey Dom João II.* Coimbra, 1950.

DE RESENDE, G. *Chronica que trata da vida de Dom João II.* Lisbon, 1545.

DIKE, K. O. *Trade and Politics in the Niger Delta: 1830–1885.* Oxford, 1956.

DONNAN, E. *Documents illustrative of the history of the slave trade to America,* vols. I and IV. Washington, 1930 and 1935.

DOUGLAS, A. C. (pseudo. NEMO). *Niger memories.* Exeter, 1937.

DUPIGNY, E. G. M. *Gazetteer of Nupe Province.* London, 1920.

DUPUIS, J. *Journal of a residence in Ashantee.* London, 1824.

EDEN, R. *The Decades of the newe worlde or west India.* London, 1555.

EGHAREVBA, J. U. *Concise Lives of the Famous Iyases of Benin.* Lagos, 1946.

— *The Murder of Imaguero and the Tragedy of the Idah War.* Sapele, 1949.

— *Benin Law and Custom.* Port Harcourt, 1949.

— *Some Stories of Ancient Benin.* Lagos, 1951.

— *The City of Benin.* Benin, 1952.

— *A Short History of Benin.* 3rd ed. Ibadan, 1960.

— *The Origin of Benin.* Benin, 1953.

EGHAREVBA, J. U. *Bini Titles*. Benin, 1956.

FAWCKNER, J. *Narrative of Captain James Fawckner's travels on the coast of Benin, West Africa, edited by a friend of the captain.* London, 1837.

FERNANDES, V. *Description de la côte occidentale d'Afrique (Sénégal au Cap de Monte, Archipels)*, trans. and ed. Th. Monod, A. Texeira da Mota, R. Mauny. Bissau, 1951.

FORDE, D. and KABERRY, P. M. (eds.). *West African Kingdoms in the Nineteenth Century*. Oxford, 1967.

GALLWEY, H. L. 'Journeys in the Benin country, West Africa.' *Geographical Journal*, vol. I, no. 2, 1893.

— 'Nigeria in the "nineties".' *Journal of the African Society*, vol. XXIX, no. cxv, April 1930.

— 'West Africa fifty years ago.' *Journal of the Royal African Society*, no. clxiii, April 1942.

— 'Benin: altars and compounds.' *Ethnologia Cranmorensis*, vol. iii, 1938.

GALVAO, A. *Tratado dos descobrimentos*. Porto, 1944.

GERTZEL, C. J. 'Commercial organisation on the Niger Coast 1852–1891.' *Historians in Tropical Africa*, Salisbury, Rhodesia, 1962.

GOODWIN, A. J. H. 'Archaeology and Benin architecture.' *Journal of the Historical Society of Nigeria*, vol. I, no. 2, 1957.

HAKLUYT, R. *The principal navigations, voyages, traffiques, and discoveries of the English nation made by sea or over-land to the remote and farthest distant quarters of the Earth at any time within the compasse of these 1600 yeeres*, vol. VI. Glasgow, 1904.

HENSLEY, F. M. *Niger Dawn*. Ilfracombe, 1955.

HODGKIN, T. *Nigerian Perspectives*. Oxford, 1960.

HUBBARD, J. W. *The Sobo of the Niger Delta*. Zaria, n.d.

JAMIESON, R. *Commerce with Africa*. London, 1859.

JOHNSON, S. *The History of the Yorubas*, ed. O. Johnson. London, 1921.

JOHNSTON, H. H. 'The Niger Delta.' *Proceedings of the Royal Geographical Society*, vol. X, no. 12, 1888.

KILGER, L. 'Missionversuche in Benin.' *Zeitschrift für Missionswissenschaft*, 1932.

KINGSLEY, M. H. *West African Studies*. London, 1899. Includes, 'A short description of the natives of the Niger Coast Protectorate, with some account of their customs, religion, trade, etc. by le Comte C. N. de Cardi.'

LABARTHE, P. *Voyage à la côte de Guinée*. Paris, 1803.

LAET, J. DE *Historie ofte jaerlijck verhael van de verrichtingen der geoctroyeerde West-Indische Compagnie, zedert begin tot 1636*. Leiden, 1644.

LANDOLPHE, J. F. *Mémoires du Capitaine rédigés sur son ms. par J. S. Quesné*. 2 vols. Paris, 1823.

LEGUM, C. 'Great Benin—the elusive city.' *Nigeria*, Oct. 1960.

LEITE DE FARIA, F. 'Os Barbadinhos italianos em S. Tomé e Príncipe de 1714 a 1794.' *Portugal em Africa*, vols. XI and XII, 1954–5.

LEONARD, A. G. *The Lower Niger and its Tribes*. London, 1906.

LLOYD, P. C. 'The Itsekiri in the nineteenth century; an outline social history.' *Journal of African History*, vol. IV, no. 2, 1963.

LOSI, J. B. *History of Lagos*. Lagos, 1914.

MACDONALD, C. M. *Report by Major Macdonald of his visit as Her Majesty's Commissioner to the Niger and Oil Rivers*. H.M.S.O., London, 1890.

MAURO, F. *Le Portugal et l'Atlantique au xvii⁰ siècle, 1570–1670*. Paris, 1960.

MICHAEL À TUGIO. *Bullarium Ordinis F.F. Minorum S.P. Francisci Capucinorum*. Rome, 1740–52.

MOLONEY, A. 'Notes on Yoruba and the Colony and Protectorate of Lagos, West Africa.' *Proceedings of the Royal Geographical Society*, vol. XII, no. 10, 1890.

MOORE, W. A. *History of the Itsekiri*. London, n.d.

NADEL, S. F. *A Black Byzantium*. London, 1942.

OGILBY, J. *Africa: being an accurate description of the regions of Aegypt, Barbary, Lybia, and Billedulgerid, the land of Negroes, Guinee, Aethiopia, and the Abyssines*. London, 1670.

OGUNKOYA, T. O. 'The early history of Ijebu.' *Journal of the Historical Society of Nigeria*, vol. I, no. 1, 1956.

OGUNTUYI, A. *A Short History of Ado-Ekiti*. Akure, n.d.

OKOJIE, C. G. *Ishan Native Laws and Customs*. Yaba, n.d.

OLIVER, R. *Sir Harry Johnston and the Scramble for Africa*. London, 1957.

OWONARO, S. K. *The History of Ijo and her Neighbouring Tribes in Nigeria*. Lagos, 1949.

355

PACHECO PEREIRA, D. *Esmeraldo de situ orbis*, ed. A. E. da Silva Dias. Lisbon, 1905, and ed. R. Mauny, Bissau, 1956.

PARRY, J. *The Age of Reconnaissance*. London, 1963.

PINNOCK, J. *Benin: the surrounding country, inhabitants, customs and trade*. Liverpool, 1897.

RATELBAND, K. *Vijf Dagregisters van het Kasteel S. Jorge da Mina*. Linschoten Vereeniging, The Hague, 1953.

RAWSON, G. *Life of Admiral Sir Harry Rawson*. London, 1914.

READ, H. and DALTON, O. M. *Antiquities from the city of Benin and from other parts of West Africa*. London, 1899.

RINCHON, P. D. *La traite et l'esclavage des Congolais par les Européens*. Wetteren, 1929.

ROCCO DA CESINALE. *Storia delle missioni dei Cappucini*, vol. III. Rome, 1873.

ROTH, H. L. *Great Benin: its customs, art and horrors*. Halifax, 1903.

ROUSSIER, P. 'Documents sur les relations entre la France et le royaume de Ouaire à la côte d'Afrique, 1784–1787.' *Bulletin du comité d'études historiques et scientifiques de l'A.O.F.*, tom. XI, 1928.

Royal Gold Coast Gazette, vol. I, no. 21, 25 March 1823.

RUITERS, D. *Toortse der zee-vaert*, ed. S. P. L'Honoré Naber. Linschoten Vereeniging, The Hague, 1913.

RUMANN, W. B. 'Funeral ceremonies for the late ex-Oba of Benin.' *Journal of the African Society*, vol. XIV, no. liii, Oct. 1914.

RYDER, A. F. C. *Materials for West African history in Portuguese archives*. London, 1965.

— 'The Benin missions.' *Journal of the Historical Society of Nigeria*, vol. II, no. 2, 1961.

— 'An early Portuguese trading voyage to the Forcados River.' *Journal of the Historical Society of Nigeria*, vol. I, no. 4, 1959.

— 'Missionary activity in the kingdom of Warri to the early nineteenth century.' *Journal of the Historical Society of Nigeria*, vol. II, no. 1, 1960.

— 'A reconsideration of the Ife-Benin relationship.' *Journal of African History*, vol. VI, no. 1, 1965.

— 'A note on the Afro-Portuguese ivories.' *Journal of African History*, vol. V, no. 3, 1964.

— 'Dutch trade on the Nigerian coast during the seventeenth

century.' *Journal of the Historical Society of Nigeria*, vol. III, no. 3, 1966.

RYDER, A. F. C. 'The rise of the Benin kingdom.' *The Middle Age of African History*, ed. R. Oliver. Oxford, 1967.

SALUBI, A. 'The establishment of British administration in the Urhobo country (1891–1913).' *Journal of the Historical Society of Nigeria*, vol. I, no. 3, 1958.

SCHEFFER, C. *Instructions générales données de 1763 à 1770 aux gouverneurs et ordonnateurs des établissements français en Afrique occidentale*, vol. I. Paris, 1921.

SÖLKEN, H. 'Innerafrikanische wege nach Benin.' *Anthropos*, vol. 49, fasc. 5–6, 1954.

TALBOT, P. A. *The Peoples of Southern Nigeria*. London, 1926.

TEIXEIRA DA MOTA, A. 'Novos elementos sobre a acção dos Portugueses e Franceses em Benin aa primeira metade do século xvi.' *Proceedings of III International West African Conference*. Lagos, 1956.

THOMAS, N. W. *Anthropological report on the Edo-speaking peoples oʃ Nigeria*. London, 1910.

TONG, R. *Figures in Ebony: Past and Present in a West African City*. London, 1958.

— 'Captain Thomas Wyndham, Tudor merchant adventurer.' *History Today*, vol. VII, no. 4, April 1957.

UGHULU, E. O. *Short History of (Esan) Ishan—Benin*. Lagos, 1950.

VAN DER WEE, H. *The Growth of the Antwerp Market and the European Economy*, vol. II. The Hague, 1963.

VERGER, P. *Bahia and the West Coast Trade (1549–1851)*. Ibadan, 1964.

VON LUSCHAN, F. *Altertümer von Benin*. 3 vols. Berlin and Leipzig, 1919.

WARD-PRICE, H. L. *Dark Subjects*. London, 1939.

WILLAN, T. S. *Studies in Elizabethan Foreign Trade*. Manchester, 1959.

Index

Names of ships are italicised

Abraka 266, 266 (n. 3), 267 (n. 2), 279, 279 (n. 1)
Abrinomy (Itsekiri chief) 246 (n. 1)
Ada, swords of state 5, 105 (n. 2)
Adams, John (ship's captain) 210 (n. 1), 206, 211, 227–9, 235 (n. 1), 236–7, 254
Adele, Oba of Lagos 226 (n. 2)
Adolo, Oba of Benin 242, 245, 247–8, 252, 255, 258, 259, 261, 262, 268
Afonso V, King of Portugal 24
Africa, Dutch vessel 166, 167 (n. 3), 169, 170
  English vessel, 197
Agbor 21, 23, 249, 280
Agwe (new yam) festival 172, 172 (n. 5), 262 (n. 2), 286; description of, 219–20
Ahenzae, Oba of Benin 110
Akabwa (Itsekiri chief) 253, 255 (n. 3)
Akassa 278
Akengbuda, Oba of Benin 21, 197, 203, 228 (n. 2)
Akengbuwa, Olu 230–1, 231 (n. 3), 243, 253
Akenzae, Oba of Benin 110
Akenzua I, Oba of Benin 20, 21, 22 (n. 1), 139, 141, 143, 145, 150 (n. 2), 152–4, 185 (n. 1), 201 (n. 2); quarrel with Boededoe, 161–2, 171; and slave trade, 168–70, 176–7
Akinbodo 267
Akintoye, Oba of Lagos 241–2
Akure 11, 14–15, 21, 259, 263, 270, 346
Alagoa, Dr. E. J. 88 (n. 2)
Anes, Afonso 70, 77 (n. 2)
Ango, Jean (French merchant) 68
Angola 29, 94, 111, 311
Annesley, G., Consul 266, 268–9, 269 (n. 1), 274, 344
Anthony, Chief of Boededoe 149–50, 151–2, 154, 154 (n. 2), 161–2, 164, 171, 174, 322, 326–7, 332, 334
Antonio, Dom (Benin trading official) 299
Antwerp 31, 38; Portuguese factor in 79,
Apa 179, 181–5, 194 (n. 2)

Arbo 88, 88 (n. 1), 90–1, 135, 158, 185, 311; missionaries at, 99, 106, 106 (n. 2), 310; Dutch traders at, 90–2, 93, 97, 124, 128, 132, 134, 135 (n. 1), 136–7, 141, 147, 151, 171, 174, 322, 324, 326–8, 334; English traders at, 90–1, 95–6, 106, 124, 197
  and Benin, 89, 136; and Itsekiris, 113, 127; and Ijos, 146, 174; burned by Dutch, 132–3, 137, 138
Ardra 73, 84 (n. 3), 87, 111, 130, 135 (n. 1), 168, 193 (n. 2), 312
Arms (*see also* Cannon, Firearms, Swords)
  7, 41, 56, 81, 297
  European coats of mail, 80, 81 (n. 1), 340
Arogho 88 (n. 2)
Asaba 263
Aulard (ship's captain) 165 (n. 3), 169 (n. 3)
Axim 163 (n. 1)

Baba (chief at Ughoton) 172, 188–9
Badagry 179, 185, 188–90, 192–4, 233–4, 242
Bahia 119, 120, 228 (n. 1), 234
Balon, Lt. (French naval officer) 200 (n. 1), 201 (n. 1), 218 (n. 2), 222
Bambergh, Arnauldt (official of West India Company) 172–4
Barbados 197, 197 (n. 3)
Bardet, Louis Isaac (official of West India Company) 135 (n. 1)
Barroso, Pero (Benin envoy to Portugal) 48, 48 (n. 1), 49, 49 (n. 1)
Basketwork 84
Batere 246 (n. 1)
Beads (*see also* Coral) 40, 90, 129, 340, 342
  European glass beads, 40, 56–7, 59, 68, 80, 82, 86, 96, 98, 98 (n. 1),138, 144, 182, 210
  Indian, 41; Benin, 37, 55–6, 295; 'conte de terre', 187, 193–4; as standard of value, 59

359

Beans 315

Beecroft, John, Consul for Bights of Benin and Biafra 240, 241, 245, 253; letter to Osemwede, 242

Beeldsnyder (Dutch trader) 126

Bells, European imported 80, 321, 240

Benin 206 (n. 3)

Benin City, name 10, 11, 36 (n. 1); descriptions of, 84–5, 88, 113 (n. 3), 254–5, 271, 313; origins, 2–3, 6; 'walls', 3, 11; wards, 4, 49 (n. 3), 250; excavations, 188 (n. 2); centre of trade routes, 22, 37, 60, 90, 264; visited by Christian missionaries, 49–50, 69–72, 101–7, 119, 309; alleged church sites, 50, 50 (n.2), 102, 116, 117; visited by Portuguese, 30, 39, 56, 64, 304; visited by English, 77–8, 82–3, 97 (n. 2), 104, 229, 233, 260, 278–9, 283; visited by consular officials, 248, 254–256, 268, 283, 344–8; visited by Dutch, 70, 143, 152, 171–3, 181, 186, 191; visited by French, 200–7, 218–220, 223–4; accommodation of Europeans, 57, 63, 85, 186, 202, 254, 303; destruction of, 8, 19; captured by British, 290

Benin, consular district 265–6, 273; Revenue, 273, 274, 278, 284 (n. 4)

Benin kingdom, descriptions of 312–15; origin and expansion, 2, 5, 7, 10, 11–15, 21–2, 72–3; contraction, 155–6, 163, 203, 245, 250, 252, 259, 263; government, 9, 9 (n. 1), 12, 17, 20–1, 51, 89, 92, 128, 135–6, 204, 205 (n. 1); trade with interior, 225, 225 (n. 1), 234–5, 258–9; relations with Itsekiris, 21, 59, 112 (n. 1), 226, 230–1, 233, 244, 274; relations with Ijos, 88, 161, 214, 219; relations with Lagos, 226, 229, 241–2

Benin massacre 285, 287–9, 292

Beninreyse 93

Benin River (Rio Fermoso) 13–14, 21, 26, 28, 44, 58, 79, 82, 88, 133, 148, 158, 205, 226, 229, 232, 239–40, 263; description, 312–13; flora and insects of, 217; captain and governor of, 236 (n. 1), 244, 245–6, 257–8, 260

Bersan (Dutch trader) 322, 324, 327

Bey and Zimmer (Hamburg merchants) 257 (n. 1), 266, 268 (n. 2)

Bingham, E. (English merchant) 79

Blacksmiths 64, 98

Blair, Vice-consul 261, 268

Blommaart, Samuel (Dutch merchant

and director of West India Co.) 87

Bloodhound. H.M.S. 241, 253, 256

Bobi 214 (n. 1), 236, 239, 241, 253; Landolphe at, 217, 219, 224, 226

Boededoe 128, 132, 135–6, 154, 158, 161–2; Dutch at, 127, 128, 151, 161 (n. 2), 165, 322, 327, 330; French at, 165; attacked by Ijos, 161, 171, 174 334

Boisragon, A. 288

Bold, E. (Liverpool merchant) 231 (n. 2 & 4), 234, 235–7

Bonaventura 166

Bonny 198 (n. 2), 232, 235, 240, 244

Bordeaux 227, 228 (n. 1)

Borgu 264

Boudakan (Itsekiri prince) 216–17

Boudakan 222

Bradbury, Dr. R. E. 1, 51 (n. 1), 262 (n. 2)

Brandy 86, 98, 145, 156, 160, 167, 168, 199, 207, 208 (n. 2), 209, 211, 321, 335–7

Brass (town) 279, 285

Brass (*see also* Manillas) sheet brass 276; basins, etc., 68, 98, 202, 207, 208, 330; neptunes, 98, 144, 173, 175–6, 181, 182 (n. 3)

Brasswork 21 (n. 1), 40, 169 (n. 2); heads, 224; crosses, 7, 72; plaques, 105 (n. 1); royal regalia, 7; fate of in 1897, 290 (n. 2)

Brassworkers of Benin City 7, 39, 40, 113 (n. 3)

Brazil 75, 119, 138, 145, 168, 168 (n. 3), 206, 208, 227, 228 (n. 1), 229, 234

Brillantois, M. (French merchant) 214, 216

Brownridge, James (English trader) 251, 252 (n. 4), 276, 281

Burton, Sir Richard 207, 233, 235 (n. 3), 245, 248, 250, 252–6, 257, 259–61, 271

Butler, Willem (Director-General of West India Company) 148, 167

Cabo Corso 171, 190, 332

Cadiz 101, 307

Calabar (New and Old) 129, 168, 226, 235, 240, 244, 285–6, 293

Calabash, as musical instrument 314

Calbeneer, Anthony (Dutch factor at Arbo) 97

Calvello, Fr. Filippo 117

Cameroons 74, 87

Campbell, Consul at Lagos 233, 242, 246 (n. 1), 250, 253

Camwood (*see* Redwood)
Cannon 43, 148, 171, 175, 332
Canoes 158; Itsekiri, 58, 213, 213 (n. 3),
215, 218, 226, 230, 258; Ijo, 13, 27,
147, 213; Lagos, 226; available at
Boededoe, 147, 149, 161, 171, 324,
326–7, 328; available at Ughoton, 89,
172, 188–9
Cão, Diogo 29
Cape Fermoso 58, 301, 305
Cape Lope Gonçalvez 133, 310
Cape Palmas 101, 307
Cape Verde 54
Capuchins chap. 4, 17–18, 124;
Procurator-General, 115 (*see also*
São Tomé, missions)
Cardamom 162–3, 163 (n. 1)
Carneiro, António (secretary of King
Manuel of Portugal and lord of
Príncipe) 42, 43 (n. 3), 44–5, 47–50,
52–3, 55, 59 (n. 1), 61–2
Carter, Sir Gilbert, Governor of Lagos
278
Casa da Mina 32, 32 (n. 3), 36, 38, 40,
42–3, 66, 74; records, 66 (n. 3)
Castile 24, 26 (n. 1), 68
Cato 197
Cavazzi da Montecuccolu, Fr. G. A.
102 (n. 1), 107 (n. 3)
Cayman Bank 332
Ceremonial, of Benin court 5, 12, 70,
77, 102, 107 (n. 3), 186–7, 255, 270,
346; of chiefs, 90, 203–4, 314; of
Ezomo, 201–2
Chanomi, (Itsekiri chief) 257, 258, 261
Chapman (ship's captain) 206 (n. 3)
Cheetham, Samuel (trader) 260, 261
Chiefs of Benin 4, 5, 11, 14, 18, 40, 104,
162 (n. 2), 205, 219, 223, 237, 251–2,
255, 269–71, 290–1, 293, 314, 325,
328, 333, 345; creation of, 314 (*see
also* Eghaevbo n'Ogbe, Eghaevbo
n'Ore and Enigie)
Chisels (imported) 199
Christian missions 19, 29, 46–50, 52,
69–72, chap. 4, 272, 307–12; reasons
for failure, 120–3
Christianity among the Edo 39, 46, 49,
51–2, 69–70; among Yoruba, 249
Clapperton, Capt. Hugh 240
Clarke, Crawford (trader) 260
Clarke, H. 289
Cloth, of local manufacture 37, 40, 55,
64, 84–5, 93–5, 129–34, 137, 140,
143, 151 (n. 2), 152, 159–60, 165–6,
173, 184, 190, 193 (n. 1), 199, 206–8,

221, 229, 234–5, 237, 322–6, 335–6;
'straw cloths', 189 (n. 1), 206–7;
manufacture, 131, 207; European,
40, 56–7, 59, 62–3, 67, 80,
82, 168, 199, 276, 295, 340;
annebaas, 94 (n. 5), 320; bafts, 208,
320; cambric, 320; canvas, 80, 340;
cholet, 208; cottons, 67, 80, 208,
340; damask, 144, 320; fustian, 40;
gauze, 335–7; gingham, 208 (n. 2);
Haarlem, 97; kannekins, 97, 335;
kerseys, 86, 97; muslin, 210, 219,
335; perpetuanas, 97, 182, 320; says,
97, 320; sheets, 97, 320, 335;
Silesian, 86; studilha, 40; table
cloths, 320; tickings, 97; velvet, 97;
'vinte e quatreno', 67; Ypres, 97;
as unit of value, 57, 62–3, 207–9,
211, 230, 335, 336–7; Indian, 97,
335; brocade, 97; Calicut (calico),
80, 208, 208 (n. 2), 340; Cambay,
40; chintz, 41, 208, 210, 219,
320; Coromandel, 210, 335; muslin,
210; nicanees, 208 (n. 2); Salempor,
320; Surat, 210, 335 (*see also* Linen,
Silk and Satin)
Cocoa 266
Coffee 214, 266
Cola 314
Coles, Alexander (English merchant)
78
Columbin, Fr., of Nantes 100
Commany 143, 147, 320
Compagnie de la Guyane 200, 216
Compagnie d'Owhere et de Benin 216,
220, 222
Company of Royal Adventurers to
Africa 87; reformed, 124
Congo 29, 30, 36 (n. 1), 46, 54, 60–1,
61 (n. 3), 65, 67; missions, 101, 109,
121; Dom Francisco, Congolese chief,
36 (n. 1)
Connah, Graham 3, 11 (n. 3), 188 (n. 2)
'Conte de terre' (*see* Beads)
Copland-Crawford, Major, Vice-consul
280, 281, 283
Copper imported rods, 321; dishes etc.,
98, 144, 340; cauldron for Oba, 68
Coral, beads, 12, 40, 56, 98, 193, 209,
219, 224, 229, 271, 276, 295, 299,
321, 340; pipe coral, 182 (n. 3), 208,
209; Mediterranean, 255 (n. 2)
regalia, of Oba, 12, 18, 223, 224, 270,
292; of Oba's wives, 291; of chiefs,
204, 204 (n. 4), 255, 314; of others,
129, 132, 202 (n. 4), 204, 314

24

Index

Coris 37, 55–6, 60 (n. 3), 62, 64, 67, 85, 88, 187 (n. 4), 295, 301, 302 (*see also* 'Conte de terre')

Corisco 74

Costa da Mina 24, 27, 29, 33, 35 (n. 2), 37, 42, 54, 55, 65–6, 74, 79, 85, 87, 94 (*see also* Gold Coast)

Costume of Oba 41, 207, 292; of Ezomo, 219; of chiefs, 40, 90, 104, 199, 208 (n. 2), 225, 255 (n. 2), 314; of messenger, 202 (n. 4); of executioners, 205; of people, 85

Cotton yarn 159, 164

Court of Equity, Benin River 257–8, 264

Cowries 56–7, 60–1, 63–4, 67, 80, 83, 95, 97, 97 (n. 3), 104, 144, 160, 166, 166 (n. 2), 173, 173 (n. 2), 193, 199, 276, 282 (n. 1), 300–4, 321, 330–1; as ornaments, 314; cowry-room (owa-igho), 202, 202 (n. 1); 'zimbos', 60; 'goats and chickens' units, 60, 61 (n. 3), 302

Cows 187, 315; sacrificial, 314

Coxon (English trader) 267, 275 (n. 2)

Credit trading (trust) 77–8, 130, 137, 139, 140–1, 208, 239 (n. 1); credit offered to English merchants, 77, 130; to Landolphe, 215; agreement on credit between Oba and West India Company, 317, 184; disputes over, 322–3, 325, 328 (*see also* West India Company); for cloth, 130–2, 141, 142–143, 151, 318; for ivory, 131, 133; for gum, 151, 161; for redwood, 151

Crocodiles 314

Crow, Hugh (Liverpool captain engaged in slave trade) 169 (n. 3), 228, 228 (n. 4)

Curamo 180

Customary payments for right to trade 56–7, 130, 173, 173 (n. 3), 184, 191, 191 (n. 1), 198, 207, 211–12, 237, 246, 276, 336

Customs duties, imposed by British 272–273

da Busseto, Fr. Giuseppe-Maria 113

da Collevecchio, Fr. Francesco 115

Dahomey 174 (n. 2), 183, 250, 271

d'Ajaccio, Fr. Angelo Maria 109, 110

da Monteleone, Fr. Francesco 111–14, 118, 126, 131, 134, 135 (n. 2), 146

da Napoli, Fr. Cipriano 115–17

d'Andrade, Fernão (ship's clerk) 298

Danish ships in Benin River 221

Dapper, Olfert 17, 40, 87–8, 88 (n. 1),

89, 90–92, 94, 96, 207, 218

d'Aspra, Fr. Celestino 119, 120, 122

d'Aveiro, João Afonso 29–32, 34

de Alicante, Fr. José 105 (n. 3)

de Barros, Christovão (governor of São Tomé) 311–12

de Barros, João 26, 33, 33 (n. 3), 46, 61, 72

de Barros, Manuel (captain of Príncipe) 311

de Caminha, Alvaro (Captain of São Tomé) 42

de Ceiros, Antonio 47 (n. 1)

de Flotte, le comte (French naval captain) 222

Deghele 257

de Hijar, Fr. Felipe 102 (n. 1), 104, 104 (n. 2), 106–7, 311

Deji of Akure 263

de Jijona, Fr. José 101–2

de la Fosse, Eustache (Flemish merchant) 26 (n. 1)

de la Palma, Willem (Director-General of West India Company) 136

de Loronha, Fernão (Portuguese merchant) 34, 34 (n. 4), 38 (n. 2)

de Marees, Pieter 84, 86–7

de Mello, Fernão (Captain of São Tomé) 42–3

de Mello, Jorge 44 (n. 1)

de Mello Puntoja, José (Brazilian trader) 228 (n. 1)

de Pamplona, Fr. Francisco 101

de Pina, Ruy 30

de Roma, Fr. Giovanni Francesco 109

de Reyke, Jacobus (official of West India Co.) 143, 147, 150, 157–8, 160, 164–5, 318–19

de Sequeira, Ruy 24

Desrud (ship's captain) 199, 203 (n. 2)

de Tolosa, Fr. Alonso 102 (n. 1), 106, 311–12

de Valencia, Fr. Angel 101–2, 102 (n. 1), 103–6, 107, 109, 121, 122, 307

de Vella, Fernão (Edo slave in service of Portuguese) 48 (n. 1)

de Viana, Fr. Bartolomeo 102 (n. 1), 106 (n. 2)

Diare (Itsekiri chief) 231, 244–5, 253, 257

Dias, Bartolomeu 27 (n. 3), 32

di Poggitello, Fr. Illuminato 120

Disease and illness, among Europeans in Benin 32–3, 101, 102, 111, 139, 181, 190–1, 212, 228 (n. 4), 326, 327–8, 331, 333; fever, 32 (n. 5), 78 150, 261,

362

322, 324, 326; yellow fever, 221; small
pox, 197; ulcers, 326–7; syphilis, 98
(n. 2); influenza, 249
Docemo, Oba of Lagos 242
Dogho (Itsekiri chief) 286–7, 290
Dogs 315
do Nascimento, Maria (inhabitant of
São Tomé) 234
D. R. (Dutch trader; possibly Dierick
Ruiters) 85, 85 (n. 1), 86, 126, 181
(n. 2)
Drugs and medicines 265 (n. 2), 333;
sarsaparilla, 98; tamarinds, 225 (n. 1)
Drums 205, 314
Dutch, first contact with Benin 84;
introduce greater variety of merchan-
dise, 95; decline of United Provinces,
165–6; interlopers, 166; in Benin
River in 19th century, 260 (*see also*
West India Company)
Dyames, Fernão (sailor) 300, 302
Dyestuff 159, 199, 222; indigo, 159
(n. 2)

Earthenware, imported European 98
Easton, Acting-Consul 258
Eben (ceremonial swords) 219
Ebrohimi 257, 274–5, 278–9; centre of
salt production, 275, 217 (n. 2)
Edaiken (title of heir apparent in Benin)
10; applied to Olughoton, 30, 199,
199 (n. 2), 200, 218, 222
Eden, Richard 76 (n. 3), 77–8, 79 (n. 1)
Edo, language and people 1, 10, 28, 39,
104, 105 (n. 3), 108, 121, 309; society,
1, 121, 122–3; character of people, 84,
100, 107, 112, 121–2, 131–2, 250–2
Edohen (an Uzama title) 4 (n. 1)
Efenmai 11
Egbini 287 (n. 1), 289
Eghaevbo n'Ogbe, (association of town
chiefs of Benin City) 8–9, 10, 17, 19,
127, 185 (n. 1)
Eghaevbo n'Ore, (association of palace
chiefs of Benin City) 5–6, 8–9, 16, 18–
19, 39, 51, 92, 107, 107 (n. 3), 153
(n. 1), 172, 204, 252, 263
Egharevba, J. U. (Benin historian) 4, 6,
7, 11, 17, 73 (n. 2), 77 (n. 2), 110, 118,
203, 228 (n. 2), 270 (n. 1), 272 (n. 1),
275, 280
Egoro (New Town) 217, 230, 236–7,
278, 344–5
Ehengbuda, Oba of Benin 14, 15, 82, 88
Eholo n'Ire (chieftaincy title) 4 (n. 1)
Ekiti 11, 15, 22–3, 258–9

Elephant-hunters 53
Elet, Jan (official of West India Co.) 180,
182
Elmina 91, 95, 96, 101, 133, 136, 157,
163, 165–7, 180–1, 190, 308, 318, 331,
(*see also* São Jorge da Mina)
Elmina Galley 185, 190 (n. 1)
Emada (Oba's swordbearers) 203, 206,
218, 255, 270, 291, 293, 346
English, interlopers 76, 78–9; trading
with Benin, chap. 3 i, 85, 95, 128,
165 (n. 2), 171–2, 176, 182, 188, 190–1,
193–4, 199, 221, 227–8, 231 (n. 4);
rivalry with Dutch, 84, 87, 90, 148,
149 (n. 2), 260; cloth trade, 93, 95;
language spoken in Benin, 218, 223;
palm oil trade, 235, 237–8, 239–40,
257; 'forward policy', 240, 256, 259
Enigie (title of village chiefs) 21
Envoys from Benin to Portugal 46–8,
56 (n. 3), 72
Erasoyen (chieftaincy title) 262
Erejuwa, Olu 217
Eresoyen, Oba of Benin 21, 192 (n. 1),
197, 202
Eribo (chieftaincy title) 90, 185, 204,
262
Ero (chieftaincy title) 4 (n. 1), 291, 292
Escravos River 26, 26 (n. 5), 27, 215,
221, 339
Esere (chieftaincy title) 6
Esigie, Oba of Benin 13–15, 40, 49
(n. 3), 73, 73 (n. 2)
Esu (Edo deity) 122 (n. 1)
Ethiope River 282 (n. 1)
Etsakor 263
Eunuchs 255, 255 (n. 1), 262
Ewart, Major 282
Ewedo, Oba of Benin 5–8
Ewuakpe, Oba of Benin 118, 118 (n.2),
119
Ewuare, Oba of Benin 7–14, 22 (n. 1),
107 (n. 3), 223 (n. 1)
Exaeve titles 204
Eyinmisaren, Ologbotsere of the Itse-
kiris 217
Ezomo (chieftaincy title) 4 (n. 1), 20,
141 (n. 6), 169, 169 (n. 2), 170, 177–9,
185, 189, 192, 201–4, 204 (n. 3), 211–12,
219–20, 223, 234 (n. 3), 250–1, 254,
256, 262, 263 (n. 1), 288, 291, 294;
Ezomo Ehennua, 168, 201 (n. 2);
Ezomo Odia, 201 (n. 2); Ezomo
Ekenneza, 201 (n. 2); Ezomo Osarogiagbon, 259; Ezomo Omoruyi, 262
(n. 2)

Fans 202 (n. 4), 283
Fante 24, 147 (n. 1)
Fawckner, James (ship's captain) 202 (n. 4), 206, 214 (n. 1), 232, 234 (n. 3), 254 (n. 2)
Fernandes, Francisco (ship's clerk) 304–305
Fernandes, Machim (ship's pilot) 56–9, 61–3, 300–1, 304–6
Fernandes, Valentim 42 (n. 4), 64 (n. 1)
Fernandez, Bastiam (Portuguese factor in Benin) 33, 37, 38, 40, 53
Fernando Po 24, 240
Fernão do Po (Portuguese captain) 26
Fiador 92, 129–32, 135, 141–2, 150, 152–3, 155, 159, 160 (n. 2), 173, 181, 184, 191, 250, 254, 276, 318, 322–3, 325–6, 329 (*see also* Veador)
Firearms 46–7, 49, 52, 68, 132, 200, 209, 211 (n. 3), 213, 225, 258; import of, 22, 114, 148–9, 150, 199, 208 (n. 2), 276, 281, 283, 321; attempted prohibition by Dutch, 148; used in defence of factories, 148, 175, 333; flintlocks, 145, 149 (n. 5), 174–5, 259; flints, 145, 209, 321; matchlocks, 189, 225 (n.1); muskets, 208; pistols, 199, 209 (*see also* Iwoki ward)
Fish 28, 315
Flanders, merchandise 78; glass beads, 80
Flint, Joseph (official of Royal Niger Company) 278
Foodstuffs 58, 64 (n. 1), 81, 315, 341; for factories at Ughoton, 141, 150, 154, 161, 191, 318, 325, 328–9; cost, 166 (n. 2)
Forcados River 27–8, 37, 44, 58, 59 (n. 1), 62, 64–5, 67, 74–5, 236, 257, 261 (n. 1), 263, 264 (n. 1), 267, 300, 305
Franciscans 69
Fraser's Magazine 248, 253
French, interlopers, 68, 71–4; trade with Benin, 68–9, 72, 75, 85, 128, 128 (n. 3), 165, 165 (n. 3), 176, 199, 216, 228 (n. 1); conflict with English, 197, 199, 203; missionary activity, 100 (*see also* Landolphe)
Fruits 220; oranges, 83; plantains, 83; bananas, 315
Frobisher, Martin 76
Fulani jihad 22, 235

Gabon 94, 133, 234, 251, 337
Galvão, António 24

Galway (Gallwey), Henry, (vice-consul, Benin) 206 (n. 4), 249, 263 (n. 2), 266, 266 (n. 2), 267–74, 279–80, 284, 344–8
German trade in Benin River 260
Gin 276, 281
Glasses 80, 206, 342
Goats 220, 315, 325, 326
Gold Coast 77, 137, 139, 149 (n. 3), 151 (n. 2), 221; slaves from, 139, 180 (*see also* Costa da Mina)
Gold trade 24, 26, 35–7, 43–4, 54, 66, 77, 79, 87, 94
Gold in Benin 138, 138 (n. 1), 163–4
Gomes, Fernão (Portuguese merchant) 24
Gonzalez, João (sailor) 300, 301, 306
Governing Council of Benin River 264
Gum 138–42, 147, 150–2, 156, 158–60, 164–5, 170, 179–80, 184, 199, 222, 318, 321–2, 324–30; 'medicinal gum'; 158–9, 159 (n. 1)
Gum arabic 268
Gum copal 80, 268, 271, 277, 347
Gunpowder 68, 145, 149–50, 154, 168, 189, 199, 208 (n. 2), 209, 211, 211 (n. 1), 225 (n. 1), 258, 276, 281, 321, 335

Hair styles 202 (n. 4), 204, 291, 313
Hakluyt, Richard 82
Haly Hutton, H., vice-consul, Benin 273 (n. 2), 344, 346, 347
Hammocks 181 (n. 2), 201, 203, 218, 254
Hanley, Dr. 344, 346
Haring, Hieronimus (Director-General of the West India Company) 142, 145, 316, 321
Harrison, John (ship's captain) 197
Harrison and Company 239, 257
Hatchets 80, 340
Hats and caps *European*, 40, 63, 80, 199, 208–9, 340; *Indian*, 56, 299
Hausas 225; troops of Niger Coast Protectorate, 261, 284, 292
Hemingway and Company 239
Henderson and Company 261
Henry (trading agent) 253, 255
Hertog, Hendrik (official of the West India Co.) 183, 185, 189–94, 194 (n. 2)
Hewitt, Edward, Consul 260–1
Heyman, Michiel (official of the West India Co.) 150–1, 157–8, 159, 161
Hides, exported from Benin 237

Hill, Sir Clement (Senior Clerk, African Dept. of Foreign Office) 286 (n. 4)

Hindoustan 274

Homens grandes (hommes grandes), principal Benin chiefs 153, 185 (n. 1), 187, 203 (n. 4), 204, 325; 'emograns', 205 (n. 1); 'homograns', 255; treaty of 1892, 345

Hoog, Willem (official of the West India Co.) 180 (n. 2), 181–4, 187

Horsfall and Company, 239, 257

Horses 7, 41, 85–6, 181, 200, 245, 259 (n. 3), 314, 315

Horsetails, as symbol of rank 40, 80, 340

Houses and buildings, of Benin City 113 (n. 3), 254–5, 271, 313; of Ezomo, 219; at Boededoe and Arbo, 128 (n. 1); European storehouses, 139, 141, 148, 160–1, 172, 174, 179, 185, 191, 194

Huela 28

Human sacrifice 22, 71, 104–5, 115, 118, 174 (n. 3), 188, 205, 206 (n. 1), 220, 223, 247–50, 268, 272, 277, 280, 282 (n. 1), 290, 292, 309, 347; crucifixion, 9, 247–8, 347

Hutton and Osborne 268 (n. 2)

Huyberts, Jacob (ship's master) 327

Ibiwe, palace association 6

Ibadan 258, 259

Ibos 1, 2, 35; western Ibos, 11, 15

Idah 13–14, 14 (n. 1), 22, 247 (n. 2), 249, 255 (n. 1), 263

Idogbo 2

Ife 258

Igala 1, 8, 14 (n. 1), 131 (n. 2)

Igbirra 1

Iginua 13, 29

Igo, (Edo name for cowries) *see* Cowries

Igo 207, 256

Igueben 245

Ijebu 74, 88, 100, 158, 162, 229, 242, 250, 274, 312; cloth trade, 93, 234

Ijebu-Ode 12

Ijos 1, 13, 21, 27–9, 35, 88, 146, 158, 161–2, 171–2, 174, 176, 184, 191–2, 213–14, 214 (n. 1), 219, 226, 229, 246, 250; attacks on shipping, 146–7, 161, 174, 188 at Arbo; 88

Ikare 11

Ilesha 15, 259

Ilorin 259

Imaguero (wife of Oliha) 14 (n. 1)

Ine Oyenmwen (chieftaincy title) 145, 185

Ingram, Anthony (English merchant) 82–4

Insurance for Benin shipping 235 (n. 3)

Interpreters (faladors) 40, 48, 52, 102–3, 110, 121, 152, 181, 186–7, 191, 197, 202–3, 211, 218, 223, 254 (n. 1), 255, 270, 309, 323, 346

Iron 41; iron bars, 95, 98, 145, 155, 193, 199, 208, 209, 211; cost, 95 (n. 4), 97 (n. 1); corrugated sheeting, 277, 283–4; ironware, 82, 168

Ishan 12, 21, 50, 163, 169, 245, 259, 263, 263 (n. 2)

Itsekiri kingdom (Warri), origin 13, 75; disintegration, 236, 243–4, 249, 312; conflict with Lagos, 226; Portuguese, trade with, 75, 113, 130, 158, 230; Dutch trade with, 88 (n. 3), 130, 213; missions, 72, 75, 109, 111–13, 116, 158 (n. 4), 310–11

Itsekiri people (Iwere) 1, 28, 29, 35, 108 (n. 1), 112, 127, 136, 158, 235, 261; in Benin River, 58–9, 88, 127 (n. 1), 175–6, 186, 197, 213, 217, 228 (n. 1), 230, 232, 236, 244–5, 257–8, 261, 265, 267, 273, 279, 281 (n. 3); relations with Benin, 75, 112 (n. 1), 113, 226, 230–1, 233, 250, 273–5, 280–284, 287; relations with Urhobo, 255 (n. 3), 267, 274, 275; relations with Ijos, 146, 219; attacks on English, 227, 253

Ivbiosakon 259, 263

Ivory trade 37–8, 53, 55–7, 61–2, 64, 67, 80, 82–5, 93, 119, 129, 131 (n. 2), 133–4, 135 (n. 1), 136–8, 140, 142, 145, 147, 153, 162, 164–6, 169, 171, 175, 179–80, 182, 188–90, 192, 196–7, 199, 206, 206 (n. 4), 209, 221, 228 (n. 4), 229, 231, 234–5, 237, 273, 295, 299, 301, 303, 317, 321, 324, 327, 332–3, 335; scrivilios (small tusks), 133–4, 135 (n. 1), 137, 142, 321, 324, 327, 332–3; as measure of value, 142–3, 145; Oba's pre-emptive rights, 206; carving, 4, 12; spoons, 84, 84 (n. 2); ornaments, 314; decoration of shrines, 219, 223, 314

Iwebo association 5–6, 89, 103 (n. 3), 187, 203, 204 (n. 3), 211–12, 223 (n. 1), 262, 280

Iweguae association 6

Iwoki (ward of Benin City) 49 (n. 3)

Iyase (chieftaincy title) 8–9, 15, 17,

Index

19–20; in reign of Ovonramwen, 288, 291; Iyase Ode, 119

Iyatsere (Itsekiri chieftaincy title) 213 (*see also* Okorodudu)

Iy-oba (mother of Oba) 90, 102–3, 106–7, 309–10

Jaja (ruler of Opobo) 22, 264

Jakpa 230–1, 234–6, 239, 245, 257

Jamieson River 283

Jamieson, Robert (Glasgow merchant) 233 (n. 1)

Jaquin 158, 183, 185

Johanna Maria 134

John (João) II, King of Portugal 28–9, 30–3, 33 (n. 3), 35

John III, King of Portugal 36 (n. 1), 69–72

John IV, King of Portugal 311

Johnston, H. H., Consul 244; view on penetration of interior, 264

Jorge, Fernão (Portuguese merchant) 61

Juffrouw Rebecca Maria 331

Junon 222

Kaolin, ceremonial use 313

'King Bernard', (Itsekiri rebel) 214

Knives, imported European 80, 98, 145, 156, 180, 207, 209–10, 321, 331, 335–7, 340

Kosoko, Oba of Lagos 241–3

Kru, carriers to Phillips' party 288

Kulfo 94

Kusei, Olughoton 253

Kwale 282

La Charmante Louise 214

Labedde 73

L'Africaine 199

L'Afrique 216, 221

Lagos (also Eko and Onim) 14–15, 72, 157–8, 180 (n. 2), 226, 228 (n. 4), 229, 232, 234, 238, 240, 242, 253 (n. 3), 266 (n. 2), 293; expedition to Benin River, 225–6

Lagos Colony and Protectorate 241–3, 261–2, 263, 266, 278, 282, 285

Lamps, palm-oil 203

Lander, John & Richard 240

Landolphe, J. F. (French sea-captain and merchant) 172 (n. 5), 181 (n. 2), 194 (n. 4), 198–228, 229, 236 (n. 1), 249, 254–5; memoirs, 198–9; plans for Ughoton factory, 199–200, 203, 212, 218; Benin River project, 216–17;

visits to Ode Itsekiri, 215, 217; establishment at Bobi, 217, 220–2, 224–7; relations with Itsekiris, 212–14, 227; hostility to English, 199, 226; destruction of his factory, 227

Lane, Arthur, (ship's captain) 196 (n. 2)

La Negresse 200, 211–12, 214

La Petite Charlotte 216, 221, 226

Lead, shot 98, 209, 210; bars, 210, 335

Lecky, A.D.C. 282

Legrand, Fredrik 151–5, 158, 160 (n. 2), 161; Journal, 322–30

Legroing, Lt. (French naval officer) 200 (n. 1), 201 (n. 1), 206 (n. 4), 208 (n. 2), 218 (n. 2), 222–4

Linen 40–1, 56, 62–4, 82, 85, 97, 144, 208, 210, 295, 299, 303, 304, 320, 340; plathilios, 144 (n. 4), 173, 320, 332, 334

Lion 76–8

Lisbon 30, 46, 48, 53, 109, 110, 113 (n. 3), 310–12, 335, 338; slave market, 36, 66; earthquake, 66 (n. 3)

Liverpool 196–7, 200, 206 (n. 3), 227–8, 228 (n. 4), 232, 235

Livingstone, Charles (Consul) 257

Locke, Vice-consul 282, 284, 288

Loebo 89, 205 (n. 3)

London, merchants trading to Benin 76, 82, 84

Looms 207

Lopes, João (sailor) 300, 305–6

Lopes, Duarte (Portuguese factor in Benin) 33, 37 (n. 1), 40

Lopes Correa, Fernão (captain of São Jorge da Mina) 36 (n. 1)

Louis XVI, King of France 216

Lourenço, Gregorio (Edo interpreter) 49, 51–2, 56, 69–70, 299

Lourenço, João (ship's master) 300–1, 305–6

Luanda, Dutch in 86

Lucas, Gregorio 228 (n. 1)

Mabbor (Mobor, Meiborg) 112–13, 126–7, 127 (n. 1), 128, 135, 137

Macdonald, C. M., commissioner to Oil Rivers, 1888 264–5, 268; Commissioner and Consul-General, 1891–1895, 265–6, 272, 279–80

MacTaggart, (agent of Royal Niger Company) 278–9, 283

Mahin 14, 65, 67–8, 73

Maize 191, 315; maize beer, 193 (n. 2)

Malabar coast 276

Malagetta Coast (Grain Coast) 77, 133, 307
Malagetta pepper 31, 157
Manillas 40, 42, 53, 55, 57, 63-4, 67, 95, 97, 144, 199, 295, 301-4, 340; brass, 86, 97 (n. 2); copper, 40, 67, 80, 82, 86; Flemish manilla, 61; cost, 95 (n. 4), 97; as decoration, 314
Manuel, King of Portugal 33 (n. 3), 41-3, 45, 47, 49, 50 (n. 1), 55, 59 (n. 2), 61, 71
Marchione, Bartolomeo (Florentine merchant living in Lisbon) 34
Marriage customs 313-14
Martinique 165
Mary, Queen of England 79
Matoso, Gil (factor at São Jorge da Mina) 36 (n. 1)
Mats, manufactured in Benin 58, 64, 84, 186, 303-4
Mbona 279
Mendes, Jorge (ship's pilot) 300-1, 305
Mercadors (see Traders)
Messengers of Oba (uk-oba, passadors) 78, 155, 174, 181, 200, 202 (n. 4), 204, 207, 222, 250, 262, 276, 283, 291, 324, 326, 329
Middelburg 214
Miller Brothers 268 (n. 2), 277
Millet 167
Minas 193-4
Mirrors 80, 98, 199, 210, 326, 335-7, 342
Mockler-Ferryman, A. F. 273 (n. 1)
Moloney, C. A., Governor of Lagos 268 (n. 5), 262 (n. 1)
Monkeys 314-15
Monopoly of trade, *exercised by Oba of Benin* 268, 276; modified to right of pre-emption, 153, 184; palm oil and kernels, 273, 277; gum copal, 277; male slaves, 168, 169 (n. 2), 334; pepper, 38, 79, 159, 339
by King of Portugal, 68; pepper, 38 granted to Compagnie d'Owhere, 216; granted to English chartered companies, 87; Dutch efforts to secure monopoly, 140-2, 147-8; French efforts to secure monopoly, 203, 222, 224
Moor, Ralph, Commissioner and Consul-General 275, 277-83, 285, 287, 290, 292-4
Mossi 5
Mouree 321
Mouree 327

Munnickhoven, Jacobus (official of the West India Co.) 165-70, 197
Musical instruments 18, 205, 291, 314

Nagtegaal 133-4
Nana (Itsekiri chief) 231, 244, 258, 261; as trader, 267, 274, 275, 279; and Protection Treaty, 1884, 259, 264; and Macdonald, 1888, 265, 266 (n. 2); defeated and exiled, 22, 262 (n. 2), 275, 278, 280, 287, 293
Nana Creek (previously Ijebu Creek) 58, 215
Nantes 199, 214, 222
Native Council, created 1897 284, 291, 293
Navigation, in Bights and rivers 26-7, 42-3, 54, 56, 76, 79, 81, 133, 148, 158-9, 169, 212, 215, 221, 235, 339, 342
New Town (*see* Egoro)
Niger Coast Protectorate 265-6, 278-9; forces of, 284-5, 290
'Niger Districts' Protectorate 261
Niger River 2, 14-15, 262, 264, 278
Nupe, 8, 11, 14, 15, 22, 94, 235, 245, 259, 263
Nuyts, Pieter (Director-General of West India Company) 136

Oba of Benin 5, 7, 14-18, 21, 71, 77, 98, 107 (n. 3), 249-50, 299, 316, 319; insignia, 31; Oba's council, 205, 224
and European trade, 39, 44-5, 53, 63, 77-8, 83, 88-90, 92, 129, 140, 164, 166-7, 173, 189, 194, 202, 218, 223, 229, 237, 251, 255, 304, 323, 325, 328, 339-40; and trust, 141-3, 151, 184, 189, 193; and missionaries, 49-50, 51, 69-70, 101-5, 107, 110, 113-121
Obadesagbon (chieftaincy title) 288
Obaduagbon (chieftaincy title) 262
Obakhavbaye, (chieftaincy title) 280 (n. 1), 287-8, 293
Obanosa Oba of Benin 229
Obaraye (chieftaincy title) 262
Obarisiagbon (chieftaincy, title) 262
Obaseki (chieftaincy title) 287 (n. 1), 291-2
Obasoyen (chieftaincy title) 185
Obayuwana (chieftaincy title) 288
Obazelu (chieftaincy title) 262
Obiariku 282 (n. 1)
Ockers, Gerrit (official of the West India Company) 170-2; letter from Ughoton, 331-4

Ode Itsekiri (Ale Iwere) 75, 88 (n. 3), 108, 112, 120, 149 (n. 2), 176, 215, 217, 227, 229, 235–6, 244, 253, 257; burial customs, 244 (n. 1)
Oere 58–9, 299, 305, 313
Ogbewekon (brother and rival of Adolo) 245
Ogedengbe (chief of Ilesha) 259
Oghene (Ogane) 7, 7 (n. 1), 14, 31–2, 72
Ogheye (Fish Town) 237
Ogiso 4, 6 (n. 1)
Oguola, Oba of Benin 7–8
Ohen, Oba of Benin 8
Ohenolokun, chief of Igo 207, 256
Oil Rivers Protectorate, Johnston's report on, 1888, 264; and Macdonald, 264–5; becomes Niger Coast Protectorate, 265; boundary, 266
Oil rivers 240
Oke Igbo, trade route 22, 258
Okeluhen, Ejimo of 119
Okorodudu, Iyatsere of the Itsekiris 213–15, 218, 226, 236 (n. 1)
Okpara 267
Okro 222
Oliha (chieftaincy title) 4 (n. 1), 14 (n. 1)
Olobe 217
Ologboshere (chieftaincy title) in reign of Ovonramwen 288–9, 293
Ologbotsere (chieftaincy title of the Itsekiris) 217, 257
Olokun (Edo deity) 89, 202, 205–7, 237, 250, 253
Olomu, chief of Ebrohimi 257–8, 260
Olu of the Itsekiris 112, 115, 146, 175, 185, 212–13, 214 (n. 1), 222, 230, 235 (n. 1), 236–7, 244; and missions, 75, 101, 108, 110, 113, 186, 231 (n. 3), 311–12; and Landolphe, 214–16, 217, 227
Olua, Oba of Benin 13
Olughoton, chief of Ughoton 13, 30–2, 39, 41, 56, 130, 199, 253–4, 299
Omakou 180 (n. 2)
Omoregboma (guide to Phillips' party) 288–9
Ondo 258, 263
Oni of Ife 7 (n. 1), 270
Onim (Aunis) (18th century name of Lagos) 225 (n. 2), 230, 234
Opmeer 134
Oranmiyan (founder of Benin dynasty) 4, 7 (n. 3), 8, 10, 107 (n. 3)
Ordeals 250
Order of Christ 69

Orhogbua, Oba of Benin 14, 73, 73 (n. 2 & 3), 77 (n. 2)
Orogu Creek 241
Orokhorho (brother and rival of Ovonramwen) 262–3
Osa (Osanobua, high god of the Edo) 122 (n. 1)
Osemwede, Oba of Benin 231, 233, 241, 244–5, 247, 252, 253 (n. 3), 259
Osia (chieftaincy title) 262
Osiers 302
Osodin (chieftaincy title) 6, 44–5, 51, 56, 62, 90, 185, 204, 244, 299; in reign of Ovonramwen, 289, 291
Osuma (chieftaincy title) 249 (n. 3)
Otsodi (Itsekiri chieftaincy title) 217
Ovenama Creek 128
Ovonramwen, Oba of Benin (named Idugbowa before accession) 262; 22, 243 (n. 2), 248, 250, 252, 262–3, 264, 268–72, 274 (n. 1), 276, 278, 280–6, 289–90, 344–7; flight from Benin City, 290; surrender, 291–3; exile, 294; trial, 287
Owo 11, 15
Oyo 8, 11, 14–15, 18, 22, 225, 234, 249, 258–9
Ozolua, Oba of Benin 12–14, 30, 35, 46, 50, 81
Ozuere, Oba of Benin 118–19, 163

Pacheco Pereira, Duarte 26–7, 28, 30 (n. 1), 32 (n. 5), 33, 35, 37, 40, 60, 71, 89 (n. 1)
Palisot de Beauvois, A. M. F. J. (French naturalist) 159 (n. 2), 199 (n. 2), 203 (n. 3), 213 (n. 3), 217–21, 249, 251
Palace of Oba of Benin 5, 16, 18, 77, 104–5, 113 (n. 3), 205, 223, 248–9, 254, 277, 309, 313; destroyed, 19, 290
Palm kernels 64, (n. 1), 257, 268, 273, 277
Palm oil 56, 58, 84, 133, 136, 167, 175, 199, 203, 221, 231 (n. 2), 232, 235–6, 237, 239, 243, 257, 273, 277, 278, 281, 297, 303–4, 315, 326; Urhobo producers, 246, 266–7; industrial uses, 235
Palm wine 83, 86, 220, 314
Palmerston, Lord 240
Pano (paan, panes pagne, pawn), Portuguese for 'cloth' 57, 132, 207, 230, 235 (n. 1), 246 (n. 2)
Papacy 30, 41, 99, 101, 115–16

Pepper trade 31–3, 38–9, 42, 68, 69 (n. 1), 74, 77–85, 93, 95, 133, 157, 159, 162, 164, 231 (n. 2), 339, 340, 342

Penteado, António Anes (Portuguese seaman) 76–8

Pernambuco, Dutch in 86, 93

Perou 216–17, 221

Pewter 98

Phillips, J. R. Acting Commissioner and Consul-General 22 (n. 2), 277 (n. 2), 281 (n. 3), 283–8

Pietersen, Claas (ship's master) 320

Pigs 314

Pimentel, Alvaro (Portuguese merchant) 38 (n. 2)

Pinnock, James (palm oil trader) 257; and Company, 268 (n. 2), 275 (n. 2)

Pinto, Lourenço (ship's captain) 113 (n. 3)

Pires, Duarte 49–51, 85

Pires, Gonçalo (sailor) 42 (n. 4)

Pistorius, Peter (official of West India Company) 173–5, 176 (n. 1)

Plymouth 78

Popo states 74

Porters 63, 82, 200, 218, 222, 251; payments to, 57, 207, 211, 303, 344

Portsmouth 76

Portuguese, trade with Benin and the rivers chap. 2, 119, 129, 134, 137, 144, 149, 172, 176, 198–9, 215, 221, 230, 234, 234 (n. 3); at Arbo, 126, 172; at Boededoe, 132; conflict with Dutch, 84, 86–7, 128, 141 (n. 4), 145–6; conflict with French, 68–73; conflict with English, 84 (n. 3); and trust, 130; Council for Overseas Affairs, 117, 120; attitude to Spanish and Italian missions, 107–11, 117, 120, 123

Portuguese language, among Edo 50, 77, 83, 92, 102–4, 187, 211, 309

Pranger, Jacob (Director-General of West India Company) 178–9

Presents, given to Oba of Benin 32, 41, 45, 56, 63, 80, 143, 172, 182, 185, 187, 219, 229, 243, 254, 261, 271, 277 (n. 2), 284, 299, 309, 342, 344, 347; to chiefs, 40, 44, 103, 160, 185, 204 (n. 3); to trade officials, 41, 56–7, 62, 130, 211; to envoys, 47; to Chief Anthony, 326; to Olu of Itsekiris, 218; given by the Oba, 36, 36 (n. 1), 90, 206, 229

Prester John 29, 31–2, 50, 312

Prices 171, 210, 299, 332, 334–8; procedures for fixing, 90, 96–7, 159, 207, 209, 274; of beads, 144; of cloths, 94–5,

97, 144 (n. 4); of coris, 62, 64; of gum, 138, 142–3, 150, 156, 160; of guns, 145; of gunpowder, 211 (n. 1); of ivory, 53, 62, 133–4, 209, 299, 301, 332; of locally-made planks and nails, 161 (n. 1); of manillas, 144; of palm oil, 235, 235 (n. 1); of pepper, 164, 340; of provisions, 57–8, 318; of redwood, 142–3; of slaves, 40, 44–5, 53, 55–6, 59–61, 63, 65, 67, 167, 198, 209–10, 211–12, 295, 299, 301–2, 332, 335–7; of tobacco, 145; of yarn, 164

Price-lists 134 (n. 2), 142, 208–9, 210–211; marktbrief, 96–7

Primrose 76–7

Príncipe 24, 27 (n. 3), 42, 43 (n. 3), 49, 67, 128–9, 198, 214, 301, 335 (n. 1); and slave trade, 36, 44–5, 52, 129, 168, 227, 228 (n. 1); and pepper trade, 38, 67; trade with Itsekiris, 75; and missions, 51, 106, 108, 310–11

Protection Treaty, with Benin, 1892 265, 268–72, 278, 281, 344, 346–7; with Itsekiris, 261

Provisioning of ships 57–8, 64, 91, 167, 169, 185, 231 (n. 2), 296, 304–5, 308, 341

Punch, Cyril (trader) 201, 205 (n. 2), 207, 217 (n. 2), 248–51, 262, 263 (n. 1), 267, 268, 276

Punishments, for losing insignia of office 129; for theft, 140, 317; for harming foreigners, 126; for murder, 132, 175; for divulging state secrets, 249

Punitive expedition proposed by Macdonald 272; by Galway, 274; by Moor, 278, 283, 285; by Phillips, 283–5; expedition of 1897, 23, 290

Raems, Abram (official of the West India Company) 185–6, 188–94

Rainbow 197–8

Ramos River 27, 263, 264 (n. 1), 306

Rawson, Admiral Sir H. (commander of punitive expedition 1897) 290 (n. 1)

Razors 199, 209–10, 335

Redwood (camwood) trade 55–6, 138, 140–3, 151, 170–1, 173, 175–6, 179–80, 184, 231 (n. 2), 295, 318, 321, 325, 331–3

Religion of Edo 32–3, 71, 100, 103, 107–8, 113 (n. 1), 114–15, 119, 121–3, 205; house shrines, 169 (n. 2), 223, 314; ceremonies, 51, 105, 315; (*see also* Rituals)

Richard of Arundell 82–4

Rio Primeiro 26

Rio Real 65

Rituals, of the Oba of Benin 6–7, 14, 16, 20, 51, 71, 104–5, 122, 172, 187–8, 205, 220, 223, 247, 249, 270, 284, 291, 313, 325; burial, 51 (n. 1), 135, 226 (n. 2); washing of feet, 202; of the Oghene, 31–2 (*see also* Agwe and Ugie-ivie)

Road between Ughoton and Benin City 201, 218, 254, 271, 289, 313, 344–5, 347

Rodrigues, Christovão (ship's clerk) 301, 304–5

Rodrigues, Francisco (ship's pilot) 76

Roth, Dr. F. L. (Surgeon to 1897 expeditionary force) 291, 294

Roupell, Captain, E. P. (Resident, Benin City) 291–2

Royal African Company, factories in Benin River 124; ships trading in Benin River, 95, 171, 196, 332

Royal Gold Coast Gazette 232, 236

Royal Niger Company 22, 263, 264 (n. 1), 265 (n. 1), 278–9; protectorate, 278, 285

Rubber 268, 277

Ruiters, Dierick (Dutch seaman and author) 86

Rum 145, 206, 254, 321

Rumbold and Company 197 (n. 3)

Sacra Congregazione de Propaganda Fide 99–101, 102 (n. 1), 109–11, 113 (n. 3), 114–15, 117, 119–20, 122, **307**

Salisbury, Marquess of 282, 284–5

Salt, local 28, 73 (n. 3), 180, 211, 217, 275–6; imported, 167, 180, 224, 335, 338

Salt Town 217

Santa Cruz de Mayo 63 (n. 1)

Santa Maria da Conceição 58 (n. 1), 300, 304–5, 306

Santiago, Cape Verde 312

Santo Antonio 66, 67–8

São João 62, 63–4

São Jorge da Mina 26 (n. 4), 27 (n. 3), 29–30, 32, 35–6, 39, 43–5, 48 (n. 1), 52, 54, 67, 79; taken by Dutch, 1637, 86 (*see also* Elmina)

São Miguel 56–8, 59, 61, 62, 295–306

São Tomé 24, 26 (n. 4), 29, 33–5, 42, 52, 59 (n. 1 & 2), 61–2, 64 (n. 1), 67, 74–5, 120, 128, 198, 233–4, 297 (n. 1), 298, 335 (n. 1); attacked by French, 68, 75; taken and lost by Dutch, 86; church, 51, 59 (n. 2); hospital, 59 (n. 2), 302 (n. 5); duties levied on trade, 56, 336; slave trade, 35–6, 39, 42, 44–5, 54–5, 65–6, 129, 168, 210, 229, 231; pepper trade, 38, 67, 69; ivory trade, 53, 67, 129; missions, 19, 51, 69, 71, 100, 109, 111, 113, 117, 120–1, 311–12

Sapele 267, 274, 277, 281, 290

Sapoba 283

Saws 80, 340

Scissors 209

Seamen, from São Tomé and Príncipe 54, 335; wages and allowances, 54 (n. 2), 56, 59; mortality among, 78, 81, 83, 84, 91, 131–2, 134, 212, 229, 335, 341; slaves employed as, 302

Senat and Company 227–8, 228 (n. 1)

Seville 101, 121, 307

Shama 101, 308

Shaw, Randall 79–81, 83, 159 (n. 1), 339–43

Sheep 218, 223, 315

Sheepskins, imported from Europe 98

Ships and boats, employed in Benin trade 38 (n. 2), 39 (n. 1), 42, 55, 76, 91, 101, 129, 165, 170, 184, 211, 228 (n. 1), 229; barques, 182, 196 (n. 2); barquentine, 182; caravels, 24, 26, 39, 43–4, 77; corvettes, 216; mail steamers, 239; pinnaces, 77, 79, 82, 167 (n. 3); schooners, 233 (n. 1), 234; sloops, 165 (n. 2), 188, 221; snow, 134; yachts, 128, 133, 147

Sierra Leone 24, 84 (n. 2), 250

Silks and satins 41, 56, 67, 144, 182, 208, 219, 229, 254, 271, 299; Indian, 41

Slaves 29, 36 (n. 1), 45, 46, 48, 60 (n. 1), 168–9, 169 (n. 3); sources of, 35, 168, 169 (n. 3), 197–8; domestic slaves in Benin, 45, 65, 201, 291; Urhobo slaves, 273; runaway slaves, 139, 176–9, 181–2, 184; risings, 165, 169 (n. 3), 197; sickness and death among, 169, 214, 216, 300; burial at sea, 59, 297, 300–1, 306; branding, 55–9; peça da India, 336 (n. 1); in service of Dutch, 139, 141, 147, 158, 163, 166, 174–6, 178, 180, 192, 193, 316; escheat of property to Oba, 178

Slave Trade, Portuguese 24, 26, 29, 31, 33, 35–7, 42–3, 44–5, 52, 54–9, 63–5, 80, 87, 120, 129, 168, 176–7, 209, 229, 231–2, 295–6, 299, 301–2, 334, 335–7;

English, 168, 171, 176–7, 182, 196–7, 200, 228, 231, 332, 334; Dutch, 86, 92–3, 130, 163, 167–70, 176–8, 197, 209; French, 165, 168, 170, 199, 209–210, 214, 221–2, 227–8; on Costa da Mina, 26, 29, 35, 39, 42–3, 55, 66; with Itsekiris, 75, 197–8; trans-atlantic, 66, 68, 129, 169, 197, 227; abolition of, 231–3, 235
Slave Rivers 26–7, 29, 33–6, 42–3
Soap 175, 180
Sobrinho, João 49, 50
South Carolina 197
Spain, trade with Guinea 307–8; trade with Benin, 128; abolition of slave trade, 231; and missions, chap. 4. i, 101, 109–10
Staffs 151, 218, 223
Stewart and Douglas (Liverpool firm) 239, 257, 276
Stokes, Lt. Comm. 253, 255
Succession, to throne 4, 8, 10–11, 16–17, 19–20, 31, 119, 244, 262, 313; to titles, 314; rule of primogeniture, 1
Sugar 224, 304; plantations of São Tomé, 39, 44, 54–5, 75; Pernambuco, 86; West Indian, 214
Swainson, J. A. (trader) 267 (n. 2), 269, 344, 346–7
Swords 199, 209

Takoradi 101, 307
Talbot, P. A. 73 (n. 2), 243 (n. 2)
Tamarind 225
Teebu 89 (n. 1)
Theft 113 (n. 3) from Europeans, 140, 155, 174, 251, 317, 329; from vessels, 52
Timbuctoo 225
Titles, chieftaincy in Benin 5, 9, 18, 22 (n. 1), 204, 205 (n. 1), 252; in Lagos, 14
Tobacco 228, 229, 314; Portuguese, 145, 321; Dutch, 145, 189; French, 199, 207–8; tobacco boxes, 210, 335; tobacco pipes, 207, 208 (n. 2)
Torre do Tombo 66 (n. 3)
Trade embargo, placed by Oba 45, 191, 193, 261, 268 (n. 3 & 5), 271, 280–1, 283, 347; on male slaves, 45, 58–9, 65, 67, 168; imposed by Dutch, 148–9, 151–5, 161–2, 175–6, 323, 325; imposed by Portuguese, 74
Traders of Benin 89, 90, 95–6, 124, 131, 190, 252 (n. 4), 276, 323, 325, 328; resident in waterside villages, 92; and cloth trade, 94, 131; free-born Edo, 130; women, 251, 314; mercadors, 129–30, 131; associations of, 258
Trading practices, of Benin 44–5, 62, 69, 77–8, 79–80, 82–3, 88–90, 92, 95–6, 129–31, 140–1, 151, 153, 170–1, 173–4, 181–2, 200, 207, 209–10, 229–30; of Portuguese, 24, 32, 34, 40, 44, 56–8, 62, 129, 295–8, 336; of Dutch, 85–6, 93, 96–7, 137, 169–70, 316–18, 329–30; of French, 228 (n. 1); of Itsekiris, 275; illicit trade of West India Company officials, 180–1, 182
Trial of Oba and chiefs, 1897 292–3
Tribute, paid to Benin 246, 347; by Itsekiris, 244, 275; by Lagos, 14, 241–2, 243 (n. 2)
Trust (*see* Credit Trading)

Udo 3
Ugboha 245 (n. 4)
Ugbini 262
Ughoton 13, 88–9, 91, 229, 237, 246, 250 (n. 1), 254, 255, 267–9, 274, 276–7, 282–3, 287–8, 290, 313, 344; and Portuguese, 30, 32–3, 36–9, 42–3, 56–8, 62, 90 (n. 1), 127, 172, 200, 204 (n. 4), 207, 229, 234 (n. 3), 299–300, 303–4; and English, 77, 79, 82–3, 171, 172, 176, 251, 261, 339; and French, 165, 199–200, 205, 212, 214, 218, 222, 227; and Dutch, chap. 5 (2–6), 128, 138, 212, 317–18, 322–30, 331–4; and Itsekiris, 175, 261 (n. 2); missionaries at, 101–3, 106, 114, 309; chiefs of, 207, 211; centre of Olokun cult, 206, 250, 253 (n. 3); markets, 90, 313
Ughoton Creek 127, 200, 267, 283, 288
Ugie-ivie ceremony (coral feast) 115, 223, 270
Ugie-erhoba (ceremony for Oba's father) 188
Ugo 21
Uhen 119
Uk-oba (*see* Messengers)
Uko (untitled palace rank) 204
Umbrella 201
Umutu 282 (n. 1)
Ureju Bay 79, 200, 211–14, 227
Urhobos (Subou, Sobo) 28; oil pro-ducers, 246, 257, 266, 274; pepper producers, 38; relations with Benin, 246, 255 (n. 3), 266–7, 273, 282 (n. 1); relations with the Itsekiris, 255 (n. 3), 267, 274–5; relations with British, 266–7; relations with Royal Niger

Index

Urhobos—*contd.*
  Company, 278; as sacrificial victims, 249 (n. 3)
Uria 267
Uromi 12, 50
Uso, (chieftaincy title) 288, 293
Usonigbe 282 (n. 1)
Uwangue, (chieftaincy title) 6, 16–17, 18 (n. 1), 51, 56 (n. 2), 62, 83, 90, 103, 185, 204, 262–3; in reign of Ovonramwen, 280
Uwangue, (chieftaincy title of Itsekiris) 230–1; Uwangue Uwankun, 231 (n. 2), 236, 243–4, 257
Uwepa 247
Uzama, (senior order of Benin chiefs) 3–4, 5, 8, 10, 205 (n. 1)
Uzebu 201, 202 (n.3), 219
Uzia 163

Valckenier, Pieter (official of West India Company) 331
van der Venne, Jan (official of West India Company) 136
van Essen, Willem (official of West India Company) 177–82
van Marken, Jan (official of West India Company) 184
van Naerssen, Revixit (official of West India Company) 139–45, 156, 158, 160–4, 189 (n. 3), 319–20
van Nyendael, David (official of West India Company) 115, 118, 124, 126–35, 146, 150, 193 (n. 2), 207, 211, 276
Veador 41, 56, 82–3, 204–5, 207, 209, 211, 214–15, 218–20, 229, 299, 333; (*see also* Fiador)
Veloz 232
vice-consulate for Benin, established 1891: 265–6
Vriesland 151

Wars, waged by Benin 7, 9, 11–13, 15, 22–3, 35, 45–6, 49–50, 52–3, 81, 163, 205 (n. 1), 259, 340; civil wars, 18–19, 20, 21, 114, 118–19, 135, 145, 150, 164 (n. 1), 168–9, 176, 198, 245, 252, 254, 259 (n. 3), 263 (n. 2); Itsekiri-

Benin wars, 113, 127 (n. 1), 186, 213, 230; Yoruba wars, 258–9, 263
Warri 108 (n. 1), 268, 277
Warri River 215
Wax 129, 133, 137
Welsh, James (ship's master) 82, 84, 189 (n. 1)
West Africa Squadron 231, 240
West India Company, (Chap. 5) formation of first company, 86; formation of second company, 87; records of, 87 (n. 1), 124, 133, 152 (n. 3), 196; at Fort Nassau, 93; treaty with Benin, 1715, 136, 139–41, 160, 177, 179, 185, 316–19; treaty of 1735, 184–5; treaty of 1737, 194, 224; and trust, 130; rivalry with other Europeans, 91, 128, 140, 148, 160, 165, 176, 189, 308, 318, 332–3; attempts to fortify river mouth, 128, 137, 148; and cloth trade, 93–5, 96–7; disputes with African peoples, 126–7, 137, 161–2, 174–6, 178; relations with Itsekiris, 88 (n. 3), 130, 175, 212; relations with Ijos, 147, 174, 184; decline, 163, 166, 174, 194–5; loss of monopoly, 179, 183
West India Regiment 290
West Indies, Spanish 66, 129; Santo Domingo, 66, 214, 216, 222; San Juan, 66; English, 196; French, 199
Whydah (Fida) 158, 166–7, 234 (n. 3), 240, 321
Wine 86, 206, 224
Wives, of Oba 6, 18–19, 107 (n. 3), 187, 291, 313
Woodcarving, craft in Benin, 4; food bowl, 64; on shrines, 202, 223, 314
Wrestling 270
Wyndham, Thomas (merchant and sea-captain) 76–9, 82

Yams 57–8, 64, 83, 167, 172 (n. 5), 185, 191, 213, 215–16, 218, 220, 303–4, 315, 325, 326
Yard, customary 299
Yorubas 1, 3, 4, 14, 15, 22, 158, 225, 249, 250, 258–9, 264, 278; 'Licomin' and 'Ulkami', 100; and Boededoe, 128, 171

The Ibadan History Series

General Editor K. O. DIKE PH.D.

CHRISTIAN MISSIONS IN NIGERIA 1841-1891

The Making of a New Élite

by J. F. A. AJAYI, Professor of History, University of Ibadan

The first major study of Christian missionary activity in Nigeria, which also touches on Sierra Leone, Ghana and Dahomey. In discussing every aspect of the missions' work and its effects, the author stresses the emergence of a new élite as their most crucial contribution to Nigerian history.

Contents: Christianity and Civilisation; The Return of the Exiles; Missionaries, Traders, and Consuls; The Mission and the State; Civilisation around the Mission House; Towards Selfgovernment in Church and State; Bishop Crowther, 1864–77; The Turning of the Tide. Appendix. Bibliography. Index.

Demy 8vo   xvi + 317 pages   Maps, Plates, Cased 42s net

THE ZULU AFTERMATH

A Nineteenth-Century Revolution in Bantu Africa

by J. D. OMER-COOPER, Professor of History, University of Zambia

A detailed study of the factors involved in the emergence of the militaristic Zulu Kingdom and its far-reaching consequences in early nineteenth-century central and southern Africa.

Contents: Bantu South Africa before the Mfecane; The Zulu Kingdom; The Birth of the Swazi Nation; Soshangane and the Empire of Gaza; The Ngoni Invasion of East Central Africa; The Invasion of the Highveld by Mpangazita and Matiwane; Moshesh and the Basuto Nation; The Career of Sebetwane and the History of the Kololo; Mzilikazi and the Ndebele; The Devastation of Natal and the Flight to the South; The History of the Fingo People; The Mfecane in the History of South and East Central Africa. Bibliography. Index.

Demy 8vo   xiv + 208 pages   Map, Plates, Cased 40s net

THE MISSIONARY IMPACT ON MODERN NIGERIA
1842-1914

A Political and Social Analysis

by E. A. AYANDELE, Department of History, University of Ibadan

The emphasis in this work is on the reactions of various sections of the African community—chiefs, educated Africans, ordinary people and slaves—to missionary activity and also to other agencies linked with it, in particular the colonial administration.

Contents: The Beginnings, 1842–1875; Missionary Enterprise and the Pacification of Yoruba-land, 1875–1900; The Missions and 'Southern' Nigerian Politics and Society, 1875–1900; The Triumph of Gin; The Missionary Impact on Society. Bibliography. Index.

Demy 8vo   xx + 393 pages   Maps, Plates, Cased 50s net

THE SOKOTO CALIPHATE

by MURRAY LAST, Northern History Research Scheme, Ahmadu Bello University, Zaria

An account, based largely on nineteenth-century Arabic documents from Sokoto, of the origins and history of the caliphate until the coming of the British in 1903. It includes, in particular, a study of the rôle of the vizierate in maintaining the administrative and the spiritual position of the caliphate.

Contents: The Establishment of Dār al Islām in Sokoto 1754–1817: 1168–1232 (The Community; The Jihad; The Early Caliphate); The Maintenance of Dār al Islām in Sokoto 1817–1903: 1232–1320 (The Consolidation of the Caliphate 1817–1859: 1232–1276; The Composition of the Caliphate; The Period of Security and Settlement 1859–1903: 1276–1320); The Vizierate in Sokoto 1804–1903: 1218–1320 (The Viziers, The work of the Viziers); Concluding Remarks. Bibliography. Index. Genealogies.

Demy 8vo   lxxxii + 280 pages   Maps, Plates, Cased 55s net

BRITAIN AND THE CONGO QUESTION 1885–1913

by S. J. S. COOKEY, Department of History, The University, Nsukka

Beginning from the emergence of the Congo Free State under the private rule of Leopold II of Belgium, this book examines Belgian interests and the consequences for the Congolese. The origins, motives and organisation of the Congo Reform movement in Britain are revealed for the first time, and its influence on British and Belgian diplomacy.

Contents: Early Evidence on Congo Maladministration; Origins of British Intervention; The Casement Inquiry and its Aftermath; The Congo Commission of Inquiry and the Royal Manifesto; International Reactions on the Eve of Annexation; the Belgian Solution; Non-Recognition; Recognition. Appendices. Bibliography. Index.

Demy 8vo   xvi + 340 pages   Map, Cased 45s net

In Preparation

NIGER DELTA RIVALRY

Itsekiri-Urhobo Relations and the European Presence 1884–1936

by OBARO IKIME, Department of History, University of Ibadan

A study of the coastal Itsekiri people and their hinterland neighbours, the Urhobo. Traditionally the two groups supplied each other's economic needs, but the author shows how Itsekiri commercial contact with Europeans at the coast gradually gave them an advantage over the Urhobo; and how the advent of British rule, the attempt to force the two groups into the same political and judicial institutions, deepened the tension between them—a tension which remains a political factor today.

Contents: Introduction—Indigenous Antecedents; Early European Activities and Itsekiri-Urhobo Relations, 1485–1883; The Régime of Chief Nana, 1884–1894; The British Penetration of Urhoboland, 1891–1914; The Native Court System and the Career of Chief Dogho, 1900–1925; The Reorganisation of the 1930s; Epilogue. Appendices. Bibliography. Index.

Demy 8vo   xviii + 288 pages   Maps, Plates, Cased, probable
price 42s net

THE INTERNATIONAL BOUNDARIES OF NIGERIA
1885–1960

The Framework of an Emergent African Nation

by J. C. ANENE, Professor of History in the University, Nsukka

A pioneer work in its field. The author has studied, from field-work, oral tradition and primary documentary sources the types of indigenous frontiers—not necessarily stable—which existed before European boundary intervention, and objectively assesses the results of that intervention and its consequences for modern Nigeria.

C   he Problems
of t   astern Boundary   undary—II;
The   ndex.

Der   price 45s net

PO   GERIA

The

by   f Ibadan

A   and English
man   which led to
the   ate.

C   he Caliphate
180   o–1900; Era
of   plomacy and
Hos   e Invasion of
Bau   estruction of
the   ex.

Der   price 50s net

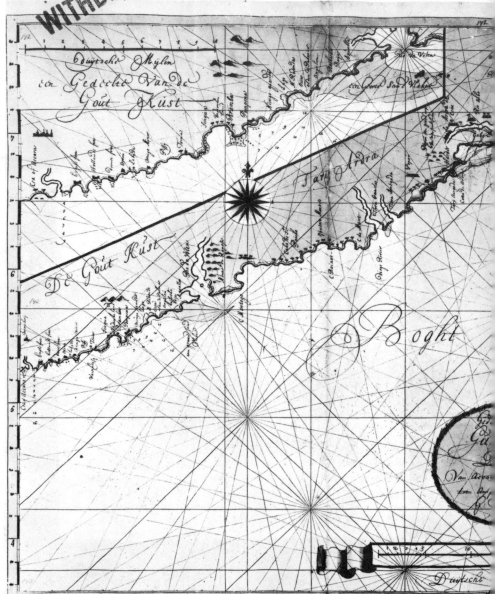